POLITICS
AND FILM

Leif Furhammar
+ Folke Isaksson

translated by Kersti French

PRAEGER PUBLISHERS
New York · Washington

Stills appear by courtesy of the following companies: Argentina Sono Films, Columbia, Contemporary, Copacabana Productions, Defa, Ealing Studios, Fama FA Mainz, Film Polski, G.P.O., Gala, Halas & Batchelor, History Today, I.C.A.I.C., London Films, Lux Films, Metro-Goldwyn-Mayer, Mirisch, Minerva International, National Film Archive, Nero Film, Nordisk, Paramount, Produçoes Cinematografica, R.K.O. Radio, Rizzoli, Sovexportfilm, Svensk Film-industri, Tobis, Twentieth Century-Fox, U.S. War Department, Unifrance, United Artists, Universal, Warner Bros.

We are particularly indebted to the staff of the Stills Department of the British Film Institute for their help in assembling the wide range of pictures used to illustrate this book.
The following chapters are by Leif Furhammar: World War I, Russia after the Revolution, Hollywood and the World, Cinema Nôvo, Hitlerjunge Quex, Ohm Krüger, Mrs Miniver, Vi er Vidkun Quislings hirdmenn, The Hitler Gang, The Battle of Stalingrad, Che!, The Aesthetics of Propaganda, The First Person Plural, Psychological Defence, Myth, Magic and Politics, Politics and Film – A Tricky Subject. The remaining chapters are by Folke Isaksson.

Contents

Preface

The old idea that films can be thought of purely as entertainment or art, or occasionally both, is today regarded with growing scepticism. It's widely realised that films also reflect the currents and attitudes in a society, its politics. The cinema does not exist in a sublime state of innocence, untouched by the world; it also has a political content, whether conscious or unconscious, hidden or overt.

Everything, in a way, is political, and a book with the title of 'Politics and Film' must, like books on politics and poetry, politics and art, or politics and religion, be marked by the writer's personal inclinations. Indeed, the general outline of this book was determined first and foremost by what its authors quite wilfully chose to interest themselves in. Consequently this is not a *handbook* on the subject of politics and the cinema. It is mainly a collection of essays on movies which have a clear political purpose, on the cinema as a weapon of propaganda.

The exclusions are determined to a great extent by what we were unable to see. Inevitably, the films of countries that are very distant geographically or culturally are least adequately covered. Literature on the cinema has not helped significantly in this respect, as film critics have until recently looked at their subject surprisingly seldom from a political viewpoint.

During the 'sixties, a new kind of political cinema seemed to be emerging in various countries all over the world. In Eastern as well as Western Europe – in Hungary, Czechoslovakia, France, Italy – films started to look at political realities with a degree of unbiased frankness. They were more subjective – and more ambivalent – than the films produced by earlier propagandists and social critics; consequently they are much more difficult to interpret. We have refrained from any attempt to summarise and analyse these developments, as the book was already threatening to expand well beyond its original limits.

Even in the time since the book was written a great deal has happened to underline that it is a retrospective survey. The heat of social conflict in the United States, France, Italy and other countries has given birth to a new brand of revolutionary cinema. The films are often produced anonymously with the very simplest technical equipment, to be distributed and shown outside the usual commercial and official channels. These 'news-reels', '*ciné-tracts*', '*cinegiornali liberi*' are sometimes simple reportage, sometimes aggressive agitprops, occasionally of a slogan-like nature with the direct appeal of a broadsheet or a poster. This militant guerilla cinema is not covered here, nor is the fact that Cesare Zavattini, who had fulfilled a similar role for neo-realism, became its prime mover and inspiration in Italy. 'It is', he has stated in an interview, 'film by many for many, a home-made Molotov cocktail.'

At the same time certain film companies, for instance in Sweden, have embarked upon the production of films with a pronounced political bias against their own society. This is taken by some as evidence of progressiveness, by others as a flagrant instance of repressive tolerance.

In Brazil, Cinema Nôvo has continued to develop, but its future and its political effectiveness are still uncertain. The Cuban cinema has advanced to a far greater degree than indicated in this book. Indeed, in Latin America as a whole, the cinema has become a weapon in the service of the revolution (see Fernando Solanas and others).

Certain changes have been made for the English language edition, mostly of a minor character, and the chapters on *The Green Berets* and *Che!* have been added.

Anyone who reads or writes about films soon realises that film literature is not always reliable; it is characteristic of the medium that people experience it differently and therefore also remember it differently. Often, things are remembered quite incorrectly, and mistakes are transferred from one film writer to another. It would surprise us if none of these errors had insinuated themselves into this work.

PART ONE-HISTORY

World War 1

In 1915, the head of censorship in Sweden, Gustaf Berg, wrote a couple of articles analysing 'The Neutrality of Our Cinema' in the newly started magazine *Filmbladet*. The general tone of the pieces is elevated:

'From the start the warring powers did not hesitate to use the visual means of the cinema to show us neutrals the base activities of their adversaries. In these sensitive times, this type of product must be considered highly explosive and consequently treated as contraband of war. And as such it was tackled by the censor . . . I am not uttering empty phrases of neutrality but expressing a fact when I assure you that neither side has any cause to boast. The emphasis in Entente films on German atrocities in Belgium can be balanced out by German descriptions of the behaviour of the Russians in East Prussia.'

During World War I, the cinema first showed its potential as a means of agitation on a large scale. Both the movies and the techniques of propaganda were still in a fledgling state, and film historians have described the cinema's early propagandist efforts with some justification as primitive.

But in this context the meaning of the word 'primitive' becomes rather unclear. It is not just the quality of the propaganda itself that determines the effectiveness of the agitation, but also the qualities of the recipient. The cinema and its audience have developed together: technical and artistic progress has created new ways of influencing people, and these new techniques have led to new demands from the audiences and fresh immunities against persuasion. The silent demagoguery of 1915 was acted out before audiences whose reactions would have been quite different from those of later generations reared with an increasingly sophisticated cinema as a natural part of the environment.

Between the most rabid of the warmongering films of the 1910's and, for instance, their Cold War counterparts forty years later, the difference in actual quality is not particularly striking compared to differences in techniques and acting methods, sound and colour, length and width. In story lines and emotional arguments we find no significant change; the basic pattern, the themes of indignation, are very much the same.

The names of the films reflect their spirit. In Germany there was, for instance, *Deutsche Frauen – Deutsche Treue* (*German Women – German Faith*) or *Auf dem Felde der Ehre* (*In the Field of Honour*) or *Das Vaterland ruft* (*The Fatherland Calls*); in France, *Les Frontières du coeur* or *Mort au champ de l'honneur* or *La Fille du Boche*; in England, *In the Clutches of the Hun* or *Under the German Yoke* or *England Expects . . .* They were stories of great chauvinistic challenge, demonstrating how beneficial the war was for alcoholics, momma's boys, snobs, intellectuals and other dubious characters, and this pattern of cinematic propaganda has persisted ever since. Then, as subsequently, the appeal of sentimental heroism was exploited. Dedicated soldiers died heroes' deaths on a decorative field of honour or avenged themselves on the enemy for his dastardly deeds, for which they were suitably decorated, according to the origin of the film, either with the Legion of Honour or the Iron Cross. Good and brave Red Cross nurses bore up with identical fortitude and dramatic gestures in all countries.

There was the mystical aspect: the moral and strategic superiority of the side by which the film was made, manifested in almost ritual conceptions like the one that even little children and dogs could outsmart the vicious and obtuse enemy. Then as now the wishful dreams of the screen could assume national proportions.

There were the idols, with whom the audiences liked to identify, and whose star appeal was used to patriotic ends. In the United States the big stars, William S. Hart, Charles Chaplin, Douglas Fairbanks, Theda Bara and others, all did their bit, both on and off the screen, as fund-raisers for Government Bonds, Liberty Loans, the Red Cross. In France the great prima donnas rallied round to embody the patriotic virtues and lend a higher dignity to grey forbearance. The most divine of them all, Sarah Bernhardt donned a nurse's uniform for *Mères Françaises*, thereby creating, if not a great work of art, certainly one of the great curiosities of film history.

There was the ridiculing of the enemy's leaders and national symbols in comedy and farce. The animated cartoon began to be used as a propaganda weapon, especially in England where the Kaiser's hubristic ambitions of achieving naval domination were held up to scorn in *Sea Dreams*, and where that new and monstrous weapon, the tank, was presented to cinema-goers in a comic but nightmarish vision called *Kinotank*, a fantasy of such shattering impact that the British War Office found it necessary to intervene and demand certain cuts.

And there were above all the great displays of indignation and outrage, the constant portrayal of the enemy's brutality and barbarism. Film upon film contained variations on the recurrent theme of virginal women, innocent children and defenceless old people being violated and tortured by sadistic enemy officers.

The Entente powers excelled above all in the propaganda of outrage. The Germans – the Boches, the Huns – were represented as slit-eyed, mustachioed, lecherous devils whose every instinct was geared towards rape and vandalism. The Central powers' propaganda was hamstrung by the lack of coordination bétween the civil and military authorities; their efforts were inapposite for the times, and so short on imagination that, for instance, the Germans, inspired perhaps by some sense of military honour, felt that they were above answering English and French propaganda on the same level of exaggerated horror. To them, the most natural way of courting public opinion was by boastful demonstrations of military power, which had a distinctly unfavourable effect on international audiences who interpreted them simply as further confirmation of Prussian ghastliness. In one particular field, however, German film propaganda got a head start on the English and the French: the newsreel.

With tendentious commentary and editing, documentary film reports from the battlefields could be used as an effective weapon in the psychological battle for the sympathies of the neutrals, while on the home front the newsreel held a particular advantage over feature films. It had the appearance of objective reportage, and kept its grip on audiences far better than did patriotic fiction. Feature film propaganda ceased to elicit audience response as the initial enthusiasm was superseded by despair and people no longer wanted to be reminded of the war when taking refuge from reality.

The German lead in the early stages of newsreel propaganda was the result of a moment of perhaps accidental foresight on the part of the authorities who, during the first months of the war, granted a film company permission to record the fighting at the front; topical documentaries could thus be exported

Stills. Above: Battle Cry of Peace. *Below and right:* Thomas Ince's Civilization.

for purposes of agitation.

Both English and French photographers were kept away from the front because the military authorities feared that revelations of the true face of war would have a demoralising effect on the home front as well as handing information on a plate to enemy espionage. Cinemas had to content themselves largely with showing archive material which was passed off as 'Newsreels from the Front'. In place of authentic material, old footage had to be dug out to show parades and manoeuvres, preferably contrasted with pictures of un-trained German recruits. Not until the war had been going for one and a half years did the authorities in England and France begin to think again, forced by the successes abroad of the enemy's propaganda documentaries. When at last the restrictions on photographers at the front were lifted, a handful of fearless camera-men went to the front line where they ran incredible risks to get their material, and the fortunate ones even lived to take it home.

Most famous of these film-making war correspondents were J. B. McDowell and G. Malins, whose most successful work was *The Battle of the Somme*. It was made on the Western Front in July 1916, and the next month it was already showing to enormous audiences in Britain, giving as true and unvarnished a picture of the war as the censor and the British War Office allowed. It was made specifically as an exhortation to greater effort directed at the workers, particularly those in munition factories. The Minister of Armaments, Lloyd George, recommended it with enthusiasm:

'Make sure that this film reaches everybody, because it is in itself an epic on self-sacrifice and heroism. Recount the deeds of our brave men all round the globe. It is your duty!'

Anglo-French propaganda soon managed to outmanoeuvre the Germans also in the field of documentaries, thanks to a rapidly developed and very efficient system of distribution. Movie-houses in the United States provided the most significant outlet for these efforts, and remained open for a remarkably long time to films from both the Entente countries and the Central powers. By the time that German propaganda finally had to admit defeat in the American arena, domestic film production in the United States had undergone a curious metamorphosis in its attitude to the European war itself, a change quite as fascinating in its effect as that of the imported films on the American public.

In the months following the outbreak of war, American films adopted an attitude of neutralism and pacifism, presenting the inhumanity of violence with a great deal of feeling. This type of film began to appear in 1914, and culminated eventually in the greatest box-office success of the period, Thomas Ince's *Civilization*, in which Christ allows himself to be reincarnated in the body of a dead submarine engineer so that he can rise again and preach his gospel of peace to the world. In an epilogue to the film President Wilson was seen offering his good wishes to Ince – and, according to the Democratic press, *Civilization* was one of the factors behind Wilson's re-election in 1916: it seemed to embody Wilson's election slogan 'He kept us out of war'. But behind the pacifist catchphrases in *Civilization*, anti-German sentiments were already clearly discernible; uniforms, badges and emblems plainly indicated who were the brutal warmongers. The Swedish censor banned the film on the grounds that it was 'unsuitable due to our country's relationship with a foreign power'.

One interesting and curious aspect of the American film industry during this period is that, from the middle of 1915, an increasing number of films were aimed at moulding political opinions to make the public clamour for American entry into the war. This happened well before the authorities had moved away from their strictly isolationist position. One reason was certainly that several film companies had intimate financial connections with businesses that would welcome American participation in the war. There were film companies with pro-German sympathies, but for the great majority an English victory was a matter of vital economic importance.

The extremely nationalistic J. Stuart Blackton, who was to produce some of the most militant of these films, set the warmongering tone for anti-German film propaganda when he released *Battle Cry of Peace* in September 1915, just in time to profit from public indignation at the sinking of the Lusitania. *Battle Cry of Peace* (in which, incidentally, Trotsky, according to unconfirmed but singularly persistent rumours, appeared as an extra; Theodore Roosevelt is said to have lent a hand in its planning) was an early example of what has subsequently been termed political fiction. It showed the Germans besieging New York from the sea and reducing the skyscrapers to ruins. Blackton's film aroused a great deal of antipathy in various quarters. The automobile tycoon Henry Ford bought up whole pages in various American newspapers to expose the economic interests of the armament manufacturers and other war profiteers that lay behind the film's activist tendencies.

The unanimous pacifism of American films in 1914 quickly turned into equally unanimous militarism; the cinemas were mobilised against Germany well before Wilson led the nation into war. For those in the film industry who persisted in pacifist or pro-German attitudes, the situation became delicate. Towards the end of 1916, a company owned by William Randolph Hearst launched the adventure series *Patria* about an imaginary war in which Japan joined forces with Mexico to attack the United States. In reality, however, Japan was fighting on the side of Britain and was consequently a presumptive ally. After personal intervention by the President himself, the Japanese scoundrels

underwent a sudden change of nationality in the last few instalments. In Walter Brenon's *War Brides* (1916), the peace-loving heroine committed suicide rather than give birth to a future soldier; the film soon came to be regarded as a dangerous work of anti-war propaganda, and was banned. *The Spirit of '76* was about the American liberation from the British and happened to be released just before the United States went to war on the British side; as a result the producer, Robert Goldstein, was given a ten-year prison sentence under the eleventh statute of the Code of Espionage.

Thus the voices of pacifism all fell silent, and after the declaration of war American

movies became a forum for wild displays of patriotism and hatred towards the Germans. As has happened so often in American films, wickedness was equated with sexual appetite, and the image of the Germans projected into everyone's mind was of lechery personified. No right-thinking American could fail to be outraged at the sight of Mary Pickford on her way to a fate worse than death at the hands of the Huns in Cecil B. De Mille's *The Little American* while, smiling scornfully from below a waxed mustache, the Prussian colonel proclaims: 'My men are in need of relaxation.' The prime incarnation of German bestiality was the Kaiser, and on him were concentrated the wildest hate fantasies. Feelings against the Kaiser reached their climax in two films from 1917, *The Kaiser, Beast of Berlin* and *To Hell with the Kaiser*. In the latter, Wilhelm II's faithful friend, Satan, encourages him to sink the Lusitania, use poison gas and bomb Red Cross hospitals.

All this may seem both naïve and primitive – a judgment that posterity, enlightened by hindsight, is always quick to pass. Although films serving the cause of patriotism were often poor even by the standard of the time, contemporary assessments of their effectiveness were so positive that most of the warring countries sooner or later made propaganda pictures.

In Austria, Imperial Headquarters ordered the production of chauvinistic films. In Russia the semi-official Skobeljve Committee with its mobile exhibition facilities was a precursor of the Bolshevik film trains. In France, the Minister of War, Alexandre Millerand, early on initiated the Photographic and Cinematographic Section of the Army, SPCA, which produced a string of successful propaganda films, aimed primarily at the American market. Many filmmakers who were later to become famous worked in the SPCA, including Abel Gance, Marcel L'Herbier and Jean Benoit-Lévy, as well as the film historian René Jeanne.

The British Government financed a number of patriotic feature films and imported D. W. Griffith from the United States to make *Hearts of the World* with the Gish sisters. The film does not rank as one of his more outstanding efforts. It was meant as a work of indignation against the Germans' infamous conduct in France, and Griffith set the story's shattered idyll against a background of authentic film from the Western Front. However, by the time it was released, audiences had become so utterly war-weary that it failed to arouse any kind of enthusiasm, and Griffith expressed his disappointment with the words: 'Taken as a drama, war is in some ways unsatisfactory.'

Curiously enough, the United States was the first country to set up a properly organised and

Stills. Left: Hearts of the World. *Bottom left:* War Brides. *Below:* The Little American.

coordinated propaganda unit, the Committee on Public Information, headed by George Creel, who was given the task of 'selling the war to America'. The CPI managed to inspire the film industry with enthusiasm for its aims by putting its staff and financial resources at the disposal of individual studios for making films with patriotic content. It offered suggestions for stories, unlimited numbers of extras for the battle scenes, military expertise and props, free publicity and advertising. This type of cooperation between the military and the film industry has been preserved to the present day in the United States, a state of affairs which does not always promote freedom of expression or artistic boldness.

A letter of 4 July 1917 from the German Chief of Staff, General Erich Ludendorff, to the Imperial Ministry of War in Berlin, gave a top level evaluation:

'The war has demonstrated the superiority of the photograph and the film as means of information and persuasion. Unfortunately our enemies have used their advantage over us in this field so thoroughly that they have inflicted a great deal of damage. Nor will films lose their significance during the rest of this war as a means of political and military persuasion. For this reason it is of the utmost importance for a successful conclusion to the war that films should be made to work with the greatest possible effect wherever any German persuasion

11

might still have any effect.'

The letter was part of Ludendorff's desperate struggle to set up, albeit belatedly, a properly organised propaganda effort. His action led first to the formation of the Bild und Film Amt (Photo and Film Office) in the Army and eventually to the massive industrial enterprise of Ufa – Universum Film Aktiengesellschaft – but in propaganda his intentions were hardly fulfilled. When Ufa emerged, there were only a few months of World War I left, and although the Ministry of War put up most of the capital, Ufa never had time to become a propaganda centre. There was, however, to be another war.

But did the cinema then – or later – really have the power that Ludendorff and others attributed to it? One might question if film propaganda actually played a decisive role in guiding public opinion, creating a state of pre-paredness and building up morale. As always, it is essential to remember that the cinema never functions in isolation, separate from other influences, that it rarely creates opinions, but rather supports them. It seems likely that the propaganda films of the First World War were a powerful instrument for conveying, to certain sections of the community at least, stark and patriotic images of the war and its causes, of motives, characteristics and behaviour on both sides, and that these images must have had some short or long term effect on morale both at home and at the front. But the ideas behind them obviously did not spring exclusively or originally from within the cinema. Emotional dramas in the cinema served as sounding boards or amplifiers for feelings and attitudes that were determined by other factors.

While films appear to have had a certain effect on the war, the war certainly had a major effect on films. For the first time, the cinema managed to shake off its cultural inferiority complex. It was lifted out of the fairground and attained a significance beyond that of cheap entertainment; it achieved patriotic prestige.

But more than simple idealism lay behind the enthusiasm with which film industries all over the world threw themselves into the national propaganda efforts. Economic in-terests are always to be watched when public opinion is emotionally charged, never more so than in the hysteria of a country going to war. Propaganda films are usually as much a means of exploiting a given climate of opinion as of exerting an influence. The public pays for the satisfaction of having its attitudes confirmed and reinforced.

World War I was a happy one for the film industry in practically every country. People needed the cinemas more than ever before. There they found an outlet for the heady patriotism of the early days of the war, and there they could satisfy the need eventually to escape from the drudgery and gloom. The boom was to recur during the Second World War.

Russia after the Revolution

Right from the beginning, the history of the Soviet cinema has, to a greater extent than that of any other country, been a history of the relationship between film and politics. The development of the cinema has been directed much more firmly by the authorities in Russia than anywhere else, and the content of Russian films has been much more coloured by the official political mythology of the day. Just as the standard American product was marked by the dream of Love, Success and the Freedom of the Open Spaces, so the favourite theme of Soviet films has been the dream of the Revo-lution, with Lenin as its central figure. To begin with, memories of the revolution were fresh, the hatred was violent and the films had a brutal reality. But the revolution became established, it turned into a memory, a national emblem. The cinema's flashbacks to the vic-tory of the proletariat over its oppressors became gestures intended to demonstrate solidarity with the past, not appeals to rise against any new misfortunes. As October 1917 has retreated into the past, films about the revolution have become increasingly mild, with Lenin turning into a gentler, almost *petit bourgeois* figure, while events themselves have been presented in a softer, sadder light.

The revolution was the great source of in-spiration in the mid-'twenties for those who created the only artistically significant style ever to emerge in films with unequivocally propagandist intentions. Several early repre-sentatives of the Soviet cinema formulated their ideas in theoretical studies which are now among the classics of film literature. The aim – both in theory and in practice – was to guide the mental processes of the spectator so that the effect of the film could only be as the director intended, which in the final analysis came down to proclaiming the absolute necessity of the revolution.

The means to achieve this aim was 'montage', a concept which came to be the pre-eminent slogan of film aesthetics. The principal idea behind 'montage' was that the viewer's experi-ence of a film depended not only on the content of its various images, but above all on the way in which they were combined. The illusory reality on the screen was not tied to reality itself, but could be constructed on the cutting table by the director using carefully chosen fragments brought together to make a combined assault on the sensibilities of the audience that would achieve the required psychological effect. The theories, however, arose from montage itself, which was in no way a product of abstract theorising, but the result of urgent necessity.

In the years following the revolution, the Soviet cinema found itself in a precarious situation. The industrialists who had carved out positions for themselves in the film business under the Czarist regime reacted with often quite open revulsion to the Bolsheviks; several producers and directors picked up their equipment and emigrated. The blockade of the Soviet Union also had the effect of creating an acute shortage of film stock which soon grew to the level of crisis.

During the War of Intervention, the government used all the stock and the rather inadequate technical resources that it could mobilise for the propaganda effort. For the 'propaganda trains' that toured the provinces and visited the front, people from the film industry were rounded up to make and show short agitation films, the so-called *agitki*, to the peasants and soldiers. Bolshevik film-makers had to turn out the most persuasive possible propaganda films using the least possible material. Apart from the short, almost pamphlet-like movies that provided simple, popular illustrations of Communist ideas and slogans, great emphasis was laid on the presentation of newsreel material – partly from the war in progress, partly older material re-edited for a new political purpose.

This primitive situation was the background to the revolutionary classics of the Russian cinema that emerged during the latter half of the 'twenties when the practical requirements for large-scale Soviet film production had at last been fulfilled.

Out of the shortage of material grew the necessity to experiment with short fragments of film which often lacked continuity.

Out of the experiments grew a realisation of the importance of the cutting in achieving an effect: juxtaposition of two separate images could create contrasts, shocks and unexpected meanings which did not exist in either image viewed separately.

And out of these insights grew the principles of montage.

Among those who worked on the experimental films for the propaganda trains and were later to pass on their experiences and even make their own films was Edouard Tissé, who became Sergei Eisenstein's chief cameraman.

There was Esther Shub who perfected the documentary compilation film with *The Fall of the Romanovs* (1927), *The Big Road* (1927) and others.

There was Lev Kuleshov, who carried out the famous experiments, usually described incorrectly in film histories, with a facial expression interpreted differently as it is shown next to a soup-plate, a naked female form and a coffin. Kuleshov became a teacher at the State Film School in Moscow. In 1924, he directed a film farce with a political edge, *The Strange Adventures of Mr West in the Land of the Bolsheviks*.

And there was also Dziga Vertov who revolutionised the documentary. He hated the false reality of feature films, but gave his own film reports and documentaries (*Kino-Pravda*) a uniquely personal form: he wanted to 'translate the visible into Communism' and did so in documentaries which blended facts, feelings and propaganda into a kind of political surrealism. He was the first to work purposefully on the idea of montage; he later did homage to the creator of the Soviet Union in *Three Songs of Lenin* (1934).

But the new generation in the Russian cinema was not drawn exclusively from the film laboratories of the propaganda trains. It was as if all the young artistic talent was drawn towards the rich possibilities of the cinema, which had so far only been hinted at and remained to be explored. Eisenstein, Dovzhenko, Yutkevitch, Kozintsev and Trauberg all came to films either from painting or from various branches of the revolutionary theatre. The poet Mayakovsky was not to make any of his more significant artistic efforts in the cinema, but he, too, was an enthusiast. In a 1922 manifesto he exclaims: 'To you films mean entertainment. To me they are almost a way of life.' The

Stills. Above: Esther Shub's The Fall of the Romanovs. *Below: Lev Kuleshov's* The Strange Adventures of Mr West in the Land of the Bolsheviks.

cinema should be turned into the new art form for the people in a country where the majority could not read or write and where political theatre had largely failed to reach the masses. The Russian cinema was infused with a vitality which was revolutionary on every level and with a will to build something entirely new on new foundations in a spirit of enthusiastic solidarity with new ideas, both artistic and political.

Political loyalty to the new regime was axiomatic to most of the film-makers. Whether they worked in fiction or documentary, their main theme was the revolution and the struggle against the counter-revolution – the ignominious acts of the rich against the poor, and the revolt of the poor; the iniquities of the Czarist regime against the proletariat, and the revolt of the proletariat; the crimes of the capitalists, the aristocrats, the military, the Church and the imperialists against the people, and the people's revolt.

Naturally, not everything or even the greater part of what was produced in the Soviet studios during their period of greatness was of merit either as art or as propaganda. Much was inspired by party directives rather than by creative talent and was coloured by the dreary, bigoted didacticism that seems to go with routine propaganda. In a great many wildly improbable tales, vanquished enemies were held up to such scorn and declared so utterly in-

competent that even the party officials reacted unfavourably. After all, if the White officers had been such a bungling lot of cowardly drunks, there would be an obvious implication of incompetence on the part of the Red Army which had needed two years to defeat them. Indeed, the period owes its importance to a handful of films which rose above the rest and established a new film style.

The Russian revolutionary cinema was unique in that, unlike the cinematic propaganda of other countries up to and including World War II, it was not geared to the middle classes in its aims and values. Film propaganda has, of course, always addressed itself to those already in agreement with its basic aims, and it is something of a truism to state that these films were directed at the working classes and did not attempt to convert the defeated bourgeoisie. Nonetheless the Soviet cinema succeeded remarkably in the extent to which it liberated itself from the established values of middle-class morality, behaviour and artistic style. It was propagandist art concerned with and addressed to the proletariat with an almost brutal sense of pride and community of feeling.

The great period began in 1924 with Eisenstein's *Strike*, which 'Pravda' described as 'the first revolutionary creation of our cinema'. The nervous urgency with which its images were presented came to form the basis for a new cinematic style. This demonstrated an almost defiant love even of what is vulgar, noisy and dirty in the lives of the working classes. The proletariat was the hero, but, by bourgeois standards, not an attractive one. The outstanding figures among feature film directors of the period were Alexander Dovzhenko, and the two best known theorists of montage, Sergei Eisenstein and Vsevolod Pudovkin.

Dovzhenko has been described as the poet among them. In his films, agitation was coupled with folklore, political vision with sensual naturalism, revolution with mystical ideas on fertility. *Arsenal* had an almost fairy-tale feeling about it, with horses which spoke and reactionaries' bullets which could not penetrate the bared chest of the Ukranian worker. In his most famous film, *Earth* (1930), Dovzhenko succeeded where the whole movement of social realism would subsequently fail: he managed to create a sense of poetry around work, collectivisation of agriculture, apples, Socialism, rain, love, death and the soil.

Eisenstein turned the masses, the People as a whole, into the hero of his films; he was the most consistent in his efforts to make individuals stand back and allow the masses to take pride of place. This was eventually to become

Stills. Left: Eisenstein's Strike. *This page: Dovzhenko — sunflowers and apples in* Earth; *below,* Arsenal.

ideologically unsound and in direct opposition to principles which he himself would be forced to accept. In 1934, he wrote about *Strike*:

'At that time it was not merely natural but even necessary to fashion the cinematic image from the basic concept of the collective, united and ruled by a common will. The deeper meaning which is demanded of films today, namely "individuality within the collective", would hardly have been able to penetrate unless the more general idea had paved the way for it.'

In his next film, *Battleship Potemkin* (1925) Eisenstein achieved perfection of the new style. Like *Strike*, it is based on an historical event – the attempted revolution of 1905 at Odessa. As in the earlier film, the class enemy is represented by heavily caricatured bourgeois citizens and anonymously stamping military boots, and the climax was again carnage, evoking passionate feelings of indignation. But where the propagandist power of *Strike* lay partly in its raw and unpolished vitality, the propaganda of *Battleship Potemkin* was contained in a classically dramatic form, and a coldly calculated precision of construction. The presentation of the massacre on the Odessa steps has remained the most widely admired propagandist sequence of all and the most perfect exposition of the theory of montage.

Paradoxically, Eisenstein's films were never accepted by the people, in spite of their picture of mass heroism. He was the 'engineer' among revolutionary directors, and his work reveals a greater interest in the expressive possibilities of film rather than in the specific problems of making the characters comprehensible, of explaining reactions or clarifying political situations. He was therefore less popular both with the public and the party than Pudovkin whose psychological intuition allowed him to infuse his films to a far greater degree with a welcoming element of human interest. The calculation which can sometimes give a mechanical feeling to the more extreme montage films was softened in Pudovkin's work by a sympathy with individuals and their reactions. His films are almost always dramas of conversion, in which we are allowed to follow step by step the development of a political consciousness from resigned apathy to revolutionary action. *Mother* (1926) described the degradation of a worker's wife and her moral awakening under the influence of her son's political conviction. *The End of St Petersburg* (1927) was about a strike-breaking peasant lad who moved from the crawling debasement of the ragged proletariat to whole-hearted Communism. In *Storm over Asia* (1928), the leading character is a Mongol who sees through imperialism during the War of Intervention and joins the Red partisans.

The theoretical expositions of montage by Eisenstein and Pudovkin diverge at various points, and their disagreement on some issues ended in polemics. Both, however, based part of their aesthetic on the Pavlovian principle of

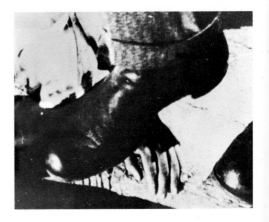

Stills. This page: images of the class enemy from Eisenstein's Battleship Potemkin. *Opposite: Pudovkin – representatives of British imperialism in* Storm over Asia; *mother and dead son in* Mother.

conditioning. Some of their speculations on the automatic functioning of stimulus and response have associations with the techniques of brainwashing and mass suggestion, but it is doubtful whether their marriage of Pavlov and politics really worked. When Eisenstein complicated his theories even further by presenting 'intellectual montage', it would probably not be unfair to say that he failed completely, at

least in his intentions of reaching a broader public with his message. Intellectual montage was most consistently applied in *October* (1928) where Eisenstein tried to provide a visual commentary to the events of the Russian revolution by means of seemingly irrelevant contrasts, chains of ironically linked associations, symbolic digressions and so on. The complex montage structure did not stand up in practice, partly because images, as opposed to words, do not seem to be able to function as abstractions and do not possess any grammar. There was nothing in *October* to suggest *how* the images should be combined to convey any meaningful message to an unsophisticated spectator.

In all its weirdness, *October* is one of the most fascinating of all films, but the People did not understand it, and the politicians accused Eisenstein of 'formalism', the gravest charge that could then be levelled at a Soviet artist. To this was added a fresh political complication. Trotsky had just been out-manoeuvred in the party leadership, and as Eisenstein had given him a prominent place in this story of the Bolshevik seizure of power, the film fell into

official party-political disgrace *vis-à-vis* official party politics. It was re-edited and soon – according to Thorold Dickinson – withdrawn altogether. Eisenstein's next film, *The General Line* (1929), was also considered politically unsatisfactory and was revamped under the title *Old and New*.

Eisenstein was not the only victim of political hazards around 1930. Works by Pudovkin and Dovzhenko were scrutinised and found wanting. *Storm over Asia*, with its metaphoric ending where the revolutionary storm sweeps across Asia, had too much symbolism and too little concern with the People. *Earth* was 'defeatist', 'pantheistic', 'counter-revolutionary' and 'too realistic'. The counter-revolutionary element of the film was to be found in the episode of the tractor that develops engine trouble before a group of scornfully laughing kulaks – excessive realism was used to show the collectivists fixing it by urinating into the radiator.

The favourable cultural climate which had made it possible for the new style to emerge, had become more severe. The dogma of social realism was beginning to make itself felt, even if its principles had yet to be formulated.

The leaders of the revolutionary film generation had unhesitatingly allowed their art to be used in the service of the new doctrine. They were to suffer a great deal under the political yoke which they had shouldered with such enthusiasm. From the early 'twenties to the end of the 'thirties the party's grip on them slowly but inexorably tightened, until finally its power over them was complete and unlimited.

At the outset, administrative, ideological and artistic guidance was exercised with great care. The film industry had of course been nationalised in principle by Lenin in 1919, but as in practice this measure tended to exacerbate the already acute crisis, it was not acted upon for a time. Censorship was still relatively mild in the mid-'twenties, and private enterprise was given fairly free rein within the film industry while Lenin's New Economic Policy lasted. However

with the perpetual and complex changes of administrative structure, things gradually changed. The first aim of the ceaseless re-organisations was to place the finances of the industry firmly under state control, but as financial centralisation was completed towards the end of the 'twenties, ideological supervision grew increasingly strict, reaching its pre-war peak in the mid-'thirties.

The growing ideological control of Soviet films was concerned with artistic as well as political orthodoxy. Bolshevik leaders and artists had long debated whether art should be guided by party authority or be allowed to develop outside any political pressures through experiments with form in an atmosphere of free criticism. Revolutionary politicians were more often than not cultural reactionaries, and like the more authoritarian artists, their ideas on style tended to be those of nineteenth-century bourgeois realism. In 1924, the controversy between the authoritarians and the liberals came to a head, but the fact that Bukharin adopted a tolerant and progressive line seemed to settle the issue for the time being. The Politburo decreed that no specific style could be regarded as particularly representative of the Party.

So the avant-garde was given a breathing space which the cinema used well. It had the further advantage of being guided ideologically by Lunacharsky, the Commissar for Information, and a great film enthusiast. His personal sympathies probably leaned towards the traditional, but his generally open-minded attitude guaranteed far-reaching artistic freedom during the first decade of the Soviet Union.

Even before the end of the 'twenties, however, Bukharin had been pushed from his position of power and Lunacharsky had left his Ministry; Stalin and his circle were in power and highly intolerant towards the arts. Both the Party Congress and the Central Committee finally defined the function of art as a political instrument. After the Party Conference on the cinema in 1928, the film authorities were not to be bothered with ideas like avant-gardism, formalism, symbolism or experiment, which had no direct relevance to the People. All films were to be comprehensible to and appreciated by the millions, and their one aim was to be the glorification of the emerging Soviet state.

In the early 'thirties, 'socialist realism' was the only style which was permitted in the Soviet cinema. Some of the basic tenets on which it was built, however, were more appealing than its application.

Art was no longer to be seen as a luxury for the privileged classes, a means of refined aesthetic enjoyment for the connoisseur. The spokesmen for social realism wanted to provide a kind of art which would be genuinely accessible to the People. At the same time, art was called upon to assist in the creation of the new society; it was to be an educational tool in the teaching of socialism. The artist was to break out of his isolation, abandon his private and exclusive vision of life to study and give shape to social and political realities. Thus, by means of his realistic art, could he contribute to the development of the Soviet state.

Of all art forms, cinema was the most important. So Lenin had said, and with the help of films people would now be introduced to Communist thought and fired with enthusiasm for their great tasks; they would take part in shaping the reality of the future, at the same time enjoying the various general benefits of artistic stimulation.

As long as theories of art could still be debated with reasonable freedom, there was lively, sometimes even bitter, controversy in the Soviet Union about the cinema, its aims and methods, theory and practice. While the victory of social realism within the party leadership can be seen as a victory for conservatism, the reverse was paradoxically the case among the film-makers themselves. The established directors of the older generation, the virtuosi of montage, and the poetic film, stood poised against the young ones, the 'prosaists'. The latter, led by Sergei Yutkevitch opposed what they saw as the ossified, academic concepts of the old school. They wanted Soviet films to be dominated not by the masses and montage, but by the individual and the actor. The debate reached its climax in the Congress of the Film Artists' Union in January 1935, during which it became clear that the general tendency was clearly in favour of the young, towards social realism and prose.

The common goal would now be the creation of film that was alive to the society it came out of, film that dealt realistically with concrete problems of direct relevance to the masses. The younger directors wanted to explain what the class struggle was about with political analysis rather than metaphysical suggestion. They wanted to get away from the predilection of traditional art for the exceptional and devote themselves to the typical problems of average people. On the other hand, though, they wanted to replace 'no-story' films about anonymous revolutionary masses with films about the individual in the mass: the new society demanded a new cinema, social realism.

Unfortunately, Socialist Realism turned to dogma; it took up totalitarian attitudes. The most comprehensive effort at centralisation in the history of the cinema degenerated into a political, moral, artistic and educational fiasco.

Socialist Realism came in practice to be realism with great reservations. Its basic principle was formulated authoritatively by the first Soviet Writers' Congress in 1934 as 'the truthful rendering of reality as caught in its revolutionary dynamics'. The reservations lay in the second half of the definition – a semantic manoeuvre which was to serve the party regime as insurance against any uncomfortable criticism. Lunacharsky had already impressed on film-makers that realism was concerned not only with visible reality but with the goals towards which Socialism was working: an emerging Soviet state could not fairly be represented as it currently appeared, because its inherent perfection lay in the future. What had been a fatherly admonition from Lunacharsky became, in the heyday of social realism, an absolute decree; what was intended in theory as an encouragement to rejuvenation became a shield for bureaucracy, a means of rendering the cinema totally impotent as a constructive political force. The social-realist fiction became a platform for apologetic whitewashing and ritual invocation, as all adversities, production delays, disastrous fires and other accidents were passed off as the work of evil-minded saboteurs. With a sensitivity that bordered on neurosis, politicians were able to dismiss even the slightest criticism of the system as being a short-sighted, pessimistic and thus counter-revolutionary view of socialist reality.

As social realism became the only acceptable style, the Soviet cinema was drained of its artistic vitality, because everything different, personal, or formally avant-garde, was identified and stamped out. Stylistic and ideological conformity was enforced through party directives. Films ceased to be the expression of freely creative minds.

Socialist Realism failed as an instrument of instruction simply because the films rarely managed to attract the masses to whom they were addressed. Certainly, the People had held no brief for the more inaccessible of the earlier stylistic experiments, but the alternative they were offered was standardised propaganda, clothed in a dreary and unimaginatively idealised 'realism'.

One of the main aims of Soviet film in the 'thirties was to show just how splendid life was for Russian workers and farmers. Grotesquely, this image of a paradise on earth was held up to a people being pressed to the limits of its endurance by five-year plans and forced collectivisation. One might regard the tractor-happy picture that social realism painted of contemporary society as a means of making people believe that the ideal society already existed, of providing some sort of communist flight from reality, or of harnessing the competitive instinct to raise production and bring the Utopian goal a bit closer. But whatever the intentions, social realism was a double educational failure. Being so massively dull, it was rarely appreciated by the People, and by falsifying reality with its romantic beautification of the struggle, it seemed to scorn the truth and humiliate the People.

The wishful dreams of social realism were not for the masses, but for the party functionaries. Their didactic purpose was blatantly expressed in works of an almost evangelical nature. 'The positive hero' became the national ideal. Playing an essential role in any work of social realism, he soon lost all human individuality and became a puppet figure. The positive hero – 'the new Soviet man' – was virtue personified; a solid, resourceful leader in a responsible position whether in the factory, the kolkhoz or the party, an omniscient being who solved every problem with courage, wisdom and socialist enthusiasm, who made no distinction between his private life and his function within the Party. He was the unreal, exemplary superman of Soviet society. The greatest of all positive heroes was Stalin.

The personal cult treatment of him in films was to reach its peak after World War II. However, he first began to appear in the mid-'thirties as a jovial, pipe-smoking adviser beside Lenin in a number of films, starting with Mikhail Romm's *Lenin in October*. At Stalin's request, this film was made in record time for the anniversary of the revolution in 1937. The Lenin films, such as the same director's *Lenin in 1918*, were propagandist enterprises. Like sequences of forged photographs or idealised paintings, they were intended to exploit Lenin's obvious popularity in order to build up Stalin and consolidate the idea of him as Lenin's natural heir.

While the classic Russian film has always been judged by its masterpieces, Socialist Realism has, perhaps unavoidably, been assessed by the great bulk of uninteresting works that it produced. As a result, its reputation, especially in the West, has been undeservedly low. It produced no great masterpieces, but especially before the political formula had hardened, there were some films which demonstrated that the new style did not necessarily exclude rounded characterisation.

Sergei and Georgi Vassiliev's *Chapayev* (1934), an exciting story from the Civil War period, became one of the great successes of the Russian cinema. Although it was one of the films which introduced the individual hero, its admiration did not degenerate into panegyrics. Indeed, Chapayev was shown to possess adverse traits like vanity, uncertainty, self-will and something of an adventurer's mentality. Both characters and events were allowed to

Still: Sergei Yutkevitch's The Man with a Gun *(1938) – Maxim Straukh as Lenin.*

retain their moral ambivalence: the representation of political acts did not become crudely propagandist.

In some happy instances, the stereotyped simplicity of the style produced an intimacy which would have been impossible with the grand, silent gestures of the revolutionary classics. The sympathetic portrait of the Bolshevik botanist Timiriazev in *Baltic Deputy* (1937) by Josef Heifitz and Alexander Zarkhi is one of the most endearing and unpretentious examples of the intimacy of feeling that sometimes raised a social-realist film above the run-of-the-mill products of the genre.

Typically, both *Chapayev* and *Baltic Deputy* looked back to the earliest years of the Revolution. Their subject matter was fairly innocuous in the political climate of the day, but still capable of exciting the imagination of film-makers and audiences alike, something which social realism was unable to do with contemporary subjects. In the Kozintsev and Trauberg *Maxim* trilogy on the evolution of Bolshevism (*The Youth of Maxim, The Return of Maxim, The Vyborg Side,* 1935–39), the most forceful sections, both as art and propaganda, were those set furthest in the past. The trilogy described the progress of a young worker from his years of poverty at the turn of the century to his becoming a council member of the People's Commissariat. The Maxim character became very popular in Russia and later appeared in films outside the trilogy.

Friedrich Ermler was among the directors who adjusted most smoothly to the principles of Socialist Realism. His silent film, *Fragment of an Empire* (1929), was already an orthodox work of social realism. However, its starry-eyed optimism has a naïve charm that makes the propaganda more touching than annoying. The main character is Filimonov, a soldier from World War I who is cured after a prolonged bout of amnesia to wake up in the new world of prosperity. He looks at its wonders with wide-eyed amazement: thriving industry, elegant ladies, enormous and functional housing estates, rushing traffic, people secure in the equality of industrial democracy,

working in pleasant conditions in factories with canteens and table-tennis rooms.

With the arrival of sound, words took over from images the function of 'carrier of the message', a process which contributed to making social-realist film trivial to the point of artistic self-destruction. In 1932, Ermler and Yutkevich made *Counterplan*, the story of an aging shop steward who, under the influence of a party official – the positive hero – learns socialist solidarity, becomes a member of the Party and contributes to the successful completion of a 'counterplan', a scheme which supersedes the five-year plan. In *Peasants* (1935), Ermler succeeded in creating a film which, unlike the majority of Russian films of the period, pleased those who worked on the land. It painted a melodramatic picture of life on a kolkhoz and the struggle against counter-revolutionaries, saboteurs and kulaks. The climax of the film is a dream in which a young woman sees herself walking out across the field with Stalin at her side; he is carrying her child in his arms, and filing past in the background are tractors – the perpetual cinematic emblem for Soviet prosperity and progress.

At the end of the 'thirties, Ermler was assigned the prestigious task of making the Soviet cinema's greatest propaganda effort to date, *A Great Citizen* (1938–9), a giant work in two parts. During its making there were constant confrontations between political fiction and reality. The film was part of the propaganda campaign against 'the enemy within' and gave the Stalinist version of the still unsolved murder of the party boss Sergei Kirov in Leningrad. The Kirov case had led to the arrest of Kamenev and Zinoviev in 1934 and gave a foretaste of the big Moscow trials that were to come a couple of years later. In common with these show trials, *A Great Citizen* emerged from an atmosphere of political hysteria. The shooting of the film became so intimately associated with the purges that actors had to be drafted to play the 'enemy parts'. The whole project was extraordinarily delicate; the script was revised several times in accordance with new party directives, and a

Stills: positive heroes and others. Far left: Mikhail Romm's Lenin in 1918. *Bottom left: the Vassilievs'* Chapayev. *Above: Friedrich Ermler's* A Great Citizen. *Right: Ermler's* Peasants. *Bottom right: Nikolai Cherkassov in* Baltic Deputy *by Heifitz and Zarkhi.*

succession of those involved in the production were either dismissed for having allegedly committed acts of sabotage or arrested by the secret police as enemies of the people.

· The circumstances surrounding the making of *A Great Citizen* were an index of the political terror which engulfed the Soviet cinema. The film industry was not spared in the wave of Stalinist deportations and purges which swept the country. Lunacharsky's successor as ideological head of Soviet films for the greater part of the 'thirties was Boris Shumyatsky, the man who was to achieve notoriety by stopping the shooting of Eisenstein's *Bezhin Meadow* for some rather murky political motive. His qualifications for the job were political rather than artistic, and he kept a watchful eye on the orthodoxy of the film-makers with unpredictable severity, but with unflinching loyalty to the Party.

It was quite in character with the general paranoia of the time that Shumyatsky himself was to become a victim of the very same methods that he had been using. In 1937 he was made the scapegoat for the fall in the film industry's productive capacity and was removed from his post as an enemy of the people who had allowed 'Trotskyite and Bukharinist agents and infiltrators for the German and Japanese fascists to damage the Soviet film industry'. Towards the end of the 'thirties, nationalist tendencies in Russian films grew markedly stronger, and domestic stories made way for subjects concerning foreign affairs. The growing hostility towards other countries were reflected with increasing sharpness.

Poland was represented as dangerously menacing, and feature films were also called upon with increasing frequency to help in the psychological build-up for the coming struggle with Nazi Germany.

Ever since Hitler had come to power, there had been a steady output of anti-fascist films, in which communism was represented as the direct and positive opponent of fascism. One of the earliest was *Deserter* (1933), in which Pudovkin experimented with new types of sound montage in telling another story of political conversion, this time about a German worker who has escaped to Russia. There he gradually realises the need for him to return to his country to fight Nazism and help bring about the revolution of the proletariat in Germany.

1938 was the year during which the Russian film industry really massed its forces to prepare for the coming confrontation with the Nazis: more anti-German films than ever before were shown in the cinemas. They included *Professor Mamlock* directed by Adolph Minkin and Herbert Rappoport, about the race persecutions, Alexander Macheret's *Swamp Soldiers*, which is set in German concentration camps, and Sergei Eisenstein's *Alexander Nevsky*. Eisenstein's first completed sound picture, this had a thirteenth-century setting which did little, however, to conceal the fact that Russian enthusiasm on the ice of Lake Peipus before the

Stills: anti-fascist films. Above: Pudovkin's Deserter. *Right:* Professor Mamlock *(top); Eisenstein's* Alexander Nevsky.

battle against the Knights of the Teutonic Order was related more to an event in the near future than to one in the distant past.

Films like these were briefly put into cold storage during the Russo–German alliance, but began to be released again after Hitler's attack on the Soviet Union in 1941. Within a couple of weeks the film industry was set to resume the *agitki* traditions from the time of the War of Intervention. Short propaganda films of widely differing characters were brought together in 'monthly albums' designed to give inspiration and edification both at home and at the front. The first year's output contained, for instance, a couple of shorts reviving the memory of the popular heroes Maxim and Chapayev, as well as an item directed by Kozintsev in which Napoleon is seen sending a cable to Hitler warning him against attempting a march into Russia.

The documentarists were put to work straight away and kept intensely busy throughout the war. As a whole, Russian wartime documentary, the work of men like Leonid Varlamov, Roman Karmen, Yuli Raizman – and Dovzhenko – adds up to one of the most remarkable achievements of the genre. The tone of the films, which cover different phases

of the war, is surprisingly factual and un-emotional, at a time when the features being made included some of the most virulent displays of indignation in the history of propaganda. It is significant that Pudovkin's film version of Brecht's 'Furcht und Elend des dritten Reiches' was considered too tame for the situation and never released.

The German ravages of occupied areas and the brave resistance of the partisans were used most frequently as the means of stirring up hatred. There was a passion in these films which seemed to cry out for revenge, and they often showed, sooner or later, pitiless vengeance being wrought against occupiers and collaborators; these cinematic visions of hate contained both a reminder and a promise.

At the same time the monomaniac glorification of the Party disappeared from the propaganda. Ivan Pyriev's *Secretary of the District Committee* (1942), the first partisan film, was virtually the only one in which the hero's position as a party official was emphasised alongside his patriotic virtues. All the attention and feeling was generally focused on the fight against the Germans, and this gave these resistance films a remarkable unity of message. In Ermler's *She Defends Her Country* (1943), the main character is a Russian woman who has lost her husband and children in the war and, confronted by the superior strength of her German attackers, fights them furiously with a hatchet. Mark Donskoi's *How the Steel Was*

Stills. Below: German occupation – Donskoi's The Rainbow (left) *and Romm's* Girl No. 217. *Opposite page: lessons from the past – two images of the war against Napoleon, the retreat from Moscow in Vladimir Petrov's* Kutuzov (centre) *and Pudovkin's* Suvorov (bottom); *top – films which had political problems, Pudovkin's* Admiral Nakhimov (left) *and Dovzhenko's* Michurin.

Tempered (1942) concerned the acts of violence perpetrated by the German army of intervention in the Ukraine in 1918, but the same director returned in 1944 with a contemporary equivalent, *The Rainbow*, a withering picture of the Germans murdering women, children and old people in their occupation of a small partisan village in the Ukraine. Mikhail Romm's *Girl No 217* (1944) is another famous film which described how the Germans treated Russian slave labour.

In the late 'thirties – and not only in the movies – Soviet patriotism had already looked for historical subjects and found its ideals in the pre-revolutionary era. During the war, this nationalist treatment of history led to Czarist generals being revalued and held up as models to the nation. World War II was in Soviet terminology 'The Great Patriotic War', a term which went right back to the war of 1812 against Napoleon, 'The Patriotic War'. It was above all to the Russian heroes of the Napoleonic wars that film propaganda referred. Memories of Suvorov's suppression of attempted Polish uprisings and his victory over Napoleon were recalled in Pudovkin's grandiose military epic *Suvorov* (1940). Vladimir Petrov's film *Kutuzov* belongs in the same category and, in 1944, was a gloating reminder of how even Napoleon's army had been destroyed when it attempted to march on Moscow.

At the outbreak of war, most of the studios moved away from the capital for safety – one of the reasons why Party pressure on the film industry eased off during the war. Afterwards, Party influence and censorship tightened again, becoming, if possible, more stringent than before. Even several films made under the eagle-eyed surveillance of the censor were later publicly branded by the Central Committee. Post-war comedies were mostly banned because, according to Babitsky and Rimberg, every joke was thought to be directed against

the regime. Many of the great directors found
themselves once more in Stalin's bad books, as
'cosmopolitan elements' were now hunted down
in the Soviet Union in the same way as 'Un-
Americanism' was in the United States.
Eisenstein was constantly harried by suspicion
while making the second part of *Ivan the
Terrible*. Trauberg, Kozintsev, Yutkevich and
many others were forced into inactivity.
Dovzhenko saw the banning of his own, un-
revised version of what was to be his last film:
he was accused of having neglected the principles of Socialist Realism in *Michurin*,
although he had been true to the fashion for
biographies of great men in Russian history.

Pudovkin devoted one of his last films,
Admiral Nakhimov, to a hero of the Crimean
War. The film was shot in 1946, but severely
reprimanded in *Izvestia* for being objectionable
to the Party. Pudovkin had to apologise and
admit to not having recognised the 'superior

purpose' of his theme. The film was revised and partly re-shot, so that the final version became something of a propaganda weapon against the Western powers. It ends with a vision in which the Crimean War frigates on the Black Sea dissolve into modern Russian destroyers. The 'cold war' had reached Soviet film studios.

Until after the death of Stalin they turned out anti-Western propaganda films no less infamous than the American anti-Communist variety. The campaign was given a powerful boost in 1948 with Mikhail Romm's *The Russian Question*, in which an American journalist travelling in Russia discovers that the politicians in Moscow are not the real warmongers. On his return home, he is persecuted by the authorities, attacked by the press, and loses his wife and home because he refuses to obey the dictates of the financiers. At the end he speaks to his compatriots: 'America's enemies are not in the Soviet Union but in Washington!'

The same tone was found in another wave of anti-American propaganda around 1950. In Romm's *Secret Mission*, American generals in league with Hitler and Himmler plan to unite against the Soviet Union in the last phase of the war. In Alexander Feinzimmer's *They Have a Country*, the Americans treat homeless German war orphans as slaves and bring them up to become anti-Russian fascists. Grigori

Alexandrov's impressive *Meeting on the Elbe*, about conflicts between the great powers in divided Germany, demonstrates how the Americans cooperate with their natural allies, the ex-Nazis. On both sides of the Iron Curtain this was the most frequently repeated argument in 'cold war' propaganda films. The anti-Americanism in the Russian cinema was supported by equally rabid attacks from other Communist countries.

The annual output of the Soviet film industry sank catastrophically after the war, reaching its lowest point in 1952 when only five films were released. The principal cause was the stranglehold of a censorship bureaucracy which reached almost incredible dimensions: every script had to be scrutinised by twenty-eight different offices before production could even begin. In consequence, the choice of subjects became limited to a few cliché themes that were considered politically safe. Apart from the anti-American demagoguery, Russian films were devoted to ever rosier kolkhoz idylls, nationally elevating biographies of great men – and to the Stalin cult.

Stills. Below: enslaved orphan in They Have a Country. *Right: Americans in Romm's* The Russian Question *(top); Romm's* Secret Mission *– American emissaries meeting Schellenberg are scared by shelling; watching is Russian agent cunningly disguised as Gestapo lady.*

The genre of epic films exalting Stalin's image – *The Vow* (1946), *The Battle of Stalingrad* (1949), *The Fall of Berlin* (1950), *The Unforgettable Year 1919* (1952) – was the absurd final phase in the development of social realism. With it the grand style returned to the Russian cinema, albeit in a grotesque form, devoid of any life. This was socialist baroque rather than social realism, and its central character was not just the most positive of all heroes. He was God.

In 1953 Stalin died. The post-Stalin thaw in the Soviet cinema was illustrated in almost laughably concrete symbols, in Grigori Chukhrai's *Clear Sky* (1961).

At the Twentieth Party Congress Khruschev spoke of the recent past:
'Our historical and military films and certain literary works make us sick. Because their real purpose is to praise Stalin as a military genius. Consider *The Fall of Berlin* and remember how he is there the only one to take action or give orders from a room where all the chairs are empty . . . Where is the supreme military command? Where is the Politburo? The film says nothing about them and their responsibilities. Stalin acts for all of them . . . Thus the whole chain of events is falsely represented to the nation. And why? In order to envelop Stalin in glory, in spite of the facts and in direct conflict with the historical truth.'
And further on:
'What knowledge Stalin had of the countryside and of agriculture, he had gleaned solely from films. These films had dressed up and beautified the real agricultural situation, and many of them described collectivisation as if it actually overburdened the farmer with turkeys and geese. Obviously Stalin himself believed that this was the true state of things.'
After this, all scenes with Stalin were cut from old films with no less scrupulous care than had been devoted to the removal of Trotsky of *Lenin in October* thirty years earlier. The history of the Soviet cinema was still a history of politics and film.

Still: The Fall of Berlin – *Stalin (Mikhail Gelovani) addressing troops in Red Square.*

Germany: the Red Front

Siegfried Kracauer viewed the German cinema in the period immediately after the First World War as a 'unique inner monologue' of a very revealing nature. It indicated a deep inner anxiety in the German nation, a state of shock (after the defeat, the Treaty of Versailles and subsequent upheavals) which showed no signs of being relieved, a traumatic fixation on negative experiences.

The expressionist films are haunted by frustrations and aggressions, by a pessimism that rejects with horror any revolt against the given order, and by dreams of a new order and of a strong man. It seemed to Kracauer that the Germans during these years of paralysis were unable to realise that there were a great many different types of society between anarchy and dictatorship. In a straight choice between disorder and order, they obviously chose the latter.

Kracauer saw Hitler in Dr Caligari. In film upon film he sees the shadow of what was to come – and of what had come (and gone) by the time he had completed his investigations. Kracauer did his equations knowing that the answers were at the back of the book, and sometimes one cannot help feeling that it all adds up too neatly. Today it seems reasonable to look at German films from 1920 to 1925 not only as an outpouring of the restless subconscious of the German people, but also as a product of the political situation of the day. If the expressionist cinema had a conservative ideological content, this was not solely because the Germans, shaken by wars and revolutions, their self-esteem severely undermined, wished for security at any price even if it meant a despot; it was also determined by the conservatism of the film producers and their power over their productions.

The dominant force in the film industry since 1917 had been Universum Film A.G. (Ufa), founded on the initiative of General Ludendorff and one third originally owned by the state. Later, the Reichswehr (the German Armed Forces) also secured an interest. The censorship regulations forbade films to contain anything that could harm German prestige abroad or in any way disturb public order. In the circumstances it was obvious that the German cinema would not distinguish itself for its liberal attitudes.

In 1925 the inflation was at last over and tensions seemed to slacken. Fresh air was let into the film industry, blowing the ghosts away. In 1930, however, the Depression hit

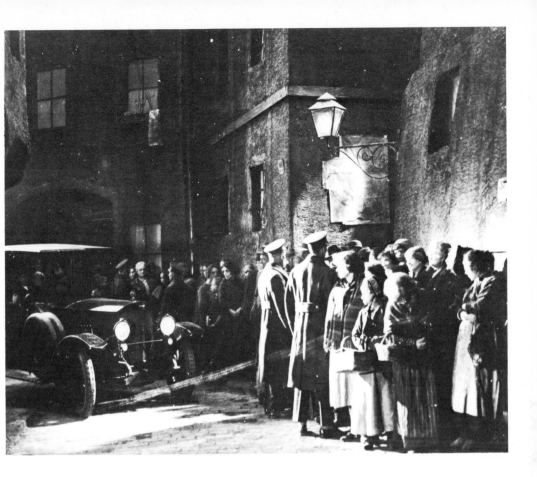

Germany. Hitler, the black magician whose coming Caligari and Nosferatu had foreshadowed, began to appear to an increasing number of Germans as the chosen one, the man of destiny who could shoulder their problems and responsibilities.

Between these two dates lay five years of economic rehabilitation and artistic expansion. Economically it was a stabilising process taking place on the edge of a precipice, artistically an amazing revitalisation between two phases of coma. When the great landslide began to move, traditions, conventions and inhibitions lost much of their hold. Some of the most daring attempts at new patterns of living and fresh artistic forms seem to be based on a need at the time to view the whole of human existence as a vast field for experiment. The old rules and regulations were suspended.

To some artists the restlessness in society was an urgent theme. It was treated honestly and incisively in Brecht's political vaudevilles and in novels like Döblin's 'Berlin Alexanderplatz'. The cinema was more like a mirror held up to society than a comment on it. In Pabst's work, from *The Joyless Street* (1925) to *The Threepenny Opera* (1931), one finds the full ambivalence of this curious transitional period, faltering between hope and despair, awareness and flippancy, solidarity and cynicism, realism and fantasy.

Pabst expressed current tendencies, whether

Still: G. W. Pabst's The Joyless Street.

revolutionary or escapist. He was not an artist of any great political awareness, and from a Marxist viewpoint he would be criticised for devoting too much time to the symptoms of evil, and not enough to the evil itself (i.e. capitalism). In *The Threepenny Opera*, in many ways a fine film, Pabst failed to transpose the author's central vision, the accusation, to the screen, and the satire was softened. Brecht sued the producer and never wanted to have anything to do with the cinema again.

Expressionism in the cinema flowered for a few hectic years, before it suddenly died away. This was not simply due to the changing times, to the stabilising of the Reichsmark, or to the fact that no one believed any more in ghosts and vampires, but also to a change in the basic conditions of the film industry. The economic structure had broken up.

In 1926 Ufa found itself in a grave crisis out of which it was pulled by Paramount and Metro-Goldwyn-Mayer with the injection of seventeen million marks. The money gave the American companies a certain influence. They bought themselves into the German market and without any compunction proceeded to buy up a great many of the stars, actors and directors who had dominated German films since the end of the war. In addition, fifty per cent of the films

31

shown in Ufa cinemas now had to be American.

Economic dependence brought a rapid adjustment to Hollywood ideals. At the same time, the old authoritarian uniformity which lent itself so well to Kracauer's analysis was splintered. Suddenly there were greater opportunities for making films about society, about people and their problems, although the best pictures of this sort were produced outside the big companies.

There seems to have been an atmosphere of freedom – a freedom, however, full of ominous portents. In 1927 Alfred Hugenberg, newspaper king and ultra-reactionary, bought his way into Ufa. 'This position he used not so much for making money as for furthering his own political interests', according to Alan Bullock. Hugenberg led the German National Party which, six years later, formed a Government with the National Socialists. In the years before Hitler's assumption of power, Hugenberg gave him financial support and functioned as the conveyor of subsidies from big industrial concerns.

Consequently, the scope given to the German cinema in the years before 1933 was both temporary and conditional. Realism, which contrasted with both the old fantasies and the new escapism, emerged in a society where the officially proclaimed and the actual liberties did not correspond. In many cases the same laws applied in different ways to different people. In two years, 327 political murders were committed in Germany. Right-wing extremists were guilty of 314 of these, and their combined prison sentences amounted to 31 years. The remaining 13 murders were committed by left-wing extremists, of whom eight were condemned to death, and the others received prison sentences totalling 176 years.

An important date in the history of the German cinema is 29 April 1926, the day that *Battleship Potemkin* had its première in Berlin.

Stills: Above: Leontine Sagan's Mädchen in Uniform. *Right: the son turns to crime in Piel Jutzi's* Mutter Krausens Fahrt ins Glück.

One month earlier, the supreme command of the Reichswehr had seen Eisenstein's film and demanded that it be banned outright. The censor obeyed, although the regulations stated that no film should be refused a showing on grounds of its political, social, religious or aesthetic content. (The regulations were a fine example of double morality, as they also decreed that films must not offend people's sense of decency nor threaten public safety.) The ban was lifted after an intense press campaign, but German soldiers were admonished in a special order of the day not to see the film as it encouraged disobedience, mutiny, uprising and revolution.

Battleship Potemkin was an immense success with both the critics and the general public. In July 1926 it was banned once more, but cleared again after only a couple of weeks, this time for good. By then, however, the censor had cut it by over three hundred feet; the famous perambulator sequence had gone, and so had virtually all the dramatic close-ups. (In the same year, Eisenstein's film was being scrutinised by the censor in Sweden and was banned altogether because of its 'inflammatory' character.)

Battleship Potemkin and the events surrounding its release were of great significance for the radical cinema in Germany. They cleared the way for other Russian films and for new tendencies in the German cinema. They opened the eyes of many intellectuals to the possibilities of the cinema. Radical opinion was activated by the debate around the censorship scandal, and in 1928 Pabst, Piscator, Heinrich Mann and others helped to form an Association for Film Art (Volksverband für Filmkunst). Its aims were to help in the promotion of progressive films and to fight against the falsification of reality which marked most of the films then produced.

For the next few years, German films were often concerned with society: some were about ordinary people, some were shot in the midst of reality itself like *Menschen an Sonntag* (1929) by Robert Siodmak, Fred Zinnemann and Billy Wilder, and some had unmistakably political tendencies, most clearly evident in Slatan Dudow's *Kuhle Wampe* (1932). They were by no means revolutionary films. The only film of a genuinely revolutionary nature, *Aufstand der Fischer* (*Revolt of the Fishermen*), was made by Erwin Piscator in the Soviet Union in 1934.

Kuhle Wampe and *Aufstand der Fischer* are exceptions. Richard Oswald's *Dreyfus* (1929) and *The Captain of Koepenick* (1931) show a great deal of caution and ambivalence in their criticism of, respectively, prejudice and blind acceptance of authority. The latter film ends, like Murnau's *The Last Laugh*, with a volte-face, an improbable reconciliation. Voigt, the habitual delinquent and counterfeit captain, has revolted against the social order and temporarily overthrown its representatives in Koepenick. He has thus committed a capital offence, but it turns out that the people in power are willing to overlook it; the Kaiser himself laughs heartily at the escapade. Voigt is given the pass he has been wanting all along: he wants to join the community, to be one of its members.

Not even in Leontine Sagan's *Mädchen in Uniform* (1931) was the existing order seriously questioned. The girls' school where it is set is typically authoritarian, but otherwise rather special, with a headmistress who is a female version of Frederick the Great. The social criticism is reformist; there is no question of replacing an obsolete society, merely of renovating it. These are bourgeois leftist films. They may preach a more humane organisation of society, but this is to be cast within the old mould.

Piel Jutzi was a humanitarian socialist, and his masterpiece, *Mutter Krausens Fahrt ins Glück* (*Mother Krausen's Journey into Happiness*, 1929), is a proletarian story with something of the slow, humble intensity of Käthe Kollwitz's portraits of workers and their wives. Jutzi has a very distinctive and completely undogmatic style. He shows backyards, bleak staircases, walls without windows – the architecture of the class system. Within it, the ragged proletariat live lives that are not totally joyless, but largely without class solidarity. The bitter social truths of *Mutter Krausens Fahrt ins Glück* are mainly about unemployment and the housing shortage. Hans, a young man, is 'one of the six and a half million unemployed'. His lack of occupation demoralises him to such an extent that he turns to crime and ends up in prison. His family cannot pay the rent and are given notice to quit. His sister Erna has been seduced by a wastrel

lodger. In desperation she tries to prostitute herself in order to find money for the rent. Her radical fiancé, who has a picture of Marx pinned up on his wall, wants to break with her, but his friend argues, with rather greater Marxist orthodoxy, that it is not the girl but her environment that is to blame. Piel Jutzi quotes Heinrich Zille, the cartoonist whose intimate knowledge of proletarian Berlin inspired the idea of the film: 'One can kill a person as easily with inferior housing as with a hatchet.'

Jutzi demonstrates calmly and factually how this society works, and what happens to people who are forced to live in conditions unfit for human beings. He shows unequivocally that the blame lies with the authorities, who are indifferent, remote and powerful. They don't know and don't want to know about the underprivileged. But the accusation is not explicit – Jutzi works consistently with understatements. His voice is clear and specific, but always low-pitched. An official warrant arrives in the post, and the camera (Jutzi is both director and cameraman) fixes on the Prussian seal, then moves to the menacing profile of the German eagle surmounting Mutter Krausen's clock.

Society is the murderer. When Hans, the unemployed son, is arrested by the police, his mother's world crumbles about her. The old woman makes herself some strong coffee, allows herself the luxury, the first in a long while, of some cream and a lot of sugar with it, and then she opens the gas-taps. In her death she takes with her a pale, weedy little child, whom nobody cares about, wishing only to spare it the squalor and degradation of life.

The younger generation are better equipped to free themselves, both because they are young and strong, and also because they have different moral values. The heraldic eagle has not caught them under the spell of petit bourgeois respectability. *Mutter Krausens Fahrt*

ins Glück ends on a note of optimism. Earlier we have seen a demonstration with placards demanding better housing carried by the marching workers, among them Erna and her friend; she is trying to keep up with him, to join in the common cause. At the end of the film we return to this image – the street, the demonstrators, two lovers who have been parted but have come back to each other, determined to throw in their lot with the people.

This final trusting note cannot, however, obliterate the underlying sadness which is felt throughout the film. It is a muted optimism – not a banal happy end, but a final aesthetic contrast.

Jutzi's *Berlin Alexanderplatz* (1931) is another film that is firmly based on reality, but it is the story of an individual rather than of a group. This film also ends on a hopeful note, but of more limited significance. The principal character's happiness seems largely due to the solitude he has achieved after abandoning the community that has treated him so badly and retreating into himself.

Kuhle Wampe has a great deal in common with *Mutter Krausens Fahrt ins Glück*, although it is different in form and general feeling. It is a film that has no reservations. Unhesitant in its declaration of faith, it is more unstable than Jutzi's picture and more heterogeneous, more aggressive and more rhapsodic.

The director was Slatan Dudow, a young Bulgarian who had earlier worked with Piscator and Brecht. The latter helped with the script and wrote the lyrics. The music was by Hanns Eisler, and one of the leading roles was played by Ernst Busch, the minstrel of the German revolution. The picture was divided into three fairly independent parts, each given a Brechtian title and introduced with an associative montage sequence. It was a partisan film made on a very small budget, a Communist Party production that various factions were interested in wrecking. No complete version exists anywhere; it can be said to have been directed partly by the censor.

In 1929, 13 per cent of German industrial workers were unemployed. In 1932 the unemployment figures stood at 43.8 per cent, and to them could be added the 20 per cent-odd only partially employed. This was an economic crisis of catastrophic proportions and the first part of *Kuhle Wampe* opens with a montage of closed factory doors, smokeless factory chimneys and screaming newspaper headlines about the situation on the labour market. Workers drift about on bicycles, trying their luck at one place after another without success. Then we are introduced to the home environment of the unemployed, and to their stagnation. Like Jutzi, Dudow picks on a single family. This time it is the young man who takes his own life after he discovers that a new law has deprived him of his unemployment benefits – he cannot bear the thought of being a burden to his family. He carefully unstraps his wrist-watch and puts it on the window-sill before plunging down.

The second part is about the sister of the dead man and tells the story of her love affair. The characters and relationships are almost the same as in Jutzi's film: Anni is warm and devoted; Fritz is politically aware and wants to preserve his integrity. Anni becomes pregnant. Earlier, she has gone the rounds of all the various authorities, trying to make them withdraw the notice to quit which has been served on her family. She has no success, and they move out to a community settlement, Kuhle Wampe, which is blessed with a kind of holiday camp atmosphere. The radio. is playing 'Deutsche Kaiserklänge', Father haltingly reads aloud from the newspaper about Mata Hari's love life, and Mother ponders over her housekeeping accounts. There is a cosy oil-lamp and an embroidered motto on the wall.

When Fritz (Ernst Busch) realises that Anni is pregnant, he does not want to marry her. But he changes his mind, and the engagement is celebrated with a beer party. The older people get very drunk, and the young couple watch their uninhibited behaviour with an

Stills. Left: Jutzi's Berlin Alexanderplatz.
Below: Slatan Dudow's Kuhle Wampe.

irritation which seems to verge on disgust. There are varying opinions about this excellent sequence – and the party, incidentally, might be thought a trifle extravagant for a proletarian story. Kracauer feels that Dudow and Brecht are playing communists against social democrats, youth against middle age, political activism against escapism and resignation. East German film critics have offered a similar interpretation. There is a great deal to support this, for it also points to the fundamental weakness of the picture: the failure to present any alternative to the betrayals and compromises of the unattractive middle-aged other than the beauty and lack of compromise of the young. The last part of the triptych in *Kuhle Wampe* is totally dominated by youthful exuberance, musical and sporting activities, a full community life from which the old and the ugly are excluded. Placards proclaim 'solidarity' and the young people sing about solidarity, but there is something exclusive and self-sufficient about their pursuits. It is like a cult, and is reminiscent of other cults, of other rites under different signs. Kracauer has pointed out this embarrassing affinity and it is only too evident.

The youth cult is apparent, too, in the epilogue, which is one of the high points of the picture. The youngsters are on their way home on the S-Bahn and get into a political discussion with other passengers. The argument gets heated and threatens to turn into a fight.

The young Communists inform the bourgeois citizens rather scornfully that they are unlikely ever to do anything about the world and its injustices. (They have been discussing the burning of the coffee harvest in Brazil.) 'Who will, then?' someone asks. 'Those who don't like it,' answers one of the girls quickly. Then the young radicals march into Berlin singing their 'Solidarity Song'.

One worrying point about this lively encounter is that it is so easy for the young people to come out on top. Their youth, faith and numerical superiority naturally give them the upper hand. There is no fight and precious little discussion. The young speak in unison, in complete uniformity, and the fact that they all have open, honest faces does not really help a great deal.

Kuhle Wampe is interesting as a document covering the various splits within the German Left and as a symptom of its illusions. It is a remarkable exception, an agitprop film from the days of Thälmann. (Even films in the social-democratic cause are rare during this period, though Ernö Metzner's *Freie Fahrt*, 1928, is one of the few electioneering films of note in the history of the cinema.) In Ulbricht's Germany it is looked upon as a classic, a progressive work and a tradition unto itself.

In its own historical context, *Kuhle Wampe* must have been regarded as refreshing or, alternatively, shocking. The authorities decided it was dangerous, and it was examined three times by the censor. The records reveal that what was considered unforgivable about this film, as compared with Piel Jutzi's picture, was the failure of Dudow and Brecht to content themselves with a critical examination of society; in making a direct, explicit appeal for political action they had gone too far. *Kuhle Wampe* gives the spectator the impression, writes the censor in his report, that 'the state in its present form is unwilling and unable to lead the mass of the population out of their misery and suffering, and that there will be an improvement only if the people help themselves and the existing society gives way to a communist world revolution.'

The political purpose of which the censor wrote might not immediately be apparent in existing versions of *Kuhle Wampe*, but this is at least partly due to the way in which the film was censored. The cuts included not only a Communist nude-bathing sequence (with church-bells tolling on the sound-track), but also some brief though essential references to political events. For instance, the young worker's suicide is not allowed to be connected with the new law abolishing unemployment benefits. The rulings on the various families who are to be given notice to quit their homes were originally read out at great speed in court: in the censored version, only a single ruling survives. A quotation about abortion from paragraph 218 of the Criminal Code, read out while Fritz and Anni walk through the woods,

has been cut out. The censor was also much agitated on the Social Democrats' account, and his indignation was shared by the Ministry of the Interior. In fairness to Dudow's film one must always bear in mind that interference from the political power structure robbed it of some of its consistency and incisiveness.

The première of *Kuhle Wampe* was on 30 May 1932. Eight months later Adolf Hitler became Chancellor. An important phase in German culture was over – a period of courageous pioneering and critical self-examination. It was followed by the dispersal and usually the emigration of German culture. In exile, new publishing houses and magazines were started up, new books were written, new symphonies composed. Emigrants from the German theatre and cinema continued their work in new groupings, and often had to make difficult adjustments, even to change their language. Most of the scientists, educationalists, publishers and artists started fresh careers in the United States. Some intellectuals of basically Socialist conviction worked in the Soviet Union. One of these was Erwin Piscator, who made his only film, *Aufstand der Fischer*, in the Soviet Union. Other films by emigré German filmmakers in Russia included Gustaf von Wangenheim's *Kämpfer* (1935) in which appeared a whole colony of German film actors, among them Ernst Busch. It is a political film, originally conceived as homage to Dimitrov, but there is something distant in its description of the fatherland where the growing darkness is enveloping both Nazi terrorism and the courage of the resistance.

Piscator had previously worked with film while at the People's Theatre (*Volksbühne*) in Berlin. He had used projected stills in early productions, but in 1925 he introduced film into a stage production, using some documentary material. In his book 'Das Politische Theater' he described the dramatic element of surprise achieved by the transition from live acting on stage to the sequences of film, and the heightening of tension created through alternation between the two. For his production of Toller's 'Hoppla, wir leben!' two years later, he let Curt Oertel make a complete original movie, and for the dramatisation in the same year of 'The Good Soldier Schweik', George Grosz made a short cartoon film.

The film passages usually represented either the main historical context or events happening in the past or the future. (In a production of Alexei Tolstoy's 'Rasputin', Piscator anticipated the murder of the Czar and his family with the help of a film sequence.) A contemporary critic likened the function of film in Piscator's work to that of the chorus in Greek classical drama; both functioned as background, as counterpoint, or as a kind of physical subconscious which could anticipate events and issue warnings.

Aufstand der Fischer is an unusual film

with a strange history. Piscator had first arrived in the Soviet Union in 1931 on an official invitation, and had originally intended to make a film of Plievier's play 'Des Kaisers Kulis'. However, Litvinov, who was then Minister for Foreign Affairs, is said to have considered the subject unsuitable in the light of relations between Russia and Germany. Therefore another novel, Anna Sehger's 'Der Aufstand der Fischer von St. Barbara', was chosen as basis for the script, although the finished film turned out to have very little in common with the book.

Piscator planned to use both Russian and German actors for his film, reserving two important parts for Paul Wegener and Lotte Lenya. The sets for the village were to be constructed outside Odessa, but there were months of delay while various items of building material arrived, and when all was ready for shooting to start, the director had to find a new cast. The subject gave him a great deal of trouble, and it is said to have been a costly production. The picture was not premièred until the autumn of 1934. Then, for years afterwards, it seemed simply to have vanished. In 1960 it was shown to Piscator in West Germany. In an interview he said: 'The Russians couldn't use it. But it saved my life.' We are told no more than that, but the film appears to have aroused unpleasant memories.

It is a strange masterpiece, the last offshoot of a great tradition, a revolutionary film that was too revolutionary to be 'used'. *Aufstand der Fischer* radiates revolutionary fervour in a more uncomplicated fashion than that of the big Russian films of the twenties. It has an intensity which sometimes gets out of control and turns into ecstasy. It is quite possible that in the Soviet Union, the film's global revolutionary appeal might have looked like Trotskyism.

This is pure guesswork. In any event this rousing hymn in praise of change must have looked quite outlandish in the Moscow of 1934, where society was being sealed off and mummified, and where the judiciary was beginning to swallow up the revolutionaries and their children.

The film gets off to an explosive start with a rapidly moving series of close-ups of fish jumping, knives cutting, hands busily working and blood pouring freely. In this initial sequence, Piscator is already putting forward the ideological content of his film, depicting the everyday life of the proletariat, their fight for existence, their exploitation. But the sequence also has a more general significance. It is an image of the terrorism of life over the living, and of the energy of a violence that goes deeper than the political conflict. Aesthetically, the sequence illustrates Piscator's efforts to direct the attention of the audience towards separate details, which are not necessarily intended to work as symbols, but rather to underline and give emphasis. It is very much a theatrical director's way of indicating what he considers significant.

Aufstand der Fischer tells a story of industrial conflict. It contains some of the conventions and clichés of the genre: wily profiteers smiling obsequiously, the guilty extravagance of the strike-breakers, the whore with a heart of gold, the fatal shot, the riot, the massacre, and the ultimate victory of the proletariat. Piscator falls back on the great tradition of Eisenstein, and makes no serious attempt to tamper with it, but he presents these conventional motifs with incredible energy. The camera is not particularly mobile, at least not laterally, but the movements within the image are particularly violent. The variations in dramatic intensity are conveyed by changes in the lighting.

Piscator clearly works in a very theatrical way in *Aufstand der Fischer*, and the acting style is also rather too much in the grand manner. But it would still be wrong to call the picture a piece of 'filmed theatre'. A contemporary critic hit more happily on the term 'film-oratorio', which conveys the deliberate as well as the spontaneous in the picture. It is a revolutionary hymn which is partially sung. Occasionally the crowd becomes a chorus. The music beats out its rhythm, the sea is roaring and the froth of indignation is rising.

With great skill Piscator guides the picture from its rather confused beginnings through to a dramatic climax. The shot has rung out, power has revealed its murderous face, and now the dead fisherman is to be buried, the man who has aroused in his brothers a new insight into the meaning of the struggle. The procession of mourners moves across the white dunes towards the church to the distorted, heavy cadences of Paul Gerhardt's Passion hymn, 'Oh head, so sorely wounded'. The black figures are silhouetted against a restless, light background – black on white, as in a Morality play.

The next scene is set in the graveyard. The priest uses the occasion to castigate the strikers. Their leader has thrown away his life. Most

Still: profiteer in Erwin Piscator's Aufstand der Fischer.

37

important of all, says the priest in his shrill, commanding voice, are obedience and order. 'The soldiers are the power, and power is divinely granted.'

The atmosphere becomes highly charged: the dark clothes, the shimmering light, the steady roar of the sea, the wildly whirling birds, the stinging heat, the women's sobs. For a single moment everything is terrifyingly still. Finally the charge must explode, the tidal wave must roar in. The oppressed people rise at last against those who wield the power. The figure of the priest and the crosses on the graves stand out darkly against the white sand, the sea and the sky, while the pages of the Bible whirl round and round through the air – an extraordinarily effective graphic contrast in the midst of the general upheaval. The film's hatred is underlined in the story, from the start the priest has been represented as an obedient tool of the exploiting classes, with only a thin veneer of godliness to hide his thirst for power. The oppressors have distinctive physiognomies. They are thin, quick-moving, sharp-featured men with cold eyes.

The theme of *Aufstand der Fischer* is that the proletariat must fight for its rights. In the final part of the film, the message is more incisive: the fight is no longer simply concerned with bread and justice, but with who is to wield the power in society.

There is a fascinating dichotomy between the political activism of the film and its conscious aestheticism, between its appeal for action and its style. This contrast gives it a somewhat forced tension; the passionate emotions become too strong for the strictly stylised framework. Although there is a stern logic about the chain of events, it smacks of hysteria: the setting is stark, tree-less, dominated by the church spire (from which a machine-gun covers the scene of the battle between the fishermen and the soldiers) and by the invisible forces determining the economic set-up. When revolt breaks out in such a place, one would reasonably expect it to be both brutal and pathetic. But in the film it becomes monotonous, for the same high pitch is maintained throughout.

In a 1935 review, Arthur Koestler speaks of the dishonesty of Piscator's film. The 'shortened projection' of revolutionary process as presented in *Aufstand der Fischer* 'is not only false, but also harmful because of the illusions it creates'. There is nevertheless something irresistible about Piscator's illusionism; this is 'the hypnotic lie of the wishful dream'.

The revolution is a dream. Erwin Piscator creates it with his own personal magic, and it has very little semblance of reality. It is, however, the very opposite of the dreamplays of the expressionist cinema, in which one was always conscious of the hovering presence of a strong man and of immutable fate.

Produced by Joseph Goebbels

In 'Mein Kampf', Adolf Hitler expounds his views on propaganda and its target, the public. He compares 'the mass' with a woman; the mass, like a woman's psyche, demands a 'complementary force', a greater, dominating strength, and prefers 'the man who commands to the man who implores'. Liberal freedom, the open market in opinion where the individual can make his own personal choice, only confuses the great mass of the people, since they do not know how to make use of it.

He pursues his argument further, with what could certainly pass as an analysis of his own propaganda both before and after 1933:

'The mass is as unaware of the unashamed spiritual terrorism to which it is exposed as it is of the scandalous abuse of its human liberty, and it has no conception of the basic madness of the doctrine. It only sees the reckless force, brutality and purpose of its expression, and in the end the mass will always bow to it . . . '

Hitlers' view of humanity was contemptuous, cynical or perhaps just pessimistic. The mass is unintelligent; it is uncritical and forgetful, and propaganda must be adjusted to this. It must be limited to a small number of points, a few ideas that can be turned into slogans and then worked into the public consciousness.

Hitler never modified this initial view of propaganda and those at whom it was aimed. This surprisingly unsophisticated philosophy became Goebbels's theory of propaganda and shaped the entire output of the Nazi propaganda machine. An expert from the opposite camp, F. C. Bartlett, contends in 'Political Propaganda' (1940) that there was nothing original in Nazi propaganda, but that the machinery itself was of impressive (or frightening) dimensions.

In general, German propaganda activities were as notable for their lack of imagination as for their persistence. It is a natural weakness. It would have been illogical for so authoritarian a philosophy to show any trace of imagination. You cannot identify with other people and other nations without attempting to understand what it feels like to be in their shoes; such flexibility could hardly be expected from members of the master race. The fatal weakness of German propaganda was its inability to adjust to different situations and different people; it always came stomping in with jack-boots, immediately recognisable as foreign and inimical.

It is significant that Third Reich propaganda for export to other countries was largely identical to that intended for domestic consumption. There was rarely any exploration of the psychological climate at the receiving end, nor of the particular need for information nor of the strength of resistance. The only concern was the choice of suitable *subjects*. Thus the efforts of the Propaganda Ministry were aimed in the United States at strengthening American isolationist tendencies; the Arab world was fed anti-British information. Lacking were psychological adaptability, a subtle use of the language and concepts of the opposite side and a pretence of sympathy. German propaganda was rarely successful in this type of infiltration. It never took off its uniform. The recipients were merely being honoured with a gracious gesture; the Great German Reich had condescended to address them and they had better listen.

In retrospect it seems odd that Germany at war knew so little about its opponents and was so poor at predicting their reactions. It has been said that the propaganda departments dealing with foreign countries were chronically short of experienced personnel. It seems more likely, though, that the difficulties lay at the psychological and political levels.

A propagandist must familiarise himself thoroughly with his adversaries arguments, must learn the enemy's method of reasoning and his opinions in order to discover the weak points and turn his own arguments against him. Such precise knowledge carries an element of risk, a danger of infection, and this apparently frightened the Nazis considerably. It was as if deep down they were afraid that the enemy's arguments might prove the stronger.

They had no ideological self-confidence, no solid basis of ideas and thought. They had their rites, their feasts and their magic emblems, but these were not effective at a distance. They were an anaesthetic that worked on their own people, but did not serve as arguments and counter-arguments.

There was consequently a remarkable gap between the size of the investment – the highly developed organisation, all the millions of Reichsmarks – and the actual results. Goebbels's ministry seems to have achieved its greatest success in the field of negative indoctrination, the propaganda of terror, which was designed to create respect for the German military machine and which painted Bolshevik barbarism in a manner of medieval descriptions of Hell.

Since 1918, the bourgeois press in Europe had been preparing the ground for this image of the Bolsheviks. But there is much evidence to

Still: Aufstand der Fischer.

suggest that this aspect of Nazi propaganda would have had a far greater effect had it not been packaged with anti-semitism. Reactionaries who did not, like the Nazis, see any obvious connection between Jewishness and Communism, were confused by this double-edged attack. Even if 'Kremlin' and 'Comintern' were concepts charged with terror for them, the message became much less persuasive. Propaganda of which part is disbelieved becomes almost totally ineffective.

Anti-semitic propaganda was largely unsuccessful outside Germany – indeed it often helped increase antipathy towards Nazism. Eventually Goebbels's propagandists learnt to make certain transpositions, to soften the anti-Jewish statements and to make an attempt at adjusting their message according to its destination. Croats and Slovaks were given information which was completely different from that going out to the Swedes and the Swiss.

But despite these manipulations, German propaganda was never particularly subtle. Hitler's idea of it suggested rape rather than seduction. In a conversation with Hermann Rauschning, he maintained that propaganda should function in the way that artillery does before an infantry advance in trench warfare. Propaganda must break down the enemy's main line of defence before the army is brought in. The enemy must be demoralised, and in the opinion of the Führer this could only be achieved through brutal aggression. In 'Mein Kampf' he writes:

'Whoever wants to win the great mass over must possess the key which opens the door to its heart. This key is not called objectivity, in other words weakness, but will and power . . .'

The key could also be called propaganda, and from the earliest beginnings of the Nazi movement a great deal of attention was devoted to it. In early days, though, resources were relatively modest. The voice of the Nazi press may have been loud, but it did not carry far; when Hitler came to power, there were 4,703 newspapers and magazines in Germany, and of these only 120 declared their solidarity with National Socialism. The radio, which was to become the most important propaganda medium, was governed by the state authorities during the Weimar Republic and was therefore inaccessible for some time. The loudspeaker technique, a prerequisite for mass meetings, was not developed until the end of the 'twenties, and as late as 1931 two people seem to have sufficed to run the entire film section of the Party. But after the seizure of power, an incredibly rapid expansion of the propaganda machinery took place. In 1934, 14,000 people were employed within this particular sector of the administration. In 1936, the film sector had been officially organised at various levels, the basic one of which comprised 22,357 minor units.

During the years of growth and consolidation, party propaganda may have been more primitive, but it had often been effective. The essential point was that the movement attracted attention. Lorries packed with activists shouting slogans drove round the streets, brass bands played in town squares, and dummy tanks advertised the party organ, 'Völkischer Beobachter'. The music was an attraction, and so were the uniformed parades, the mass meetings, the aggressive atmosphere surrounding these manifestations and the physical violence which often accompanied them.

The so-called 'Party days', or rallies, held at Nuremberg, were aimed above all at the edification of party members. They were like gigantic conferences given by a political revival movement, but because of their spectacular character their propaganda value went far beyond this. Every year, the rallies grew in size, and the stage direction of them became ever more precise. Every detail of the production was considered and weighed in relation to the whole: the musical element, the standard-bearers, the emblems, and the human architecture composed of uniformed formations. The 1934 rally, which Leni Riefenstahl preserved for posterity in Triumph des Willens, according to Hamilton T. Burden, ' . . . marked the beginning of a new tradition of carefully staged visual propaganda. The Chancellor's speech was timed so that his closing remarks coincided with the arrival of darkness, and during the last words of his address, bonfires were lit along the horizon, and innumerable searchlights sent their broad beams into the sky, creating the illusion that the entire field was surrounded by a vast forest of luminous columns.'

The rally was a ritual of emotion, a ceremony through which, according to one enthusiastic eye-witness, 'the mass' was freed from its 'formlessness' and the individual from his 'lack of context'. It was a religious festival, a collective spiritual baptism and an annual sacramental confirmation. The strict form, the symmetry, was an expression of the Nazi movement's spirit, its fondness for abstraction and its fundamentally inimical attitude to people. It also served as a psychological tie, a force which held everyone together and forbade any individual departure.

The main director of these spectacles was Joseph Goebbels. Chief architect was Albert Speer, later Armaments Minister and one of the most capable men in the Hitler regime. From 1933 until the outbreak of war in 1939, the rally arena outside Nuremberg was the most massive construction in the Third Reich. It represented an embodiment of the self-confidence and power fantasy of National Socialism, of its 'reckless force' and its 'basic madness'.

From 1930 onwards, the intensity and scope of Nazi propaganda was significantly increased. In May 1928, the Party had received over 800,000 votes in the general elections and captured twelve seats in the Reichstag This led a year later to the alliance between Hitler and Hugenberg. During the 1930 election campaign, the Nazis were supported by the National Party press, and Adolf Hitler was provided with helpful publicity in the Ufa newsreels. At the elections, the National Socialists got 6,407,397 votes and won 107 seats. Following this success, a steadily increasing number of willing donors swelled the party funds, and Hitler cut down on the 'Socialist' content of his message to make the industrialists happy.

During the election campaign of 1932, the leader of the party took to the air. He flew about 30,000 miles, speaking at two hundred meetings. Otto Dietrich, the Nazi press chief, testifies: 'This tidal wave of propaganda appealed to the sporting instincts of the mass and satisfied their hunger for sensation, as well as stirring up their political opinions.'

The Party also began to make its own films. One of the first was *Hitler's Flug über Deutschland* (*Hitler's Flight over Germany*). The movie enthusiast Joseph Goebbels arranged for one of his own speeches to be filmed and shown at open air meetings around the country.

Almost immediately after the seizure of power, a bureaucratic machine was established for the cinema. In July 1933, a Film Office was created, later to become the National Film Office with ten subordinate departments. This was one section of a larger organisation, the National Cultural Office. The President of the latter was Goebbels, and in his department, the Ministry for Enlightenment and Propaganda, there was a special film section. All the threads were gathered in the hands of the Minister of Propaganda; he also controlled the party's propaganda centre, which had its own film department. 'We are convinced', wrote Goebbels, 'that films constitute one of the most modern and scientific means of influencing the mass. Therefore a government must not neglect them.'

From the start it seems to have been decided that the emphasis should lie with the production of documentaries. *Deutschland Erwacht* (*Germany Awakes*) was released in time for the March 1933 elections; it was about the National Socialist movement, its struggles and its victory. In August 1934, a plebiscite was held to confirm Hitler's assumption of Hindenberg's functions as chief of state (on which occasion over four million Germans dared register their dissent), and before the event an election film called *Unser Führer* (*Our Fuehrer*) was distributed.

There was a high rate of expansion within the organisation and the film output rose. In 1934, 129 feature films were produced in Germany. In the same year, according to Curt Belling, a member of the party propaganda committee, twenty million Germans saw Leni Riefenstahl's first party rally picture *Sieg des Glaubens* (*Victory of Faith*) and *Blut und Boden* (*Blood and Soil*), a film by Rolf von Sonjewski-Jamrowski about German land and German farmers in the miserable past and the happy present.

In 1935, the State invested forty million

marks in the theatre and the cinema. Initially' only the production side of the film industry was completely nationalised. According to Nazi theoreticians, German film before 1933 was characterised by a lack of national spirit. It glorified all things foreign and exotic; it speculated in sin and encouraged crime. (There were outstanding exceptions, indicated by Goebbels in a speech in 1934, for instance in Fritz Lang's *Nibelungen* pictures and Luis Trenker's romantic national epic, *Der Rebell*, which had its première two weeks before Hitler seized power and which the great leader himself had seen four times by August.)

The blame for this scandalous lack of balance could be laid squarely on the Jews. In his book 'Der Film in Staat und Partei' (The Film in State and Party), Curt Belling quoted a great deal of statistical material. He had worked out that between 70% and 80% of the scripts for films made in the early 'thirties were written by Jews. Half the finished films had Jewish directors, and Jewish financial interests controlled almost 90% of the distribution.

The party's fight against un-German films had met with great success in December 1930, when it managed to halt screenings of Lewis Milestone's *All Quiet on the Western Front*, an

Still: un-German movie — Lew Ayres and Raymond Griffith as World War I German soldiers in All Quiet on the Western Front.

American movie based on the notorious work by a 'marxist-pacifist' emigrant writer and produced by 'a Jew who originated from Württemberg'. According to the Party chronicles, forty thousand National Socialists gathered for a protest meeting outside the Berlin cinema where the première was held. Giving in to this storm of indignation, the censorship authorities banned the picture on the grounds that it was harmful to Germany's reputation abroad.

The National Socialist cinema was naturally patriotic. In *Heimkehr* (*Return*, 1941), a picture about persecuted Germans who return to the Reich, Paula Wessely delivers an ecstatic monologue during which she tearfully mentions

Stills: early Nazi features. Hans Westmar – *communist rioters being prevented from attacking the hero's coffin (above); Westmar (right); Paul Wegener as the Lenin-like chief communist. Far right:* SA-Mann Brand. *Bottom right:* Friesennot.

Deutschland 36 times. The first Nazi features, however, did not concern themselves so much with the nation as with the Party. They were surprisingly few, really only three; *SA-Mann Brand*, *Hitlerjunge Quex* and *Hans Westmar*, all made in 1933. Fritz Hippler, for many years the leading figure under Goebbels in the industry, complained in his book 'Betrachtungen zum Filmschaffen' ('Reflections on Film Making,' 1942) about the soullessness that marked the cinematic treatment of National Socialist ideas. It does seem, though, as if the propaganda leadership rarely encouraged script writers and directors to expound their National Socialist faith in their films. At any rate, they were not to shout out their ideals. In a speech in September 1934, Fritz Scheuermann, the president of the National Film Office at the time, said that 'great National Socialist propaganda films' should still be made, but they were not suitable for export. Films to be exported should be works of art.

Thus the revolutionary phase in the history of the Nazi cinema was just an episode. Films were adjusted to the political situation of the

day, and amongst the anti-Russian and anti-Polish films, there were a few in which Russians and Poles were actually represented as ordinary human beings. One of these is *Der Postmeister* (1940), based on a Pushkin short story. The hostile *Friesennot* (1935), though, was banned on 7 September 1939, two weeks after the signing of the Russo-German non-aggression pact. In 1941, when Germany was at war with the Soviet Union, the ban was lifted and the film re-released under the more expressive title of *Dorf im roten Sturm* (*Village in the Red Attack*).

During the last two or three pre-war years, Hitler spoke a great deal on the subject of peace. The Berlin Olympics were a gigantic exercise in respectability; the signs saying 'Jews Not Wanted Here' were removed from restaurants and hotels, and 'Der Stürmer' was briefly unobtainable from the newspaper kiosks. In 1937, Karl Ritter, normally a noisily outspoken

party man, made a sympathetic, restrained picture, *Urlaub auf Ehrenwort* (*Leave on Word of Honour*), showing German soldiers faithfully reporting for duty even when obstacles are put in their way, but they are presented in a very relaxed manner as a bit frivolous, sometimes faltering in their determination, and cursing and swearing. The most remarkable feature of the film, however, is the presence of two communists, one intellectual and one worker, who are part of the group. As Gosta Werner has written; 'They believe in their cause, and the others respect their convictions. Both would have been impossible in a German film made from 1933 to 1935.'

Of the 1,097 feature films made in Germany from 1933 to 1945, only 96 were initiated by the Ministry of Propaganda, the so-called 'Staatsauftragfilme'. To this group belong two of the most significant films of the period, Veit Harlan's *Jud Süss* (1940) and Wolfgang Liebeneiner's *Ich klage an* (*I Accuse*, 1941). Harlan's picture is part of the anti-semitic film campaign launched in 1939 with the apparently innocuous comedy *Robert und Bertram*. *Jud Süss* was apparently shown to the Aryan population in the areas of Eastern Europe to which the Jews were to be moved while awaiting transport to the extermination camps. Under an order issued by Heinrich Himmler on 30 September 1940, and still preserved, the whole of the SS and the police corps were to see the film. And the press was notified by the Ministry of Propaganda that *Jud Süss* was not to be described as anti-semitic.

Ich klage an has a hidden purpose of a different kind. On the surface it is a very humane story about a love that conquers all. A beautiful and vivacious young woman, married to a successful professor of medicine, contracts a fatal disease, the last stage of which is two months of horrible agony. The woman deteriorates before our eyes, while her husband works desperately to find a cure. She asks him to let her die and he helps her to slip away. Her death is beautiful; her husband holds her lovingly in his arms while in the next room a close friend is playing music by Beethoven. Then come the court proceedings. While the jury is deliberating, an old huntsman tells the rest that he has had to destroy his dog. He asks: 'Are we supposed to treat people worse than animals?' Somebody else says that a law demanding that sick people suffer is inhuman. The president of the court rules that individuals cannot be left to decide in these questions, but that the responsibility lies with the state authorities. There is a need for new and more humane laws.

Before the war, the 'racial policy' department of the Party had had a few informational films made about the euthanasia programme. *Ich klage an*, a popular film full of noble sentiments and with well-known actors, must be seen against the background of the killings which, on the Führer's orders, were now being stepped up in the interests of the economy and the

Stills. Top left: Heinrich George in Der Post-meister. *Bottom left: Heidemarie Hatheyer and Paul Hartmann in* Ich klage an. *Above: leading actors in drag for* Robert und Bertram. *Below:* Urlaub auf Ehrenwort.

race. Directives from Goebbels' Ministry to the press noted that the problem should be treated with the greatest tact and that the term 'euthanasia' was not to be used in any reviews.

Most of the films of the Goebbels period, however, were fairly innocuous. In a register published in 1951 by the Allied Control Commission, 141 feature films were described as politically debatable. According to Arthur Maria Rabenalt, director of a number of popular films (such as . . . *reitet für Deutschland* (*He Rides for Germany*, 1941)), the escapist element in the cinema was encouraged by the authorities during the greater part of the war. There was a curious discrepancy between the doctrinaire principle of conformity and the absence of political directives for the major part of film output. If we are to believe Rabenalt, it was often difficult to know what was allowed and what was not. Cinema audiences seem to have preferred the 'unpolitical' films. Certain war films were also very popular while the war was still going well.

During the last phase of the thousand-year Reich, an interesting change of approach occurred. By then, Joseph Goebbels had become the principal spokesman for the régime. From the autumn of 1942 onwards, he used a propaganda method somewhat reminiscent of the manner in which Churchill spoke to the British nation in its moments of crisis. Goebbels made no secret of the difficulties: he admitted that a German defeat was possible and rejected all the comfortable notions of certain victory. On that basis, he went on to fire his audiences with enthusiasm for the total involvement that total war demands. It was no longer a matter

of revivalist ecstasy – but rather of a factual approach, which extended to films. Ideologically speaking, this new cinema of resistance could be seen, according to Rabenalt, as a move to the left. There was even the odd instance of the word 'proletarian', so long unspoken, being heard. With this trend, the National Socialist cinema recaptured the spirit of simplicity and concentration on the great cause that had characterised *Hitlerjunge Quex* and *Hans Westmar*.

Goebbels appears today to have been the most interesting of the Nazi leaders. His biographers Roger Manvell and Heinrich Fraenkel consider that he originally showed a certain inclination towards Marxism. During his early days in the Party, when he was close to the Strasser brothers, Goebbels was more anti-capitalist than anti-Communist, and entries in his diary

show that as late as February 1926 he was horrified by Hitler's 'reactionary' attitude to the Soviet Union and to private ownership. But eventually he adjusted to the Führer, almost to the point of romantic devotion.

Goebbels, like Hitler, was interested in the cinema, and on two occasions even recommended *Battleship Potemkin* as a worthy example for German film-makers to follow. It was a great work of art and a fabulous piece of propaganda. ('Someone without a firm ideology could become a Bolshevik through seeing this film.') Sergei Eisenstein acknowledged this praise in an open letter, commending the propaganda minister's wisdom in allowing his film-makers to be trained by the enemy. He added that the closeness to life which Goebbels had recommended to the German cinema in February 1934 was an excellent guiding principle which, in this case, would have strange consequences. Truth and National Socialism were incompatible; realistic German films would have been about terror, about prisons and torture, about concentration camps.

Goebbels's *Battleship Potemkin* was *Ohm Krüger* (1941), directed by Hans Steinhoff, in which the minister invested 5,400,000 marks and to which he devoted an intense personal interest. He might possibly even have contributed to the script himself. 'Certain lines,' write Manvell and Fraenkel in their biography,

'seem to come straight from Goebbels's pen'.

There is evidence to indicate that Goebbels was also actively involved in work on other films. One of his pet projects was *Kolberg*, Veit Harlan's historical spectacular in colour about a German town holding out against an enemy of vastly superior strength. It had its première in Berlin and La Rochelle (an enclosed fortress like the historical Kolberg) on 30 January 1945, exactly twelve years after Hitler came to power. It had cost close to nine million marks, and according to the director's memoirs, 187,000 soldiers and 6,000 horses took part in the production.

Goebbels's State Secretary, Walter Funk, had written the last words of the script of another Harlan film, made in a sunnier phase of National Socialist history. In *Der Herrscher* (*The Sovereign*, 1937), the industrialist Clausen, played by Emil Jannings, is making his will. The old man disinherits his children and donates his large business to the 'people's community'. One day, he ponders, someone will rise from the depths to shoulder the responsibility 'because,' he says in the final line, 'the man who is a born leader needs no other teacher than his own genius.'

It is a pronouncement typical of Goebbels, and, emanating from his Ministry, an expression of the leadership cult, of Goebbels' love for the Ruler, and possibly an expression of his anti-bourgeois attitudes, his curious 'folksiness'.

Doctor Joseph Goebbels did not desire absolute power for himself. He dreamed instead of a future as a free intellectual. When the war had been safely won, he planned to devote himself to a theoretical work on film that was to be as crucial to the development of the cinema as Lessing's 'Die Hamburgische Dramaturgie' had been to Romantic drama.

Stills. Left: Emil Jannings in Der Herrscher. *Below: the French charge in* Kolberg.

The Spanish Civil War

In 1931, Spain was a country with twenty-four million inhabitants of whom half could not read or write. There were eight million impoverished peasants and two million who possessed no land of their own. Twenty-thousand people owned more than half the country, and some land-owners even had entire provinces in their private possession. A labourer could earn from one to three pesetas in a day, and two loaves of bread cost one peseta. In Spain at the time there were 20,000 monks, 31,000 priests, 60,000 nuns and 5,000 convents. There were 15,000 officers, among them 800 generals. In 1934, one of these, Francisco Franco y Bahamonde, led the brutal quelling of a workers' uprising in Asturias. During the next two years, national tensions grew progressively more acute. The 1936 elections were won by the Popular Front, but the resulting government was drawn mainly from the bourgeois left.

On 17 July 1936, a group of officers rose against the lawful government. When Franco finally emerged victorious in the spring of 1939, half a million Spanish houses were in ruins. Over a million people had been killed. Two million Spaniards were in prison and another half million had fled the country.

Spain at the beginning of the 'thirties was a feudal society and in some ways almost mediae-val. Luis Buñuel's documentary *Las Hurdes* (*Terre sans pain* or *Land Without Bread*, 1932) describes a society which goes even further back into darkness, 'outside culture and civilisation, outside our time, outside our present world' (Artur Lundkvist). In Las Hurdes, a remote part of Estremadura, there is nothing but suffering and ignorance. It is a sterile ravine around which are scattered a few dwellings. There is no flicker of freedom, beauty or hope in Las Hurdes: it is a nightmare of apathy and stagnation.

School is the one manifestation of 'the present' which has reached the place. Here, where no one possesses anything, the children are taught to write on the blackboard: 'You must respect other people's property.' It is a typical Buñuel comment. In this section of the film there is at last a suggestion of light, but at the same time Buñuel shows that the light of knowledge can be manipulated in such a way as to confirm ignorance and bondage. Another note of sarcasm is introduced by the softly flowing music of Brahms and by the brisk commentary; these are contrasting effects serving to emphasise the remoteness of the world and the ability of people to shut themselves off from the suffering of others.

Las Hurdes is a picture of an extreme kind of life, of realities that are so improbable that they seem to have a place among Bunuel's surrealist creations. It is a social documentary which superficially draws our attention to an ethnic curiosity. Las Hurdes, however, is also a reality which is not shaped simply by its geographical conditions and the barrenness of its soil, but by the ignorance and indifference of the authorities, and by the remoteness of power from individual suffering in pre-revolutionary Spain. The authorities certainly considered that this curious social documentary embodied an accusation which was rather too far-reaching.

Stills: Spanish peasants, real from Buñuel's Las Hurdes, *and played by Henry Fonda in William Dieterle's* Blockade.

Not until 1936 could Buñuel's film be shown in Spain during the Civil War and then only on the Republican side.

Blockade (1938) is an American feature film set in Spain, 'a story of love and adventure' in an operetta-type landscape of painted backdrops. Henry Fonda plays a young, noble peasant, Marco, who is something of a progressive as he is actually on the point of getting himself a tractor. According to the credit titles, it is spring 1936. There is the sudden noise of guns, shattering the idyllic picture of peasant life. People are seen fleeing across a bridge. Marco speaks to the people, and his heart-felt appeal dissuades them from running away. To a background accompaniment of choirs and military music they put their bundles down and set to work repairing the damaged bridge. The tide turns in their favour; they close ranks and march off with guns on their shoulders towards the enemy.

It is nothing more than operetta with an element' of folklore. The military action is broken up with musical numbers. There is a village tavern complete with dark-eyed señoritas and the romantic sound of guitars. At the same time it is indisputably a Civil War story. It is stated in the introduction that the film does not in any way take sides, but this is merely a dutiful phrase; in reality the sympathies in *Blockade* are firmly with the Republicans. The film is directed by William Dieterle, a militant human-

Stills. Above and right: Blockade *with Henry Fonda and Madeleine Carroll. Top right: Gary Cooper, Akim Tamiroff and Ingrid Bergman in* For Whom the Bell Tolls.

ist, and the script is by John Howard Lawson, who, a decade later, as one of the 'Hollywood Ten', was to see himself black-listed by the American film community.

Blockade may be simple-minded and moralising but it is nevertheless of interest because of its passionate appeal to the world. Lawson and Dieterle never mention the names of any of the combatants. The enemy is anonymous but he stands condemned by his own actions. The fascists in this film which never mentions fascism (or socialism for that matter) are the true enemies of the people; their war is mainly directed against the civilians. A Republican officer makes an impassioned little speech about the ruthless bombardments, the blockade and the attempts at infiltration. His own soldiers are frank and warm-hearted, casually dressed, but always ready for resourceful action.

The obligatory love-story is acted out between Marco, man of the people, and Norma, a White Russian emigrée. She has no roots and momentarily looks like choosing the wrong side. She has always thought that 'war was only about slogans and flags', but realises that this particular conflict is about liberty and the dignity of man.

The end of the film is remarkable. Marco, now a lieutenant, turns towards the audience. This war, he says with vibrant sincerity, is not war but murder. He appeals to humanity, his honest gaze meeting ours. 'Where is the conscience of the world?'

In 1938, the position of the anti-fascist forces in Spain was becoming precarious. The one-sided effects of the policy of non-intervention had isolated the Republic, and in April, Franco's forces broke through to the Mediterranean, driving a wedge between government-con-trolled areas. It was high time for the conscience of the world to wake up.

In distant Hollywood, *Blockade*, a Walter Wanger production, seems to have been seen as a commercial experiment. 'Variety' wrote that the film's reception would be of particular interest to those producers who had so far hesitated to tackle subjects of a politically controversial character. In spite of various protests, it was a great box-office success. A project with quite opposite intentions – a Fox film on the siege of Alcázar – was stopped by a campaign from the left.

Hollywood returned to Spain in 1943 with *For Whom the Bell Tolls*, Sam Wood's colourful spectacle freely adapted from Hemingway. This film, too, avoids calling political facts and actions by their right names. James Agee believed he caught the term 'fascist' at one point. Apparently this naughty word was used right through Dudley Nichols' script, but was replaced in the finished film by the word 'nationalist'. The producer, Adolph Zukor, called *For Whom the Bell Tolls* 'a great film without any political connotation', adding re-assuringly, 'we are neither for nor against anyone'.

According to Agee, Franco's ambassador in Washington made approaches to the State

Department in an effort to stop Zukor's film. In Spain, of course, it has never been shown. The Spanish authorities still showed the same degree of sensitivity twenty years later when they banned *Behold a Pale Horse*, a pallid film by Fred Zinnemann, which, although set in the present, had a leading character who had been an anti-Fascist hero during the Civil War.

A fascist film with a Spanish Civil War theme is the Italian *L'Assedio dell'Alcázar*, directed by Augusto Genina in 1939. It is not a major work of art, but contains a couple of scenes which belong among the high points of political cinema.

The subject is heroic, concerning the fortress at Toledo, the Alcázar, and its defenders who for sixty-eight days managed to hold out against superior forces. In his description of the military course of events, Genina seems to have stuck to the historical facts, although we are naturally not told about the hundred civilians, all members of the Republican families in the town, who were taken hostage as a precautionary measure. In this film, soldiers and civilians are all one big family, sustained by the same beliefs.

It starts out harmoniously: children are dancing and playing in a yard inside the fortress. Then come the Republican planes; bombs are dropped in an act of vandalism, not just against civilians, but also against a national monument. Later there is a conversation in which it is stated that one cannot expect anything else from people who are deficient in both national conscience and aesthetic sensibility.

On the whole, however, the attitude to the enemy in *L'Assedio dell'Alcázar* is tolerant rather than vindictive. The Republicans are a mass – they storm forward like Indians in a traditional Western. An officer from the Alcázar who plans to get through to the nationalist army, dresses himself up as a Republican. He dons a baggy uniform, asking jokingly: 'Doesn't it suit me?', and ruffles his hair. It is a good-natured joke about people who have no style. More serious accusations are advanced, but less clearly spelled out. No rumours are spread among the defenders about the 'reds' raping women or using weapons forbidden by the Geneva Convention. On the other hand, Genina lets the disguised Franco man, travelling on the back of a lorry, overhear a conversation between two Republican soldiers. 'If it was up to me,' one of them says, 'we'd start using poison gas'. He also mentions the possibility of poisoning the drinking water.

At a later stage, a member of the Republican parliament comes to the Alcázar to persuade the commander, Colonel Moscardó, to give up. The adversary is represented as a sympathetic man who, however, feels unable to guarantee on his honour that women and children, if given safe conduct out of the fortress, would not later be used as hostages against the Alcázar's defenders.

When bidding farewell, he asks to shake the hand of the commander. Colonel Moscardó then asks for a priest, saying very calmly, 'If you have a priest who is under sentence of death, please send him over to us.' The implication seems to be that the colonel (who was forced in an earlier scene to sacrifice his son for the Alcázar and Spain) is a greater hero than any on the Republican side, and there is also a suggestion that the other side is in the habit of killing off priests.

Aiming at positive indoctrination, Genina dwells on the virtues of the Alcázar's defenders rather than on the crimes of the enemy. There is no indulgence in invective, no talk of bolshevism, hardly even of 'the reds'. The opponents are quite simply another kind of people, another class, and it is typical of the view of humanity in *L'Assedio dell'Alcázar* that the republican officers are depicted with a certain amount of respect and understanding, while the private soldiers are given very little individuality and certainly no attractive qualities. A stronger note of indignation is noticeable only towards the end of the siege, when the Alcázar is threatened by Republican mines. An officer at the enemy's headquarters looks sadly out of the window towards the fortress, saying: 'I am sorry about the women and the children.' From the depth of the fortress vaults rises the muffled noise from the Asturian miners' drills. Somebody exclaims vehemently, in an echo from *Blockade* and possibly (even probably) in answer to Henry Fonda: 'This isn't war. It is murder.'

At the beginning of the film there has been another, even more, startling echo. A superior Republican force is advancing on Toledo, and the 'nationalists' are getting ready for them. 'They'll never get through!' somebody vows. An officer defending an advanced position repeats the solemn declaration to the commander of the Alcázar: 'They will not get past us!' Here they actually use the battle-cry of the Republic, the promise given by the heroic city of Madrid: *No pasaran!* It is a subtle psychological trick. The director robs the enemy of his insignia, and thereby disturbs the pattern of emotional communication. An audience with

vague sympathies for the Republican cause might become hesitant at this point, as the roles have been so cleverly switched. The heroism is attributed by Augusto Genina to the fascists, and the ruthless war against civilians is waged by their enemies.

There are two high points in the Alcázar film, both underlined by music. In the first the radio operator is told that relief is finally on its way. There is a great eruption of joy: people rush about in a state of individual excitement which is soon orchestrated by the music into an expression of communal happiness, with men, women and children rocking rhythmically from side to side.

The other high point is on the eve of the attack. The priest has come over from the Republican side, dressed in an ordinary suit, and now dons the robes of his office. He officiates at a service which is accompanied by solemn and emotional music. The congregation kneels, and the camera moves more or less in a circle from face to face, softly, almost like a blessing. The organ music changes to gentle choral singing while the priest gives the sacraments to the wounded. A dying hero wants to be married to his beloved.

The end is abrupt and very compressed. Suddenly the whole landscape is filled by the quietly approaching liberators. Then there is joyous tumult, a flourish of trumpets and an exchange of Fascist greetings (the only one in the film) and the commandant reports: '*Niente di nuove di Alcázar*.' Whereupon the whole picture freezes into static images: the camera dwells on the ruined walls, symbols of tradition, honour and duty.

André Malraux's only film, *L'Espoir* (or *Days of Hope*) also deals with a communal experience.

Malraux arrived in Spain on the third day of the Civil War, taking command of the airborne forces of the International Brigade, an outfit which played a vital part in the Republican achievements during the initial stages of the war. After being wounded in an air-battle, he wrote 'L'Espoir', one of his greatest books, during his convalescence. Two of the central episodes of the novel formed the basis for the film which Malraux apparently made at the special request of the Spanish government. Shooting began in June 1938, in Barcelona, and was interrupted in January 1939, the day before Franco's army marched into the city. The picture was later completed in France, but was not publicly shown until after the end of World War II.

The film of 'L'Espoir' is more activist than the novel, one might even say more 'socialist', but inferior from an artistic viewpoint. In parts it is fairly inept. Too much of the action is narrated in the titles; they recount what is

happening in the meantime and carry the story over from one episode to the next. In certain respects Malraux seems to be an instinctive neo-realist. He uses third-rate actors and amateurs, but many sequences have a stylised character in sharp contrast to the realism of the faces and the soundtrack.

Three sequences are important, for in them a feeling of reality forces its way through the fictional events. The first concerns an enemy gun which covers the entrance to a threatened town and consequently must be silenced. A young Republican sacrifices himself; at breath-taking speed he drives a car straight into the fascist artillery post, blowing both it and him-self up. This scene has terrific emotional power as well as an undertone of romantic existentialist activism.

Another sequence involves a bombing raid against a well camouflaged enemy airfield. The crew has taken a farmer up with them as he alone knows the area and has seen where the fascist planes are. From the air everything looks different, and the assignment at first appears impossible. During the approach, the plane comes under anti-aircraft fire; never did a plane seem as fragile as this, nor the flying itself appear so hazardous, so incredibly heroic.

The ending is famous. One of the Republican bombers has crashed on the sierra after success-fully carrying out its mission; a long line of people is making its way down the mountain with the wounded and the dead. This proces-sion filing across the landscape has strong cinematic associations. First comes a mule carrying a simple coffin; instead of a wreath it bears on its lid the machine-gun from the crashed plane. Old peasants stand by the side of the road greeting the procession with the Republican salute. Down by the church a big crowd has gathered, and even the women give the clenched fist salute.

The feeling of this sequence grows out of the utter silence of the mountains and the people. Its low-keyed realism gradually seems to assume a symbolic significance.

Malraux depicts a political reality, sometimes

almost casually, and sometimes with great emotion. Our own feelings rise and respond, if we relate emotionally to that particular phase of history. Perhaps also the film contains an element of genuine tragic grandeur which can move even the neutral spectator.

The rather mixed experience that L'Espoir provides today might be due to the proximity we feel to war through television. Compared to what we can see of events in Vietnam, the military action in Malraux's film seems carefully arranged. The inimitable flavour of actuality is clearly evident in many documentaries of the Spanish Civil War, even though technically they were not generally of a high order.

The most remarkable of these films is Joris Iven's The Spanish Earth, which is considered in detail elsewhere. A less important film, but similar in its quiet observation and appeal, is Herbert Kline's Heart of Spain, made in 1937 for an American–Canadian Relief Commission. It shows the bombs, the ruins, the weeping women, the dead and the relief workers, and ends with a political–humanitarian appeal: 'We must give more!' followed by a single clenched fist, more clenched fists and a paso doble.

Russian and English documentary film-

makers were also at work on the scene of the Civil War. Roman Karmen sent home a long series of weekly reports under the general title of What Is Happening in Spain, and from this rich material Esther Shub later put together Spain (1939), one of the masterpieces of the compilation film and very influential, not least on Frédéric Rossif's Mourir à Madrid (1962). A left-wing British company, Progressive Film Unit, produced two films: Behind the Spanish Lines and Spanish A.B.C., the latter directed by Thorold Dickinson. With Norman McLaren as his cameraman, Ivor Montagu made a 16 mm film in colour and black-and-white, The Defence of Madrid, which was shown at pro-republican rallies all over England.

In his book on compilation movies, 'Films Beget Films', Jay Leyda also mentions a film compiled from documentary footage by Luis Buñuel, and made at the request of the Republican government. This film, Espagne 1937, long thought to be lost, was rediscovered a few years ago. Jean-Paul Le Chanois was the director, and Buñuel was supposedly responsible for the production and the commentary. So far no further analysis seems to have been made of this remarkable item.

On the fascist side, Karl Ritter directed a documentary feature called Legion Condor, the première of which was planned for the autumn of 1939. It was to tell the story of the German

Stills. Opposite page: L'Espoir – *the suicidal drive; the bombing raid. Below: a precedent from* Battleship Potemkin.

Flying Corps in Spain. Ritter, who is said to have been a fighter pilot during World War I, and made the flying films *Pour le Mérite* (1938) and *Stukas* (1941), must have been the right man for the job. In a letter from Berlin to the Stockholm newspaper 'Svenska Dagbladet' during the summer of 1939, the project is described as 'a moving and grandiose picture reportage which is said to have never been equalled'. The film was to have ended with the triumphant entry of the Condor Legion into Berlin after the victory. But the première never took place.

William L. Shirer offers an explanation in 'A Berlin Diary', under 4 February 1940:
'A big German film company completed last summer at the cost of several million marks a movie based on the exploits of the German Condor Legion in Spain. It was a super-film showing how German blood had been shed in the holy war in Spain against Bolshevism. Hitler, Göring, Goebbels, Himmler, saw it, praised it. Then came the Nazi–Soviet pact last August. The film is now in storage. It was never shown to the public.'
Shirer's information seems reliable. But he never explains why *Legion Condor* was not released two years later, when the campaign against 'World Communism' was resumed and the 'crusade' against the Soviet Union began.

Another picture about 'German volunteers in Spain' was *Im Kampf gegen den Weltfeind* (*In the Fight against the Common Enemy*), an anonymous reportage film, with a strong political bias. It opens with clips from newsreels, accompanied by a very loud commentary, to illustrate Republican 'excesses': a raging mob burns churches; priests and monks are murdered. No political distinctions are made, the enemy invariably being described as Communists or Bolsheviks. The political situation before the outbreak of the Civil War is summed up in the words 'Spain's last hour had come', followed by a picture of Franco, saviour of the nation.

The material included also contains some unique pictures of members of the International Brigades who have been taken prisoner. (They are asked: 'Why do you come here to kill us?') Apart from that, it is all about the Germans, the Condor Legion who have come to fight international communism in a foreign land, and who will 'spread the fame of Germany'. After many military operations and much gathering of booty, it ends with a victory parade. It is March 1939: Franco mounts the podium to speak.

Some political films from World War II included interesting references to this war-before-the-war. In a 1942 Vichy propaganda film, *Français, vous avez la mémoire courte*, alleged Republican atrocities and wanton destruction of cultural monuments (shots of corpses and burnt-out churches) were used as an argument in support of the authoritarian form of government in France. The second part of the American series *Why We Fight* was called *The Nazis Strike*, and as it examined the development of Fascism up to the German attack on Poland, it might have been expected to quote the Spanish Civil War as evidence against Hitler and Mussolini, using their intervention in defiance of all international agreements, as well as crimes like bombing Guernica. But Capra and Litvak mention the Civil War just once in their film, and then only in passing: 'The fire which started in Manchuria and spread to China, Ethiopia and Spain . . .' There is no reason to believe that this omission was not politically motivated; as late as 1943, the Spanish Civil War was still a subject of debate in the United States, and as the issue of the moment was the gathering of national strength, there was no point in breathing new life into old controversies.

In 1962, two films with a left-wing bias made intelligent use of documentary material from the Spanish Civil War: Rossif's *Mourir à Madrid*, which was a great box-office success, at least in France, and Kurt and Jeanne Stern's *Unbändiges Spanien* (*Untameable Spain*), an East German production. The latter opens with the war itself; there are numerous ironical comments about the Western democracies and expressions of gratitude to Russia for sending experts and weapons (with images accompanied by the Brecht–Eisler 'Solidarity Song'). Then, surprisingly, comes the whole of Joris Ivens's film on Spain, followed by a final sequence which begins with the triumphal march of the Condor Legion through Berlin and then moves on to the second deception practised on Spain by democracy after 1945. *Unbändiges Spanien* even mentions West German investment, and a picture of Erhardt is linked with those of Hitler and Franco. Finally, we are faced with the Third World, in which hundreds of millions of people have thrown off the yoke of imperialism. Cuba is a hope and a reminder, and the Sterns quote a line of poetry: 'When Fidel flies through a century in one minute, I think of Spain.'

In *Mourir à Madrid*, the commentary by Madeleine Chapsal has a very important function. It guides us through the story of the conflict and also through the background. It does not interpret events, but it establishes an atmosphere which is solemn and serious, but with underlying passion; it plays on our emotions. It is a nostalgic summary, not a picture for those who neither know nor care about Spain; it is a film which confirms an experience.

The weakness of *Mourir à Madrid* is a tendency to aestheticise; its logic turns into rhetoric. Too much of the involvement is conveyed not by images but by actors' voices; they anticipate the visuals, emphasising and drawing conclusions. They are rather too well trained; there is a certain disharmony between the directness of the images – someone is carried off to die, someone else is crying, another

Still: image of destruction wrought by the Nazis in the second part of Why We Fight, The Nazis Strike, *a survey notable for its omission of Spain.*

clenches his fist – and the classic French of the voices. It is surprising that Rossif did not employ · everyday language to create some feeling of proximity. He used hardly any of the documentary soundtracks that were available.

Mourir à Madrid seems to have been viewed by the Spanish authorities as an uncomfortable reminder. On 18 July 1965, a counter-film with a similar title, *Morir en España*, was simultaneously premièred in all Spanish provincial capitals. According to a review in an emigré magazine, the Basque 'Gudari' in Caracas, the commentary tries to clear Franco's supporters from accusations of fascism, and there is only passing mention of the German and Italian relief effort. The main characters on the enemy side, Azaña, Prieto, La Pasionaria, do not speak with their own voices. They do not even have the voices of actors, but those of naughty children.

La guerre est finie, Alain Resnais's film based on a script by an emigré Spanish radical, Jorge Semprun, is about Spain after the war. This sad, thoughtful picture is concerned with the ageing both of a man and of ideas.

Diego (played by Yves Montand) is a courier for a Spanish resistance organisation in France. He belongs to a communist group, and returns to Paris at the beginning of the film, having spent a year underground in his homeland. In Paris he soon finds himself in conflict with his taskmasters: revolutionary theoreticians and old-time Communists who have been dreaming up a Spain which bears little relation to reality. Diego is alone and longs for the quiet life, a woman and a home. He gets to know some young people, romantic student revolutionaries who are planning to frighten the tourists (fourteen million a year) away from Spain by planting bombs, and they, too, look upon him as a traitor. Diego regards others with scepticism and himself with despair. He is hesitant on almost every issue, but wholly convinced that the revolution must come from within.

La guerre est finie is, as a Swedish critic has written, 'one of the most defeatist political films to be made in recent years.' In spite of this pervasive feeling, the film's nomination as the official French entry at the Cannes Festival of 1966 was taken as an unfriendly act towards Madrid. The French, sensitive to Spanish reactions, withdrew Resnais's picture. In 1967, Serge Roullet's *Le Mur*, a Bresson-influenced version of Jean-Paul Sartre's short story, was rejected by the selection committee nominating French entries for the festival, apparently less on aesthetic than political grounds. (The short story and the film describe a group of republi-

55

cans under sentence of death and their last hours in a Franco prison.) The war is not over.

The Spanish Civil War also appears as a motif in two Swedish films. Hampe Faustman's *Främmande hamn* (*Foreign Port*, 1948) is set in Gdynia ten years earlier and is about a conflict of loyalties. A boat loaded with weapons for Franco is ready to sail, but the crew mutinies and defeats the commercial interests. This was a Socialist's declaration of solidarity with a good cause, but it came rather late in the day. The film conveys feelings of both faith and impotence, because in the event, the effort was all to prove in vain. The strongly emotive acting seems to be a genuine expression of Faustman's personal despair.

Vilgot Sjöman's *I am Curious, Yellow* also combines idealism and emotion. The Spanish Civil War is a significant biographical fact in the life of the central character, Lena; her father went off as a volunteer but returned home having made no contribution whatsoever. His daughter shows her contempt for him by hanging a picture of Franco on her wall and by assiduously ticking off each day the time that has passed since his return from Spain. In his book on the making of the film, Sjöman explains:

'I want people to feel that the Spanish civil war is the first big defeat for democracy. To feel what an abomination it was that Franco won and is still head of state, guarding a Spanish society based on privilege.'

This is one of the political motifs that do not get lost in the film. Sjöman carries it through in Lena's lightning interviews at Stockholm Airport with some of the fourteen millions who put sun before justice. Out of the twenty she asked, only two or three had a firmly negative attitude towards Franco, according to the director's journal. He writes:

'Well, the Spanish holiday is one of the comfortable features of Swedish life. Then, suddenly, idealism appears out at the airport asking angrily if we are not ashamed. A girl's voice demands that we sacrifice a little bit of comfort for political reasons. There is annoyance and uneasiness: a tremor runs through the general smugness.'

The picture ends, however, with Lena Nyman piercing the eyes of Franco's picture. It is a 'ritual murder', patricide via an effigy, the settling of a private score, not a political act.

In the final analysis, attitudes to the Spanish Civil War depend on date of birth as well as on political affiliations.

It was a war which offered unique opportunities for identification, for both the right and the left, because the dividing line was so clearly drawn. For once the fighting did not appear to be about frontiers, bases, natural resources or interests, but about different conceptions of society, about conflicting ideologies. The left was divided – this was one of the main reasons for its defeat. The right was more strictly disciplined, but far from united in its notions of how the war should be fought, or of the way in which society should be organised afterwards. Yet this war still seems to have been a confrontation of two nations within a nation, two nations with distinct and contrasting personalities.

For the European left, the Spanish Civil War was a conflict of open minds against closed, the pure of heart against the deceitful, in which great promise emerged among the confusion. At the same time it was overshadowed by threats from outside: Spain was a practice ground for the fascists and a sacrifice to the weakness and treachery of the democratic nations. It was a war in which individuals could still conquer machines (as they can again in Vietnam). It was also a war which led to an even bigger war, a war which will not come to an end until the fascists have finally been defeated: in Vietnam, in Angola, in Bolivia, in Greece, in Spain itself.

For two or three generations of the left, the Spanish Civil War looks like no other war (except perhaps the war in Vietnam although the differences are great). The opportunity for identification remains, and somewhere within us we have not accepted the defeat. Madrid is still a battlefield in our hearts.

Still: Yves Montand in La Guerre est finie.

56

Hollywood and the World

There exists a basic formula for film propaganda on which there are innumerable variations, an almost universal pattern of action. Broadly speaking it comprises three consecutive phases:

1) we are shown an idyll of quiet, harmonious contentment, which wins our sympathy;
2) a force from the outside threatens the idyll, seeking to destroy it by some abominable means;
3) heroic attempts are made to defend it.

This formula can be seen in propaganda films from every country, but it also appears in other contexts. The great box-office successes, from *Birth of a Nation* (1914) to *The Sound of Music* (1964), follow this basic pattern with some regularity.

The numerous similarities between propaganda films and box-office successes should not surprise us too much. The reinforcement of established attitudes is an important factor in conditioning responses. The business of satisfying cinema audiences is very closely connected with their aesthetic, religious and political preferences and norms. Judging from the box-office returns, ideological factors play a significant part in achieving success. The liberation of the Jews in *The Ten Commandments*, the struggle of emerging Christianity in *Ben Hur* and *Quo Vadis*, the subjugation of the Confederacy in *The Birth of a Nation* and *Gone With the Wind*, the coming of the Nazi terror in *The Sound of Music*, the Bolshevik revolution in *Doctor Zhivago* are all events whose treatment implies an element of political or at least ideological content. Nor is the fact that this content is often retrospective and conservative particularly surprising. In order to satisfy the greatest possible number of people, popular successes must be based on safely established values – as is most often the case with propaganda.

This applies particularly to propaganda in American movies, and for obvious reasons. The cinema had become the fourth most important industry in the United States, and the measure of a successful product was how it fared at the box-office. Even during World War I it was still possible to speculate in indirect gains greater than the profit from the sale of tickets. There was even the chance to risk antagonising large sections of the community to create attitudes to controversial issues – for instance, America's entry into the war. As the industry expanded, its relationship to various pressure groups grew more delicate, and the difference between public success and failure became more marked and assumed greater financial significance. To challenge existing opinion meant gambling with vast sums of money. In order to protect their interests, the large film companies came together in the early 'twenties to form the powerful Motion Picture Association of America, the M.P.A.A. This worked out the famous Production Code which had the purpose of sparing the movie industry from boycotts or similar financial hazards and established definite limits to freedom of expression. The result was that if commercial features took up a stand on anything, it was almost exclusively on causes that were generally sanctioned by authorities and public alike.

The loyalty of American films to existing society can hardly be said to have been any less stringent than that of the Soviet cinema. The Production Code which was to govern the attitudes of Hollywood for several decades may have been inspired mainly by commercial considerations, but in practice it became a declaration of faith in a particular social system. Consequently, products of the American film industry, while uncontroversial, still have attitudes and values. An entertainment industry so firmly geared to the satisfaction of *all* is bound eventually to develop a whole imaginary world that both shapes and is shaped by the collective value judgments of the public. It does not necessarily advance any political theses, but it reflects and preserves the imagined aims and favourite myths of society by presenting them in attractive forms. Whether because of or in spite of its will and intention, such an industry therefore becomes political.

Entertainment becomes indirect propaganda and propaganda becomes entertainment. The relationship between the two has been revealed in times of hot or cold war, when American films have gone all out to edify the nation.

Still: The Birth of a Nation.

For propaganda purposes, several standard entertainment genres have willingly accommodated slight modifications to their basic patterns or extra touches to accord with the demands of the political situation.

When the United States entered World War II, the war movie had already been given its shape; it only needed to be anchored firmly to current events and be given a greater patriotic emphasis. But there were other forms, like farce, which were easily harnessed to propaganda, and several musicals struck a political note without compromising their credentials as entertainment or their stylistic tradition.

The Invisible Man became the Gestapo's number one enemy in *Invisible Agent* (1942). Donald Duck was exposed to Nazi terror in *Der Fuehrer's Face* (1943). Tarzan fought German soldiers in *Tarzan Triumphs* (1943). The adventures of Sherlock Holmes lifted him to the level of international politics in a series of films from the war years (i.e. *Sherlock Holmes and the Secret Weapon*), and when the *Desert Song* was filmed in 1943, it was given a slight face-lift in that the villains became Nazis.

At the same time the heavies in adventure films became German agents, and the gangsters in thrillers were Nazi fifth-columnists. The character actors who had earlier specialised in heavies acquired German accents and began working for Hitler, just as they would go on playing similar roles, but change uniforms,

Stills. This page: left – Conrad Veidt and Humphrey Bogart as 'Gloves' Donahue in All through the Night; *right – Donald Duck in* Der Fuehrer's Face; *bottom – Peter Lorre, Sir Cedric Hardwicke and Jon Hall in* Invisible Agent. *Opposite page: top –* The Return of the Seven; *bottom – Bruce Cabot and Dennis Morgan in* Desert Song.

when the Gestapo villains turned to communists in the Cold War.

But American gangster mythology also has its heroic criminal, and there are models of patriotism even in the underworld. Humphrey Bogart's 'Gloves' Donahue in *All Through the Night* (1942) and Richard Widmark's pickpocket in *Pickup on South Street* (1953) are not the only criminals to become representatives of American democracy and to fight it out with respectively Nazi and Communist infiltrators in order to defend their existence as free entrepreneurs of crime.

The Western, too, has often proved itself particularly well able to symbolise current nationalism on an allegorical level. Strong, silent, lonely men ride in from the prairie, conquer their aversion to the use of weapons and, without profit to themselves, defend freedom-loving farmers against gangs bent on grabbing land and power – this national myth fitted the United States to perfection when the Truman doctrine against communist expansion was proclaimed; it turned up in such films as *Shane* (1952). Some years later, in *Return of the Seven* (1966), the framework has been developed so that the Western plot offers the perfect filter through which to look at the Vietnam war.

But the favourite setting of standardised propaganda fiction in the 'sixties was the spy movie, which successfully glamourised a new kind of fascism. The other side is generally a hierarchy of scoundrels, the top ones often of Asiatic origin. The tone is flippant and has a suggestion of parody; the underlying purpose is not necessarily deliberately propagandist. But spy films have exploited a specific political mood, simplifying and embodying widely held notions. They give the spectator a magical

sense of satisfaction by encouraging the conviction that the overpowering menace from the East would ultimately be immobilised by our agent – i.e., by the West. The air of parody is a safety valve to reduce the fears implicit in the subject-matter and stop them undermining its success as entertainment.

With the arrival of the Production Code, the film industry formally and collectively proclaimed that the American cinema intended to be non-controversial. On the whole it has rarely departed from this course. The Hollywood *community*, however, has been at the centre of political controversy and all sorts of demagoguery. Movie celebrities have often been actively engaged in politics. Among the great generation of stars, Jane Wyman, Henry Fonda and Joan Bennett have all worked for Democratic candidates, while Bing Crosby,

Gary Cooper and Robert Montgomery have all worked for the Republicans.

But Hollywood has also been shaken by more serious political activities, of which the witch hunts of the early 'fifties were by no means the first. Back in 1934, America was in the throes of the Depression. Roosevelt was in his first term of office and had launched the New Deal to fight poverty and unemployment, but the movie industry had already come through its crisis and was booming in the midst of the general depression. In the election for the Governorship of California, Upton Sinclair ran as Democratic candidate, supporting Roosevelt and the New Deal. He was a well-known critic of capitalism as well as of Hollywood and the movie industry; his platform reeked of Socialism. His nomination as candidate threw the movie industry into a panic. The companies started a violent anti-Sinclair campaign, distributing nasty little election films, and adding force to their message by threatening to move their Hollywood operations from California to Florida. Upton Sinclair was not elected governor.

But Roosevelt was president, and Roosevelt was St George fighting the dragon of Depression. His plans were obviously not very popular with the tycoons, but then tycoons did not make up a large proportion of cinema audiences; in terms of ticket sales their economic significance to Hollywood was small. The Sinclair episode is interesting, though, because it contrasts so sharply with the popular idea of Hollywood's cordial attitude towards New Deal policies. This image was most clearly focused in Frank Capra's extremely popular comedies of the 'thirties and is not at all false – in the case of the films, that is.

There is no reason to doubt that Capra made a genuine PR contribution to the New Deal and the new spirit. His contemporary stories exuded a sense of security and optimism

Stills. Top left: Henry Fonda and Jane Darwell in John Ford's The Grapes of Wrath. *Bottom left: the lynch mob storms the jail in Fritz Lang's* Fury. *Above: Humphrey Bogart in Archie Mayo's* The Black Legion. *Below: Paul Muni in Mervyn LeRoy's* I Am a Fugitive from a Chain Gang.

through their belief in the strength of democracy, in freedom of expression, in the American desire for progress and the Big Chance. Idealism was blessed by fate and luck: Gary Cooper became a millionaire through an inheritance in *Mr Deeds Goes to Town* (1936) and grappled with professional politicians, bureaucracy, corruption and big business. But Capra did not make controversial films. His new film deal was against crooked capitalism, but was not anti-capitalist. It upheld the ideas of politics and the United States that were most attractive to true Americans. It was blue-eyed and healthy, the expression of an American myth.

Another film from the early 'thirties, Walt Disney's *Three Little Pigs* (1933), is well known for its relationship to the Depression and shows how simplification and political reality can combine with a mythical element to popular effect: the Big Bad Wolf became a symbol of the Depression, and the refrain 'Who's afraid of the big bad wolf' served as a sort of campaign song to fight off despair. One can spot many similar nostrums, some involving an almost hallucinatory fixation on money, in the musicals made during the Depression.

Not until *The Grapes of Wrath* (1940) was the Depression shown straight in a Hollywood feature. John Ford's picture was one of the highlights in the tradition of social involvement in American films which had managed to survive in spite of unfavourable conditions. The range of social criticism within this tradition has rarely been uncompromising or politically

challenging – even *The Grapes of Wrath* sprinkled its realism with little touches designed to eliminate any risk of identification of specific targets. However, it has managed to direct the attention of audiences to various outrages even if it has not been able to do more. Even gangster films had a kind of social involvement. One of the most celebrated of them, *Scarface* (1932), put the question straight to the audience: 'What are you going to do about it?' During the 'thirties there were also exposés of barbaric prison conditions (*I Am*

a *Fugitive from a Chain Gang*, 1932), lynch-law (*Fury*, 1936; *They Won't Forget*, 1937), American fascism (*The Black Legion*, 1936), slum conditions (*Dead End*, 1937) and other social evils, all depicted with a genuine feeling of indignation. These and similar films had a degree of urgency and concern; they may seldom have been courageously controversial or free from romantic tendencies but undeniably they had political implications.

They were films made in a socially aware but still isolationist America. And while the United States as a whole remained isolationist, Hollywood movies were isolationist too. The clouds were gathering in the Far East, in Italy and in Germany – but such political matters were almost never touched upon in Hollywood films.

But this is not to say that Hollywood was totally oblivious to events abroad: the mid-'thirties saw the formation there of an anti-Nazi association which eventually reached a membership of four thousand people, among them some of the most brilliant writers, actors and directors. But even then, the content of Hollywood movies remained insulated from developments abroad. It was some time before it was considered opportune in terms of public

Stills. Left: pictures by Robert Capa from 400 Millions *(Joris Ivens and John Ferno). Below: William Wyler's* Dead End. *Right: Anatole Litvak's* Confessions of a Nazi Spy.

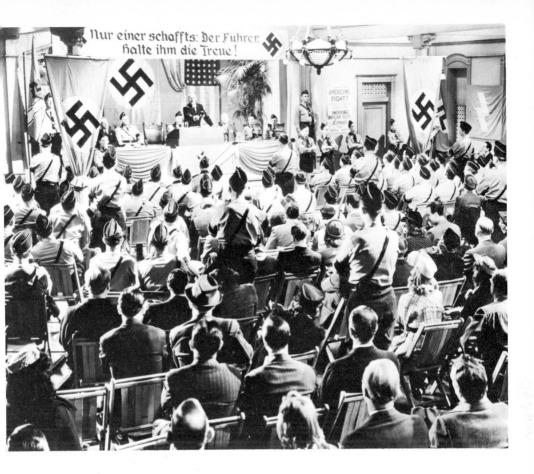

opinion to take a stand in the movies themselves on events outside America.

At roughly the same time as the formation of the anti-Nazi League, another political event of quite different character and indeed of ominous significance came about in Hollywood. The House Committee on Un-American Activities was set up under the chairmanship of Martin Dies and it was decided that one of its tasks would be an investigation into subversive radicalism in Hollywood. The extremely reactionary Edward F. Sullivan led the hearings, and something like forty movie personalities – among them the eight-year-old Shirley Temple – were branded as tools of Communism before the activities of the committee were interrupted by World War II (temporarily as it turned out).

It could never seriously be suggested that radical film-makers left a clear imprint on the Hollywood cinema. Uncompromising attitudes to events in Europe were found mainly in independent documentaries which displayed a fierce personal involvement on such subjects as the Spanish Civil War (Joris Ivens's *The Spanish Earth*, 1937), the Sino-Japanese war (Ivens's *400 Millions*, 1938–9), and Hitler's militarism and the consequences for Czechoslovakia of the spirit of Munich (Herbert Kline's *Crisis*, 1938). Working in the area somewhere between the film industry and journalism, Louis de Rochemont introduced his current affairs series, *March of Time*, which consisted half of reportage, half of reconstruction, and in 1938 one of its more sensational instalments, *Inside Nazi Germany*, was devoted to recent developments there.

However, the feature film industry cautiously and loyally sided with the country's official neutralist policy. Pressure groups, censorship authorities and foreign diplomats were not to be challenged by the M.P.A.A. It was 1939 before the word 'Nazi' appeared in the title of a film – Anatole Litvak's *Confessions of a Nazi Spy*. The first test of the public's tolerance to politically *engagé* films had been *Blockade* in 1938. The action was of course presented without any explicit mention of dangerous political names but the film took an emotionally unequivocal stand on the side of the anti-fascists.

Blockade was a success with the public, but there were signs of conflict. Protests from Catholic organisations like the National Legion of Decency indicated that powerful pressure groups were still against Hollywood taking up any political stands of its own. Added to this was the risk of unpleasant reactions ' from insulted foreign governments, and so the cautious approach stayed even after the outbreak of war in Europe, although by then public opinion had largely taken sides in the conflict.

Caution was not entirely inappropriate and when Chaplin dared to make *The Great Dictator* in 1940, it was banned, for instance, by

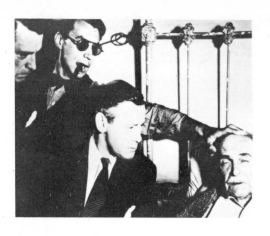

the local censorship body in Chicago that had previously forbidden de Rochemont's *Inside Nazi Germany*.

The other great crime against Hollywood's silence was committed by another immigrant from Britain. This was Alfred Hitchcock, whose *Foreign Correspondent* was a thriller in his celebrated English style, but it was also a surprisingly powerful challenge to American neutralism. The title-character of the film is used as an ironic caricature of the American position when asked in the very first scene of the film about his opinion of the European crisis. 'What crisis?' he answers uncomprehendingly, but he is nevertheless dispatched to the other side of the Atlantic to report on developments during the summer of 1939. He is confronted with the blinkered Munich mentality, brilliantly visualised in the allegory of the umbrella scene, a classic piece of Hitchcock. A few months later, the foreign correspondent, Joel McCrea, stands in a London broadcasting studio at the beginning of the 'blitz' broadcasting his message to the American people in the final scene of the film. His words add up to an undisguised appeal to the United States to enter the war. This did not happen for some time, but when it did, and not until then, the floodgates opened to release a mighty stream of propaganda from Hollywood.

Propaganda and information were indeed sorely needed when the war began. After Pearl Harbor, the American authorities were faced with the tricky problem of curing the population of the after-effects of isolationism. A will to fight had to be fostered; the aims of the war needed clarifying; arguments had to be developed and anchored to generally accepted values. There was a need to instil solidarity with the allies and hatred for the enemy.

One of the main weapons in this adjustment campaign was *Why We Fight*, a series of documentary films started in 1942 under the aegis of the U.S. War Department, by a group of film-makers led by Frank Capra, Anatole Litvak and Anthony Veiller. The series comprised seven films. The first, *Prelude to War*, concerned the rise of fascism during the 'thirties

in Germany, Italy and Japan; the second, *The Nazis Strike*, was about the build-up to the war, ending with Germany's attack on Poland; the third, *Divide and Conquer*, was the story of the first war years. The three that followed were expressions of solidarity with the resistance in Britain, Russia and China: *The Battle of Britain*, *The Battle of Russia*, *The Battle of China*. The last, and least known, took as its subject the mobilisation of the United States itself, under the title *War Comes to America*.

Although the films were made under great time pressure, the *Why We Fight* series was considered such a success that several parts received theatrical screenings in spite of having been intended purely for military training purposes. The first four are classics in the history of documentary montage films. *The Battle of China*, however, was seen as a failure; it was never given a public showing and was soon withdrawn even from educational use. One of its shortcomings was that it did not satisfactorily manage the precarious political balancing act between Chiang Kai-shek and the Communists. The unqualified tribute paid to the Soviet Union in *The Battle of Russia* caused this film, too, to be regarded, in the changed post-war climate, as a political accident.

The twin aims of the series were to guide the emotions and to inform. A tolling bell with the word 'Liberty' engraved on it – the Liberty Bell, which had proclaimed the Declaration of Independence in 1776 – appeared in each film as an emotive element in the prologue, which established a lofty emotional tone with invocations of freedom, democracy and the word of God. Certainly the *Why We Fight* series is not restrained and low-pitched as has been suggested in certain film histories which have helped to give it a not entirely deserved reputation for objectivity.

The first two films, in particular, are pretty blatant pieces of demagoguery. They rely to a surprising extent on artificial juxtapositions, which are endowed with a facile symbolic significance. Their visual material is not purely documentary but includes extracts from features and reconstructions which have a strong studio atmosphere about them. Using tricks of photography, lighting and music, *Why We Fight* tries to solve the underlying dilemma of most documentaries on war: the tendency of all photographed history towards anonymity. In documentary, wars seems to turn from specific events into generalised visual impressions lacking in concreteness. *Why We Fight* only succeeds in parts in capturing that rare feeling of immediacy. Its persuasive power depends less on visual impact than on the purposeful force of the commentary.

Stills. Left: Alfred Hitchcock's Foreign Correspondent. *Right: German footage used by the Americans in the* Why We Fight *series –* The Nazis Strike *(top) and* Divide and Conquer.

In *Why We Fight*, the image is an accompaniment to the commentary rather than the other way round. Large sections of *Why We Fight* were made up of sequences taken from Leni Riefenstahl's films, from German newsreels and documentaries, as well as from their Italian and Japanese equivalents – now put to work as propaganda for the other side. The effect is of course partly achieved through careful selection of material and intelligent editing, but even more by the commentary, which can succeed in making a military parade into a magnificently ridiculous spectacle.

The commentaries of the series became increasingly unacademic, folksily unsubtle and unsentimental, and attained their artistic peak in the rather grim lyricism of *The Battle of Russia*. There the narrator was Walter Huston, a 'fellow American' who, in a friendly but insistent tone, addressed other 'fellow Americans.' All in all, *Why We Fight* added up to a brilliant series of lectures, a didactically planned survey of the preliminaries to the war and of its early stages which is still unsurpassed. Animated diagrams, maps and charts are intelligently used in conjunction with documentary material on historically important incidents

Still: John Huston's The Battle of San Pietro. *Right: two Conrad Veidts in Jules Dassin's* Nazi Agent. *Bottom right: Lewis Milestone's* All Quiet on the Western Front.

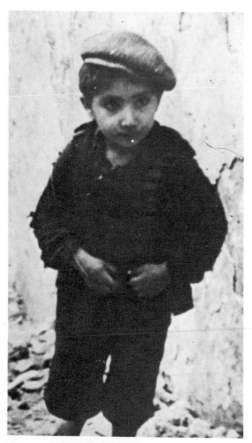

and from the various theatres of war.

Great things were expected of the *Why We Fight* series, and the War Department decided to test its effect in the most carefully planned research project ever devoted to measuring the exact influence of film. The results, however, were discouraging. The social psychologist C. I. Hovland and his team of collaborators did find that the films had been relatively successful in spreading information about the causes of the war, but that the information tended to be remembered by audiences only for a brief time. In certain respects they found that attitudes had been influenced in the direction intended, but to a lesser degree and more infrequently than had been hoped for. The project found no indication that the film propaganda had succeeded in its principal aim of increasing the enthusiasm of soldiers for war service. Thus, the most authoritative of scientific investigations set no great store by the ability of film propaganda to influence people.

However, discouraging results like these are sometimes worth treating with a certain amount of scepticism. The psychological effects of a film might be impossible to assess through the use of established testing methods perhaps the most significant areas of influence lie beyond the scope of knowledge tests and ability assessments. It is also obvious that films never function as an isolated agent, separated from all other sources of influence. In a situation like the one in which *Why We Fight* had to operate, every attempt at an interpretation of the evidence gathered in research runs up against a problem of relativity. The individual is exposed to so many opinion-shaping factors working towards the same goal, that the *separate* effects of these factors are necessarily difficult to measure. They are also insignificant in relation to the effect of the collective onslaught of all the various forces.

Three years after Pearl Harbor, the film producer Walter Wanger could, in a moment of excessive self-satisfaction, sum up the contribution of the movie industry to the war effort as follows:
'When future historians write the story of World War II, a bright chapter will be assigned to the contribution of America's motion picture industry in winning the war.'
It is certainly true that when the United States was finally forced into the war and the nation's psychological and material resources had been mobilised to conquer Germany and Japan, Hollywood, too, mobilised unconditionally. During the three years that followed, almost its entire output seemed steeped in propaganda. The patriotic films were often noisily heroic, grotesque and naïve, sometimes foolish, often filled with highly threatening fantasies in the manner of horrid fairy-tales, and, just occasionally, compassionate, perceptive or brilliant.

In this enormous offering of propaganda as entertainment – Hollywood Quarterly estimated that of the total film production for the years 1942 to 1944 about 375 Hollywood movies had a more or less openly expressed patriotic purpose – many of the names of the film-makers have been forgotten, and were indeed hardly ever worth remembering. But a majority of the most important directors were also involved in the psychological war effort.

Some of them were formally enrolled in the forces and produced remarkable documentaries. These films have rarely been given any commercial distribution, but many of them belong among the greatest achievements of the documentary cinema; John Huston's *The Battle of San Pietro* (1944) managed to a unique extent to convey the physical experience of war.

Among the officers who made movies for the armed forces were (apart from Major Huston) Colonel Frank Capra, Lieutenant-Colonel Anatole Litvak, Colonel William Wyler and Commander John Ford. Walt Disney put his staff at the disposal of the Army to make propaganda films of an instructional nature, while at the same time his cartoon characters were mobilised for service in anti-Nazi satires. Other celebrated directors remained in Hollywood feature film production, but were no less patriotic in their work.

Jules Dassin made his debut in feature films with *Nazi Agent* (1942), and Edward Dmytryk established himself as a director with a series of propaganda films, the most successful of which was *Hitler's Children* (1943), which was backed by an extensive radio campaign and gained further appeal from some pretty pornographic footage of half-naked women being whipped by sadistic Nazi officers. Billy Wilder's second directorial assignment was *Five Graves to Cairo* (1943), in which he let Erich von Stroheim concoct a new variation on his old starring role as a Prussian officer. 'The Field Marshal' in the film was a respectfully satirical portrait of Rommel. Delmer Daves also made his direc-

torial debut in propaganda with the submarine movie *Destination Tokyo* (1944), with Cary Grant – an anti-Japanese effort which was considered so successful that it was used as an instructional film in the US Navy. Another newcomer among the Hollywood directors – and, like Wilder, of German origin – was Fred Zinneman. His screen version of Anna Seghers's novel, *The Seventh Cross* (1944), was one of the few American films in World War II that emphasised the existence of 'another Germany'. Spencer Tracy played the concentration-camp prisoner who escapes through Germany to freedom and is helped on his way by Germans who have not lost their human dignity. It was such a low-keyed work that it was considered a danger to American morale at a time when hatred of Germany was the order of the day.

Among the established major directors, one of the most productive propagandists was Lewis Milestone – the man who had originally become famous with the pacifist film *All Quiet on the Western Front* (1930), which contained the now suddenly inopportune line 'When it comes to dying for your country, it's better not to die at all.' Another prolific worker in the field was Michael Curtiz, a great virtuoso, who could make propaganda enormously attractive by creating on the screen the emotions that audi-

ences love to feel, for instance in the splendid *Casablanca* (1943), with Humphrey Bogart and Ingrid Bergman in the leading parts.

Alfred Hitchcock had brought with him from England a clever and well-tested thriller formula which worked well for the purposes of propaganda. In his British picture, *The Lady Vanishes* (1938), he had already warned about the danger of Hitler, and he continued this anti-Nazi line using the same thematic pattern in *Foreign Correspondent* and *Saboteur*. But in his next film, *Lifeboat*, he chose a semi-allegorical theme with which to express an uncompromising view of the German question.

The other master of the thriller in the United States, Fritz Lang, devoted three films to propaganda against the country from which he had escaped a decade earlier, while Ernst Lubitsch, also a German emigré, created Hollywood's sharpest satire on the Nazis, the flippant and marvellously entertaining *To Be or Not to Be* (1942). Howard Hawks's version of Hemingway's *To Have and Have Not* (1944) turned out to be about the struggle of Caribbean Frenchmen against Vichy agents. Jean Renoir saluted his homeland with *This Land is Mine* (1943), in which Charles Laughton personified the French Resistance as it moved out of its period of dejection and into the offensive.

In the same way – but often in a more naïvely heroic form – every allied nation, each resistance

movement, every occupied country, was given its own romanticised panegyric on film. In every branch of the armed forces, in every area of battle, in the desert and in the air, at sea and on land, chauvinistic war films found stories of nobility and courage which were then contrasted with the enemy's barbarity.

These films sprang less from reality than from currently popular preconceptions which, in turn, they served to reinforce. War was an exciting adventure; politics a superior form of romance; morality a matter of morale. In this treatment, death was painless, decorative and even, ultimately, a blessing.

Gradually the emphasis changed. The movie

Stills. Left: Hitchcock and Nazism – Paul Lukas in The Lady Vanishes *(top); Robert Cummings and German agent in* Saboteur. *Above: Humphrey Bogart in Howard Hawks's* To Have and Have Not. *Right: Dana Andrews in Lewis Milestone's* A Walk in the Sun.

image of the war became increasingly cruel and horrifying. This was partly due to a progressive adjustment on the part of the audiences which had to be compensated for with harsher effects, more powerful realism and more brutal shocks. But it was also a question of changed attitudes, of an increasingly factual approach. The war was de-glamourised and eventually ceased to have any patriotic value in fiction.

In 1945, when victory was near, it was no longer necessary to maintain the encouraging and dishonest wishful image of the war. Nor was it desired by war-weary audiences; the reality had become so intense that war was no longer a subject for escapism. Towards the end, despair, exhaustion and reality break through the mythical treatment in film's like Raoul Walsh's *Objective Burma*, in which even Errol Flynn loses his romantic aura, Milestone's *A Walk in the Sun* and William Wellman's *The Story of G.I. Joe* – all from the last six months of the conflict.

With the war over and all the demonic villains of the past few years removed from the scene,

the American people were faced with a new and different set of problems which had to be solved, problems of a political and social nature. Quality film production geared itself to post-war problems as subjects for serious scrutiny and debate. A realist style was established by such directors as Elia Kazan, Henry Hathaway, Jules Dassin and Edward Dmytryk in problem pictures, which often worked with the conventions of the crime picture but managed to draw

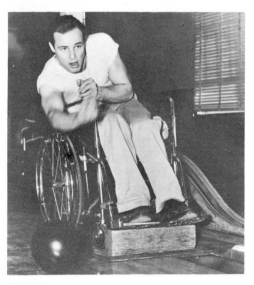

attention to everyday misery and social collapse. For the first time, racial problems were tackled in films which at least attempted to view the issue clearly. Difficulties of readjusting to civilian life were treated with remarkable frankness in William Wyler's *The Best Years of Our Lives* and Fred Zinnemann's *The Men*. Political corruption and fascist tendencies received fairly uncompromising treatment in Robert Rossen's *All The King's Men*, Abraham Polonsky's *Force of Evil*, Stuart Heisler's *Storm Warning* and Jacques Tourneur's *Stars in My Crown*.

But the post-war world soon became a bad place for socially involved, radically oriented film-makers, and it is remarkable that some of these problem pictures were made after 1947. The new war, the cold one, had become the great political issue in America and was also directed inwards, against everything which could be seen as 'un-American' – a label which was attached to most things which carried even

a hint of social criticism. When the House Committee on Un-American Activities resumed its activities in 1947, one of the first places it bore down upon was Hollywood.

During the war, a number of people with leftist sympathies, mainly writers, had been brought into the film industry. They had very seldom made any noticeable personal impact on their films, but the reactionary groups behind the Republican Congressman and HUAC Chairman J. Parnell Thomas indicated that they had noticed disturbing radical tendencies in Hollywood pictures. The fact that cinematic villains were frequently represented as fat and rich was interpreted in the general tragi-comic hysteria as a subversive attack on the very basis of American society. Any kind of social criticism, liberalism or radicalism was associated with communism – and the classification of communism as a conspiracy and not a political party was to be confirmed by the Supreme Court in 1951.

The suspicions of the Committee 'were directed in particular against the Screen Writers Guild, and the Committee's opinion that the Guild was a centre of conspiratorial communist activity was willingly confirmed by a number of 'friendly witnesses' who put themselves at the Committee's disposal, emphatically declaring their concern about the increasing flow of Un-American ideas into filmmaking. Many of them were also helpful when it came to pointing out suspects. Some of the more cooperative witnesses were the tycoon Jack L. Warner, directors Sam Wood and Leo McCarey, actors Adolphe Menjou, Robert Taylor, Gary Cooper, Ronald Reagan . . .

Nineteen suspected Un-American film personalities, the 'Unfriendly Nineteen', were put up for questioning before the Committee in Washington, mainly to answer two specific questions: 'Are you a member of the Screen Writers Guild?' and 'Are you now or have you ever been a member of the Communist Party?'

Out of the nineteen who were called, eleven were heard; the Committee felt that was enough for the time being. One of the eleven, Bertolt Brecht, considered that as the nation's guest, he was under an obligation to reply, but he denied Communist Party membership (and left the country the following day). The remaining ten, the 'Hollywood Ten', refused to answer any questions regarding their political affiliations and opinions, falling back on the American Bill of Rights with its guarantee of freedom of opinion and speech, and they further claimed that the Committee's activity was by the same token illegal.

The ten were punished with prison sentences for their disobedience; they were Alvah Bessie, Herbert Biberman, Lester Cole, Edward Dmytryk, Ring Lardner Jr., John Howard Lawson, Albert Maltz, Samuel Ornitz, Adrian Scott, and Dalton Trumbo.

It was a time of moral humiliation for the American cinema. The film world certainly did not face the accusations silently, but even the protests tended to turn into surrender under the principles of the inquisition. Several pro-

Stills. Left: Ginger Rogers in Storm Warning *(top); Marlon Brando in* The Men. *Right: Broderick Crawford in* All the King's Men. *Below: Beatrice Pearson and Thomas Gomez in* Force of Evil.

ducers and senior officials defended their industry indignantly, proclaiming its politically unsullied state – but in so doing they accepted the purposes of the hearings. Five hundred prominent actors, directors, writers and other film professionals launched a protest action, The Committee for the First Amendment, but many of the five hundred, among them Humphrey Bogart, drew back and recanted when the prestige and power of the Thomas Committee grew stronger: Many of them were eventually called before the Committee themselves. Some were cleared, others blacklisted. Others, again, turned informer; among them were Elia Kazan, Lee J. Cobb, Budd

Schulberg, Sterling Hayden, Clifford Odets and – at his own request after serving part of his sentence – Edward Dmytryk, one of the Ten.

On the other hand, in 1954, three black-listed artists created a sensation with a rousing socialist film made by an independent film company in New Mexico: the producer Paul Jarrico, the director Herbert Biberman and the script-writer Michael Wilson made *Salt of the Earth*, which ran up against varying degrees of resistance from American conservatives.

Although the M.P.A.A. had gone so far in 1947 as to issue a declaration denying that anything un-American had ever occurred in films, it promised at the same time to fire immediately and not to re-employ any of the 'unfriendly witnesses' until such time as they had confessed the error of their ways.

The hearings on film people were resumed in 1951 with a new and even greater zest that reached its peak in Senator Joseph McCarthy's days of glory. In the previous couple of years, the Committee had compiled a list of 212 names of people actively at work in the movie industry, whom the companies obediently black-listed. Joseph Losey, Jules Dassin, Robert Rossen, Carl Foreman, Michael Wilson, Lillian Hellman, Ben Maddow and many others were forced to get out of American films, at least for the time being.

These attacks on the film industry and the subsequent black-listings and emigrations con-

Stills. Above: Salt of the Earth. *Opposite page: top – Clark Gable and Hedy Lamarr in King Vidor's* Comrade X; *bottom – Dana Andrews in William Wellman's* The Iron Curtain.

siderably weakened the socially conscious aspects of Hollywood film-making. But it is probably wrong to assume that the activities of J. Parnell Thomas and company were a necessary prerequisite for the flow of rabidly anti-communist propaganda which began pouring out of Hollywood after 1947, reaching its peak in 1952 when there was an average of at least one feature film per month with clear propagandist tendencies. This new development was a symptom of a political hysteria which Hollywood obviously would have tried to exploit even if the House Committee on Un-American Activities had not chosen movie people as the first object of their investigations. Another point here is that the attempt was not particularly successful: very few anti-Communist movies did well at the box-office. The cycle began with William Wellman's *The Iron Curtain* (1948). With it the attitude of American movies to the Soviet Union was to undergo a remarkable metamorphosis – not, however, the first in its history.

As late as 1920, the U.S. Government used films in attempting to influence the outcome of the civil war in Russia. With the aid of various

72

remains of George Creel's World War I propaganda department, anti-Bolshevik films continued to be exported to cinemas in the parts of Russia that were still controlled by the White Army.

America was hardly in need of such propaganda as Communism, the red peril, was already surrounded by an aura of terror, but the movie industry, always quick to spot easily marketable values (and undoubtedly from conviction, too), reinforced the general feeling in feature films which spectacularly demonstrated Russian barbarism and Bolshevik godlessness, without taking any particularly strong attitude over the Czarist regime's misuse of power. Films also had the great deterrent effect of showing the famine and the lack of freedom in the Soviet Union. Gertrude Jobes, the author of an industrial history of the American cinema, thinks that this campaign against the communist danger was intentionally complemented by another celebrating the pleasures of American consumer society. Hollywood movies were starting to favour stories with lavish and luxurious settings, stories which came to be typical of the American cinema for some time.

In the early 'thirties, possibly due to the fact that the U.S. Government had recognised the Soviet Union, the hostile attitude was softened and the output of films about modern Russia tailed off. The number of anti-Communist films coming out of Hollywood at the end of the decade might have been connected with the wave of horror which welled up at reports of the Stalinist terror, but strangely enough these films were invariably light-hearted comedies; a good-natured mockery of Communism. They were films without rancour, which by means of simple arguments that were often quite irrational and politically meaningless, they laughed off both the terror of Communism and Communism itself. Two of them have become minor classics: Ernst Lubitsch's *Ninotchka* (1939) and King Vidor's *Comrade X* (1940).

Ninotchka is a vastly reactionary satire which playfully advanced the thesis that no one with a bit of sense in his head and a heart in his body could remain a Communist after once tasting the glorious fruits of capitalism. Greta Garbo plays a Soviet woman Commissar on a mission in Paris. On her arrival she comments on the Stalinist purges with the words 'There will be fewer and better Russians left.' But then she gets seduced by the heroic representative of free enterprise, a charming and irresponsible playboy. She is 'de-indoctrinated' by the strains of the waltz, love, the Paris air and capitalist light-heartedness, until, drunk on champagne and romance, she renounces her ideology, and the portrait of Lenin on her bedside-table begins to smile knowingly and encouragingly.

'Let us form a party where we greet each other with a kiss and not with a clenched fist,' exclaims the reformed Ninotchka. *Comrade X* was based on approximately the same emotional

premise, but became more of an anti-Soviet than an anti-Communist film. The heroine, an attractive Russian bus driver, qualifies as a security risk in Russia as, unlike the party bosses, she actually has practical Communist ideals. When *Comrade X* was released in 1940, the Russo-German non-aggression pact was still in force, but in the autumn of 1941, the film was suddenly provided with introductory titles explaining that the satire on the Soviet Union was merely a harmless joke. By then Hitler had marched into Russia, and American public opinion had swung round. The disclaimer was the first turn in the sharp change of course which Hollywood was to make during the following years.

Beside the idealising documentaries which reached a peak with *The Battle of Russia* – the film which was intended to wash away decades of stored-up hatred of Russia from the minds of the soldiers – Hollywood did what it could on the home front to popularise the new ally in the fight against Nazism. The image now presented was no less fanciful and exotic than that from the years of mistrust. In 1942, 1943 and 1944, American audiences were presented with

a succession of dutiful celebrations of the Russian way of life – cheery, well-meaning and unreal fabrications. The Soviet Union was still a story-book land, though no longer filled with ghastliness and terror, but with happy folk-songs, smiling kindness and well made-up, heroic people living in neat studio landscapes, for instance in Lewis Milestone's *The North Star* (1943), Michael Curtiz's *Mission to Moscow* (1943), Gregory Ratoff's *Song of Russia* (1944), and Jacques Tourneur's *Days of Glory* (1944).

These naïve expressions of solidarity were to become a grave liability to Hollywood, not through their inferior quality, but for their suspected communist propaganda, for in 1947,

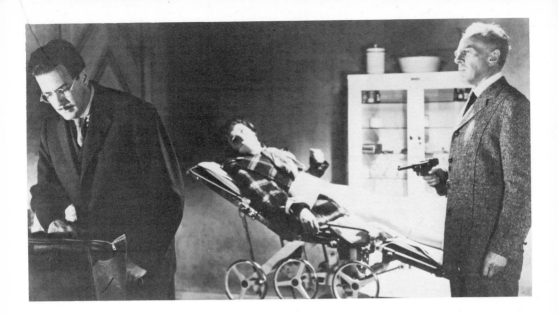

Stills. Opposite page: top – Walter Huston meets Stalin in Mission to Moscow; *bottom – Cyd Charisse and* Silk Stockings; Days of Glory. *Right: Frank Lovejoy being a Communist for the FBI. Above: Raymond Burr in* Whip Hand.

with the war over and the ex-ally now the enemy, the Committee on Un-American Activities bore down on the cinema.

The year 1947 was also that in which the Truman doctrine was proclaimed. It encouraged anti-Soviet feelings, out of which was now to burgeon a flora of primitive cinematic horror scarcely equalled before or since. Hollywood again adjusted its mythical patterns in accordance with the current political situation, abandoning itself with as much zest to the hatred of Russia as it had done to the earlier panegyrics.

The film industry appeared to take upon itself the task of keeping the spirit of the doctrine alive and meaningful for the public: the United States was pictured as becoming the defender of freedom wherever there was the threat of communist expansion.

Just a few of the many titles: *Whip Hand* (1951) was a lugubrious story, staged by the designer William Cameron Menzies, showing the communists running a prison camp in a small provincial American community with the object of testing biological weapons on the inmates. In *I Was a Communist for the FBI* (1951), an FBI agent manages to infiltrate the Communist Party where he meets, among others, Gerhardt Eisler, head of the East German security service, who is provoking riots; one of the members tells how they caught up with Trotsky who thought he'd got away, and that Jan Masaryk was thrown out of a window – people thought it was suicide. In Henry Hathaway's *Diplomatic Courier* (1952), Tyrone Power was the hero who, thanks to his superhuman intelligence, manages to uncover and thwart the plans drawn up by Russian bandits for the occupation of Yugoslavia in 1950. The most unsubtle propaganda of all was possibly found in *Walk East of Beacon* (1952), based on a book by the head of the FBI, J. Edgar Hoover, and put together with the help of the Bureau. Nunnally Johnson's *Night People* came the year after the East Berlin uprising and told a story of communist kidnapping in Berlin. André de Toth's *Man on a String* (1960) dealt with the Berlin problem and was still able to profit by the feelings aroused by the crisis. *Ninotchka* was re-released in 1947, and later in the general anti-Russian fervour, two new versions of it were shot within the space of one year: Rouben Mamoulian's musical, *Silk Stockings*, and the Katherine Hepburn / Bob Hope comedy, *The Iron Petticoat*. The latter was produced in 1956 and financed with British capital – in both Britain and West Germany, the film industry contributed actively to anti-Communist feeling at the time.

The attitude of American films towards Germany changed radically as Russians and Communists took over the heavy roles formerly reserved for Germans and Nazis. The vanquished enemy had become an ally, and even World War II stories were turned into face-saving exercises on his account and saluted the German forces and their honourable officers. In the interests of NATO, they were presented as magnificent fighters, and also as being firmly anti-Hitler, as for instance in *Rommel, the Desert Fox* (1952), *The Sea Chase* (1955) and *The Enemy Below* (1957).

The excesses of hate in war films were transferred to other fronts. Around 1950 came a notable series of flashbacks to the fighting against the Japanese in the Pacific. *Sands of Iwo Jima, Halls of Montezuma,* and *Flying Leathernecks* all echoed with the strains of the rousing patriotic march, 'The Halls of Montezuma'. These violent and aggressive lessons in the art of war expressed hatred of the Japanese. But this was not directed primarily against the former enemy, but in general at all the alien and beastly creatures of the jungle – the Asiatics.

In 1949, Communism won a definite victory in China. A few months afterwards, the Sino-Russian friendship pact was signed; a few months later still, the Korean War broke out, and Hollywood was supplied with another lively setting for its illustrations of the Truman doctrine.

But there was also a strong fear of the enemy within, of Communist infiltrators inside the United States, a fear which found its most panic-stricken expression in McCarthyism and which seems to have reached the height of its naïvety on film in *The Red Menace* (1949), which provided intimately detailed information about communist blackmailing methods, psychopathy, godlessness and promiscuity. Accusations of conspiracy to overthrow the government, of sexual anarchy, atheism and neuroticism came thick and fast in anti-Red movies. Ideological communists were frustrated intellectuals whose readiness to be deceived was exploited by unscrupulous (and extremely rich) budding dictators who were surrounded by beautiful and evil women distinguished by their contempt for the appeals made by their pious parents. That devoted reactionary John Wayne produced one of the rawest B-feature expressions of the hatred of communists, *Big Jim McLain* (1952), in which the paranoid ideas then current were paraded, confirming that the movement was 'a conspiracy to enslave humanity'. We see how Communists planned to poison the water in the harbours, and that their leaders were intending to liquidate all their ideologically cumbersome comrades once they had come to power. Wayne himself played the part of the triumphantly violent Communist-hunter, McLain – the

name's echo of McCarthy was hardly accidental – and the film was an express tribute to the maligned Committee on Un-American Activities.

Anti-communist paranoia was not by any means the sole prerogative of the B-feature. Mark Robson's *Trial* (1955) – in many respects, well made – appeared on the surface to be

Stills. Above: John Wayne hunting commies in Hawaii in Big Jim McLain. *Below: honourable adversary – Curd Jurgens with Robert Mitchum in Dick Powell's* The Enemy Below. *Right: Burt Lancaster in John Frankenheimer's* Seven Days in May.

confrontation with McCarthyism but at the same time encouraged all the prevailing anti-Red prejudices. The same ambivalence between hysteria and anti-hysteria could be seen seven years later in John Frankenheimer's bizarre movie, *The Manchurian Candidate* (1962), which at the outset alluded with massive irony to Joseph McCarthy's career, but proceeded to show, in an extraordinarily spectacular climax, how communist conspirators all but succeeded in assassinating the future President of the United States.

The détente in the relationship between Russia and America came in the mid-'sixties, and again movies adjusted to the new climate of opinion. The Russian gradually became a less demonic character. Comedies like *The Russians are Coming, the Russians are Coming* (1966) were one of the indications that a swing had occurred: another was the co-operation between Russian and American agents in episodes of *The Man from U.N.C.L.E.* (e.g. *A Case for U.N.C.L.E.*). The Russian was succeeded by the Chinese as the favourite screen heavy. The Russians as represented on the screen may have been grotesque, but the characterisation of the Chinese was monstrous, to say the least. Unlikely horrors seem to become less improbable the greater the racial and geographical distance and the more exotic the subject.

But Hollywood was producing more than

horror propaganda on the subject of politics. The serious problem movie had not died out completely during the period of starvation at the end of the 'forties. The most celebrated of later problem pictures was Sidney Lumet's *Twelve Angry Men* (1956), which showed a real concern about the ills of American society. Stanley Kramer treated a number of political, social and ethical subjects. In addition, John Frankenheimer (*Seven Days in May*), Otto Preminger (*Advise and Consent*) and Frank Schaffner (*The Best Man*) worked with fictional themes set in the sphere of domestic politics, and all these movies carried some message and raised interesting issues. Stanley Kubrick's *Dr Strangelove* (1963), Sidney Lumet's *Fail Safe* (1964) and James B. Harris's *The Bedford Incident* (1965) were sharp reminders of a world situation in which the pressing of a button could bring about total annihilation.

And Hollywood is still the scene of political action away from the screen. Charlton Heston, Marlon Brando, George C. Scott and others make appearances as spokesmen for left-of-centre ideas, and John Wayne, Bob Hope, Shirley Temple and others remain faithful to their reactionary views, campaigning for Goldwater and supporting the Vietnam war.

The governorship which was denied to Upton Sinclair thirty-two years earlier was won, in December 1966, by the right-wing ex-film star – Ronald Reagan.

Britain: Democracy at War

World War II gave the British a sense of solidarity that cut across class barriers and increased awareness of national identity. The British recognised in themselves a certain strength which, when viewed from the outside – and especially from Berlin – could be interpreted as weakness. British films of this period, documentaries as well as features, are particularly fascinating because so much of what happens in society is of necessity reflected in the cinema.

It was a period without masterpieces. The pictures are characterised not by depth or brilliance, but by a lack-lustre ordinariness, a factual approach which is both natural and deliberate. They are made by people seeking to inform an audience rather than to induce an emotional state. They do not inspire intolerance. Their representation of the enemy is tendentious, but does not strip him of all humane traits. The difficulties of the situation (the material superiority of the Germans in the early stages of the war) are not glossed over. There may be a kind of escapism in these films, but it is never dominant; they contain no extravagant flights of national ecstasy.

The period involved was only three or four years, and the films that were made were never important in the development of the cinema in other countries or at other times. However, the best British films made between 1940 and 1944 have a very distinctive character.

First came the documentaries. When a country suddenly finds itself in a new political situation, in this case faced with a deadly threat from an outside enemy, it is quite natural for the cinema to assume a purely fact-recording function. The camera is used to determine what the new reality looks like, what exactly is happening, and which values are being threatened.

A message or an educational emphasis can be added to the reports once the authorities and the public have been made aware of the significance of the change and have begun to understand the demands of the situation. Thus a film can show the burning capital and also the courage of the firemen; it shows the extent of the bomb damage and takes a fleeting look at the victims, but also points out the spiralling column of black smoke from a plummeting enemy bomber; it can suggest that the nation will not be conquered by terrorism directed against defenceless civilians. The camera settles on calm, determined faces, confirming the general sense of community, and quietly shows how the clearing-up begins the moment the all-clear has sounded. It might also sweep across the landscape, perhaps indicating the village church and hence tradition, the common background. But the next moment, the sky is filled with British bombers taking off from their well-camouflaged base.

This is the second stage of development. In a later, more stable phase, the message is built into a fictional framework; ever since the earliest days of the cinema, fiction has gripped the general public much more than recorded reality.

There were also practical reasons for documentaries leading British film production in World War II; they were already in a state of preparedness. In the decade preceding the outbreak of war, a large number of documentaries had been made under the auspices of the British Government, many of them concerned with social issues. For some years, John Grierson headed the General Post Office Film Unit and led a group of documentary film-makers, including Alberto Cavalcanti, Arthur Elton, Humphrey Jennings, Paul Rotha, Harry Watt and Basil Wright, all of whom were engaged in reportage work.

Their films were unpretentious, frequently with a touch of gentle lyricism and optimistic undertones. They were quietly Labour-orientated films, paid for by a Conservative government, and according to Cavalcanti they were tolerated only because of their modest approach. They were honest but never provocative. A film like *Forty Million People* (1939) could open with a long quotation from Karl Marx, but this did not mean that the film itself, or any others like it, contained any demands for a change in the economic structure of society. These documentaries embodied reformist social criticism – a criticism of chosen aspects of society with little attempt at a conclusion or analysis in depth. Furthermore, they were more than balanced by feature films which were conservative in spirit and attitudes, and in which nothing was questioned. More than a hundred features were made each year in the pre-war period; in 1937 no less than 225. The documentary film was a remarkably attractive but very marginal phenomenon.

When the war began, however, documentary film-makers were better equipped than feature film directors for the task of capturing the new reality. Their equipment was lighter and they were used to working fast. They had learnt to get close to people and events. They knew how to tell a story directly.

Initially the talents of documentary film-makers were not particularly well exploited. A certain confusion seems to have reigned at the planning, decision-making and financing level,

Stills. Top: Harry Watt's Squadron 992. *Above: Alberto Cavalcanti's* The First Days.

and Grierson's men were given little or no work. Producers opted instead for the innocuous: Alexander Korda produced a hollow, jingoistic film, *The Lion Has Wings*, in which (according to Cavalcanti) German pilots 'screamed with fright when they came in over London and discovered the anti-aircraft balloons'. But it appears that the GPO film-makers quickly took matters into their own hands. Watt, Jennings and Pat Jackson, under Cavalcanti's supervision, made *The First Days*, and Watt on his own made *Squadron 992*, a short and unpretentious film describing an anti-aircraft balloon unit in training and on active service.

These were isolated efforts; the initiative for an ambitious film project on the influence of the war on British society came from outside, from the Rockefeller Foundation. A dozen documentary film-makers were brought into this project. But the British cinema did not become seriously preoccupied with the war until the war started drawing closer to Britain.

The turning point came in the summer of 1940, with the establishment of the Crown Film Unit, a state-controlled organisation for documentary films attached to the Ministry of Information; after this, production got under way in earnest.

To judge from Sinclair Road's assessment of it in Rotha's 'Documentary Film', the attitude of the authorities seems to have been that the documentary was a propaganda weapon, an instrument for national edification and for the teaching of special skills, while feature films were still meant to offer escapist entertainment. It is probable that the authorities saw the documentary above all as an educational tool; it was extremely useful for instruction in the handling of new weapons, or in demonstrating the minding of complicated technical machinery when there was suddenly nobody around to work it. The documentary film was an important audio-visual aid and became extremely significant in the field of adult education during the war.

But political instruction was also important. The British people saw an unusual number of films during the war years; it has been estimated that roughly half of the population went to the pictures at least once a week, and apparently performances often carried right on in spite of air-raid sirens. Information was conveyed in 'flashes', messages or appeals lasting about a minute, in the course of short or long documentaries, newsreels and, eventually, even in feature films. Information and opinion was also conveyed directly to people's places of work through special magazine films, like *Worker and War-Front* (1942–5).

Typical of the initial phase was a documentary by Watt and Jennings, *London Can Take It*. The subject was one of the first big bombing raids on the capital and took the form of a news bulletin delivered by the American correspondent Quentin Reynolds. Addressing a sympathetic audience in the United States and the British Commonwealth, the speaker describes the stoicism of the British in the face of danger. He spans the distance with feeling but without sentimentality, while the flares from anti-aircraft guns light up the night sky.

London Can Take It seems to have inspired confidence; and it was not just the title that was reassuring. The film spoke not so much of military as of moral preparedness. It appealed to people who adhered to the same values as the British. It warned them that they, too, were threatened.

In spite of the aptly demonstrated determination, *London Can Take It* was a defensive film. In Watt's *Target for Tonight* (1941), Britain, under the inspiration of Churchill, moved into the offensive. According to the Balcon–Lindgren–Hardy–Manvell survey in 'Twenty Years of British Film, 1925–1945', the picture came 'at the psychological moment', when audiences had begun to long for an aggressive response to aggression.

In fact, it is a very low-keyed and sympathetic film. It tells the story of a bomber squadron on its way to a target in Germany, the bombing, and the homeward journey, during which the radio operator is wounded and the radio goes dead. The non-professional cast play themselves; they hold the same positions and perform the same tasks as in a real life raid. It is a documentary feature in which large sections are as straightforward as an instructional film. It contains an extraordinarily clear exposition of the radio link system, with interior shots from the ground control room where reports of bombed targets and missing planes are received and acted upon as calmly as if it was all an ordinary peace-time exercise. There is no suggestion of acting; it is a straightforward report of an event and a particular strategic technique.

The framework is broken when Watt briefly lets the enemy appear. German anti-aircraft guns start shooting, tongues of fire reach up from the earth and others stab downwards in answer; then we see *them* down there, screaming, black silhouettes milling about in confused activity. In the calm, informative, reassuring context of the film, this feverish scene becomes something of a caricature. These featureless figures take on an aura of unreality as we switch back again to the bomber crew. The men in the plane are a closely-knit group who, confined within a tiny space and face to face with danger, calmly set about their various tasks.

The men are not made to look like heroes, but the railway station at Freihausen burns fiercely, and when the bullet-riddled plane

Stills. Below: war-time magazine film, Worker and War Front No. 7, Shop Stewards' Banner. *Right: aircrew member in Harry Watt's* Target for Tonight.

comes limping home, once more over English soil, the uneasy silence is broken by music.

One of Our Aircraft is Missing by Michael Powell was made a year later. It is Watt's film over again but with bigger resources: a feature film with professional actors, a proper script, and more high-pitched excitement than was probably usual on a routine flight over enemy territory.

Here, too, all human relationships seem utterly relaxed. While flying towards their target, the members of the crew chat to each other. They are not discussing Adolf Hitler or the German as a soldier. One of them played football in Stuttgart before the war, and some-one else's nanny came from there. Their conversation conveys an impression of secure and well-adjusted lives. They have an inner calm which is in itself an almost challenging contrast to the reality outside – the enemy guns, the difficulties of the mission. Today one marvels at this self-possession in *One of Our Aircraft Is Missing*. Was it really possible before El Alamein and Stalingrad? Certainly, the men in charge of British film production during World War II were intent on fostering this kind of confident assurance. It could be a true reflection of reality and also serve as a model. It might involve a dangerous under-rating of the enemy, but above all it provided a secure foundation. With such confidence, one could take careful aim.

In Powell's film, the beginning is factual but the end is inspirational. The plane has crash-landed by the Zuyder Zee and, after encounter-ing various hazards, the crew is being cared for by a Dutch resistance group. (Some of the complications are almost farcical.) The film is dedicated to Holland, and it ends with the Orange coat of arms, the lusty national anthem, and the slogan 'The Netherlands will rise'.

Previously we have listened to a high-minded conversation between the English airmen, or rather their spokesman from the upper class, and the delightful Mrs de Vries, secret agent. She raises her glass, saying: 'We have no food, but we still have hope', and she translates the royal device *Je maintiendrai* as the rather more

folksy 'We can take it'. The Englishman replies solemnly, 'We have nothing to give you but our gratitude.' But he promises that they will soon settle the score with the Germans. And straight away the piercing scream of air-raid sirens is heard, followed by the roar of British bombers. The Germans scatter like sheep, and Mrs de Vries says proudly, half-turning towards the audience and momentarily detached from the fictional context in order to assume the role of representative spokesman: 'Do you realise what it means to us when we see the masters of the world hiding under the tables? It is like oil on the burning flame in our hearts.'

This is followed by an epilogue. It is two months later, and the crew is back on active service. The planes are newer and better, and the target is now Berlin.

Thus the pendulum can swing from the factual to the emotional within one film. Much has happened in the course of two years; British confidence would certainly not have manifested itself quite so noisily in 1940 as in this film of 1942. The Germans are viewed from above, from an attic window, and there is no escaping the fact that 'the masters of the world' have begun to look rather ridiculous. They are not regarded with hatred, they are not 'Huns', but they have no style. This gentlemanly attitude also turns up in other films.

The enemy had been more subtly drawn in the film Powell had made in the previous year, *49th Parallel*. The Germans were very much the subject of the film, but were of varying character. The men of violence confronted the men of peace, one faith stood against another. (The action takes place in Canada, where a group of world conquerors are drifting about after an unsuccessful submarine raid. They attempt to infiltrate a colony of pious Herrn-huters, but are soon revealed in their true colours.) It was a commercial feature film, partly financed by the British Government, and seemed to suggest that the Germany which the democratic world was engaged in fighting was unrighteous, but that nevertheless another Germany existed.

Two simple feature films of the year before had been devoted to the decent Germans who formed the resistance and with whom it would be possible to cooperate when the tyrant had been brought down. They were Anthony Asquith's *Freedom Radio* and the Boulting Brothers' *Pastor Hall*, the latter with a religious resistance hero loosely based on Martin Niemöller and a script freely adapted from a play by Ernst Toller.

The aristocratic attitude to Germans and German-ness was adopted with devastating elegance by Leslie Howard in *Pimpernel Smith* (1941). This is a very special propaganda film. Initially the star, who was also the director, seems to play along with the German mis-conception; he is *their* kind of Englishman, just as slight and whimsical as they have imagined

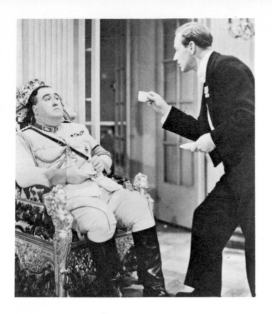

and represented him. But then behind the comic mask we discover an ice-cold tactician, a diabolical psychologist, a man who was stout-hearted and fearless.

The obvious danger of the film is that everything is too easy for Pimpernel Smith: he displays infinite resource while his adversaries are constantly clumsy. Von Graum, a farcical Himmler–Goering composite, is always being hoodwinked, and in the marvellous final scene, when he announces with total confidence that his nation will march on Poland that very evening, he is duped again, like a dim schoolboy tricked by a bright one. There are no intelligent villains here. At the psychological moment they are either led in the wrong direction or leave some loophole.

The outstanding characteristics of Pimpernel Smith are equanimity, self-confidence and refinement, which have been cultivated through the generations. During the escape he talks to Ludmilla about his country while the other passengers on the train are sleeping. He quotes Rupert Brooke, and an English fog drifts into the German third-class compartment. Everything becomes dream-like and emotive. In the final scene, Pimpernel Smith at last slips over the frontier into the mist, and speaks to us directly, in quiet but intense tones; he does not evangelise, rather he confesses his faith. It is one of those democratic sermons of World War II in which the hero turns to *us* and, looking us straight in the eyes, tells us what the war is all about. Pimpernel Smith talks of the strength of the weak and its superiority over violence. He also speaks about the ultimate victory, not about the hour of revenge, but about the inevitability of what will happen. It is worth asking whether *Pimpernel Smith* was really a salutary picture for Britain at the time, or whether it gave the nation a soporific dose of entertainment and inspiration. Rune Waldekranz argued that it 'illustrated the tendency of the English to underrate their adversary'. He adds:

'There were still people about who were under the illusion that victory would come quickly and unexpectedly. Germany would collapse from within, it was thought. English films from the earliest war years often reflect this vain hope.'

It is always hazardous trying to isolate serious intentions within a comedy, and it is not at all certain that the unsuitable confrontation of opposites in Leslie Howard's film – intelligence versus smug self-deception, and so on – was accepted at face value. It seems much more remarkable that this university don and secret agent is presented as such an aristocrat, both in behaviour and outlook. He is so refined as to be almost transparent. More questionable is his faith in the individual, the upright and exceptional individual who makes a stand against evil and will eventually turn the tide in Europe. There is a touch of the *übermensch* philosophy here. In any event, Pimpernel Smith does not rescue any ordinary middle-class or working-class people.

In Carol Reed's thriller *Night Train to Munich* (1940), the hero went to the aid of a beautiful girl and her father, a Czech inventor. Here, however, the motive of patriotic heroism seems to have been more clearly spelled out than in *Pimpernel Smith*: the Czech was shown to be of great value to the British war effort.

Life and Death of Colonel Blimp, directed by Michael Powell and Emeric Pressburger in 1943, was also concerned with Anglo-German relations. The story starts in 1902; two young officers, a German and an Englishman, fight a duel over a beautiful woman and end up as firm friends. In 1918, shortly before the Armistice, the German is in England as a prisoner of war. His English friend is married and with his wife comes to visit him at the camp, but he refuses to see them. The camp orchestra is playing and Blimp's wife sighs: 'Aren't they strange. They write poetry and music, and suddenly they start a war. There they are in their butchers' uniforms listening to Schubert.' Later, however, the German telephones them from Victoria Station and Blimp (real name

Stills. Far left: Leslie Howard's Pimpernel Smith. *Left:* Life and Death of Colonel Blimp. *Above:* In Which We Serve.

(Clive Wynne-Candy) picks him up and takes him to his club.

In 1938, Blimp's German friend returns to Britain of his own accord. He has escaped and tells the story of his life to unbelieving immigration officials. His children have gone over to Hitler. 'In Germany the criminals threw the decent people into gaol.' Before Wynne-Candy's arrival, he makes a serious little speech, staring straight out at the audience past the official who is facing him. By stepping out of character and addressing himself directly to us, he becomes the representative of something resembling an idea. (He is played by Anton Walbrook, a Central European immigrant. In *49th Parallel* he stood for the 'good' Germany as the leader of the Herrnhuter community.)

Then comes the outbreak of World War II. Against his will, Blimp is retired. A radio lecture he is preparing on the fall of France is stopped by the authorities. Blimp had wanted to say that it is better to lose than to win with the kind of weapons the Germans are using. His German friend takes him to task on this issue. Struggling to control his emotion, he delivers a sermon about democracy at war. In the face of Nazism, you cannot follow the rules of the game. 'This is not a gentleman's war.' This is war against evil itself, and if the democracies were to lose, it might take a hundred years before the oppressors were crushed.

It is hard to say whether this speech should be seen as an attempt to justify the bombing war against Germany during which, as is well known, there was no room for gentlemanly considerations. Be that as it may, it is certainly an interesting idea to have these grave and significant words spoken by someone coming from the other side: a German teaching an Englishman, a German instructing the English on how to fight the war and on what the enemy is like.

Following this confrontation, Blimp takes a decision. He swallows his pride and becomes a Home Guard leader. However, during a combined civilian and military exercise, the army uses debatable methods. Blimp is ignominiously arrested while having a Turkish bath. Flushed and agitated, he says to the arrogant young officer defending him: 'But the war starts at midnight.' This is something of a showdown between two generations, and for the second time this comedy film earnestly emphasises that, if need be, any means may be used to defend Britain.

The ending implies reconciliation. There is an army parade, and Blimp stands to attention. He himself cannot change, but he realises that the country must do so. He is a curiosity. At the same time, in a way he is Everyman. Although his attitudes are strange and obsolete, he has become a symbol of endurance.

Blimp may be an awkward hero, but Noël Coward's captain in the film which he directed with David Lean, *In Which We Serve* (1942), is a practical gentleman with elegant manners, cool judgement and great firmness in the exercise of his command.

An English destroyer, HMS *Torrin*, is torpedoed and sunk in battle off Crete in May 1941. Its story is told in flashbacks. We see how Britain awakens, closes its ranks and prepares for war. We see her being tested at Dunkirk and her subsequent growth in strength and confidence. HMS *Torrin* stands for the nation; she has her officers and crew, those who command and those who obey, loyal subjects on all levels but with one unfortunate exception, the man who forsakes his post under fire. (In the end, however, he mends his ways and dies a hero's death.)

All in all, they are an attractive lot, but they might perhaps be considered a bit old-fashioned. This is a society founded on class in which all the roles are predetermined. The captain has his bridge. His social isolation may be broken momentarily, but the overall pattern does not change. After the crew's rescue, the captain thanks each member on the quay at Alexandria. They step up to him one by one to shake his hand. It is an incredibly gripping scene because the dead are also present, standing behind the living, and because we know that this fellowship is now to be dissolved.

This scene makes a further call on our emotions: it seems to represent the sudden emergence of the British nation. The anonymous millions are given a face; the people are stepping out from the background. At the same time, though, the ceremony seems patronising. It is a big moment, but there is no question of any change in the social order; it is simply a tangential contact between two social groups.

In Which We Serve never suggests that the war might be about anything other than a defence of existing values and value judgments. There is no hint that there could be individuals who wish they had a different place in society, a different set of relationships, and that there are movements working for change. The working-class homes shown in the flashbacks have an unmistakable authenticity, but it seems that the differences in background between officers and crew are only economic, cultural and linguistic. Beyond that they seem to have the same kind of values. There is, of course, no mention of political opinions or parties.

A more egalitarian society emerges in a number of feature films which show a stronger documentary influence. A more important film in spite of its modesty, or maybe because of it, is *Millions Like Us* (1943) directed by Frank Launder and Sidney Gilliat. As the title suggests, it is about everyday heroism on the home front, about ordinary people, mostly women.

The story of a group of people is brightly told, with quiet humour. It begins before the war; it is summer and the greatest problem around is next week's football pools. Then, suddenly, comes the black-out, and trains arrive with soldiers from Dunkirk. The idyllic and the serious co-exist. Mines are laid along the coast and someone says drily: 'We'd better remember not to swim around here after the war.' It is bedtime in a middle-class home and children are happily playing, but on the doormat lies the pamphlet 'If the Invader Comes'.

Seriousness takes over, but the undercurrent of cheerfulness remains. Women are called upon to make a contribution to the war effort. The nice young girl from the middle-class family we have met at the beginning of the film, and have since been following, goes to enrol for service. Having indulged in Walter Mitty-type reveries, she does not want to work in a factory, but hopes to join the WAAF. The elderly lady interviewing the applicants says sternly: 'Mr Bevin wants another million women.' The romantic young lady ends up manufacturing spare parts for aeroplanes. *Millions Like Us* presents England as one great integrated community. Different social groups meet and exercise a friendly influence on each other. The old division of roles is no longer taken for granted, and it is almost as if this equality produced fresh energy.

There is, however, no question of a genuine confrontation. There is a single representative of the ruling classes, a haughty young woman

Stills. Below: Millions Like Us *by Frank Launder and Sidney Gilliat with Eric Portman, Anne Crawford and Patricia Roc. Right: Humphrey Jennings's* A Diary for Timothy.

who feels seriously insulted at having been forced down among the people in this way. Shrugging her shoulders, she pretends not to be capable of coping properly with the machine. The foreman, who feels that her attitude is sabotaging the war effort, has repeated arguments with her. They get on each other's nerves, but it all ends, naturally, on a note of harmony, maybe even of love. The middle-class girl turns out to possess not just a sense of humour but even a sense of social responsibility.

In the final scene all individuals and classes get together in a hearty sing-song. All join in, even the girl from the beginning of the film who has just lost her husband over Germany after being married for just a few days. The RAF come roaring over the factory on their way to Hamburg or Berlin, on the road to victory, followed, as at the beginning of the film, by the opening chords of Beethoven's Fifth Symphony.

Millions Like Us stands far to the left of *In Which We Serve*, but it is still very mild. There are no bad people, and Launder and Gilliat, too, seem to believe that differences between individuals are largely of an external nature. Some girls in the dormitory go to bed in their underwear, while others wear pyjamas and use cold cream.

It is as if responsible film-makers of the period were governed by a silent agreement to the effect that deeper divisions would be better treated on some later occasion. An armistice reigned in domestic politics, and the struggle was not between Churchill and Attlee, but between Churchill–Attlee and Hitler.

Nevertheless a few isolated films touched on more explosive issues. John Baxter treated the unemployment problem in *Love on the Dole*. It seems rather unlikely that a feature film on this serious subject could have been produced before the outbreak of war. (Richard Griffith even contends that such a project would not have been approved by the censor.) Now it had become acceptable. But in 1941 it was not a particularly vital issue.

The democracy fought for in these British films of World War II is consequently a democracy with reservations. It is democracy in principle rather than practice, a democracy expressing itself in a tone of voice or in new forms of social behaviour, but without any real political or economic significance. 'Democratic' in these films means rather 'kind, tolerant, pleasant, free of cant'; it is a morally charged word rather than a political concept. Democracy stands for unity, for individuals working together in unison for a common goal. It is a time for action, but the concept of democracy is passively interpreted – no backward look reveals anything but idylls, and there is no forward look, no proposed course of action, no programme, no vision of a new Jerusalem, or even a new London.

It has been said that the wartime cinema discovered the 'lowest common denominator' of the British people. It was of course a re-construction, a beautiful piece of mobilisation poetry. The military situation demanded that internal social conflicts be checked. They existed all right, in spite of all the smiles that were exchanged across the barriers of the class society. In the films, there's a pretence that the conflicts did not exist except on the level of anecdotal distinctions, accessories, habits and liguistic variations.

The parallel course of documentary films ran closer to so-called reality. For a number of years, British documentary film-makers had been working rather in the style of sociologists. While reality itself became dramatic, they retained their factual approach. They made low-keyed films of the tumult and did not comment on the progress of the war as much as on the everyday life of ordinary people in the shadow of the war. In their magazine, 'Documentary News Letter', they set out their aims. In their opinion, there could be no better propaganda for Britain itself as well as for the rest of the world, than 'a thorough analysis of the effects of the war on our democratic society' and of the constructive efforts being made or prepared in the midst of destruction.

In the films themselves, these ambitions seem rather tentatively realised. The documentary may well be, as Grierson suggests, an essentially social democratic art form. However, in the real life stories that his disciples produced before and during the war, Socialism emerges as something very vague and undefined: a gentle belief in progress, a form of humanism.

The belief in the capacity of the individual seems particularly strong in the most highly esteemed of the documentarists, Humphrey Jennings. His films, from *Listen to Britain* (1941) to *A Diary for Timothy* (1945) are a kind of invocation to democratic man, especially in Britain. Jennings is a social story-teller and poet, an excellent listener who catches the

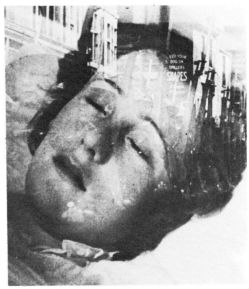

universal note in seemingly total diversity and who establishes connections everywhere. There are no breaks in his films between then and now, between big and small, between one image and another; he creates one billowing movement, a complete harmony that at times burgeons forth like an anthem. They are patriotic films from a nation at war, but without uniting symbols, fiery slogans or spectacular military feats. Humphrey Jennings's heroes are not the soldiers in the Libyan desert but the firemen of London. To them he made an unpretentious memorial in *Fires Were Started* (1943).

Characteristically, Jennings ear fails him in *The Silent Village*, also made in 1943, a work of indignation about Lidice, but transposed from occupied Czechoslovakia to Wales. In this film, however, his gentle associative technique does not work. What is elsewhere his strength becomes a fatal weakness.

As Eric Rhode has pointed out, Jennings was an apolitical person. He was a republican who felt the need for monarchy, and a Socialist to whom Conservative symbols seemed a genuine expression of the spirit of the nation. These inconsistencies made him a fitting spokesman for an attractive country led by a coalition government. He almost became the lowest common denominator. But when, in the Lidice picture, Jennings attempted to present a conflict of ideologies, he revealed his lack of political feeling and awareness. He could be truly interested only in what he loved.

In the same year as *Fires Were Started* and *The Silent Village* came *Desert Victory*, a long documentary film by Roy Boulting on the triumph of the Eighth Army over Rommel's Afrika Korps. There was no longer any doubt as to whose was the ultimate victory, and Boulting's film is a rather self-satisfied demon-

Still: Humphrey Jennings's Fires Were Started.

stration of strength. It does not depict people, friends or enemies, but military action and war machinery; it is coldly efficient and has none of the human intimacy that distinguished the art of Jennings. There is a distancing effect in the description of war which is actually reminiscent of *Sieg im Westen*. The film ends with the national symbol, the Union Jack.

The war had entered a decisive phase, but with the immediate threat against Britain past, a reaction set in. At any rate, the films begin to show considerable evidence of battle fatigue, and from 1943 onwards the character of feature films changes. 'The influence of the documentary film gets weaker,' Rune Waldekranz points out, and 'the collectivism gives way to a fresh and purely escapist note.' In 1944 only two features seem to have been directly concerned with the war. A growing number were about lonely hearts, and there was a decrease in the number of pictures about 'society'. There was more talk of love than of heroic deeds, and cinematic plots were more often acted out in historical costumes than in battle-dress.

Psychologically this is a natural development. If one is to accept the evidence provided by the cinema, the need for aggression did not grow stronger in Britain during World War II. There was instead a need for a sense of security, but after El Alamein the cinema was no longer needed for reassurance.

During the war years 'Documentary News Letter' had exercised pressure on the authorities; the documentary film-makers wanted to be able to campaign more forcefully on a political level. In an editorial of March 1942, British film propaganda was described as a failure. It had suffered not only from shortage of funds, but even more from lack of purpose. The article went on to say that in a time of violent change there was a need for revolutionary tactics. But British documentary had persistently retained its inhibited and insular character.

The authorities seem to have been unmoved by these appeals, and after the end of the war the limited resources were to shrink even further. In his preface to the third edition of 'Documentary Film', Paul Rotha speaks of the Labour Party's betrayal of documentary. The Labour Government did not want films that gave a critical analysis of the housing situation throughout the country; they required instructional films on how to erect pre-fabs. Rotha sums up grimly:

'Between 1946–51 the Labour people threw away one of their strongest aids to interpret and make acceptable the aims and ideals of social democracy, not just to Britain but to the world.'

In a postscript he records the epitaph of British documentary. On 29 January 1952, the Conservative Government decided to dismantle the Crown Film Unit. Thus an era which had begun in 1929 with John Grierson's *Drifters* came to an end.

Cesare Zavattini

Still: Vittorio De Sica's Bicycle Thieves.

Cesare Zavattini, a small man, but weighty, has been a key figure in the Italian cinema, pouring his indefatigable energy into it for over two decades as the practical philosopher of neo-realism. Analytical and encouraging, he has been a source of inspiration and moral authority. He writes films, and collaborated on perhaps almost half of the best Italian films from 1940 to the time about twenty years later when Fellini with *La Dolce Vita* and Antonioni with *L'Avventura* left behind the cinema of Vittorio De Sica, Zavattini's director. He is an artist who has never been afraid of coming out with a message, a man with something to say. He is saying it at this moment, eagerly and with such lively gestures that his chair seems in danger of toppling over.

Rome, one day in the summer of 1963. I have come to see Zavattini – with an interpreter, an intelligent young man who is of the opinion that Zavattini is *vieux jeu*, an opinion which will have changed after the meeting.

Language barriers are quickly broken down, for Zavattini has no difficulty in establishing personal contacts. He is as talkative as a bar-room politician but with greater powers of concentration; he is as solid as one of his leather armchairs, and his manners are easy and natural.

A man of the people and working for the people, he is not at all a sentimental socialist; he does not idealise the people, but feels they are closer to reality than the bourgeoisie, and reality is all.

The dialogue of film scripts first lives in Zavattini's mind as the language of the common people. The characters all speak in popular dialect. In this way they become properly keyed to their actions, and when they have come alive within him as real people, he can then translate their lines into literary Italian. Total realism is impossible in the cinema, even in the country of neo-realism.

This is an admission that Cesare Zavattini does not make gladly. He is a practical man and a theoretician, and neo-realism is a philosophy expressing his experience of society and his concept of what part the cinema could play in this society. He has tested his ideas in films which others – De Sica above all, but also Blasetti, Emmer, De Santis and Visconti – have made from his scripts in the closest collaboration with him. He is an idealist who has been forced constantly to revise his vision because of the limitations of the medium and because of the form's debasing dependence on capital and technology.

Such are the realities of the cinema, and Zavattini never pretends that they do not exist. Nevertheless, he nurtures within him a dream of independence. He would like to make films about everyday life, films which would have the courage to confront reality at close range. A film could be about an ordinary day in the life of an ordinary human being. A two hour film might, for instance, take as its subject a mother buying a pair of shoes for her little boy. In reality this is an act lasting about ten minutes, but when the camera is confronted with reality it finds new depths and ramifications. The scriptwriter and the director must try to demonstrate what makes a person act and how different actions are interrelated. In analysing the purchase of a pair of shoes, one can see opening up before one, according to Zavattini, 'a vast and complex world, pregnant with meaning and with practical, social, economic and psychological values'.

In 1952 Zavattini discussed the conditions and possibilities of the cinema in an important statement which amounts to a manifesto. (It was actually an interview by Luigi Chiarini for 'La Rivista del cinema italiano'.) He is ruthless with himself and at the same time almost touchingly optimistic, taking note of failure and then looking defiantly ahead. Genuine neo-realism, like genuine communism, has never yet been achieved. Films like *Open City*, *Paisà*, *La Terra Trema*, *Bicycle Thieves* and *Umberto D* are a beginning, a few steps on the road towards a new realism, but they are not 'neo-realist' because the 'documentary attitude' has not yet won through.

Films made so far, in all countries and periods of film history, have been unliberated and artificial. A 'story' implies a flight from reality, an assault on reality and an attempt at shuffling the cards to conceal human defeat. A new attitude to the material, to the environment, must involve, among other things, a new narrative technique. Zavattini is utterly sick of the old restlessness, the chasing from one scene to the next, the unnatural effort to create a chain of dramatic climaxes. The outstandingly obvious must no longer be of the greatest importance. One must be able to stay with a scene, to wait, to rest, and then delve down deeper or expand sideways. Nor does Zavattini want films which are concerned with 'exceptional' people. 'It is about time,' he says, 'that we let the audiences know that it is in fact they who play the leading role in life.'

The cinema has betrayed reality, and in so doing has impoverished itself. To Zavattini reality is enough, and the task of the scriptwriter and the director consists of forcing people to take stock of their situation and to find their feet within their own reality (which means becoming politically conscious). He feels that the cinema needs not only 'brains' but also people with a moral backbone. Reality is a moral problem, and to produce poetic versions of it instead of describing, reporting and documenting it, is just escapism. Zavattini himself believes 'in fantasy and in solitude', but even more firmly in 'reality and people', and although there is a poet inside him, he has decided to sacrifice poetry. Or at least it must be subordinated to reality.

The subject that touches him most deeply lay close at hand in the Italy of the early 'fifties: poverty. It is not a popular topic either with the mass audience, which has become accustomed to escaping from reality, or with the minority holding economic and political power, for they prefer that people are not reminded of social injustice. But Zavattini is convinced that if Christ were living in our midst and owned a film camera, he would show up the good and bad of our time. He would be a social critic, a neo-realist. He would give us 'close-ups of those who embitter the lives of their fellow men, and of the victims, if the censor allowed him to.'

There is a great deal to be said about censorship in the Italian cinema after 1945. It is clear that radical film-makers have rarely been able to realise the ideas that touched them most deeply. This has not just been a question of outright banning, although the Italian film industry had a code of morals copied from Hollywood. More often there appears to have been censorship by the producer rather than censorship by the censor, compliance by the film industry with the wishes of the spiritual and civil powers and, as everywhere else in the world, self-censorship

Stills: neo-realist films. Below: Pietro Germi's Il Cammino della speranza. *Opposite: De Sica's* I Bambini ci guardano.

by scriptwriters and directors, in accordance with their experience of what is and is not feasible. Yet there are still outstanding works of art, hypnotic images of reality which rise above the mass of indifferent pictures – the bulk of the post-war Italian cinema. They indicate the courage, intelligence and persistence of a few individuals, as well as the intrinsic vitality of the material. The realities of Italy were not easily shut out, but elbowed right through the clichés.

Early neo-realism was a reaction against the hypocrisy of the years when the new directors were learning their trade and attaining awareness. Fascism was a tragic farce. To the cinema it meant first of all a dynamic building programme (a film city, a film school), and then colossal films like *Scipio Africanus*, historical and drawing-room romance, chivalry and white telephones. A few more realistic movies were also produced. In 1942 Luchino Visconti made *Ossessione*, and Alessandro Blasetti, an older director, *Quattro passi fra le nuvole*. Blasetti's picture, like Vittorio De Sica's *I Bambini ci guardano* from 1943, was based on a Zavattini script, and these films inaugurated a phase which was to culminate in (and conclude with) *Umberto D* in 1952.

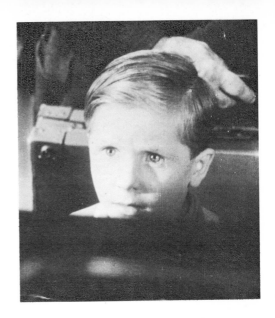

The new films turned against the false myths offered by Fascism, against the misery into which it had plunged the country, and against the confusion and nihilism it had left in its wake. The pent-up energy broke forth with a moral indignation directed both against conditions which could be blamed on a particular form of government and a specific political leader, and also against the absurdity which seemed to be the human condition: the helplessness of man, the vanity of dreams, and death which parts all lovers.

There was a metaphysical problem posed in many of these films, whether they were made by sensible Marxists or radical Catholics. In spite of its social concern, this was an individualistic cinema; as a rule it told the story of isolated individuals and of individual tragedies. There were films about groups – the Sicilian fishermen in Visconti's *La Terra Trema* and the miners who in Germi's *Il Cammino della speranza* walked north with their families to find work – but hardly any collective stories in the Russian manner. De Sica has said that what struck him most at the end of the war was people's loneliness.

Society is not easily pinned down in Italian post-war films. It is a state of chaos in which the good and the bad, the clear-sighted and the confused are trying to find their way, or alternatively it is an anonymous prison-like institution. This simultaneously amoral and authoritarian community has as its victims the simple people who do not know how to manipulate the economic-political machinery and do not as yet know their own strength. The neo-realist cinema emphasises both man's solitude and the importance of solidarity, yet it contains no urge to revolution. It points out injustices, most effectively in demonstrating the vulnerability of children. The films mirror and examine a situation; they combine critical realism with a humanitarian appeal. Their openness and sincerity were to many filmgoers around 1950 something approaching a revelation.

These films were written and directed by communists or communist sympathisers, but never seemed to be shaped according to any particular party line or trimmed to fit any ready-made scheme. They were made by politically conscious people, but they did not politicise. They were political films, says Karel Reisz, 'only in the sense that they treat problems that are subjected to jurisdiction and political control; but they do not offer any solutions nor have they got any particular programme.'

From the end of the war up to May 1947, Italy was led by a coalition government linked to the resistance movement. Both Nenni and Togliatti were members of the cabinet, the latter as Minister of Justice. During this period there seems to have been no censorship of films; there were quite simply no laws allowing for that type of control, except those made by Mussolini. A new, Catholic-inspired censorship code was tabled after the dissolution of the coalition government, but was not effectively applied before 1949.

In 1948, *Bicycle Thieves*, a simply told but moving story, attracted vast audiences. 1948 was also the year when a quarter of the Italian working population was unemployed. As De Sica's film became known throughout the world, so did some of Italy's social ills, which did not particularly please the new government. In 1949 a governmental body, the Direzione Generale dello Spettacolo, was set up, with a mandate to subsidise suitable films and to forbid the export of films which 'might give a false idea of the real conditions in our country'.

This decision had unpleasant repercussions for the new ambitious cinema. Neo-realist films had met with resistance from Italian finance and had been largely paid for by export profits. The government now possessed the means to direct all film-making as it wished; it could encourage tendencies sympathetic to its aims and steer producers and directors away from controversial subjects. It was a subtle form of dictatorship, influencing film production through subsidies and credits. There were certain subjects that the authorities regarded with disfavour. For instance, it soon proved very difficult to get a script through which treated or even mentioned Fascism. The Christian Democratic regime apparently did not want to risk any comparisons.

In his book 'The Sociology of Film Art', the American film historian George A. Huaco places this development quite firmly in a wider political context. 'The increasing distaste of the Italian government for the neo-realist cinema,' he writes, 'was at least in part a consequence of Italy's position in the "cold war".' In March 1949, Italy had joined NATO.

The situation was becoming increasingly difficult for films concerned with reality. When De Sica had made *Umberto D* (the film Zavattini considers closest to the neo-realist ideal), Giulio Andreotti, dictator of the Italian cinema, sent him an open letter expressing the displeasure of the regime. Andreotti wrote, with characteristic aplomb and lack of clarity: 'We ask the man of culture to feel his social responsibility, which should not be limited to description of the abuses and miseries of a system and a generation . . . If it is true that evil can be fought by harshly spot-lighting its most miserable aspects, it is also true that De Sica has rendered bad service to his country if people throughout the world start thinking that Italy in the middle of the twentieth century is the same as in *Umberto D.*'

De Sica did not unbend, but he made his next film for an American producer. He returned to working more as an actor than as a director, and although he went on to make his own, sometimes very successful, films, it would not seem unreasonable to assume that his subsequent artistic decline might also have been political in origin.

Zavattini is a more robust character. In an interview from this period his tone becomes very stern. He turns to his colleagues within the film industry, scriptwriters, directors, actors, technicians, imploring them to get organised, to give the government and the financiers a definite answer, and counter blackmail with blackmail. He declares himself, too, prepared to make the necessary sacrifices. He has made sacrifices and still does, although the major battle must now be considered over.

What Zavattini has been forced to sacrifice above all else is ideas. He has a vast number in his mind and occasionally speaks of a film which has never existed as more than a concept. His greatest project was given the proud title of *Italia Mia*. (It preoccupied him in 1951 and 1952 and came from an earlier idea about a film journey round the world.) It was to have been a journey with a camera right through Italian society, a living fresco of episodes, snapshots, fragments of lives. It would concern itself not with the picturesque Italy but with the hidden one, more real than that shown to tourists. *Italia Mia* would show the lives and feelings of simple people, how the war ends and everybody begins to work again, how hope returns and also eventually the fear of another war, uneasily co-existing with the dream of peace.

The film was intended to give us a genuine understanding of these people. Zavattini contends that the lack of love in the world is due to our insufficient knowledge of each other. He now feels more than ever that his task is not to create fictitious worlds, but to increase people's knowledge of the existing one. In a 1953 report on this project he adds:

'A time will come when we will partake [in the cinema] of a person's everyday preoccupations, watch him at his most menial tasks, and we will follow all this with the same attention that the Greeks devoted to the works of their great playwrights.'

It was to have been a film without a story and without a script, created in the present tense and with all the immediacy of reality. Unfortunately nothing came of it. The financiers hesitated, De Sica got an offer from Hollywood, and the volcanic Rossellini, who was bubbling over with enthusiasm, soon forgot *Italia Mia*.

On this summer's day in 1963 I ask Zavattini if it is easier to make films of social interest now that the political balance has changed and the 'left' has achieved greater influence. Zavattini is optimistic, albeit with certain marked reservations. True, there is no longer any official resistance to realistic film art. On the other hand it is really no easier than before to finance such films. Furthermore, Italian society has a built-in braking mechanism, and one must not expect too much from any apparent progress.

Zavattini goes on to develop this theory of Italy's national disease. The Italian is progressive in principle, and inclined towards change. He travels quickly and happily towards a goal but usually develops scruples as it comes within reach. The normal pattern is two steps forward and one back; it recurs in all sections of society and every political group. Italians are slaves to convention and their own sensual nature. What we need is a shattering crisis, says Zavattini, briefly assuming the tones of a public orator.

Possibly there is a crisis already. Italy has developed very quickly into a modern industrial state, but few of the population have gained appreciably from the overall increase in pros-

Still: perhaps the last neo-realist film, De Sica's Il Tetto *(1956), scripted by Zavattini.*

perity. At the same time, Zavattini contends, something of value which existed in the old system has been squandered. He defines it as a deep sense of reality, a feeling for the substance of life, that is characteristic of ordinary people. He has faith in a human capacity for good, but knows, too, how easily man can be led astray.

Some of the films scripted by Zavattini in the early sixties referred to these problems, but the arguments lacked sophistication. *Il Boom* (1963) is a grotesque comedy, containing an urgent message that is under constant threat of being entirely swamped by laughter. The comedy is overplayed in *Boccaccio '70* (1961) and the action preaches a primitivism that seems rather heartless. Society has changed and it has been suggested that conditions no longer call for films like those made at one time by Zavattini and De Sica. Nothing is that simple any more; the conflicts are no longer so clearly defined. The new Italy is more faithfully reflected, it is said, in films like those of Antonioni, for instance.

That is obviously not how Zavattini sees it. I ask discreetly, but no, he has no axe to grind with Fellini or Antonioni, with the young Italian and French directors. On the contrary, they have brought greater mobility to the cinema and have had the courage to break with many cinematic conventions. He can see several of his own theories realised in their work. He thinks they have good eyes, but they should be even bolder. They are extremely talented, but Cesare Zavattini cannot quite understand their attitude to the task. He gesticulates eagerly, making the sunlight flicker on his round, shining face. He has spoken somewhere about the cinema's 'hunger for reality'. Now he says that films must exploit 'the intrinsic vitality of the medium'. Most of all, the new films lack force rather than observation, sensitivity or subtlety.

Out of all these explanations and gestures one basic idea emerges quite distinctly: Zavattini feels that the new film-makers have forgotten about commitment. They are too sophisticated, and lead a narrow, private existence. But film is a window looking out on the world. He himself feels a responsibility, stemming from his origins, experiences, politics and temperament. He is a social utopian; he wants to make the world a better place and recognises the need for this. He has recently been teaching future directors, sharing with them his knowledge of the cinema and his ways of looking at society.

In spite of his determination, Cesare Zavattini has become less exacting. From his films and his ideas on film, he was never a near-sighted realist. He was something like a realist mystic;

91

to him there is a magic about reality. André Bazin writes that the film-maker's function, according to Zavattini, consists of 'making things light up from within, and liberating from them a shining brightness which might turn our attention to them, and our feelings and thoughts'. To Bazin it is also clear that Zavattini's philosophy is the concept of a poet and not of a realist.

If this is correct Cesare Zavattini presents a dilemma. He is not a realist but wants to be one, Bazin suggests, and is a poet without wanting to be. It would be fairer, I believe, to see him both as a realist *and* poet, a richly gifted man whose combined talents are ideal in principle, but not really fitted to the present situation in the cinema; absolute realism is no more appropriate than exaggerated lyricism. No imagination can be given complete freedom while the film industry is even as restrictive as it still is today, and there cannot be critical freedom when the cinema operates in and serves capitalist society.

Zavattini is aware of the conflict; it seems as if he is now resigned to it. He possibly feels that he made the wrong choice. He should have been a director – if indeed he ought to have been in the cinema at all. The Zavattini he knows within the depths of his innermost being is neither a political animal nor a satirist but, he suggests, a man of imagination and melancholy. He flings out his arms and then strikes

his forehead; he is of course really a poet, a dreamer. The cinema forced him to become aggressive, to look critically at reality, to turn himself into a realist. And he was and still is, but his imagination has suffered. Now at last he wants to give it a chance.

Zavattini smiles behind his glasses. He seems charged with youthful energy, although he was born in 1902 and has been writing film scripts since 1936. He keeps huddling up and stretching in the brown armchair while he is talking, at once forceful and relaxed. He is a serious clown, a world reformer with a funny name, and behind the imagination and the critical intelligence one can sense a deep love of life and a ruthless desire to make the world a better place.

Zavattini is an emotional radical, a communist without dogma. His pathos is not noisily conspicuous. His best film stories have a tender melancholy and are about lonely and unprotected people. There is Umberto D, the old-age pensioner abandoned by the whole world except his little dog, and there are the worker and his son in *Bicycle Thieves*, shivering in the rain, walking through a society where everyone is pushing and shoving and where charity is but the faint glow of morning flickering weakly amid threatening clouds and grey smoke.

Still: the De Sica–Zavattini partnership hits the big time with La Ciociara (Two Women).

Cinema Novo: Brazil before the Revolution

Until the 'sixties, Latin American films were generally thought of as mass-produced, low-level entertainment, a poor imitation of the standard escapism from North America. There were very few exceptions. Some of Luis Buñuel's most highly respected films were made in Mexico. At times he was able violently to express his contempt of bourgeois institutions and opinions. In Argentina, Leopoldo Torre-Nilsson managed to achieve international acclaim as a social critic in the mid-'fifties. Despite melodramatic plots and a visual style that was stiffly baroque, his political involvement was taken seriously, at least in Europe. He attacked corruption, reactionary social ideas and Catholic sexual morality in films like *La Casa del angel* (1957) and *Fin de fiesta* (1959), but radicals in Latin America mainly regard him as a bourgeois opportunist.

A revolutionary cinema started in Cuba in 1959. Its aims were to enlighten people and increase their awareness, to provoke and inspire. It was supported by a lively national film institute which, in harmony with the country's vast information and education projects, laid great emphasis on documentaries. A school of directors was trained to concentrate on reportage, 'pamphlet montage' and essay films. The group includes Santiago Alvarez, with his description of the great hurricane disaster of 1963, *Ciclón*, and the anti-American shorts, *NOW* and *Hanoi, martes 13 diz*, Fausto Canel, director of a formally sophisticated documentary on a Cuban hero, *Hemingway*, and Manuel Octavio Gomez who made *Historia de una batalla* about the campaign against illiteracy in mountain districts.

Beside the documentaries, Cuban features in the spirit of the Revolution are also emerging. Humberto Solas's *Manuela* (1966), a love-story set among guerillas, attracted a certain amount of attention outside Cuba, as did Tomás Alea's *Historias de la revolución* (1960) and *Memorias del subdesarrollo* (1968). *La muerte de un burocrata* (1966), by the same director is a burlesque on his country's bureaucracy, with a satirical attitude that eloquently counters any suspicion that the Cuban cinema is all revolutionary smugness.

One only expects to find a revolutionary cinema where the Revolution has already triumphed, as it has in Cuba. The exposed system of commercial film distribution provides few opportunities for working in the shadows, where revolutions begin. Most governments have developed institutional means of suppressing unwelcome propaganda long before it

Stills: Latin American films. Below: La Casa del angel. *Bottom:* Ciclón *(left);* Historias de la revolución.

reaches an audience. The most efficient controls are found among those who most fear upheaval, and military dictatorships would seem to offer the very worst conditions for the production of revolutionary films. So it is paradoxical that Latin American films have become internationally known, largely through a school which has been called revolutionary in the political sense: the new Brazilian cinema.

Under the collective name of 'Cinema Nôvo' a group of outstanding young directors has grown up outside Brazil's stagnating commercial cinema. Most of them began, without any previous professional qualifications, as documentary reporters of poverty. And poverty and misery remained their subjects when they pooled their resources in a concerted effort which succeeded in turning them into leading film-makers. French critics called their work *Cinéma de la faim* – the cinema of hunger.

North-eastern Brazil contains one of the world's most under-privileged areas. There on vast prairies – the *sertão* – the population scrapes a living from the most primitive forms of agriculture constantly undermined by catastrophic periods of drought. Every year, large numbers of people leave these areas for the big cities, and in Rio de Janeiro these fugitives from starvation merge with a different proletariat crammed into the *favelas*. These slums are no more than a conglomeration of dwellings made out of cardboard boxes, boards from broken

crates and sheets of corrugated iron. The *sertão* and the *favelas* were the worlds whose people Cinema Nôvo first made its own.

In 1955, Nelson Pereira dos Santos, an ex-lawyer, managed to get a privately produced, semi-documentary feature, *Rio quarenta graus*, shown in the cinemas. It was a story of the big city in the neo-realist manner, linking episodes in a number of lives on a hot day in Rio de Janeiro. The misery and hardship of the *favela* is contrasted harrowingly with the affluence of the rich and the heartlessness of the authorities. A film of this kind could hardly fail to make some impact, although parts of it appeared amateurish. Nelson Pereira became a kind of father figure for his younger colleagues, and inspired them to make films themselves. After some stilted early efforts, they developed a purposeful assurance in handling film. Cinema Nôvo became both a style and a social outlook.

Roberto Farias made another sort of *favela* picture in *O Assalto ao trem pagador*, a gangster film that has clear affinities with *Rififi*, but uses suspense to convey an evident challenge. It works by forcing the audience to side with the impoverished robbers against a society which has deprived them of any chance of carving out for themselves a worth-while and dignified existence. The tragic irony lies in the fact that the stolen money has no value for the poor, since their destruction is preordained as soon

Stills: the two settings of Cinema Nôvo – the sertão in Nelson Pereira dos Santos's Vidas secas; *the* favela *in Roberto Farias's* O Assalto ao trem pagador (The Train Robbers).

as they attempt to live above the level of bare subsistence society has allotted them.

The other main category of early Cinema Nôvo films has a greater feeling of homogeneity. It takes as its theme the suffering of the *sertão*. The sun-bleached pallor and oppressive atmosphere of the peculiar desert landscape keep recurring and reflect a state of mental desolation and misery, drought and endless spaces. The environment lends pain, oppression and monotony to the films, but the monotonous rhythm comes from a suppressed energy which must sooner or later explode in vain outbursts of blood-shed and cruelty. Violence is much in evidence in Cinema Nôvo, but it is not the violence of the Western. It is not attractive as entertainment and carries no metaphysical meaning: it has the blindness of rage, a state rather than technique.

Nelson Pereira whose *favela* picture had marked the beginning of Cinema Nôvo, made one of the very best *sertão* films, *Vidas secas*, based on a novel by Graciliano Ramos. The film begins with the title '1940', over a shot of a little family group on the horizon. They approach with painful slowness through a sun-ravaged landscape – four people, starving and resigned,

carrying their home on their backs. The man gets a job as a cattle-hand and this provides two years' grace from the fatal drought. But it returns eventually, and the family walks out again into the same desert and the same hopelessness. The last scene recalls the first and the title '1942' appears as the little group disappears towards the horizon – this walk will recur year after year with the same monotony, unless . . .

During the deceptively carefree period when the family in *Vidas secas* are living a fairly good life, though at the mercy of a feudal landowner, the film is occasionally delightful, sometimes funny and always beautiful. But there is pain in the beauty; the comedy foreshadows brutality, the charm hovers on the brink of despair. The family's lovable dog Baleia is almost starved to death and then injured by a bullet from which it eventually dies – an almost unbearably painful sequence. When the son of the family overhears the taboo-laden haranguing of an old medicine woman he asks curiously what all the words mean. In answer he gets a ringing clout across the head and runs away crying, defiantly muttering the new words about hell, death and torment. We hear his whispered words about hell on the soundtrack as the camera sweeps over this land of humiliation and injustice, and the boy's words become the message of the film. On another occasion the family attends a festival in the nearby village, but the holiday mood is cruelly shattered when the local representative of authority demonstrates the power at his disposal by having the father beaten up and thrown into jail.

Religion has come to represent a reactionary force in this culture, with its promises of *another* and better life and its mystical expressions of ecstasy that impede social revolution by sublimating the instinct to rebel. Its functions are, however, diffuse and sociologically complex. The theme of religion is central in Glauber Rocha's powerful *Deus e o Diabo na terra del sol*, for example. Here the church emerges as an ally of feudalism against a semi-religious, semi-revolutionary popular movement around 1940. Religion often recurs in *sertão* pictures as a phenomenon that has complex associations with the psychology of violence, a relationship deeply rooted in the bandit tradition which can be seen, in a certain sense as a forerunner of later revolutionary efforts.

Religion also lies behind the Cinema Nôvo picture that is perhaps the most wilful, angry and *engagé* of them all, Ruy Guerra's *Os Fuzis*. The action is set in 1963. The starving inhabitants of the *sertão* gather around a 'prophet' and his sacred ox which will, he tells them, bring rain to save the country from drought. The prophet and his followers are in a small town when the mayor calls in the soldiers to protect his bulging grain-stores from the starving, unruly crowd. The people are overpowered by the soldiers but, submitting to the existing order of things, they vent irrational fury on the unfortunate cow. A child dies of hunger. *One* solitary human being revolts in individual, bloody, furious protest. The rhythm, which has up to that moment been slow and ponderous,

Stills. Below: Brazilian politics in Glauber Rocha's Terra em transe. *Right: the prophet (Mauricio Loyola) and followers in Ruy Guerra's* Os Fuzis.

explodes into scenes of violence that have never been equalled in the cinema, a panic of incredible power and pent-up fury.

But the *people* do not take part; the lonely revolt becomes a desperate gesture which can only result in death.

Oddly enough, until 1964 Cinema Nôvo had been able to work in comparative freedom – sometimes even with the financial support of the authorities. In April of that year the moderately leftist Goulart regime was overthrown by a military coup and the situation changed dramatically. The authorities halted work on a number of projects, censorship became stricter and the police were empowered to oversee film production. In November 1965 some film directors were briefly imprisoned for their direct involvement in demonstrations against the new régime.

But Cinema Nôvo did not stop and, apart from a few incidents, the group has been allowed to continue its politically embarrassing activities. The Brazilian directors are still, at the moment of writing, among the most fascinating and promising film-makers in the world, although distribution problems make it hard for us to follow their development. The scope of subjects was enlarged from the *favelas* and the *sertão* to include the political situation of the bourgeoisie and the intellectuals. This led to a demand for more complex dramatic conflicts and more sophisticated social analysis than before. The new subject matter was not immediately as dramatic as the themes from the disaster areas. In *O Desafio*, Paulo Cézar Saraceni dealt with the sadness and despair which Brazilian intellectuals suffered after the military coup. Although the film was cut by the censor and had trouble getting an export permit, it was widely discussed in Brazil. Glauber Rocha's *Terra em transe* also concerned the mood of political indecision among intellectuals,

nd it, too, ran into censorship and export
roblems in 1966. *Antonio das Mortes*, Rocha's
ext film, is a gory, dogmatic melodrama in
olour, aimed at revolution. It probably escaped
eing banned through appearing as an official
ntry in the 1969 Cannes Film Festival.

The relative freedom of the Brazilian cinema
s still sufficiently unexpected to make us
onder why, *if* there is a genuine basis for
alling Cinema Nôvo revolutionary, these
lirectors are allowed to produce and exhibit
heir films in Brazil. Cinema Nôvo's critical
ttitude to the authorities cannot seriously be
uestioned. When a succession of films appear
n which a whole group of directors present an
nvarying image of misery and outrage that
vidently compromises the regime and are ex-
licit about the totally unfair distribution of
ealth and economic assets, the authorities
ust logically regard them as subversive. In
ddition, Cinema Nôvo directors have spoken
ublicly of their aims with a fair amount of
rankness in other countries. Their most vol-
ble spokesman, Glauber Rocha says, for in-
tance, in a *Cahiers du Cinéma* interview that
hey want to make their pictures explosive and
ope to 'make a contribution to the revolution'.
number of films even give openly sympathetic
ccounts of attempted revolts against the
egime. And still the films are allowed. They
re even supported by a state film institute. The
ituation is something of a mystery.

Saraceni has hinted at an explanation. The
regime chooses the lesser of two evils: they let
the film-makers carry on rather than challenge
international opinion. Thus a democratic façade
can be maintained. Apparently the challenges
contained within the films are considered less
dangerous than the effects of demonstrable
political censorship. There are various complementary factors behind this assessment.

Cinema Nôvo films combine artistic honesty
and ambivalence. Their view of people has a
profound and intricate complexity that inhibits
their power as political weapons. They do not
present any easily recognised reality with clearly
identifiable crooks and heroes. In addition, the
films all share an elegiac atmosphere that non-
Brazilian audiences, at least, find alienating. In
spirit, the films are also humanist rather than
socialist. They depict a scandalous social situation without showing any political causes for
it, or any clear ideological alternative. The
revolts that we glimpse are not visions designed
to inspire any hope. Either they finally fail to
materialise or else they are suppressed by the
authorities, channelled into religious submission, or occasionally they are the work of
isolated, desperate individuals while the passive
masses hold back. Finally, the masses – the poor
and under-privileged themselves are not the
ones who see the films. They do not want to be
confronted with their own misery in the very
places where they go to escape from it.

New Babylon

The Paris Commune of spring 1871 was a tragic episode in the history of socialism. The workers took over, established their own administration, made their own laws and governed for ten weeks before being crushed by the armed bourgeoisie.

Marx saw the Commune as the foretaste of an entirely new society, and Engels regarded it as the realisation of 'dictatorship of the proletariat'. To Lenin, the Paris Commune was the first popular uprising of modern times. In 'State and Revolution' there is an analysis of this attempt to crush the old order, 'the bureaucratic-military system'. He returns again and again to the failure: the lack of unity among the revolutionaries themselves, their indecision and lack of ruthlessness. When he makes his own revolution he is not going to be held back by any feelings of inadequacy or any scruples. The final atrocity of the Paris Commune – the murder of twenty thousand workers by the punitive squadrons of Marshal Macmahon and General Gallifet – taught him that the ruling class has no pity on those seeking to rob it of its privileges.

The Communards possessed a strong sense of the meaning of symbols: they pulled down the column which had been erected in the Place Vendôme by Napoleon I for his own glorification and staged a public burning of the guillotine at the foot of Voltaire's statue. The Commune itself has become a symbol for Communists in the Soviet Union and elsewhere. When Lenin died, he was wrapped in a gunpowder-stained flag which had fluttered over one of the last barricades at Belleville. Forty years later the crew of Voskhod I took with them three treasures (or fetishes) on their journey into space: a portrait of Marx, a portrait of Lenin, and a strip torn from a red flag that had been flying in Paris during the Commune.

Considering its status as a symbol of revolution, it is not surprising that the Paris Commune has been the subject of a big Soviet movie. However, New Babylon (Novij Vavilon), directed by Grigori Kozintsev and Leonid Trauberg, is not a sweeping revolutionary epic. It is an important work of art in a symbolic-expressionist style which is all its own, combining forceful expression with reticence. It includes titles in the form of exclamations and images which have an emblematic density of meaning. The greatest strength of this virtually unknown masterpiece is also its most decisive weakness: the emphasis lies on the separate images – it becomes a maze of individual details, like Eisenstein's October.

Kozintsev and Trauberg do not primarily set out to tell a story, attempting instead to illustrate a whole concept. Apparently they want to invest each image with the utmost significance, aiming not for a gradual build-up of effect, not 'development', but instant illumination. The succession of static images produces harmony or dissonance.

This kind of musical or poetic method does not lend itself particularly well to an account of political events. Isolated details can have a shock value of their own, like carefully used adjectives or metaphors in a literary text; they possess a kind of energy which can be transmitted in the written page or in a sequence of film. But the great social novels of Balzac, Tolstoy and Dreiser are not written in luminous prose; their effect is achieved through subordinate elements, observations and statements which together form a meaningful whole. Many of the images in New Babylon are startling. Some have the appearance of strange tableaux where every gesture and effect has been carefully considered. We cannot escape the conclusion that a less showy presentation and more concentration in the film on verbs rather than adjectives might have given greater revolutionary dynamism to this film about revolution. In a fragmentary form, a political attitude can certainly be discerned in the film. It does, however, seem as if political involvement is invariably subordinated to aesthetic considerations.

In 1870, the German press described Paris as a 'modern Babylon' which should be destroyed. In the Kozintsev and Trauberg film, New Babylon is a big department store apparently containing its own restaurant and vaudeville. (As a subjective narrative technique has been chosen instead of objective reportage, it is sometimes hard to tell exactly where the action is taking place at any given moment.) The story begins before the Commune. during the final phase of the Franco-Prussian War, in an Offenbachian orgy of pleasure. The casual extravagance is in outrageous contrast to the social situation, to the life of the working classes, and to the political developments as the Germans approach Paris. We catch a glimpse of washerwomen lit as if in a Daumier painting, and in an extraordinary night sequence Andrei Moskvin's camera picks out th

Still: New Babylon.

caps and lances of the Uhlans shining in the dark.

These are effectively contrasted images, but life at *New Babylon* is still the principal theme: trading, eating, dancing, love that can be had at a price and its potential customers. '*Il nous faut de l'amour/Nous voulons de l'amour*' from La Belle Hélène' is the ironic leading motif in the musical accompaniment to this silent film. The frilly skirts of the can-can girls billow wildly; the whirl of pleasure becomes increasingly frenzied until it verges on hysteria. Suddenly the atmosphere is rudely shattered. A man loudly proclaims the grim news of the French Army's ignominious defeat at Sedan. The music stops and within a few moments the stage and the auditorium are empty.

Clearly, this is dramatised social comment, a piece of political satire. But Kozintsev and Trauberg seem particularly fascinated by the external trappings of drama, the choreography and the props, and satire gives way to a series of scenes from cultural history. Contemporary Russian critics appear to have noted this aestheticism or formalism without actually using these condemning terms.

Apparently the directors had gone to Paris to make a careful study of locations. It is not known whether Kozintsev and Trauberg also examined the historical accounts of the events.

The actors had to prepare themselves by reading Zola. But only fifty pages of 'La Débâcle' (1892) are concerned with the Commune, and in his political journalism of 1871 Zola's radical conscience is much closer to reactionary Versailles than to revolutionary Paris. If Kozintsev and Trauberg made actors read Zola it must have been for the sake of local colour. (They should have read Lissagaray, the great chronicler of the Paris Commune.)

New Babylon is more the picture of a period than a story about people. A number of individuals personify different sections of society. Even minor characters appear to represent something more than themselves. There is a representative of the shoemakers' guild, one from the tailors and so on. Louise Poirier, played by Elena Kuzmina, is a salesgirl at the big store, a young woman of the people who eventually becomes aware of her ties with the working classes and dies a true daughter of the revolution, a proletarian Marianne. She is also beautiful, and the owner of New Babylon, a grotesque little capitalist in a top hat, tries to buy her affections. He is rejected, and Louise falls in love with Jean, a farmer's son who has become a soldier. He is like the Russian *moujik* who does not want to be liberated by the revolution although it is his only means to achieve human dignity and a decent life.

In addition to this representative trio, there is a member of the so-called intelligentsia: the

journalist who announces the collapse of the army and eventually becomes one of the Commune fighters. (He is played by Sergei Gerasimov, better known today as a director.) There is also a young lieutenant. We first meet him at Versailles, where Thiers's government is gathering an army to crush the Commune.

These characters are not drawn with any particular psychological depth and do not fit together with great harmony. They are characterised above all through their actions, and their individuality is only a reflection of the events in which they are involved. Louise Poirier, however, is a complete portrait. Maybe Ebbe Neergaard is right in suggesting that the action of *New Babylon* is seen through her eyes. Certainly, she enlivens every frame she is in. But the confused and pathetic Jean also plays an important part. He is a victim of his belief in authority, one of the ignorant masses which the powers (the 'bureaucratic-military system') exploit and humiliate. In a central scene, which offers an isolated, deeply perceptive observation of human behaviour, Jean hesitates as love and class solidarity conflict with his natural instincts of obedience. Louise begs him to stay, but Jean frees himself from her embrace and walks off down the muddy road to report back for duty at Versailles.

At the end, the two meet again, just before the collapse of the Commune. The darkness is impenetrable, the rain is heavy and cold and there is thick mud. At Père-Lachaise, where a few remaining Communards offered some resistance, a tribunal is in progress. The lieutenant in charge wants to spare Louise; she may go free if she confesses to being a prostitute. But not even then can Louise Poirier be bought. She slaps the officer hard across the face, and an expressionist title spells out D E A T H. Then Jean appears. He is given a spade and ordered to dig Louise's grave. Mud, rain and the shots being fired.

Neergaard claims to have seen a final scene in which the repentant Jean swears a horrible revenge over the body of his beloved. In the version of *New Babylon* on which our description and analysis are based, the final scenes are acted out in a mood of black fury, and there is no room for protestation; nothing beyond a cry of 'Vive la Commune!' from the dying, slumped against the wall. There is nothing in these sequences that points to revenge and final victory. Everything is directed towards the collapse of the Commune and the mass grave, but the anger which is activated during these sequences could be felt as a positive force. It is not until this moment that the film becomes revolutionary.

New Babylon is of interest not only because of its creators' skill in the first part of the picture, and the moral and political indignation that they manage to express towards the end. There re also some omissions that are worthy of note. Kozintsev and Trauberg depict the people's enthusiasm in an effective montage sequence, but we are told hardly anything about the reasons for their joy, about the self-confidence that they gain from the feeling of being their own rulers, or of the programme of social reform which was fifty, even a hundred years ahead of its time. We join a meeting of the Commune and follow Delescluze, the patriarch of the Communards, out of the hall. The camera focuses insistently on his trousers and shoes in a close-up which might be intended as a demonstration of the man's simplicity, and a sign that the people who have been awakened are now on the move. The detail is symbolic of the whole, but this rhetorical detail does not work in the context. It does not have the same unmistakable political import as the pince-nez of the drowned ship's doctor in *Battleship Potemkin*. Here it is just an aesthetic frill.

Consequently, *New Babylon* is both a success and a failure. It is dazzling rather than politically effective, yet parts of it have a remarkable propagandist force. In many ways the film is an isolated case, and it never became stylistically influential. It is about a revolution before The Revolution and concerns one of the myths on which the metaphysics of revolution are based. It is untypical not only in style but above all in its foreign setting. The fact is that, with very few exceptions, the Russian revolutionary

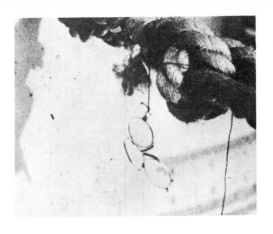

Stills. Above: Battleship Potemkin – *pince-nez. Others:* New Babylon; *Pudovkin in a small part as a merchant (below).*

cinema is not about world revolution but about the Russian revolution; like the American Western, it is a national genre. The Paris Commune is a challenging example, an emotionally laden symbol, but it is not part of the reality in which the propagandists of the Soviet cinema erect their monuments to the glory of Socialist heroes. They do not make revolutionary films about Spartacus, Thomas Münzer or Charles Delescluze, but about Lenin and Stalin – and Lenin again.

Hitlerjunge Quex

'A film about young people's spirit of sacrifice' is the subtitle of *Hitlerjunge Quex*, a most stirring Nazi hymn to youth, martyrdom and the swastika. The music behind the credit titles is 'Unsere Fahne', the battle song of the Hitler Youth with words by Baldur von Schirach; it recurs, like an impassioned revivalist hymn, right up to the ecstatic final vision of the picture. Reich Youth Führer von Schirach himself stood behind *Hitlerjunge Quex* which was made under official Party sponsorship in 1933 and directed by Hans Steinhoff It is thus one of the earliest Nazi feature films, produced while it was still necessary to build a National Socialist spirit on what was left of the values of the Weimar Republic. The old had to be replaced by the new. Gentle and sophisticated methods of persuasion are used in *Hitlerjunge Quex* to guide the audience towards ultimate enthusiasm. It *insinuates* a new content into old patterns, carefully moulding the new spirit with traditional ideas, religious and secular.

The religious overtones become increasingly noticeable as the film nears its end, but they are well established from the outset. Martyrdom can be predicted from the start for poor, frail little Heini, the film's saintly hero. He grows up in a poor Berlin family, and although his mother is a good woman, his unemployed father has been led astray by socialist ideas. Little blond Heini is drawn into communist youth activities, and 'the commune' will obviously be seen later on in the film as the negative pole in opposition to the wonderful Hitler Youth, but it is indicative of the film's psychological tactics that the communists are portrayed at first with some sensitivity and the gradual transition into caricature is so subtle as to be almost imperceptible. With elaborately disarming tactics, Stoppel, the leader of the commune, is introduced as a sympathetic, authoritative element of security in Heini's impoverished existence, only to be gradually revealed as a seductive force, destructive and evil.

Heini and the audience meet the Hitler Youth for the first time when Heini is spending a weekend hiking in the woods with the communists. The two groups confront each other in an emotionally charged scene on the railway station. The Hitler Youth are the image of candour, discipline and harmony, very personable and trim. Heini is struck by the sharp contrast with his noisy, unkempt companions who stand with their hands in their pockets, smoke, flirt and swill coffee. At night Heini creeps wistfully out of the young communists camp to share, from a distance, the sacred fellowship of the Hitler Youth, their healthy joy and solemn sincerity, their songs and their banners. Next morning the tune of 'Unsere Fahne flattert uns voran' ('Our flag is fluttering before us') resounds in him, and even in the presence of his brutal father he doesn't manage to keep his new-found happiness to himself but quietly hums the song at home, too. With this we come to the first sequence of painful conflict: his father forces him to sing the Internationale, which he does hoarsely, with tears rolling down his cheeks.

The father is not really an unsympathetic character but a deeply unhappy man, the victim of an evil social order, i.e. that of Weimar. This fact makes the audience's suffering even more acute, for it is only the father's despair that makes him cruel to his son. At various levels, the film exploits the theme of pain, and thus probably has a special appeal to adolescents with their anxiety in emotional relationships, their fear of exclusion from a group. The most insidious development of all is Heini's rejection by the fellowship to which he aspires most fervently, the Hitler Youth. After a series of misunderstandings, they suspect him to be a spy from the communist side, but *we* feel, indeed know, that this boy is incapable of deceit – his rejection becomes our pain. Simply because he is refused entrance to it, membership of this brotherhood becomes even more passionately desirable.

This idea of loss finds a parallel in the death of Heini's mother. This film appears to have been deliberately influenced by the established image of depression in the Weimar period seen slightly earlier in the films of Piel Jutzi. Heini's father is almost identical to the rootless worker in *Berlin Alexanderplatz* (and both are played by the same actor, Heinrich George), while the mother's fate looks like a detailed copy of *Mutter Krausens Fahrt ins Glück*. Overwhelmed by her circumstances, she attempts to gas herself and her son. She dies but Heini survives and is taken to hospital, where he experiences the greatest happiness of his life. A delegation from the Hitler Youth comes to visit him as a friend and present him with a uniform. The pessimistic Jutzi pastiche is transformed into prodigious Nazi optimism.

In spite of intimidation, Heini cuts all his links with the communists and becomes the most devoted National Socialist in the whole Hitler Youth group, earning the honourable nickname 'Quex' ('mercury'). He always asks for the hardest and most hazardous missions – and they are hazardous indeed as the communists stop at nothing to crush their enemies. Heini's idealism is limitless, but his boss (who seems to us, nowadays, an incredibly distasteful character chosen, apparently, as embodying the SA ideal – brutal, square jawed and steely eyed) is reluctant to allow Heini to oin the fight as he is really too young. Heini ppeals to his military past: 'When you were n officer, did you stop your soldiers from oing to the front?' Smiling with sad, paternal dmiration, the SA man allows his disciple to undertake the distribution of electioneering pamphlets in the most dangerous parts of the city.

There Heini's martyrdom is achieved. In a equence which is set up like the climax of an American gangster picture, he wanders through the back streets of the communist held Berlin lums. Alone and unprotected he walks into a rap. From every corner and every alley the enemy pours forth, sheltered by the darkness hat symbolises their intent. When dawn breaks he Hitler Youth arrive, and Heini's friends ind him dying. With a happy, distant smile he

whispers: '*Unsere Fahne . . . flattert uns . . . voran.*' As he dies, a vision grows within him of thousands upon thousands of uniformed Hitler Youth in endless columns, and behind them the swastika which gradually grows into a monumentally emotive final emblem. Here is an ecstasy of image equalled only in other Nazi films, a vision of infinity with metaphysical implications and an emotional strength built on un-earthly joy. In the Nazi cinema death is the way to the millennium.

> Our flag is fluttering before us,
> One after another we march into the
>   future.
> We march for Hitler through night and
>   through need
> With the flag of youth for freedom
>   and bread.
> And the flag leads us into eternity,
> Yes, the flag means more than death.

Stills: Hitlerjunge Quex – *a Hitler Youth get-ogether (top); Heini gets his uniform.*

Triumph of the Will

The immediate circumstances of Hitler's death and the fall of the Third Reich, resulting in partition of the country and the Nuremberg trials, were followed by silence and oblivion. Then came the questions. How did it all actually happen? How could such a man have gained this power? And how could a group dedicated to triumph through the annihilation or subjection of all others, almost have succeeded in conquering the world?

The attempts at an answer usually concern junker ideal and the opposition of the new romanticism to rationalism, and go on to mention Wagner and Nietzsche, the Versailles Treaty and inflation, political divisions in the labour movement, industrial magnates who became exploited by those they had planned to exploit. They even invoke a trauma in the German national soul or the evil inherent in man. The final answer will have to be left to historians, although important documentary clues to Nazi psychology can be found in the autobiography of Hoess, commandant of Auschwitz, or in Eichmann's bureaucratic, mechanical mode of expression where his lack of humanity cannot be concealed by all the euphemisms and abstractions. However, terror and blind submission still do not explain how ordinary, decent people chose to follow a band of criminals and were turned into criminals themselves.

One German film demonstrates better than any other artistic work of the period the seductive magic of Nazism. It shows both the upturned faces and the ones looking stiffly ahead, bound by magnetic attraction. The principal character is Adolf Hitler. In a way he is also the originator of the film.

Leni Riefenstahl's *Triumph des Willens* is one of the greatest achievements, perhaps the most brilliant of all in the history of film propaganda. It is a magnificently controlled work of art, and, at the same time, a document on an event captured in all its terrifying immediacy. There is still a sense of ecstasy wildly building up, while events in the film have a significance which lies beyond them. It is impossible to regard *Triumph of the Will* simply as a record of what took place in Nuremberg during a particular week in September 1934. Subsequent events, too, are involved. Beyond the Führer and the masses under his spell lie the victims. The smoke from the torches recalls the smoke from the gas ovens. Behind the well-drilled columns of fair-haired youth we sense the

ghostly parade of prisoners from Stalingrad. Behind the triumph stands defeat.

Consequently we cannot consider the film simply as a chronicle, a work of art, or even as both. It constantly frees itself from its given context. Our image of the film is not unified but fragmented, for we find ourselves not just in its present tense of 1934, but later in, say 1944 when the action is of a very different nature. And we are also in our own time, the present tense as we watch the film; perhaps we are even projected into the future, to 1984.

This is an important element in the picture's continuing fascination, and also complicates any assessment of it. It is impossible to examine one's attitude to *Triumph of the Will* without also examining one's attitude to Hitler, Nazism, the authoritarian personality, mob psychology and the capacity of the cinema to influence an audience. It is a complex experience.

The film's impact is further complicated by the use of footage from it in numerous later films, to achieve entirely the opposite effect. The images which in Leni Riefenstahl's picture convey the idea of *Ordnung* – rigidly straight columns of marchers, young men with a purposeful look and so on – suggest machine-like terror in *Why We Fight*, *These Are the Men*, Alain Resnais's *Nuit et brouillard*, Erwin Leiser's *Mein Kampf* or Mikhail Romm's *Ordinary Fascism*, and become a grotesque ballet in *Germany Calling*.

The beginning is not predominantly visual. The audience's expectation is heightened by music, which also strikes the right note of solemnity. Then there appears the collective symbol of the eagle, the national emblem and sign of authority. After that come credit titles, from which it emerges that *Triumph of the Will* was not just officially authorised; it was specially commissioned by the Führer. The film describes an event twenty years after the outbreak of World War I, sixteen years after the humiliation at Versailles, and nineteen months after the nation's rebirth through Adolf Hitler. In the prologue he is seen flying to Nuremberg to attend the sixth National Socialist Party Rally. It is 4 September 1934.

The film begins in the sky – amid clouds that move dramatically to windswept, stormy music. Through a break in the clouds we see the plane dominating the air. The diffuse clouds get more sharply defined, and the overture to 'The Mastersingers' slowly merges into the Horst Wessel Lied, just as the old Germany has given way to the new. Then the Renaissance façades of Nuremberg loom out of the mist. Hitler is about to descend from the sky, and the music which up to this moment has been in the background swells into a hymn of praise. Far below, the waiting crowds have already begun to march.

The triumphant journey from the airport has a different atmosphere. The god has come down to earth and is moving among his people. We see workers' wives, children pushing their hair out of their eyes, hands being lifted, mouths opening. It is not the Party we are meeting here, nor the citizens of Nuremberg, but the People, the enthusiastic masses. Leni Riefenstahl follows the procession; she is at every corner with her camera. For a few seconds she even makes the picture swing like a church-bell, merging the walls of houses, banners and faces in a wave of joy. She gives the picture a breathing-space; it moves from calm to storm (or nearly storm) and back to calm, from day to night and then to morning again. She knows how to wait. The forward motion is accelerated, but Leni Riefenstahl still defers the climax. She has constructed the film in stanzas. Each part can be seen as a whole. Each entity· has a marked musical rhythm and the solemnity of a hymn.

The leader has come to his own, and the ritual follows. First a séance at night: torches, faces lit by the flames, military music, an atmosphere both of triumph and of oath-taking. Dawn follows, windows are opened, mist rises from the roofs, flags wave gently, coming to life again. In the awakening city, fashioned by the Middle Ages, the Renaissance and modern times, the camera flits about like light itself;

Stills: Triumph of the Will – *the Führer meets the people; below, camp-site ritual.*

it seems completely weightless. But Leni Riefenstahl does not linger on this breathless note. She interrupts it with a sequence showing simple every-day activities in a light-hearted manner. Before reveille, we get a bird's-eye view of a camp-site with its strictly geometrical pattern of paths and tents. Then there is a piece of realism, albeit against a background of military marches: the young Germans shave, wash and exchange friendly jokes as they sit down to breakfast.

The people parade through the streets of Nuremberg: farmers, women in national costume, children. The first evening has come, and Rudolf Hess appears to open the festivities. While he is speaking, the camera glides briefly along the row of foreign diplomats present. After this, there is total concentration on the Party and its leader. His look sums up everything, but first his henchmen have their say. Rosenberg, Goebbels, Ley, Darré, Todt, the press chief Dietrich, and Hierl, leader of the Labour Front, all make short speeches. Hans Frank, Commissioner of Justice, says: 'There is no other justice but the will of Adolf Hitler.' It is only Streicher who really has the look of madness in his eyes. This is before the witches'

Stills: Triumph of the Will – *the parade through the streets of Nuremberg; the* Arbeits-dienst *salute; Himmler, Hitler and Lutze march down the aisle to the memorial.*

sabbath, and Nazi Germany still has the feel of a workers' state. The annexations have yet to come. It is four years before the 'night of broken glass'. But re-armament has started, and Dachau is already functioning as a place for re-educating enemies of the people.

Then follows the ceremonial of the mass demonstrations. Fifty-two thousand men of the Labour Front (the *Arbeitsdienst*) have gathered on the Zeppelin Field, holding spades, to cheer Adolf Hitler. Drumrolls are heard. Someone asks in a loud, clear voice: 'Where do you come from, comrade?' and several voices name the various corners of the German nation

from which they come. With this established, the summation comes in a ringing chorus of '*Ein Volk, ein Führer, ein Reich!*' shouted in unison.

Ceremony then turns to ritual, the atmosphere grows calmer, more attentive and solemn. Flags are lowered as the names of battlefields are read out: Tannenberg, Liège, Verdun, Somme, Flanders. The music begins to play '*Ich hat' einen Kameraden, ein' bessern' finds't Du nit*' ('I had a comrade, you'd never find a better one'). And fifty-two thousand people are filled with new vigour and defiance.

A voice recites lines about dead comrades from the Horst Wessel Lied for the others to repeat in unison, and the flags are raised high as they all shout together: 'You are not dead, you are alive in Germany!' They lift their spades, as if presenting arms. The people are united. Resolute faces are seen in close-up, ready for sacrifice.

It is nightfall again, and the old soldiers gather for a firework party. Lutze, Röhm's successor as leader of the SA, speaks to his comrades. Rhythmic singing, hands, torches, an enormous bonfire and fireworks shooting up into the sky. The next section is devoted to youth. Baldur von Schirach introduces Hitler, saying: 'As you yourself are the most perfect expression of unselfishness, our young people too want to be unselfish.' The Führer begins: 'My German youth.' The young hold the

greatest promise, and in them he can trust. They are his youth, the Hitler Youth, a group whose hearts he can fire to great deeds or inspire with any emotions he may choose. They are one body, they have the same face, fair and determined. Their singing has a revivalist feeling. Each puts aside his personality, the things that make him different, so that he can join in the common faith. Individuals can no longer be distinguished and the crowd is a background for the Führer, a chorus of acclamation.

Here *Triumph of the Will* seems to grow more sombre, and the cheering has a menacing undertone. From now on, we chiefly see paramilitary organisations. (The armed forces, however, appear only briefly, and the General Staff was so displeased at this that the following year Leni Riefenstahl had to make a film *Tag der Freiheit – Day of Freedom* specifically about the German Army.) Columns of the SA and the SS form giant rectangles in the Luitpoldhain, 11,000 men in black and 97,000 brownshirts. The camera is placed so that the scene looks like an eighteenth-century palace garden with a vast expanse of trimmed hedges. Three men, Himmler, Hitler and Lutze, march solemnly along the wide central aisle to the memorial monument, as if officiating at an altar. Muffled drums are heard. In this Wagnerian celebration with its 21,000 swastika banners, we no longer see faces or bodies but

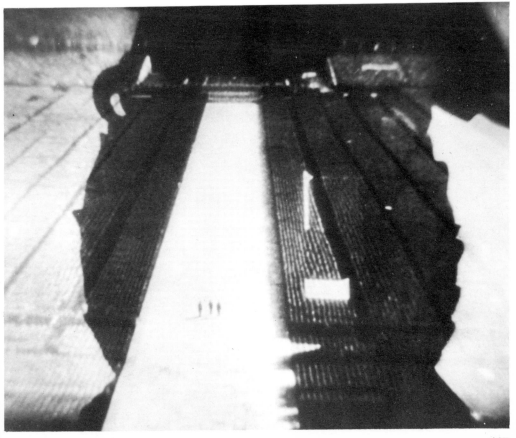

groups and emblems in a menacing geometry. Hitler speaks of unity, of the continuing strength of the SA (a passing reference to the suppression of Röhm's opposition the previous June). Behind the platform, cannon are fired. Then the SS march through the city, looking tough, with the skull and cross-bones on their peaked caps, swinging their right arms in an energetic goose-step. They carry their equipment as if on their way to the battle-field.

The final speech is heard in the Conference Hall. Again the camera links Hitler with the crowd. Then he takes command. He works up to a new level of fervour, and for the first time utters the word 'eliminate'. He threatens but also reassures, speaking of yesterday, today and tomorrow, he is both calm and impassioned. 'This Reich will stand for thousands of years,' Adolf Hitler cries and is loudly acclaimed by great waves of cheering. Hess ends the rally, saying 'The Party is Hitler. But Hitler is Germany, just as Germany is Hitler. Hitler – *Sieg Heil!*' Banners are raised and everyone sings the Horst Wessel Lied. The camera fixes on the swastika at the centre of the stage.

It is difficult to write about all this without some feeling of nausea. However, the film provides insights into events which were to culminate a few years later in Warsaw and in Auschwitz, and end on the gallows, at Nuremberg on 16 October 1946. In *Triumph of the Will* we catch a brief glimpse of the monster

lying in wait. Here, Hitler is not Chaplin's Great Dictator nor is he a raging demon. He appears neither ludicrous nor terrifying. It would not even be correct to describe him as entirely unsympathetic. There is something attractive about his personality, that gives an occasional impression of good humour. Today we know the character hidden below the surface, and how it emerged. But when the film was made, people were rushing to join this Pied Piper. One and a half million people were gathered at Nuremberg, to be led away.

The most striking thing about Leni Riefenstahl's Führer is his magic, the Piper's tune. Hitler speaks. He is a demagogue, flinging his

Stills: Triumph of the Will.

arms around. He is a pedagogue, wagging his finger instructively in the air. He is a prima donna, happy and smiling. He is a holy man, folding his arms across his chest. He can get any reaction he wants. He has conditioned the reflexes of the crowd; he guides them from the platform, calling for acclaim, receiving it and quelling it with a gesture as if silencing the storm.

At one curiously unguarded moment during the big final speech, deafening cheers force the speaker to pause, and for one and a half seconds we see a gleam in his eyes. Hitler is smiling to himself. There is an element of satisfaction, but it is not quite that simple. His smile certainly reflects the joy of power but also perhaps, a sense of wonder. His authority has been granted by the overflowing hall, the ovations, the ecstasy. At the same time this amounts to a limitation. Here is an exclusive fellowship rejoicing with the Chosen One that they have been selected, and storming against all those who have not shared the spiritual baptism.

This exclusiveness might, in spite of everything, make *Triumph of the Will* less dangerously seductive than has sometimes been suggested. It is a hypnotic experience for the converted, but not for others. It is unlikely that anyone would, or did, become a Nazi simply through watching *Triumph of the Will*. The film can equally well arouse excitement, perplexity or horror. Its power is largely the achievement of Leni Riefenstahl. She has miraculously escaped the monotony that ought to have been unavoidable in describing such stunningly uniform activities: hundreds of thousands ceaselessly marching, or watching others march. It does appear, however, that the Nuremberg Rally of 1934 was a particularly well organized occasion. The event itself had its directors. There is indeed much to suggest that it was staged with the cameras in mind from the outset. Kracauer compares 'this staged show, which channelled the psychic energies of hundreds of people' with the cardboard villages built by General Potemkin on the Ukrainian plains, for the benefit of Catherine II. In the same way, he says, the Nuremberg Rallies were a fraud fabricated from elements of real life. These *tableaux vivants* were designed to create illusions for the German people. After such demonstrations of strength and order it would not be reasonable to have any doubts. Apart from being useful as training and psychological reinforcement, the rallies were also an aesthetic creation, a kind of ritual theatre. 'I had spent six years in St Petersburg before the war in the best days of the old Russian ballet,' testified Sir Neville Henderson, 'but for grandiose beauty I have never seen a ballet to compare with it.' Alan Bullock, who quotes the old ambassador in his biography of Hitler, sees the spectacle as a deliberate show of power; the complement to it was 'the compulsive power of the Gestapo, the SS and the concentration camp.'

The Nuremberg Rally was a spectacular festival, but fundamentally it existed for the sake of the terror. It is significant enough that it was in Nuremberg that Hitler called the Reichstag to a special session and in 1935 presented the so-called Nuremberg Laws, which were unanimously approved, to deprive German Jews of their citizenship and forbid marriages between Jews and Germans.

Leni Riefenstahl deserves a chapter to herself. She was born in 1902 and began her career as a dancer before becoming an actress. In the 'twenties she starred in a number of romantic films directed by Arnold Fanck and set high in the Alps. They preached a peculiar philosophy of fate, the elements, and the exceptional, heroic individual – a precursor of Nazi metaphysics. But this beautiful, stubborn, talented heroine was soon making films herself. In *Das blaue Licht* (*The Blue Light*, 1932), which she made in collaboration with the film theoretician Béla Balázs, Leni Riefenstahl played a young girl who chose a dream instead of life and was unable to withstand the demands of reality. When he came to power, Hitler, who had seen this beautiful film, summoned the director. He ordered her to make a film and himself provided the title. (No other word, according to Bullock, was uttered so frequently by Hitler as 'will'.) When the picture was finished he accorded it his own recommendation. It was, the Führer wrote on 7 March 1935, 'an outstanding and unparalleled tribute to the strength and beauty of our movement'. It was also his film.

At the outset, Leni Riefenstahl appears to have had doubts about the project, objecting that she knew nothing about politics. Hitler, however, did not want a film made by some

party hack, and managed to talk her round. She first experimented with a short film on the rally of 1933, *Sieg des Glaubens* (*Victory of Faith*), a rather confused and sketchy effort. Even the event itself seems amateurish compared with that of the following year; the marching is undisciplined, the performances lack rhythm, and there is no steady mounting of tension. On the other hand, a newsreel about the rally of 1937, *Festliches Nürnberg*, shows the spectacle in all its horrifying excess and indicates the faultless control of every moment of the proceedings. (A small-scale battle is fought out in the arena by anti-aircraft guns and attacking fighter planes.) This anonymous film amply demonstrates the superior talent of Leni Riefenstahl. Flags are marched in and then taken round towards the sides in a movement identical with that in one sequence of *Triumph of the Will*. However, in *Festlisches Nürnberg* the relationship of camera to object is totally lifeless.

After the war Leni Riefenstahl became a political outcast. Today her films are shown with increasing frequency in film clubs and film societies. She herself gives interviews. She is embittered about the misunderstanding and persecution she has suffered. *Triumph of the Will* has led to many years of imprisonment, she told Cahiers du Cinéma adding that she was forced into obscurity. It was not, after all, a real propaganda film. She claims that it was a documentary record taken from contemporary history, simply a piece of *cinéma vérité*. The event actually occurred as a symptom of something which world opinion did not then condemn as it does today. Even Winston Churchill had a good word to say for Adolf Hitler in those days. And she herself was just a young girl, without any interest in politics. She loves all that is 'beautiful, strong, healthy and alive'. On the other hand, 'I am not interested in purely realistic, slice-of-life, every-day

ordinariness'. *Triumph of the Will* was an assignment like any other. The film cost 280,000 marks, and was shot with only two cameras.

Unfortunately, this is a mixture of lies and half-truths. A picture album by Leni Riefenstahl entitled *Behind the Screens of the Rally Films* (Zentralverlag der NSDAP, Munich, 1935) begins with a pedantic description of the set-up. There were 135 people on the staff; thirty-six of them are listed as members of the camera crew, i.e. as photographers and assistants. Hand-held cameras were operated from firemen's ladders; bridges and towers were built and tracking rails laid for filming. They had an aeroplane and an airship, T/PN 30, at their disposal for the aerial shots. Thirty-seven men of the SA and SS helped maintain order. The young girl in control of production was in fact thirty-two years old.

There are other inconsistencies in the *Cahiers* interview. At one point the sun reappears from behind the clouds, just as Hitler steps up. 'Hitler Weather,' Leni Riefenstahl exclaims. She describes the state of feverish excitement in which they all spent those days, and there is a breathlessness about her style, with not a single sentence to suggest distance or hesitation. In one passage, Leni Riefenstahl explains how she saw *Triumph of the Will* during the shooting. It was not a work of reportage, because such an approach could not be attuned to the 'heroic style' of the events nor to the 'inner rhythm of what is visibly happening'. In fact she described reality only as Hitler wanted to see it. Leni Riefenstahl created a hymn to the Führer's greatness, the Party's strength and the nation's unity, a brilliant, cinematic oratorio. But here beauty really is, in Rilke's words, 'the beginnings of horror'.

Stills: Leni Riefenstahl in mountaineering movies. Left to right: S.O.S. Eisberg, Stürme über dem Montblanc, Das blaue Licht.

The Spanish Earth

Joris Ivens, like Robert Flaherty, has the gift of simplicity, though this can sometimes appear as naïvety. His humanism is often vague and his poetry bland. It is hard to tell whether the weakness of his films stems from lack of resources (in technical expertise as well as time and money), from the inhibitions that come with his political loyalties or from some defect in temperament. In Ivens' best films, *Zuiderzee*, *Borinage*, *The Spanish Earth*, his humanity and his political opinions work together effectively; it appears that the films in which his emotions are strongest are also the most perfectly controlled. He has been making films since 1928, working in over twenty countries, including, recently, North Vietnam and Laos.

To him, documentary entails setting down a record of reality and organising his observations in the light of his political involvement.

In February 1939, at the première of *400 Millions*, his film about China at war, Ivens discussed the documentary film-maker's job and his attitude to his material. On the important question of the director's subjectivity or objectivity, he asked, 'Would you rather see the two sides in the Spanish Civil War brought together in one film or look at the events in two different pictures, one from the Government side and one from the Fascists'?' To Ivens the answer is clear. On issues of life or death, democracy or fascism, the true artist cannot be objective.

Ivens had taken sides long before he went to Spain in January 1937, and he went there on a definite assignment: to make a film which would give moral and financial support to the Republican forces. The original plan had been to use newsreel material. But it turned out that such material as could, with difficulty, be obtained came from the Franco side. The film's backers soon realised that it would have to be shot on location by Ivens and formed a company, Contemporary Historians, to produce it. Ernest Hemingway, John Dos Passos, Archibald MacLeish and Lillian Hellman were among those involved in this altruistic enterprise.

Ivens arrived in Spain with a complete synopsis. It was very dramatic. At the beginning, King Alfonso was to be seen on his way into exile. Then in some Berlin sanctum, we would see the German and Spanish military authorities discussing the coming campaign against democracy in Spain. With the outbreak of the Civil War, the underlying class conflict would come to the surface, a village would fall and

later be regained. It was a scheme worked out at a desk on the basis of preconceived ideas.

Ivens realised almost immediately that the current situation of the war and the move towards Socialism in Spanish society was much more fascinating than any historical reconstruction. He also quickly grasped that soldiers involved in battle could not be expected to turn into actors. So he made a new plan, retaining one important idea from the first outline – prominence was to be given to a village somewhere on the road between Valencia and Madrid; its people were to be working on an irrigation scheme. Ivens and his collaborators found just such a village, called Fuentedueña.

The Spanish Earth begins with a song and images of a calm, imposing landscape. Then we learn about the village, the arid soil and the irrigation scheme that will solve all the peoples' problems. Hemingway's precise commentary speaks for Fuentedueña:
'Water – and this barren earth will give good crops. For fifty years we have wanted to water it but they did not let us. Now we shall give it water and bring forth food for the defenders of Madrid.'

The film's two settings, the poor village and the Spanish capital, are linked by Julian, a young peasant soldier. We first see him as he sits down to write to his parents, during a lull in the battle for the university town outside Madrid. Then he goes home on leave and is welcomed by his family. In the evening, Julian instructs the village boys in army drill.

Julian is to some extent a representative figure, but nothing in his character is overemphasised. He is not the soldier on a recruiting poster but simply one human being among many others, a young man on leave who will soon go back to the front. His function in the film is as an identification figure for the

Stills. Left: Borinage (*Joris Ivens and Henri Storck*). *Above:* 400 Millions (*Ivens and John Ferno, photographed by Robert Capa*). *Right and below:* The Spanish Earth.

audience. It is easier to get involved with a strange environment through a recognisable character, whose behaviour we can observe, than through some anonymous figure from the crowd. Ivens envisaged the end of *The Spanish Earth* with Julian back as a soldier in the trenches, but when these scenes came to be shot, he had disappeared and all efforts to find out what had become of him failed. Ivens therefore settled for an unknown face, a bearded soldier taking aim and firing, an eloquent image that does not so much state as embody the film's meaning – a man aware of the meaning of the fight, with his rifle at his shoulder. Over this are the words of Hemingway's commentary: 'These men who had never before fought a battle, who were not trained in the use of arms, who only wanted to work and eat their bread, are fighting on.'

The Spanish Earth was intended as a 'film of peace about the war', a reportage in which the

Ivens is a poet of brotherhood; he is at his most convincing when he can show his love, when he can establish linkages. In *The Spanish Earth*, he dwells on the conditions of community life in war, the close relations between civilians and soldiers, communications between village and capital. One concrete line of communication plays an important part in the action. The Republican Government has been established in Valencia, but the decisive battle is being fought in Madrid. The Republicans must hold the road between the cities if the republic is to be saved.

No more than the outlines of major events can be studied in diagrammatic form, reducing the people to statistics, lines and arrows. Ivens allows us only a glimpse of a map. For him important events exist in small ones, and he quickly returns to Fuentedueña. Farmers look up from their furrows to listen to the sound of the guns that are defending Madrid. They are also defending them. In Fuentedueña lies the true cause of the Civil War, the fundamental clash between the rich land-owners and the exploited ones without their own land. Here is visible motivation for the struggle, evidence that the sacrifice has some meaning. In Fuentedueña, the people are improving their lot. For the first time, farmers are cultivating their own land. Ivens expresses this social revolution in very lucid visual terms.

Ivens was determined to emphasise the

battle of Madrid and the work in the fields at Fuentedueña were presented as interdependent aspects of the same event. Food production was essential to the defeat of Franco. At the same time, the farmers of Fuentedueña knew that if the Republican soldiers lost, their village would revert to its former state. The soldiers were fighting for peace and progress; the farmers' peaceful work was part of the war effort.

Republican soldiers' solidarity with the people and the people's trust in the soldiers, the unity within a civil war. This picture of harmony corresponded with his own vision. He would have been more objective had he also considered the differences, the conflict between the efficient Moscow Communists and romantic revolutionaries like the Trotskyites of the POUM group. But he had not been asked for objectivity. His film was intentionally subjective, for a political statement can never be effective if it attempts to do justice to everyone. Ivens is too deeply concerned to pretend detachment.

The Spanish Earth, then, shows the fighting Spanish-Republic as Ivens saw it, and the way his backers wanted to see it. It does not claim historical accuracy; it is a work of politically committed reportage which also has something of the quality of an epic poem. With great simplicity and palpable feeling it tells us of ordinary people fighting a war machine, of people defending themselves against an enemy from outside – from Nazi Germany, from Fascist Italy and from North Africa (the Moroccan mercenaries) – as well as against their traditional oppressors, the parasitic social classes. Yet there is no sense of the audience's feelings being manipulated, perhaps because many viewers are in complete agreement with Ivens's attitude to the Spanish Civil War even before seeing the film.

However, this preconceived attitude is surely not essential to finding *The Spanish Earth* outstandingly sympathetic and authentic. Ivens has the ability to highlight details without losing sight of the whole. He also appears to be uncommonly honest: Socialism and the Spanish Revolution are matters of deep personal concern to him, and he speaks for them, but it seems unthinkable that he would lie for the sake of the cause. He may be committed and subjective, but being also truthful, he is no demagogue.

The Spanish Earth is Ivens's most important film and one of the best of its kind ever made. The construction is firm but not rigid, with gentle changes in tempo and setting. He has an admirable talent for using association. At one point in *The Spanish Earth* he shows us a van that has been turned into a barber's shop, with soldiers having shaves and haircuts. Then we see an armoured loudspeaker van broadcasting a frenzied *paso doble*; according to Hemingway's commentary the sound carries as much as two kilometres. (The implication is that the enemy must be less than two kilometres away.) The next step takes us to more serious matters, the battle for the university town, a strange mixture of frenzy and calm. On the soundtrack, the stirring music, and the machine-gun fire, contrast with Hemingway's matter-of-fact voice. Julian is seen with the Commander, Martinez de Aragon who, the commentary tells us, was killed on the day they were filming there. In a film about reality, there is no illusion to be shattered, and when you watch a man living, talking, working, at the same time as you hear a description of his death, you can hardly feel that this piece of information is gratuitous.

From the front line, we move to a band of soldiers in a political group. They have gathered to elect delegates to a meeting occasioned by a merging of Republican forces into a Popular Front. Then the speakers: Enrique Lister, Carlos, José Diaz, Gustav Regler, La Pasionaria. Back to the loudspeaker van which is now broadcasting La Pasionaria's address. A survey of the battlefield; the commentary mentions the enemy's courage and his lack of inner motivation (referring to the Moroccan mercenaries). The People's Army, Republican soldiers are coming home on leave from the front. Julian is among them. This is the last link in the chain.

The associations can also be simple. Later, Ivens alludes to the Republicans' regard for the cultural heritage of Spain. During the salvage of works of art in the Duke of Alba's palace, which has been damaged by the enemy, someone leafs through an old illustrated volume, which turns out to be 'Don Quixote' In the next shot, Don Quixote himself materialises,

Stills: The Spanish Earth.

standing motionless among the sandbags, holding a small red flag. He, too, is fighting for freedom since the true Spain is Republican.

It is subtle propaganda to represent the republic as the guardian of 'good' traditions, countering the Fascists' view of the Republican iconoclasts, wrecking cultural monuments, burning churches and murdering priests. (These descriptions had made an impression on American public opinion.) The rest of the film covers the Fascist terror: bombs over Madrid, buildings in ruins, a dead accountant, murdered children.

The Spanish Earth ends with a double triumph. The enemy is driven back from the road to Madrid, and at the same time water begins to flow in the dry fields at Fuentedueña. The water runs freely and all the little rivulets sparkle in the sun. Farmers straighten up as passing soldiers wave from their lorries. There is a controlled optimism in these final scenes, a powerful elemental poetry. There is no hint of the tragic defeat that is to come, but the confidence is tempered with solemnity. Audiences are meant to sense the spirited and determined defiance of this democracy fighting for its life. Such is Joris Ivens's own experience, his reality as seen through his commitment.

The film made an impact. Roosevelt saw and admired it. It was a commercial success in the United States and eighteen field ambulances were bought with the profits.

Der ewige Jude

Der ewige Jude (*The Eternal Jew*), directed by Dr Fritz Hippler and from an idea by Dr Eberhard Taubert, is probably the most evil film ever made. It is a *Kulturfilm*, a cultural film in the German sense of the term – an educational documentary on 'the problems of world Jewry'. It had its première at the UFA-Palast am Zoo in Berlin on 28 November 1940 before an elegant audience, which included representatives of the civil service and the armed forces, Nazi Party members, artists and scientists. The programme opened with a short, *Ostraum – deutscher Raum* (*Eastern territory – German territory*) and the orchestra played Beethoven's 'Egmont' overture before the main film. At the end of the show, according to Deutsche Allgemeine Zeitung, there was a great ovation.

This was almost fourteen months after the defeat of Poland and a year after the decree which made wearing the Star of David obligatory for Jews in occupied Polish territories. It was just over seven months after the invasion of Denmark and Norway and almost seven months after the establishment of the Lodz ghetto. It was five months after the capitulation of France and six weeks after the decision was taken to establish a ghetto in Warsaw. Eight months later, the Endlösung project really got under way – the 'final solution' to the Jewish problem.

Der ewige Jude is almost unknown today, and a fairly detailed account of it might therefore be of value. It is not brilliant, though dubious, like *Triumph of the Will*, and it seems that it became regarded as totally unsuitable for exhibition after the war because of its general depravity. Even film archives possessing a copy of Hippler's film are very wary of showing it publicly.With German thoroughness, *Der ewige Jude* demonstrates, in its various sections, subsections and parentheses, the inferiority of the Jews. Stills and sequences are followed by explanations, sometimes emphatically stressed. The commentary allows no alternatives. It progresses in a determined frenzy, supported by images and music. The spectator is not meant to consider and form his own opinions. He is meant to swallow the material whole.

The film begins with a statement in the credit titles that 'the civilised Jews we have known in Germany' give us a false idea of the Jewish character. Then it goes on to say: 'Here we shall see what they really look like behind their masks.' The 'reality' is Poland. Hippler speaks of better Jews (German) and bad Jews (Polish), quickly adding that both represent the same lower form of humanity. He then compares the Jews with their 'hosts', the Poles, whom he had previously represented as weak and deceitful in a film called *Feldzug in Polen* (1939). We catch a fleeting glimpse of the war. The commentary asserts that the defeat was felt more strongly by the Poles than by the Jews, who just sat in their 'calm ghettoes' and resumed trading an hour after the end of the fighting. We see Jewish faces, men with enormous beards and strange eyes in authentic shots of the Lodz ghetto taken by German photographers. 'We look at all this', says the narrator 'but now our eyes see more clearly.' Earlier the Jews might have been regarded as comic characters, but by now every sensible person must realise that they are a danger, a pestilence, a threat to humanity.

'Their home life lacks dignity' becomes the message as the camera goes inside a house. There is a close-up of flies on a wall, a crawling black mass. The speaker describes the Jews' lack of hygiene; they are sufficiently well off to keep themselves and their houses neat and tidy, but this happens to be the way they like it. The image of flies is significant. It has been brought out that Jews are unclean but this shot takes the argument a step further, associating the Jews with vermin. Decent, hygienic people can draw their own conclusions. (When the Nazis began to 'solve' the Jewish question a few months later, they used Zyklon B, which was initially a pesticide.) This is an image for the subconscious, but Fritz Hippler lets the conclusion wait. Meanwhile, he concentrates on reinforcing the arguments.

We go outdoors again. 'All community life takes place in the street', the commentary remarks, and we find ourselves among people who are all involved in some outlandish argument. They rarely work, Dr Hippler claims, and then they do so only under pressure. We see some Jews unwillingly at work, and they really do rest on their spades. We cannot tell the reason for this. In any case it is used here to prove that Jews are lazy and ungrateful. Instead of working, they spend their time haggling. We see some street-trading: someone tries on a pair of stockings; someone else offers bootees for sale. (Here, Jews are blamed for the primitive conditions that the Germans created in this artificial walled town.) Hippler refers to their racial character; the Jews carry on bargaining only because they have always had a particular aptitude for that sort of thing. Scenes with quarrelling women, men buying second-hand clothes – handling, feeling, tugging at the cloth – illustrate the vulgar image of the rag-trading Jew. Excited Yiddish voices, against a background of Aryan music, create drama as well as distance. There is filth everywhere. A woman in a bloody apron is trying to sell some emaciated chickens. Children are also trading, 'proud to be like the grown-ups'. Jewish children are not touching, like other children. The young ave no ambitions – 'They are not idealists, like our youth.'

The lecturer pauses before moving from the worthless to the admirable. 'The Aryan individual finds dignity in every action. He seeks to create something.' His words are accompanied by images of Germans at work. Shots of hands imply diligent craftsmanship. There is a low-angle shot with the sky as background; a visionary feeling that in the context of the film seems strangely solemn and idealising.

For the Jew there is nothing in life but money, according to Hippler. He shows us a junk merchant and his goods. 'This is how the little Jews start, and soon they get quite a good stock.' A steady growth is suggested, until finally we are shown luxurious houses: if nobody stops them, Jews will soon move into the very smartest neighbourhoods. (A threat of financial exploitation – Jews are equated with capitalists and usurers.)

Hippler is now ready to describe infiltration by the Jews. 'But whenever they get to be too many in one place they move out across the world. They need a market and they are not productive.' Jews are not useful to society, they are a race of parasites. 'That is how it is in Poland; that is how it was in Germany.' (The implication being that there is still a lot to be done in Poland.) After describing 'the facial characteristics of the eternal Jew', Hippler provides a map showing his origins and present distribution. Jews have been restlessly moving around the world for centuries because 'such is their character', and are unwelcome wherever they go. Their 'mobility neurosis' brought them to Spain, Germany and, with the new 'colonisation of the East', to Poland. Unfortunately, the nineteenth century, 'with its vague notions on human dignity and equality', gave the Jews a false respectability, and they settled almost everywhere. This is illustrated as a dense network over the map. Then follows an analogy. Like the Jew, the brown rat, which has a similar Asiatic origin, has also spread across Europe. Map and close-up of a milling army of rats.) Factual commentary: 'They carry disease.' Aesthetic-moral commentary: 'They are ugly, cowardly, and move about in groups.' The commentary underlines the parallel. Then the camera is back among the Jews, faces in the crowd at the Lodz ghetto.

After this brutal demonstration, the description becomes more rhapsodic and the didactic method more lax. Hippler piles on the examples. He shows us Jewish criminals, with statistics and pictures of unshaven chins and feverish eyes, commenting: 'These physiognomies make nonsense of the theory of equality.' 'Civilised' Jews with their high society life are also alien elements. He then deals with capitalism in a long section on the Rothschild family, their double loyalties, their manipulation of politicians and their war-profiteering. Hippler moves on to the bustling New York Stock Exchange, where influential Jews, financiers and states-

men, are 'masked' to look like Americans. Also fitted into this sequence are Léon Blum and the British Secretary for War, Hore-Belisha. The next section – on German politics – accuses Rathenau and others of having brought about Germany's humiliation. We are shown Jewish administrators, financiers and publishers.

Demonstrations with red flags give the commentator the opportunity to say that youth here has lost all the nobler values, '. . . all this because of a Jew, Karl Marx'. After the still of Marx come Lassalle, Rosa Luxemburg and three political assassins of Jewish origin.

But the Jews are at their most dangerous, we are told, when they try to corrupt art and religion. Our cultural heritage is invoked: a Greek temple, classical sculptures, Gothic faces, Botticelli's 'The Birth of Venus' and a Bach chorale on the sound track. Hippler claims that Jews cannot grasp the Aryan concept of beauty. Instead they give their Jewish character free rein in tasteless manifestations like cubism, expressionism and jazz. A satirical montage with a Renaissance religious figure. An image of the smiling Christ child is shattered by the intrusion of a six-pointed star out of which emerges the figure of a modern woman, a loathsome monster. According to the commentary, 'One cannot easily credit it, but this used to be the only acceptable form of art. Jews decided what could be called art and culture.' The taste wreckers are held up to scorn: Kurt Tucholsky, Alfred Kerr, Max Reinhardt ('the Jewish dictator of the stage') and others. Even Albert Einstein, called the 'relativity Jew', appears among this bunch.

The German film industry is represented as a playground for Jewish intellectuals. One of the contentions in *Der ewige Jude* is that a Jew is instinctively interested in all that is sick. The pernicious pre-1933 cinema tried to win sympathy for the criminal by shifting the burden of guilt on society. Jews, then, corrupt not only art but also justice. They might well be suspected of anything. Why not infanticide, for instance? In *Der ewige Jude* the child-murderer in *M*, played by Peter Lorre, is made out to be Jewish.

Religion (and Bach once more). Christianity has unfortunately conveyed a deceptive image of the Jews; in Christian art, biblical figures have been represented as human ideals. 'We must correct this impression,' shouts the narrator, embarking on a short demonstration of the Jewish religion. Trading is carried on in the synagogue during services. Praying figures rock back and forth. Rabbis are called 'masters in the art of deception' and carry out political indoctrination. Hippler concludes, 'This is no religion. It is a conspiracy against all the peoples of the world.'

Moreover, the Jews are not only a threat to humanity but also to animals. After a title warning all 'sensitive *Volksgenossen*' to leave the cinema, we are shown some 'original film' of Jewish ritual slaughter. A cow bleeds to death

117

from a knife wound in the neck, and the butcher wipes the blood off the knife with his hand. An assistant digs inside the living cow to make the heart pump out the blood more quickly. The butchers are laughing. The head is practically severed from the body, but the cow is still moving in a pool of blood. Press cuttings follow, showing the National Socialist campaign against ritual slaughter; they tried to have it banned before 1933. Liberal and socialist newspapers defended this dubious practice. Idyllic shots of living animals – a herd of cows and calves, a flock of sheep – are followed by slaughter: slashed throats and leering Jewish butchers.

Enter Hitler, delivering his big speech in the Reichstag on 30 January 1939. If the Jews plunge the world into a new war, he yells, it will not be the end of the world but it will be the end of the Jews. We look at Hitler and his people: Aryan faces, young, fair and attentive; rows of resolute faces against a background of sky. The SS and SA march through Nuremberg. 'In this spirit,' say the final words of the commentary, 'the German nation is marching into the future.' Finally come the symbols: flags and enormous banners.

To determine the effectiveness of *Der ewige Jude* as propaganda, it is necessary first to establish what the film was intended to achieve.

The aim was presumably quite specific: all

Still: the most famous of anti-semitic films. Veit Harlan's Jud Süss *with Werner Krauss a. Rabbi Loew.*

this 'documentation' was supposed to justify the genocide which was being planned by Himmler and Eichmann and which began a few months later in Eastern Europe. *Der ewige Jude* is a film for people who know the way things stand. The sermon works from the axiom that Jews are a lower form of humanity, an idea which had been familiar since the publication of 'Mein Kampf'. Hippler's film is a spurious dossier on the Jewish people, an indoctrination course for murderers – and the potential murderers made up a large audience.

Goebbels's Ministry of Propaganda was otherwise careful about anti-semitic propaganda in films. Racist films like *Die Rothschilds* and Veit Harlan's notorious *Jud Süss* (both 1940) were not made after the early years of the war, and references to the regime's anti-semitism were often removed from the versions of German films intended for foreign distribution. This happened, according to Kracauer, in the case of the American versions of *Feuertaufe* (*Baptism of Fire*) and *Sieg im Westen* (*Victory in the West*). There must have been some anxiety lest the visual presentation prove too strong to the extent of making those who were being vilified appear sympathetic. The insistent message of *Der ewige Jude* might have aroused mixed feelings in some Germans. But the majority of those already indoctrinated were unlikely to have any second thoughts. These Jews were neither German nor middle class and were so remote from German cinema audiences of 1940 that they must have seemed too debased to qualify as objects for identification.

The film was also shown in the occupied countries. Its French title, *Le Péril Juif*, had been used before the war on the cover of a classic document of anti-semitism, an infamous forgery called 'The Protocols of the Elders of Zion.' In Holland, a decree was issued on 22 August 1941 to order a screening in every cinema in the country by 30 April 1942. In January 1941 it was shown in Lodz (Litzmannstadt), where a large part of the documentary material had been shot. The magazine Film-Kurier wrote:
'The film camera walked through Litzmannstadt's ghetto before the German authorities had intervened, bringing some order with them and cleansing this Augean stable, and thus it could give an unvarnished picture of the stinking quagmire from which a steady flow seeped into world Jewry.'

The director of the film deserves some comment. Fritz Hippler was born in 1909 and joined the Party in 1927 as member no. 62,133. From September 1939 until May 1943 his power over German film-making was second only to that of Goebbels. He was given titles like 'Reichfilmintendant', 'Ministerialdirigent', and became head of the film department in the Ministry of Propaganda. He produced a number of pictures including *Jud Süss*, and had the power to decide which films would be made and what would be said in them.

In a pamphlet entitled 'Betrachtungen zum Filmschaffen' ('Some Thoughts on Film-Making') published in 1942, Hippler develops his new conception of films as both art and propaganda. A film must be the clear expression

Stills: the result – ghetto footage shot by the Nazis from Erwin Leiser's Mein Kampf.

of a message. 'In the cinema the audience must know with greater certainty than in the theatre whom to love and whom to hate.' In an anti-semitic film the Jews must appear unsympathetic and all other characters must inspire at least some degree of sympathy. A film appeals first to the senses and emotions, Hippler says in a different context. It is an art for the masses, frequently more effective in its teaching than church, school, press or radio. It would, therefore, be irresponsible of the authorities not to assume control of this important instrument.

Whether Hippler's policies were actually his own, is difficult to tell. In the period immediately following Hitler's accession to power, he had been one of Goebbels's protégés as a student leader in Berlin, actively fighting for a radical approach to art. He publicly declared his loyalty to 'degenerate' artists like Nolde and Barlach, helped to organise an expressionist exhibition in July 1933 and became involved in a cultural debate when he attacked the academicism, whether naturalistic or historical and literary which National Socialism was encouraging. These activities appear to have met with Goebbels's approval, but they came to be regarded as a splinter action. The exhibition was closed after three days, and Hippler lost his political position for a time, a victim of the final battle with the group of intellectuals who believed in the independence of art and the continuity of political revolution. They were the Trotsky-ites of Nazism and could not be tolerated. In July 1933, Hitler declared that the National Socialist revolution was complete, and at the Nuremberg rally of 1934 he scornfully attacked both Goebbels's artistic radicals and Rosenberg's reactionaries, deluded souls who were still living in 'the Germanic dream world'. Now there was a clear distinction between what was permitted in art and what was not.

In his youth, then, Hippler appears to have been a 'liberal' National Socialist. He adjusted himself to the Party line, achieved a great deal of power and lost it. Veit Harlan claims in his memoirs that Hippler was fired from the Ministry of Propaganda for hiring Erich Kästner as a scriptwriter (uncredited) on *Münchhausen* with which Ufa was to celebrate its twenty-fifth anniversary. His approach to film-making is fairly unconventional; in 'Betrachtungen zum Filmschaffen', at any rate, he opposes anything artificial or far-fetched and prefers filming on location to work in the studio.

Hippler was an SS officer. His face is hard to describe: it does not lack strength or attraction; his photograph calls to mind a picture of some actor playing a political leader. In 1949 his testimony for Veit Harlan, who was on trial for directing *Jud Süss*, confirmed that it was indeed dangerous to go against the wishes of Joseph Goebbels. He himself was apparently never made to account for *Der ewige Jude*. According to an East German source he worked after the war on some West German documentaries with militant nationalist tendencies.

Ohm Krüger

1941 saw the institution of an honorary title, 'Film der Nation' (Film of the Nation), the highest cinematic distinction that Nazi Germany could award. The first winner was Hans Steinhoff's *Ohm Krüger*. It could scarcely be denied that *Ohm Krüger* is a brilliant propaganda film. It combines courage and wit, intimacy and huge effects, dignity and pathos, human warmth and infamous behaviour. Goebbels's dream of seeing a Nazi equivalent of *Battleship Potemkin* never came nearer to fulfilment than in this picture.

The character of the hero and the historical material made a fitting theme for Nazi propaganda. Stephanus Johannes Paulus Krüger was president of the Transvaal Free State at the turn of the century and led the Boers in their war against the British. He possessed a great many noble Germanic characteristics, taking great pride in his ability to father vast numbers of children, a noisy, authoritative patriarch, a führer.

He led a model nation which seemed to embody the rousing German slogans of 'blood and soil' and 'strength through joy'. Above all, he was fighting a heroic war, to the everlasting shame of the British arch-enemy. Here was a theme that gave cause for icy indignation over unavenged atrocities.

The film introduces Ohm Krüger in the manner reserved since the days of Griffith for saints and legendary statesmen. We see only the back of the armchair in which he is sitting. The scene takes place in a Swiss hotel, because Krüger has been forced to leave his country in brutal British hands, and spend the rest of his life in exile. As he turns towards the camera we gather that he is very old and blind. A nurse is reading him an article from The Times that describes him as a murderer and war-monger. The old man remarks with a deep sigh: 'If a lie is repeated often enough, people will come to believe it in the end.' It is ironic that these words formed one of the basic tenets of Nazi propaganda.

Ohm Krüger looks back across the years. He sees sturdy pioneers building a country for themselves in South Africa, but the Boers are prevented from living in peace and cultivating their soil by British imperialists. The British are shown to be devious, degenerate capitalists, spreading the aura of their seedy civilisation wherever they go. Their moral decadence is embodied in the sly, effete Cecil Rhodes, whose best agents are missionaries – pious-looking charlatans distributing Bibles to one row of negroes in the chapel, and rifles to the next.

Stills: Ohm Krüger – the opening scene (top), below, Ferdinand Marian as Cecil Rhodes (left)

The Boers themselves display rustic simplicity; their pleasures are modest and pious. They lead the simple, natural life on their farms, and are on the best of terms with the natives. Their leaders are colourful individuals playing games and planning foreign policy with equal enthusiasm in farmhouses and pioneers' kitchens. Steinhoff contrasts this with the luxurious British Court, where a senile Queen Victoria totters around swigging Scotch, surrounded by arrogant statesmen who resent the old lady's interference in their conspiratorial activities. Joseph Chamberlain, played as a brilliantly vicious caricature by Gustaf Gründgens, explains to her why Britain must crush the Boers

Stills: Ohm Krüger, *Queen Victoria (Hedwig Wangel) with Joseph Chamberlain (Gustaf Gründgens). Opposite – rotten corned beef.*

and take control of the Transvaal gold: 'We British are the only ones capable of carrying the burdens of wealth without becoming ungodly.' Victoria is slightly deranged but the only British character to be treated at all sympathetically: she possesses visionary powers which warn her that Britain will be punished some time in the future. She even takes the initiative for a conciliatory meeting with Krüger in London, and their confrontation is given a burlesque treatment that verges on tenderness.

Brief relaxed moments – for instance, when the two old people withdraw from the official programme and sit down together for a quiet chat about their rheumatism – set *Ohm Krüger* apart from the frenzied run-of-the-mill efforts of Nazi progaganda. Despite the film's chauvinism and hatred, the main character has a deceptive air of humanity. It is doubtful whether Emil Jannings ever achieved a more moving and impressive portrait of an old man than this. 'If I didn't know that I am Ohm Krüger, I would think I was Emil Jannings,' said the caption to a good-natured caricature of the role in *Simplicissimus*.

Krüger has a well-loved son, Jan, who returns home after his studies in England. He is pleasant and sincere but has been indoctrinated with flabby notions of pacifism. He is a prototype of the intellectual weakling who becomes a man of action through the beneficial influence of war. Father and son engage in angry arguments about British political ethics and Jan harks back to his historical studies for proof that the British keep their promises, but his father, who knows better, retorts with patriarchal assurance that history is not something that you study, it is something you *create*. Events will show that the father's idea of the British is the correct one. British soldiers break into Jan's house and an officer attempts to rape his wife. Jan kills the man, and the Boers respectfully mumble, 'So he was a Krüger after all'.

The war begins with a victory for the Boers filmed in enormous panoramas of the battle that leave Veit Harlan's large-scale effects standing. After the battle, Ohm Krüger conducts a thanksgiving service, but in London, Lord Kitchener assumes responsibility for the future conduct of the war, and immediately abandons all humanitarian principles, ordering vandalism and destruction without pity even towards women and children. It is total war – a British invention, like the concentration camps, where Boers are dying of starvation and typhus.

A prison camp is the setting for the climax of the film, which is inspired by the Odessa steps massacre in *Battleship Potemkin*. It starts with a reference to Eisenstein. The prisoners cannot eat the rotten food they are offered, but the sadistically leering camp commandant declares on examining it that it is definitely edible. To add emphasis he shoots one of the hunger strikers through the stomach.

Jan Krüger is to be hanged from a tree which stands on a hillock in the middle of the camp. His wife is made to stand by the tree to watch him die, and all down the white slope behind her, dark-clad prisoners stand waiting. At the top of the hill, British soldiers parade in their white uniforms. The scene is stylised and almost abstract in conception; the allusion to Golgotha charges it with heavy foreboding.

Jan Krüger is hoisted on the rope, but as he dies, he screams a violent curse on Britain. His shouts are echoed by the people on the slope, releasing unsuspected forces among them in their utter degradation. They merge into a black mass and storm up the hill towards the white uniforms. A shot rings out, killing Jan Krüger's wife. This signals the beginning of a terrible massacre. From the top of the hill, the soldiers march down with rifles raised, firing on the unarmed Boers, who scatter in panic. At the end, only the dead are left on the field, sprawled on the white sand, and from somewhere comes the whimpering of an abandoned baby.

In his Swiss hotel, Ohm Krüger himself is waiting to die. Like Queen Victoria on her death-bed, he has a vision of the future. One day revenge will come, and Britain will be crushed by a nation stronger than the Boers.

Emil Jannings said about his part as Ohm Krüger: 'I played him because he had been chosen to start a struggle which will be concluded in our time.'

Mrs Miniver

Mrs Miniver is an award-winning and extremely popular American movie made in 1942 about the brave British allies. Like so many other successful films with a strong emotional appeal, it begins with an idyll. The Miniver family is happy in the hot summer of 1939. Mrs Miniver herself is beautiful and charming, with a weakness for extravagant hats. She is happily married, and her handsome husband, who dotes on her, is sufficiently rich to indulge his passion for exclusive and expensive cars. The children are as attractive and well mannered as their parents, and their surroundings indicate their secure position somewhere above the middle of the British class system. The eldest child, Wyn, is at Oxford, where he has been absorbing some radical notions. The two younger children are full of fun. Wyn eventually finds a sweetheart, Carol, a lovely girl with dancing eyes. Her aunt, who owns the local manor, is a forbidding but good-hearted old woman.

This picture of the world indicates the film's basic values; our sympathies have been aroused by a particular way of life. It is an idyll where minor irritations only uphold the harmony, in which economic injustice is a minor matter to be solved some time in the future, and members of all social groups happily cultivate their roses in evident acceptance of their conditions, of Britain and of the class system.

There is time to contemplate the meaning of this idyll, before it is darkened by war. It is a delightfully false and idealised image of England; the distortion is neat but thorough and barely disguised. The class system is gently caricatured even as it is being glamorised. There is a suggestion that the upholders of feudalism and those of radicalism are really on the same side and will sooner or later be united, so that for the time being we can regard both with amused tolerance. But the idyll does not merely embody a set of emotional values which must be defended; another psychological function may have had even greater importance in the success of the film.

The idyll revealed to us is *too* happy, too unspoilt not to start off reactions in the audience. The happiness of the Minivers is a form of arrogance which must be paid for before we can give them our whole-hearted sympathy. One of the film's attractions is the way in which war restores a balance by upsetting this blissful existence. Mr Miniver's filthy and exhausted state when he returns from Dunkirk is gratifying, not just because of its heroic aspect but because his life has been so unbelievably cushy. When Mrs Miniver is forced to make do, we do feel sorry for her but at the same time we enjoy her penance. It is

Stills: Mrs Miniver. Left: English life goes on. Above: in the Minivers' shelter.

a lot easier to feel strongly for the Minivers – i.e. the English – once they have atoned for their good fortune.

How does this affect our attitude to the war? It means that, though war is bad in principle, it can become acceptable on a moral level: it inflicts tragedies but it also creates a kind of balance in the distribution of happiness and suffering. All war propaganda has this curious dual purpose, but no medium attains it as simply as the cinema, where war becomes an exciting adventure even when the lines spoken refer only to hell and madness. William Wyler's method in *Mrs Miniver* is unusually sophisticated.

War does not come to the Minivers with the cruelty of the unexpected. Some masterly dramatic construction brings war gradually closer. The tension mounts steadily as we are led from the delights of the idyll to the in-evitable horror. When the war first appears, it is as a distant and intangible fact. The villagers are in the church on the Sunday when news arrives of Chamberlain's radio announce-ment that Britain is at war. It all seems remote and unreal, but the moment is full of the deceptively muted tension that the fictional cinema is so suited to evoke in situations where heroism is involved.

The idyll continues uninterrupted. Nobody takes the threat really seriously; the hope of a quick end to the war outweighs the fear; the sun is still shining. In a wonderful proposal scene – the climax of the whole idyllic sequence build-up – Carol promises to marry Wyn before he goes to war as a pilot in the RAF. Class barriers are not insurmountable. England is a good country full of well-mannered people.

The war comes a step nearer. Mr Miniver is ordered to take his boat on a secret mission in which thousands of other Englishmen and thousands of boats are involved. Their meeting in a steadily growing fleet is a moving sequence of feelings being shared in the face of a common destiny – Dunkirk.

However, we stay behind with Mrs Miniver and see the war from her viewpoint. It is still too distant to be frightening. But is drawing closer, and one day Mrs Miniver finds a German pilot lying exhausted in the garden after his plane has crashed. And bombs start falling. The Minivers huddle with the children in their garden shelter, reading 'Alice in Wonderland' aloud. They make Alice more important than the bombs exploding outside. Although we hear the war, we do not see its effects until the following day, and even then no one makes any comments.

Finally the war is all around: Mrs Miniver and Carol are in a car with planes crashing and fire all round them; the whole town is in flames. Carol is killed. For the first time, Mrs Miniver is genuinely distressed. At last she has paid for her happiness. We – the audience – can now love her and England without reservation. Since we ourselves do not have to suffer, we need only enjoy our feelings of compassion. Carol's death is not painful; she dies quietly and beautifully, with a sigh. Mrs Miniver does not lose her composure. Nothing distasteful occurs; it is all very dignified and discreet. These are people who know all about the comforts of life but who can also take mis-fortune in their stride, without losing their self-control. Their performance has earned our sympathy. We can now forgive them for having been too comfortable.

Carol is not the only victim of the raid. Ballard, the stationmaster, dies, as the con-ventions demand of everyone who has become linked with an object that can stress some symbolic message by surviving him. Ballard is

a rose grower, and he has named his finest rose after Mrs Miniver. When the war come she says that 'there will always be roses and there will always be an England'. He represents common-sense and utters all the crucial words of wisdom in the film. Before dying, he comments thoughtfully that people who fail to realise that the Bible contains more profound ideas than any other book, can never win the war. He is of course referring to Germany.

His words express the religious values behind the film. The war is introduced during a service, and the film ends in church. A service is held the day after the catastrophe. The church has been badly damaged in the

Stills: Mrs Miniver. *Above: the final sermon. Right: Mrs Miniver and the German pilot.*

raid. Carol's aunt is sitting in her pew, lonely and brave; the stationmaster's seat is empty. 'Why were they sacrificed?' the vicar asks in a fiery sermon. The answer is that this war concerns the people and it must be waged by all. Gazing far into the future, the congregation sings a hymn. The camera tilts up towards the gaping holes in the roof through which we can see 'our' 'planes on their way into battle again. The hymn merges with the roar of the 'planes and turns slowly into the strains of 'Land of Hope and Glory'.

126

Vi er Vidkun Quislings hirdmenn

The Germans occupying Norway in 1940 needed to take over all existing propaganda channels, including cinemas and distributors. There was no difficulty in gaining control of the Norwegian cinema since between them, local councils owned almost the whole network of theatres, and as Quisling's men took over local government, they got a well developed film administration into the bargain. The Nazis established a State Film Directorate which was given absolute power of censorship and took control of distribution and production. Its first chief, whose functions were determined by the 'leader' principle, was one of the major figures in the Norwegian cinema, the veteran director Leif Sinding.

The Resistance answered by attempting to stage strikes, to force Norwegians first to avoid seeing German films, and later to boycott the cinemas altogether. Both attempts failed. The cinemas flourished as never before. People flocked to the movies, which included a record number of Norwegian productions. The escapist urge was not to be denied. And escapism became the main characteristic of Norwegian films during the occupation. The films made under the Film Directorate's control showed hardly any of 'the new spirit' and were useless to the Nazis for this reason. Most of the productions were feeble farces and painfully soulless comedies.

The only Norwegian director to involve himself seriously in Nazi propaganda was Walter Fyrst, an experienced film-maker and a National Socialist ever since the formation of the Norwegian Nazi Party in 1933. His *Vi er Vidkun Quisling's hirdmenn* (*We are Vidkun Quisling's Brethren*) is interesting if only because it is so ineffectual. It is a documentary which attempts to recapture the exhilaration of *Triumph of the Will*, but the result is pathetic because the original enthusiasm is lacking. There are no massive, spectacular or demonic resources to draw on. The big Nazi gesture merely looks awkward in this provincial reproduction: Riefenstahl in clogs.

Vi er Vidkun Quisling's hirdmenn – the title is in rune-like characters – begins with stormy seas, Viking relics and the Norwegians' age-old battle against nature. When Nordic culture was at its zenith, Norway had not been weakened by liberalism, Marxism and monetary power. Viking blood is not yet completely watered down; the new Norway must be built on firm Norwegian ground. With Vidkun Quisling the old has joined faith with the new. After this prologue about the mystical properties of blood, earth and the sea and the resourcefulness of earlier ages, we are presented with the élite who are now preserving the glorious heritage and demonstrating that the Norwegian people have withstood the effects of parliamentary rule and other destructive forces of civilisation. They are the *hird* – Quisling's new Viking tribe.

They are shown in training. A healthy mind in a healthy body is a goal always held up by Quisling for his men to seek: athletics play an important part. The *hird* men are coached in boxing – to a background of hearty folk music. We see parades with the 'Norwegian Legion' and, later, scenes of battle. Most of the music is paraphrased Grieg – Norway's cultural tradition siding with the martial exploits of the present. There is peaceful fellowship of a healthy character, also marked by ancient Norwegian customs. People gather to have a good time: folk-dancing in national costumes. People from all classes of society join the Norwegian Nazi Party. The visuals could have come from almost any idyllic context. The message is in the commentary – we must keep the race pure; we must guard our Germanic character and our idealism. A people without idealism is like straw in the wind.

We see today's answer to the spirit of olden days. The *hird* swear an oath of allegiance to Vidkun Quisling in front of Oslo University: unswerving loyalty unto death. This is the climax of the film but its effect is ghostly rather than inspiring. A little parade of *hird* men with banners and torches. In the darkness surrounding them are scattered groups of spectators. There are no natural sounds, no real voices, only the grinding voice of the speaker describing the scene as if it were a tribal gathering. Even Quisling's speech is only reported rather than recorded. A picture in bronze relief of Quisling emerges from the torch-lit procession. That is all.

Det brinner en eld

This Swedish Resistance film dating from 1943 was directed by Gustaf Molander. The producer, C. A. Dymling, declared in the programme notes that 'the film has no direct or indirect political purpose whatsoever'. However, a diplomatic report to Berlin in October 1943 described *Det brinner en eld* as 'that infamous anti-German film from occupied Norway'. At that time, thirty-five of Stockholm's fifty-nine cinemas were showing American films. Only three were showing German films and those were politically innocuous.

What must have annoyed the Germans about *Det brinner en eld* (*A Fire is Burning*) was its attitude to the new order and its unmistakable sympathy with the struggling democracies. The film's real intentions are never in doubt even though the director has tried to use details to create a little confusion. A steel helmet is the mark of the oppressor, but in *Det brinner en eld* the occupying soldiers wear helmets that look more Swedish than German. The cut of their uniforms is Swedish, too, except for the wide epaulettes which look more specifically Russian. The sympathetic military attaché, Colonel Lemmering (played by Lars Hanson) wears a Swedish-style cap but the badge on it is a star, not a cockade. The names have an anonymous sound, as is usual in allegories, but are German-Swedish in character: Lemmering, Falkman, Brenner, Bernt, Albert, Winter, Wollert, Bruhn. The name of the theatre group to which most of them belong, the 'National Theatre', contains an allusion towards Norway.

The occupying forces are characterised by the speech and gestures of individuals among them, but even here Molander uses stylisation. This is natural in the conditions under which the film was made – its manner had to be vague, things could not be given their real names – but it could also have something to do with the fact that the cast were mostly stage actors who might have been unable to shake off their theatrical mannerisms. The Germans are stage stereotypes, jutting out their chins, yelling in staccato voices, banging doors and stamping. A caricature of a civil servant enters, carrying a brief-case. He is an obsequious 'Herr Doktor' type with thinning hair, rimless glasses and an icy smile. He wants to involve

Still: Det brinner en eld – *soldier and theatrical company (including, at right, Inga Tidblad as Harriet Brandt, and Victor Sjöström).*

he National Theatre in propaganda and tries to negotiate this with its head (Victor Sjöström), saying at one point, 'Propaganda is as likely to produce disbelief as belief'. When Victor Sjöström refuses to adjust his theatre to the cultural views of the occupying forces, the Herr Doktor blows his whistle and policemen in black uniforms enter the room. They look like Gestapo, but they behave like Swedes and wear Swedish-style peaked caps.

The cultivated Colonel Lemmering, who is in love with the theatre's leading lady, Harriet Brandt (Inga Tidblad), is put in the difficult position of having to act on behalf of this faceless authority that all honest people must detest. He himself is the 'good enemy', hesitant and restrained, caught in the conflict between his emotions and his duty, half sympathising with the Resistance. The strain is reflected in his face, and his way of speaking is somehow sadly reserved, painfully controlled. Lemmering has to sacrifice his love and cannot, like his beloved, offer it up to a great cause. When these two loving, compatible people split up, it is apparent that his life involves total lack of liberty, while she is free to choose to give him up. Perhaps this is the most important point of all – not that the occupiers rule with brutality but that love cannot exist under their domination.

The end of the film is full of pathos; it is reminiscent of Griffith in the way it follows separate but parallel actions, frantically joining the various strands. The actress is reading a poem over the free radio: 'Somewhere someone else will take my torch.' There are shots of listeners: farmers, workers, middle-class people, a nation-wide gathering to hear the cry for freedom. Across the border, in freedom, her brother Georg switches on the radio. At the same time colonel Lemmering walks through the darkness with his soldiers. His beloved stands at the microphone, calm and glowing. The patrol closes in; rifle barrels and radio equipment glint in the darkness. The informer (Stig Järrel), suddenly overcome with remorse, tries to warn the freedom fighters but is shot down. Georg listens in freedom. Harriet Brandt reads on. Outside, the shooting has begun. Her reading light shatters and she falls to the floor. Colonel Lemmering enters as she whispers the last line of the poem: 'But the fire, the fire.' She dies in his arms.

Det brinner en eld belongs somewhere between *Rid i natt* (*Ride Tonight*, 1942) a costume drama which openly discusses the question of freedom and oppression, and *Excellensen* (*His Excellency*, 1944), in which Lars Hanson dies in a concentration camp and everything is stated about the evil except its name. *Det brinner en*

Still: Det brinner en eld – *Colonel Lemmering (Lars Hanson) and Harriet Brandt.*

eld represents a degree of commitment which, although limited by diplomatic considerations, must have had a liberating effect on many people at the time. Reviews speak of the longest ovation ever heard at a Swedish première. The audience must have received this soul-stirring sermon as an expression of solidarity with the Norwegian Resistance and anti-Nazi forces in general. At last dawn was breaking. Nevertheless the pathos reflects doubt and a sense of remoteness; there is a hollow ring about these declarations of freedom. *Det brinner en eld* has something to say about Norway and Germany in the early 'forties but even more about neutral Sweden, the people's hopes and feelings of guilt, their isolated and anxious existence in the shadow cast by the power that still ruled a great part of Europe.

The suggestion of a guilty conscience cannot be proved; it seems to be duly present, in Molander's film. Possibly, faults in acting and technique could contribute to this feeling with the inadequate expression of genuine emotion (and much reliance on film cliché and theatrical convention). Yet it is not simply a matter of awkwardness. There is something dutiful about *Det brinner en eld*. This Swedish hymn to democratic ideals differs remarkably from some of the British features of the same period and with the same message. With Gustaf Molander, one can see the intention and feel the effort. The work of his British colleagues contains the same pathos without the melodramatic means. The Swedes of 1943 were democrats who had been involved for some time in dubious trade with enemies of democracy and had been spared the distressing trial of war. Perhaps this is why the message of freedom in this film from neutral Sweden has such a high tone. It is both a confession and a piece of rhetoric.

Still: Det brinner en eld – *Harriet Brandt's last broadcast. Opposite:* The Hitler Gang.

The Hitler Gang

Many films have been made about Adolf Hitler but few have achieved more than a grotesque portrayal of him. The Führer's personality does not invite a balanced characterisation. And balanced is scarcely the word for John Farrow's *The Hitler Gang*, with Robert Watson, a little known actor with an uncanny likeness to the man he portrays, in the leading role. The film has a consistent but almost undefinable tone somewhere between the authentic and the fantastic. James Agee said that it fascinated him 'as all waxworks do'. Waxworks is a fitting term to describe *The Hitler Gang*, but these models are so sublime in their resemblance to reality that both truth and fabrication have a bewitching quality.

Naturally the characterisation takes the form of caricature; Hitler and the men around him are seen through enemy eyes. When the Kaiser abdicates, Corporal Hitler stealthily snips the droopy ends off his moustache. He is positively delirious when the mighty Ludendorff establishes contact with his organisation immediately before the Beer Hall Putsch. He is superstitious, silly, cowardly, megalomaniac and crouches in a wardrobe, trembling from head to foot after the putsch has failed. The devoted Hess waits on him in prison, delicately shielding him from vulgar curiosity when he is revealed in his long underwear. The fawning Goebbels has a limp and Röhm indulges in some cautious importuning. Göring is raving for morphine in a Swedish hospital. Streicher, looking just like a pig, carries a whip. Rosenberg brims over with smugness when Gregor Strasser has bullied him about being a provincial fanatic and the Führer defends him by saying that National Socialism needs fanatics. Himmler, the blackmailer, hints at Hitler's secret vices, and Hitler's beloved niece Geli, who is murdered later in the film, provides substance for the subtle suggestions of perversion that surround Hitler.

But the remarkable thing is that these beastly little sketches appear in settings of amazing authenticity against a background that is scrupulously correct in every detail; they never contradict the ideas we already have of them. Instead they quietly intermingle with our existing views, merging with them, influencing them, exploiting our need for simplification and clear psychological outlines.

When the film was shown in the United States in the spring of 1944, it must have provided edification for the haters, relief for the war-weary, security for the anxious, con-

rmation for the contemptuous. Seeing *The Hitler Gang* would certainly affect anyone's image of Hitler and his associates – not drastically, perhaps, but it certainly emphasises their pettiness. (I once watched a pompous German newsreel of the Nuremberg rally of 1937 immediately after seeing *The Hitler Gang* and I had the impression that I could recognise the real despots behind the façade of their official appearance; I felt I was aware of their motivation, their vanity and insignificance. The version the feature had given, invested the documentary with new meaning and coloured my view of the characters. The Farrow film, for me, had created concepts, and thus provided a basis for interpreting reality.)

The Hitler Gang employs the narrative technique of a gangster movie. It is by no means the only American film with propagandist inventions to do so. It harks back to a tradition of earlier gangster films in which an infantile and hostile psychopath surrounds himself with a gang of similar hoods, forces himself into a position of power and eventually becomes 'the shame of a nation', so that the powers for good seek revenge and destroy the criminals. The ultimate fate of these characters is always predictable and it seems likely that those behind *The Hitler Gang* counted on audiences to complete the process although the film ended with the situation as it was in 1943.

The image that emerges of the Hitler gang is entirely one of mediocrity, but it also appears psychologically illuminating, like the gangster films of the 'thirties. This inevitably weakens the film's power to inspire hatred, partly because there is a danger that experiencing the film will in itself soften the indignation: we get close to the criminals who turn out to be absurd and irritating, but also entertaining. But above all, the difficulty is that the film makes their perversions seem insignificant in relation to reality. There is no sense of horror at the power of these people to carry away a whole nation and threaten the rest of humanity. Even at the peak of their power they are little more than a noisy bunch of small-time traders and intriguers. Although we hear them expounding grand ideas about world domination and genocide, they remain gangsters plain and simple, because their minds seem too petty to hold any grand visions. Their brutality is that of *Little Caesar*, not of the Nazis.

It might have been the realisation of this that decided the makers of the film on the measure – which is inconsistent with both style and plot – of suddenly forsaking the purely dramatic form for a documentary presentation with spoken commentary. Only with the help of a disembodied guiding voice can the film raise its plot to the level of reality. Only by destroying its fictional basis can it convince us that these people really *are* plunging the world into disaster.

The Battle of Stalingrad

An exhausted general in Russian staff quarters at Stalingrad says despairingly: 'If comrade Stalin only knew what a difficult time we are having.' Someone nearby whispers confidently and solemnly: 'He knows.' Fade-out.

Nowhere else in the cinema is there a counterpart to this two-part film apotheosis, made in 1949, which carries the Stalin cult to its most pompous extreme. It is only too easy now to dismiss Vladimir Petrov's wild panegyric with sarcasm. It is actually a film of complete stylistic consistency, and is unusual and surprising as film art has hardly ever, before or since, tried to create an equivalent to the hieratic style expressed in the pharaonic sculptures of Egypt.

Reality in *Battle of Stalingrad* is stylised into a lofty geometrical harmony. Stalin's movements are measured and dignified. The rhythm is majestic. The dialogue is presented in solemn tableaux, which take on a liturgical tone with the careful recitation of lines by one person at a time, with no overlap or interruption. The people are certainly a positive force but the conception of them is aesthetic. They are firmly relegated to the background and have no charisma of their own. The rigidity is not, however, a technical failure on the part of the director but a deliberate style. It is not a film designed to arouse enthusiasm. It is a monument to a victory and the victor.

The battle is mythological as well as historical, a ritual Armageddon, in which forces of good and evil clash. *Battle of Stalingrad* is enacted on three strictly separate levels. At the top is the god, working out a strategy for the forces of good in Olympian seclusion. In the lugubrious darkness at the lowest level live the forces of evil. Between them lies the level of the ordinary people, where the struggle between good and evil will take place. The battle itself is depicted in incredibly costly fake documentary sequences and presented mainly in panoramic scenes which make the war seem very far away. It is seen from above, as if from a heavenly viewpoint, remote from the painful details of reality. This elevated position is the Kremlin, where Stalin strolls in majestic solitude, thoughtfully smoking his pipe in front of large maps of the world. He is the god. With him on occasion is Marshal Vasilevsky, who has the sole function of admiring Stalin's wisdom and thereby saving him from the indignity of talking to himself.

Stills: The Battle of Stalingrad; *lavish recon-struction and patriotic tableau.*

Sänt händer inte här

The headquarters of Hitler and von Paulus is a lurid place darkened by grim shadows, in pointed contrast with the Kremlin which is always bathed in a glorious light. Hitler is a mad, sweating, hysterical demon, von Paulus a gloomy megalomaniac. Neither seems danger-ous. They are demons, but from the outset their appearances are marked by the destruc-tion ordained for them.

The portrayal of Stalin is remarkable because it so obviously – and totally in keeping with the style – lays no claims to credibility as a human being. His figure has the solid dignity of an official portrait. He speaks in aphorisms, and every sentence he utters has an authoritative emphasis that kills every trace of intimacy and spontaneity. Even the pointedly human traits demonstrated in episodes inserted expressly for this purpose have a curious air of unreality. During one of the most critical days of the Stalingrad battle, he spends a few hours talking about Tolstoy with an old friend, a man of the people. The scene is suffused with a mythical, superhuman glow; it does not humanise Stalin but rather conveys his divine calm.

The actor Alexei Diki embodies the Stalin myth, a myth does not operate with realistic characters and techniques. The figure of Stalin is reduced to its most representative and monu-mental characteristics; reality is stripped of all irrelevant detail. This is why the war is so re-mote; there is no place here for individual suf-fering and trivial incidents. The war becomes an abstraction rather than a historical reality, and the isolated events reproduced are heroic episodes which have already become an intrinsic part of the legend in the 'Chronicle of the Great Patriotic War of the Soviet Union'.

In a memorial like this, barbed wire is not a painful barrier but a decoration. The suffering is a gesture, not a sensation. Here war is an oratorio; and organ notes, exploding bombs, martial music and rhythmic cutting all combine to make a minute-long fanfare of unequalled joy, in both image and sound, at the point when the forces of good begin their decisive attack.

Ingmar Bergman hates discussing his political opinions in interviews. He is certainly not the type to carry a banner. He is scornful of his critics, of the Swedish intellectual climate, of pretentious debates, of art with a political message ('a girl in a raincoat singing about Vietnam'), and of the young theoreticians who keep announcing fresh approaches to the theatre. On the other hand he worships the classics, artistic craftsmanship, and his audience. He senses great opportunities within those who are not yet aware – children and the poorer classes – all those he would wake up if only the authorities dared to give him a really big alarm-clock. He does not worship politicians, possibly regarding the whole area of politics as a badly directed farce.

In the theatre, Bergman is humble, attentive and rational. When making films, however, he seems to work more ruthlessly. He almost always writes the script himself, doing so with a lack of inhibition usually reserved for private diaries or polemical debates, while expressing his meanings indirectly under the camouflage of epic or dramatic form; he also likes to tell a story. His own face is to be observed among the others in his films. His dreams and his night-mares appear, too. Bergman may not have a clear political philosophy, but like most people he seems to have political nightmares. Not that he necessarily shares with the fisherman, Jonas Persson, an unbearable terror of the Chinese atom bomb (expressed in *Winter Light*), but on occasion he has shown a landscape of fear that bears a certain resemblance to political reality. The strange country in *The Silence* might be something more than a simple metaphor for an existence in which God is silent; it also suspici-ously resembles the idea many people had in the 'fifties of what lay behind the Iron Curtain. It is a country where people do not smile, where every act is prompted by caution and where human communication occurs only in the form of violence and terror. It is a fantasy dictator-ship without sun where no Swedish manufac-turer would consider starting up a shirt factory.

The fact that such an interpretation of *The Silence* is possible, does not make Ingmar Bergman some kind of belated anti-communist fanatic. He might be called a cynical mystic or a bourgeois individualist, but he does not in-dulge in political propaganda. Nevertheless, political thought can insinuate itself into any picture. Bergman, like everybody else, is part of the political situation. He presents a concept (of the Communist world) conditioned by knowledge, misconception and anxiety (whether justified or false). The false anxiety is the kind that people need when living in a vacuum. (They need something on which to project their unease.) The genuine anxiety is produced by a real threat. For a time, the Soviet Union behaved threateningly; it was a closed country and seemed to express little human feeling. Later, and particularly perhaps in the case of a small country, the icy suspicion between the two super-powers might have come to seem nightmarish. The situation today is completely changed but fantasies of terror can emerge in dreams even after the terror itself has been overcome, and *The Silence* is a dream-play.

It Couldn't Happen Here (1950) is a political thriller. The script is by Herbert Grevenius, and according to Jörn Donner in 'Djävulens ansikte' (The Personal Vision of Ingmar Bergman) the film was 'quite simply a commissioned work, produced in the space of a few weeks'. It is not the worst film Ingmar Bergman has made but decidedly the weirdest. Parts of the plot are ludicrous. The film opens with a background of dark clouds and a commentary spoken by a soft, ingratiating voice about 'a small country . . . that has wanted to make itself indistinguishable'. A man called Atkä Natas arrives in idyllic Sweden from Liquidatzia. The name of his country means what it says and lies somewhere to the East, beyond Helsinki. The man's name can also be read backwards (Äkta Satan means 'the real Satan'). He is the representative and the victim of evil.

Natas (played by Ulf Palme) is an agent who has decided to defect – and the first thing he does in Stockholm is to 'phone the American Embassy. He has a showdown with his wife Vera (Signe Hasso) in their hotel room, and it turns out that he has informed on her parents. Natas tells her exactly what he thinks: her father was useless, a naïve man who supported the revolution. 'He didn't realise that all revolutions are won by the dark elements, the professional murderers.' Natas earlier worked for the Germans and has four thousand lives on his conscience. In the society that employs him this is regarded as a virtue. Vera is filled with disgust, while Natas goes on drinking and boasting. When he has fallen asleep, she injects some form of poison into the back of his neck. But agents die slowly and Natas eventually wakes up again. He is carried off by his own men who flash dark looks from beneath pulled-down brims of their big hats.

The Liquidatzian agents are not only preoccupied with liquidating traitors but also with persecuting refugees. An anonymous letter arrives: 'Refugees! Don't imagine that you are safe. The Third World War will soon break out.' Some refugees are celebrating the wedding of a young couple who have recently arrived by boat; they do traditional folk-dances. A priest says: 'Tonight we are back again in the villages we were driven away from.' Then a message

arrives: an old woman has died, killed by the shock of the anonymous letter. In another scene, the same refugees confer behind the screen of a cinema. (A Donald Duck film is being shown, and the incessant chatter from the soundtrack forms a noisy background to their excited conversation.) Someone reports on the situation in their occupied country. An electric fence is rumoured to have been put up all around Petersdorf, a big town. The informer in the group is suddenly revealed to be the young bridegroom. When the others hit him, he tells them that he was tortured in his cellar. 'They demanded more and more.'

Meanwhile Natas is being questioned by the Liquidatzian agents. The brief-case he was to deliver to the Americans contains a list of all Liquidatzian agents in Sweden and directives for the infiltration of the mining areas in the north. Natas is in trouble but manages to extricate himself. A little later, we see him sitting in a suburban house with Vera and Almkvist (Alf Kjellin), a kindly policeman who works in intelligence. He loves Vera and is looking after her. The conversation is strained. 'Do you know much about the Middle Ages?' asks Almkvist. 'I've lived through them,' answers Natas darkly.

The end is confused. Almkvist has been knocked out by Liquidatzian agents and Vera has disappeared. As he lies semi-conscious on the floor, the radio plays happy, summer music. Someone with a sinister voice gives him an incomprehensible message over the telephone. He struggles to get up and a moment later we find him sitting on the plinth of Charles XII's statue with a colleague from the security police. There is a group of children with an officious woman teacher; the warrior king is pointing eastwards. Suddenly Almkvist remembers the words: Mrofnimok Gadyn. They rush down to the quayside and raid the boat which is ready to sail. Around them are dark, suspicious faces. Vera is found and the sun shines over Stockholm.

The name of the ship, like Atkä Natas's name, can be read backwards – Kominform and Ny Dag the name of the Swedish communist newspaper. It is a rather poor joke. The movie contains a number of such humorous details. Indeed, it is hard to take the film seriously. Superficially it looks like one of the most virulent anti-communist films ever made anywhere; everything can be clearly identified – Liquidatzia is the Soviet Union and nothing else, and the refugees come from the Baltic states (their roles are taken by professional and non-professional actors with Estonian names). The film was made during the paranoid era when Josef Stalin ruled supreme over the Communist world and Senator Joseph McCarthy had begun to guide American public opinion. It gives some idea of the political atmosphere in Western Europe after the 1948 Prague coup, though it is not ideologically conscious. It uses politics only as a source of suspense.

The director himself seems to have felt rather unhappy about *It Couldn't Happen Here* and for a long time refused to have it included in any retrospectives on him. Lately the ban appears to have been lifted. Bergman may well feel that we have progressed far enough from the atmosphere of 1950, which no doubt coloured this film, to be able to see it now as a piece of confused fiction from a confused period in history. It says almost nothing about Ingmar Bergman as he is today.

At one point, though, *It Couldn't Happen Here* does ring true. It contains some harsh words about Sweden which Ingmar Bergman could just as well be saying today. One of the representatives of Liquidatzia is standing at an open window. He looks out over Stockholm, saying ironically 'I like this country; it is full of intelligent people who don't understand anything. They are Sunday people. If you were to tell them what is happening they'd say: "It couldn't happen here".' Jörn Donner has pointed out that this criticism of Swedish prejudice and innocence can hardly be interpreted as an urgent message in view of its peculiar context. Politically, Ingmar Bergman himself has been fairly innocent at times.

Still: Sånt händer inte här – It Couldn't Happen Here; *Ulf Palme as Atkä Natas.*

Únos

Únos, a Czech film by Ján Kadár and Elmar Klos dates from 1952, one of the coldest of the Cold War years. An airliner on its way from Ostrava to Prague is hijacked by a group of Czechs and made to land in Munich. At the airport there are gum-chewing Americans and a mob of news-hungry reporters. The Americans expect the Czechs to choose freedom. First they are taken to a US Training Centre and tempted with food. They all turn it down except a young jazz musician who is clearly shallow and unstable. His opposite is an unyielding Communist from the State Planning Commission, who is also a member of parliament. Also in the group is the engineer Prokop, a skilled technician who is sceptical of the new society. (Somebody hints that this is because of some personal tragedy.) In his brief-case are the plans for some vital industrial projects, and these are the primary interest of the Americans. The hijacking was organised by the CIA, here called CIC.

The Americans take it for granted from the beginning that Prokop is willing to co-operate. They arrange for him to meet some German colleagues from the Bavarian Metal Works, but their cynicism worries him. They are not

engaged in production for peace; tanks are lined up in the factory compound. Contrary to accepted international rules, the Czechs are prevented from contacting their consul in Munich. Their leader, the member of parliament, is questioned by a CIC agent. When he proves unco-operative, the agent starts to threaten him, with the help of an unpleasant Sudeten German in a leather coat, who already has the deaths of thirty people to his credit.

The group is subjected to other forms of pressure: there is an attempt to make them succumb to the frivolous side of western life. They are taken to an open-air show, complete with high-kicking chorus girls (it is the Munich Follies); a comic negro climbs up a lamp-post, falls down and is struck by a policeman. The engineer is about to give in, but the colonel handling the negotiations with him is so boastful that he cannot resist showing off photographs of his bombing raids. Prokop lost his wife and child during the bombing of Ostrava. In an emotional speech he says that the Americans have killed his child and 'millions more'.

By now the Americans are fed up and ask the Czechs quite brusquely to make up their minds which side they want to be on. All except the musician want to go home. They are searched and somebody's Party badge is confiscated. The Czechs protest by humming the Internationale. The member of parliament manages to escape and alert the consul. Public opinion is aroused; there are protest meetings and workers go on strike. But when the Czechs are eventually about to leave, Prokop is missing. He is in the hands of the CIC, who torture him and try to convince him that the others have left him behind. In the end, an American general intervenes; he himself is very bitter about the CIC. The Czechs do some folk-dancing before gladly leaving West Germany. The jazz musician, though, is having a rotten time in a refugee camp and bitterly regretting his folly. There is an epilogue in the UN General Assembly where the Czech delegate speaks of 'thousands' of similar provocations.

Únos (The Hijacking) is a typical product of its period. Almost identical films were made at the time in the United States, except that it was the communists who were devious and morally corrupt enough to employ ex-Nazis in their shady activities. As in Únos, the settings were hostile and there was a desolate feeling that one might at any moment hear the rattle of iron gates.

The genre seems to lack subtlety: it is often coarsely demagogic and loaded with insinuation. As Prokop is on his way to the Bavarian Metal Works, the tune of the Horst Wessel Lied is sneaked into the score. On the return journey, he sees a troop of soldiers. They are young Germans dressed in American uniforms, and singing just as they used to: 'Es ist so schön Soldat ze sein, Rosemarie.' Behind them an invalid slowly crosses the road in the opposite direction. The message is clear: West Germany is re-arming with American aid, and the old spirit is still alive. But traces of the previous collapse also remain. The Germans will lose once again if they embark on further reckless adventures.

Films like Únos are not persuasive, nor are they really intended to be. Their main function is to reinforce existing opinions. In German folk tales the noble prince is fair and his evil adversary has a dark countenance. In the same way, here the Americans are shown as people completely divested of dignity. This premise is fixed before the film has even begun. The one American soldier who possesses some trace of decency is typically of Czech origin; he is ashamed of his profession but would have been unemployed had he not enlisted.

Movies of this kind are manifestations of weakness rather than strength. They are also of dubious value in creating a state of readiness. If you turn the enemy into a grimacing puppet, you are unlikely to recognise him when he appears as an ordinary human being.

Something should be said about the background of the film. Even during the 'liberal' period between the liberation in 1945 and the Prague coup of 1948, Czechoslovakia was governed according to Socialist principles. A vast nationalisation programme was carried out in the months after the end of the war, and the film industry was nationalised by special decree of President Beneš. At the free elections in 1946, the Communists received 38 per cent of the vote and their leader, Klement Gottwald, became head of a coalition government. The film industry was organised in roughly the same way as in Socialist Poland, with independent production units. The film school set-up at the time was to have greater significance for the Czech cinema later. After the events of 25 February 1948, everything changed. A supreme arts council started to scrutinise all films from an ideological viewpoint and in accordance with Zhdanovian principles, effectively filtering off all critical opinion and personal initiative. Filmmakers became anxious and their work mediocre. The new conformity had a disastrous effect on the cinema both in quality and quantity. Between the wars, Czechoslovakia with fourteen million inhabitants had been a small country with a large output of films. In some years over fifty features were produced. During the good years after the end of World War II, the annual production was about half that. In the early 'fifties, it was virtually non-existent; only a handful of films every year. One of the subjects that could safely be treated, in strict accordance with the Party line and in perceptive harmony with tendencies in the Soviet cinema, was anti-Americanism.

Still: Man on a String – *Boris Mitrov (Ernest Borgnine) and Vadja Kubelov (Alexander Scourby, left) as guests of the Bensons (Ed Prentiss and Colleen Dewhurst).*

Man on a String

This cliché-ridden American film (also known as *Confessions of a Counterspy*), directed in 1960 by André de Toth, has a dramatic opening: a man is tossed off a train after a brief fight. The commentary explains that he was an agent whom the CBI, the American secret service, had almost managed to place in the Kremlin.

After this bit of violence we see a headline: 'Soviet Spy Ring Shattered' and a rather elaborate presentation of the leading characters, their background and basic conflicts. Boris Mitrov (played by Ernest Borgnine) is a Hollywood film producer of Russian origin. His father has just arrived from the Soviet Union, but Mitrov has no news of his brothers. He is contacted by Vadja Kubelov, head of Russian espionage in North America, who hints that the brothers, too, will be allowed to leave. The two men begin to meet socially. A millionaire, Benson, and his wife, both devoted communists, are among their friends.

The CBI begin to take an interest in Mitrov and his companions. Secret Service methods are outlined in a documentary section. Conversations can be overheard from a good distance with electronic equipment. (An agent with a gadget of this sort is seen among the trees outside Mitrov's house.) The CBI have also installed microphones, and watch what happens inside Mitrov's house on a television screen. The commentary explains and justifies this procedure. The serious conflict in which the secret service organisations of the two great powers are engaged forces the CBI to resort, in certain cases, to means which are not available to other departments. The CBI use some compromising pictures to persuade Mitrov to enrol as a counter-spy.

Mitrov arrives in West Berlin, and stress is placed on the city's precarious position, surrounded by the Communist bloc. Shooting is held up on the film Mitrov is to make there. A mysterious accident occurs and one of the production directors, Grünwald, is fired. The fact that Grünwald is a Communist agent is revealed to Mitrov by a distinguished musician, who is an old friend, but this is not news to the audience as the commentary has already revealed both this and Grünwald's earlier career as an informer for the Gestapo.

We pass into East Berlin through the Brandenburg Gate. Here Mitrov has to testify at the trial of the old musician who has been abducted from West Berlin by the KGB.

Mitrov returns to the West where he complains about the situation to his colleague Bob Avery; he feels vaguely guilty of having helped to kill someone. Avery, who is a CBI man, answers that in this line of work one has to disregard all human feelings except love of one's country.

The Communists have confidence in Mitrov, who now goes to Moscow. The camera zooms in to the Ministry of Foreign Affairs as Mitrov enters. He talks with a general in the secret service who bears the name of a Communist movie hero, Chapayev. The general gives a lecture in the spirit of Khruschev about the inevitability of ultimate Soviet victory due to technical and economic supremacy. Mitrov walks around the Russian capital waiting for an assignment. One day he visits a training establishment for secret agents outside Moscow, and questions a class of students who are soon to be sent into the United States on forged passports to carry out special assignments. They have done their homework. Mitrov himself now receives systematic training and has to memorise the names of his American contacts.

Suddenly the Bensons arrive in Berlin; they are convinced that Mitrov is not playing it straight and plan to inform on him. Avery calls Mitrov back. He lands in East Berlin, kills a policeman and escapes to freedom. A man tries to shoot him from a roof opposite his hotel in West Berlin. A hand-to-hand struggle follows between Mitrov and Grünwald and the latter is killed. There is a happy ending. Mitrov's information proves extremely valuable to the CBI. Agents from the Russian spy school arrive in the United States and are immediately arrested.

Man on a String is interesting partly because of the crudeness of its construction but also because of a curious uncertainty in its attitude. It tells the American public what McCarthy and Dulles have already taught them, that Communism is evil, that the Kremlin is out to undermine the American way of life, that Russian diplomats are really Soviet agents, that the Communists are no better than the Nazis, and that there is no grimmer place than East Berlin. These statements are presented as unarguable fact.

The film preaches anti-communism: the whole scene in the gloomy, nightmarish courtroom in East Berlin suggests that communist society is not only merciless but also underprivileged. We never hear the sentence passed on the accused, the old musician, but we hear of his death soon afterwards. (Obviously, there is only one possible outcome of involvement with the KGB.) Elsewhere the indoctrination is more subtle. In Moscow, Kubelov tells Mitrov that an agent, if need be, might easily smuggle into the United States a 'bomb' to be detonated later by remote control, as nowadays the smallest are no bigger than a grapefruit. This is said in an offhand way, but this kind of line is probably all the more powerful for being spoken without any special emphasis. The words inspire disbelief and fear (spoken in this way, they must be about an atom bomb). The fear, however, is counteracted by a quick dose of reassurance. The commentator, who plays an important role in the film, hurriedly assures us that the CBI have all the necessary equipment at their disposal to enable the country to survive the threat of communism. (This probably refers obliquely to the 'missile gap' debate in the United States during the late 'fifties.)

Man on a String is based on *Ten Years as a Counter-Spy*, an autobiographical account by Boris Morros, a film producer whose work includes Julien Duvivier's *Tales of Manhattan* (1942). The film operates both as an ordinary spy-thriller and as a fictionalised documentary on the political situation. Location sequences of New York, Berlin and Moscow are meant to convey a feeling of authenticity, and the commentary is spoken in the breathless manner of an American newscaster. It indicates and emphasises, without necessarily achieving its desired effect; it is almost too insistent.

The movie's other great weakness as a propaganda weapon is a certain hesitancy, and ambivalence. Communism has traits that are less than humane, but surely there is also a lack of humanity in the machinery of the CBI, whose working methods are here demonstrated with such childish pride. Communists are evil in 'de Toth's picture, but sometimes they look confusingly like ordinary human beings.

In the American cinema, the rich communist represents the very worst form of decadence; he has betrayed 'the American way of life' and his corruption must be exposed. While Avery, the CBI man, meets his wife and children at Tempelhof airport, proving that his job and the sentiments he has expressed earlier do not preclude human feelings, the communist millionaire Benson appears totally to lack moral strength. He is childless, and now married to his third wife who is having an affair with Kubelov.

For Communists in the Soviet Union, the treatment is different. General Nikolai Chapayev is respectfully portrayed. In Moscow the milling crowds do not appear to be living in a nightmare but in a reality that includes laughter. (There are shots of beaches which could have been taken at Coney Island, although the appearance and activities of the Russian crowd seem less standardised.) In 1960, horror propaganda will no longer do; people may believe that communism is inhuman, but not that Russians are fiends disguised as humans. The film is so undecided whether it is recording or indoctrinating that it fails to make any clear and lasting impression. The audience is given time to think, which is fatal in this kind of context. *Man on a String* is a McCarthy film in the wrong decade. The phantoms have lost their power.

Torn Curtain

It is just possible that Alfred Hitchcock is a political innocent who imagines that his films are not about politics. In the interviews he gives nowadays, it looks as if, like Ingmar Bergman, he carefully is avoiding any discussion of the subject. However, during the period from *The Man Who Knew Too Much* (1934) to *Lifeboat* (1943), Hitchcock's films seemed to be greatly concerned with politics, even if the particular demands of the thriller pattern into which political situations were skilfully woven meant that a great deal remained obscure or only partially stated. These films were nevertheless quite clearly about Nazism and the cold shivers that ran through Europe when political criminals became heads of state, when terror established its ministries in one country after another and some people adjusted themselves to the rule of force while others united to resist it. In these films Hitchcock expressed the confused state of political opinion at the time. But he was also a fighting democrat, as he showed with particular clarity in *Foreign Correspondent* (1940).

Apart from a prologue and epilogue, Hitchcock's fiftieth film, *Torn Curtain*, is set in the German Democratic Republic. The director himself has said that he originally planned to set it in Poland, but that a Polish-born friend made him change his mind. The director, then, is not trying to describe the atmosphere of a specific country: he has simply decided to make a film in which the action takes place somewhere inside the Communist bloc. East Germany has the advantage of being an unexploited background where novel situations can still be set up.

The German Democratic Republic has had a bad press in the United States. To the United States it appears an irritating phenomenon; it does not exist, but demands recognition, presenting the additional threats of dour efficiency and the Berlin Wall. As a Communist state, it may no longer have its Stalinstadt or Stalinallée, but is still led by a man who enjoyed Stalin's confidence. In the German Democratic Republic, some of the old spirit lingers, and might therefore lend weight to the argument which allows an American film set in that country to use some of the stereotypes favoured by the West in earlier films about Socialist countries.

Poland would certainly have been a more demanding choice, involving more subtle nuances of characterisation and setting. The audience's preconceptions would have been more complex, for in the American imagination, Poland is a sympathetic country governed by the wrong regime, a bohemian-aristocratic nation. (In *Torn Curtain* it has a touching representative in Lila Kedrova's dizzy countess who longs to escape from East Berlin to an imagined paradise in the United States.) There is a pressure group of Polish nationals whose patriotism continued irrespective of the political situation in their native land. This makes it hard to accept that the East German setting was as accidental as Hitchcock has claimed. In some ways it was probably a wise decision. Apart from a brutally prolonged murder, *Torn Curtain* contains few moments of real tension. The suspense rests on the hero's constant danger that his duplicity will be discovered by the enemy.

Colour is an important element in *Torn Curtain*. The original plan was to make grey the predominant colour as soon as the action reached East Germany. Fortunately, Hitchcock decided on a more subtle method of presentation. Professor Armstrong (Paul Newman), the American scientist who claims a desire to defect, is welcomed at Berlin-Schönefeld airport by East German dignitaries and security officials. They stand around in a circle, all dressed in black; it is clear to us that Michael Armstrong will have a hard time here, whether he happens to be sacrificing his country or sacrificing himself for it on an extremely hazardous mission for the CIA. At this point, we do not know all the facts, but the composition and colouring suggest that Professor Armstrong stands for idealism and individualism, while the men surrounding him represent the machinery of government.

The colour warns, emphasises and characterises. The interiors of the Hotel Berlin where Armstrong and his devoted secretary Sarah Sherman (Julie Andrews) are staying are in cool and subdued blues, greens and browns. There is a claustrophobic atmosphere that seems the more threatening after the Norwegian fjords of the prologue. Ruins can be seen silhouetted through the hotel windows. Sarah's red nightdress has a striking warmth in this gloomy setting. Hitchcock has often enjoyed ironic contrasts. In *Torn Curtain*, red does not stand for revolution, socialism, or danger, but for escape and liberation. It is the dominant colour in the ballet at the end of the film; red stage flames prompt Armstrong to shout 'Fire', thus creating total chaos in which his pursuers lose sight of him. It is the colour of the stage door behind which Armstrong and his secretary take refuge. And finally the fugitives warm themselves by a glowing red fire in the Swedish town of Trelleborg when the danger is over.

Lack of freedom is at first depicted with some restraint. As far as we can judge, the East German standard of living is reasonably high. Gerhard, the security chief, receives official visitors in an elegant, comfortable room with large windows. But through the windows we again see ruins. Our suspicions should be aroused about the power which Gerhard represents: the luxury surrounding him as a

Party official reflects his Party's isolation.

Gerhard himself is intelligent and efficient, although naturally he is outwitted in the end. He gets obeyed without needing to raise his voice and has the air of a very competent technician. Gromek, one of his thugs, who acts as Armstrong's bodyguard, on the other hand, is an unsavoury character, though he does have a personality – when Armstrong is forced to get rid of him, he is not killing a monster but a human being. But Gromek also has his cliché aspects which render his murder acceptable psychologically. Superficially he is immediately identifiable as a crook; he slouches around, unshaven and chewing gum, in a black leather coat. We have come across his kind before, in the underworld and the Gestapo and know that according to the rules of the game, he must be eliminated. In his conversations with Truffaut, Hitchcock has explained the purpose of the 'unintentional murder' of Gromek. It is a prolonged scene, and, as Truffaut says, 'since it is played without music, it is very realistic and also very savage'.

Hitchcock did it in this way because he felt 'it was time to show that it was very difficult, very painful, and it takes a very long time to kill a man.' It is possible to impute a moral significance to this key scene. Michael Armstrong at this point commits a fascist act of liquidation. We have identified with him, followed his progress through East Germany,

shared his experiences, sympathised with his distress and participated in his decision. Hitchcock might be forcing us to do some soul-searching.

Soon after the murder of Gromek it begins to look as if Hitchcock has lost interest. He no longer worries about whether the film looks convincing and instead of making jokes and insinuations with colour, he switches to crude polemics that would have been more acceptable in an American movie of the early 'fifties. East German police shoot wildly in the centre of Berlin, but no one is hit. It is comforting to know that the cruelty of the enemy is hampered by his incompetence.

At times, the improbabilities become offensive. On the way from Leipzig the yellow bus carrying refugees is stopped by Russian deserters, who are identified as such by their epaulettes, weapons and accents. They demand 'money, not jewellery and watches'. An East German motorcycle policeman arrives on the scene later, apologising that 'there have been so many robberies lately'. For purposes of indoctrination, this kind of statement is more effective when it comes from a representative of the regime than from an enemy or an out-

sider. It has now been suggested to the audience that the atmosphere of gloom in East Germany is made worse by lawlessness and, further, that there are discipline problems in the Red Army. Here Hitchcock is using the old trick of belittling the enemy and giving the audience some reassurance when they have been frightened. But the situation is not very topical. The Soviet Union and the other Warsaw Pact countries are no longer the enemy they once seemed.

In an interview Hitchcock has described *Torn Curtain* as a 'film filled with compromises'. He had originally planned to describe 'the tragic element in espionage', a subject to which he returns in *Topaz* (1969). In the ending originally planned, Armstrong manages to get to Trelleborg with the formula for rocket fuel but then throws the paper on which it is written into the fire. But such an exercise in pointlessness could scarcely be allowed in a film that cost six million dollars, and certainly not as the final gesture. Hitchcock realised this and fell in with the conventions of the industry. He is unhappy about it but feels that there is also 'an ethical side to the question'. He says: 'The future of a number of people depended on this film. What was I to do? In a way my problem was the same as Paul Newman's in the film.' There is of course another 'ethical' aspect. A film like *Torn Curtain* helps to create and confirm political misconceptions.

Ordinary Fascism

Mikhail Romm's *Ordinary Fascism* (1965) is a sixteen-part lecture. Romm himself has said in the magazine 'Sovietski ekran', that he did not intend it as the sort of didactic account which had already been provided by Erwin Leiser, Paul Rotha or the Thorndikes. Yet another description of events seemed to him superfluous. On the other hand he felt there was an opportunity to go more deeply into the significance of Fascism, using documentary film material. He attempted to uncover the motivations behind Fascism and the mystique surrounding it, as well as the ways in which it has survived. Romm studied the face of power – a third of the five million feet of German newsreel material that he and his team examined covered Adolf Hitler himself. But he also studied the faces watching, mesmerised, as their leader passed. The unofficial side interested him most – not the leader or the marching columns but the people, enthusiastic or silently obedient, according to the state of Germany's military fortunes. It took Romm a year of intensive work to select stills and sequences. He combines this material with a critical commentary that is occasionally reminiscent of Chris Marker, and with Godardian chapter headings. This is no objective lecture; it is difficult to approach Fascism without preconceived ideas But Romm does not indulge in preaching or emotionalism; he prefers to observe an ironical distance.

Nevertheless *Ordinary Fascism* cannot help but disturb. It contains much new material, horrific images of inhumanity which have not yet become hackneyed and lost their human impact. Eyes gaze out at us: a naked Jewish woman in a Nazi pogrom; concentration camp prisoners shown in a sort of rogues' gallery. The spirit of resistance and a strange human dignity still lives in these eyes. But we are reminded that our sensibility has become dulled. We have been exposed to so many images of suffering that we register whether a picture is new to us or not, rather than responding to the reality they convey.

Ordinary Fascism is the literal translation of the title; it could perhaps have been rendered better as 'Everyday Fascism'. Ominous signs appear, but it is not a pessimistic film. The director has faith in man, and furthermore the Soviet Union stands as a guarantor for peace. We begin with the present: summer in Moscow and Warsaw. A woman carries her child across the road; the scene comes from a life which is founded on affection. Romm freezes the image. It loses all its warmth and is linked with a still we have seen before, one of those still pictures that come to life in their simplicity and horror: a German soldier kills a Polish woman with a baby in her arms. There follows an account of industrialised annihilation and some of its end products, including female hair. Then come Hitler, the parades and the mass psychosis. The commentary says: 'These are people, too.'

Chapter II is headed 'Mein Kampf – or how to prepare calf skin' and contains part of a grotesque short about the printing and binding of a copy of 'the Germans' book'. The following chapter talks about the book's author. It has a light-hearted irony, that demonstrates Romm's incredibly skilful use of cutting and commentary to make his point, and shows how capricious he allows himself to be. He gives a rapid account of Hitler's rise to the chancellorship,

Stills: Ordinary Fascism.

with an amusing digression in which his predecessor, Hindenburg, a walrus-like figure, loses his way while inspecting a guard of honour and fumbles around for a small coin with which to tip the chauffeur.

Chapter IV is titled 'In the meantime . . . ' and concerns life in the democracies between the wars. It contains a choice selection of entertaining nonsense, like women's wrestling, and a motor race with a plethora of crashes. Kings and presidents trip about to the Chicken Polka, and the Swedish king, 'Mr G.', is seen playing tennis. While Mosley's Fascists are demonstrating in London, fighting breaks out and the police appear to side with the Fascists. In Marseilles, King Alexander of Yugoslavia and Prime Minister Barthou are murdered. It is quite clear that the Western world is superficial, corrupt and doomed. After this, Romm goes on to talk with tougher sarcasm about the seductive nature of Fascism. He shows us a fantastic torch-lit parade spreading over an entire landscape, saying: 'They turned people into savages with great solemnity.' He shows us the bookburnings and the dominance of uniforms in the German Academy of Science. He also shows us the absurdity of the racial doctrine. There is a racialist lecture on biology, in which Ayran and non-Aryan skulls are shown. This is followed by Romm's own demonstration. He indicates a

few degenerate physiognomies – Pushkin (who had negro blood), Tolstoy, Chekhov, Marx, Mayakovsky, Einstein – and invites us to compare them with a few Aryan examples, typified by the heads of Röhm, Streicher and Bormann.

This superficial and rather grotesque approach carries through to Chapter X, which deals with the indoctrination of children and the ritual oathtakings which bound the German nation to the Führer. Chapter XI, 'But there was also another Germany', has German socialism as its subject. Karl Liebknecht speaks, there is a socialist demonstration and the police charge. Romm's commentary is restrained, without the sweeping ideological judgments on

German social democracy that always came with earlier Soviet accounts of the period. 'The German workers' movement was split, and it was easiest to crush a section at a time. It was defeated, and *he* reaped the benefits of the defeat.'

Three chapters are devoted to World War II. We are presented with key situations and visual shocks rather than a full account of political and military developments. Chapter XIV is the title section. It depicts the slaughter and is built on contrasts. Smiling Germans are photographed with their victims. Laughing soldiers, bathing in the nude, build themselves a woman out of sand. In the pogrom, naked Jewish women wait to be exterminated. A 'Strength through Joy' tourist jaunt visits the Warsaw ghetto. German women weep with joy after listening to one of Hitler's speeches.

Chapter XV is 'The End of the Third Reich'. Goebbels presents Germany with the idea of total war. The masses are listening, but Romm discloses something new in their faces: 'They are thinking.' This is the kind of revelation that a documentary can offer; something much more vital than the papers a scholar normally has to work with. But it might also be a meaningless image that acquires significance and expression from its context and/or lighting. Here we may have thinking Germans, as Romm would have us believe. But their appearance could equally well come from the photography or the effects of food rationing and lack of sleep. The com-

Still: Ordinary Fascism.

mentator has a position of great power and can carry the unwary with him. He, too, can lead people astray.

Romm's final chapter is concerned with Fascism today. He makes a crude comparison between life in the German Democratic Republic and life in the Federal Republic. In the West, people seem to be reverting to the decadence of the years between the wars. 'People want to love each other – but with boys these things can happen,' Romm says and proceeds to show footage on the US Marines from François Reichenbach's *Les Marines* (1957). He shows parades of former SS men in West Germany, Mosley and renewed street fighting, desecrated Jewish tombstones, George Lincoln Rockwell, torch-light processions of so-called exiles from East Prussia and Silesia. Then the West German monopolists: 'See how smug and aristocratic they look!' One of the film's contentions is that Capitalism and Fascism go together. We are shown rockets and the mushroom cloud which could envelop the world; then children playing, eager, happy, serious; and the dead – once again those eyes looking out from the archive pictures of concentration camps.

The film is gripping but problematic. Like Harry Martinson and Hannah Arendt, Romm has set out to reveal the banality of evil – in itself probably a good place to start. (Evil is lack of empathy and lack of human maturity.) Sequence after sequence demonstrates the limitations of Nazi thinking, and the way in which people let themselves be taken in by clowns, crooks and men of straw. It is an effective didactic method but also a dubious one, because Romm dares not (or cannot, for ideological reasons) make a film which brutally shows us the implications – that we, like everyone else, have a capacity for evil, and that social and political environment decide whether it is to be realised. This is not necessarily inconsistent with Marxist principles, but it would be difficult to discuss such complex matters in a film. Romm does not take the risk of losing track of his argument. He wants, quite rightly, to play down the demonic myth of Hitler and his henchmen. However, he falls short of target in failing to make these people real enough and thus close enough. We ourselves are on the right side, unless we happen to live in West Germany. There is no question of any disagreeable process of identification.

Ordinary Fascism therefore becomes much less frightening than it might have been. Fascism is represented as a homogeneous movement with unpleasant repercussions in the present. There is no suggestion that its contempt for humanity might become reorganised in different forms. Here the evil-doers are on one side, against the good, warm-hearted people who can be found everywhere, not least in Socialist countries.

The evil ones are not just evil but pathetic as well. Romm wants to demonstrate their pettiness, but for the sake of clarity he has dramatised it. This seems to me to be a major error. Romm emphasises the grotesque aspects of Nazism and the Nazis; he skilfully picks out the frames which reveal them. But at these points Adolf Hitler unfortunately does not display his malevolence – it is much more evident on any page of Eichmann's accounts. Instead Hitler is exposed as a fool and we are given an opportunity to laugh at him. But laughter liberates us from the evil. What was frightening has become grotesque, and now the grotesque turns comic: the Führer becomes a clown. The moral approach is replaced by an aesthetic one which puts everything at a distance.

Romm makes too much of Hitler's way of folding his hands around the lower part of his stomach on ceremonial occasions and the slavish imitation of the gesture by his entourage. It is entertaining but ill-advised. Certainly Hitler appears ludicrous in these scenes, but his ludicrousness makes him inaccessible. He becomes a film comedian. Chaplin's dictator, with a confusing hint of humanity. One cannot have a serious discussion about such a character. This means that the inhumanity of Adolf Hitler's crimes, though illustrated more forcefully here than in any other picture of this kind, is ultimately obscured rather than illuminated.

The Green Berets

The American film industry has always fought shy of subjects regarded as controversial in the United States. Consequently the Vietnam War, as distinct from, for instance, the Korean War, has not inspired Hollywood to any patriotic offerings. Some Americans view the involvement in Vietnam as a crime and others, perhaps the majority, just do not want to know about the whole distasteful business – their consciences are uneasy enough already without being disturbed further. But for the considerable minority who approve of the war, a couple of independent producers have made films in a traditional vein, with their own side as nobility personified and the enemy as vile murderers. In *Commandos in Vietnam* (1965) the director, Marshall Thompson, is at pains to emphasise the role of the United States as adviser and helper. This harmonises perfectly with the official propaganda fiction aimed at justifying the war effort with the argument that South Vietnam, as a small, free country, has asked a great and generous nation for protection against terrorists and infiltrators. 'We are here at the request of the Vietnamese Government,' states an American military spokesman in the movie, going on to mention the threat presented by Red China.

Commandos in Vietnam has a characteristic attitude of discretion among all the clichés: the killing is all done by the Asians, Vietnamese against Vietnamese, while the quiet American acts as an observer. At a critical moment, however, he does step in to save his companions, in a sort of improvised counter-guerilla group, from the evil little men in black pyjamas. This is a cheap propaganda film, but the conventions are put to skilful use. It is always difficult for the spectator to resist the appeal of heroic acts by a small group of people and the attraction of daring, resourceful incursions into enemy territory. It is to be noted that the help of the Directorate of Psychological Warfare is gratefully acknowledged in the credits.

The Green Berets (1968), based on a novel and a famous ballad, is produced and co-directed by John Wayne. He stars in it, and the film undoubtedly expresses his attitude to the war. It is a statement from the extreme right that celebrates the individual bravery of the Special Forces, whose selfless fight for a good cause has been criticised by certain misguided peace-loving characters.

'This would be a wonderful country if there wasn't a war,' says Colonel Mike Kirby, looking out across green slopes and mountains with all the melancholy that Wayne can convey. (War is a sad business, but the job has to be done and it takes a man to do it.) Kirby is on a tour of inspection in the Vietnamese jungle and visits an American base, A107, also called 'Dodge City'. The enemy is lurking unseen somewhere in the vicinity, and the defenders, Green Berets and South Vietnamese paratroopers, prepare for the expected attack. They are putting out pungi sticks, with points capable of penetrating the heaviest marching boots. These were first used by the NLF, but 'we don't poison them the way *he* does.' He – the enemy – is called Charlie, Victor Charlie, VC or Viet Cong.

The NLF is represented as a terror machine. The inhabitants of the mountain districts are systematically robbed of their rice, their chickens and their young men. The wise old village chief talks of his hatred of the Communists. It is decided to bring the villagers into the camp for protection, but before the rescue operation can be carried out, the village is destroyed by the enemy. In the soft light of dawn, the women huddle, with soot-blackened faces, around the old man who has been tied, bleeding all over, to a tree and left to die. The huts have been burnt down and all the young men have been abducted.

Later, a child's body is discovered in a thicket outside the village. It is the chief's little grand-daughter, who was introduced earlier in a highly emotive scene. There is a clear sugges-

tion that she was raped before being murdered. This is the turning point of the picture, in that it provides a focus for indignation. These sequences of outrage are intended to justify the subsequent brutality directed against the guerillas.

There is a good deal of violence, but the obvious sensationalism does not prevent the most nerve-racking moments from attaining a kind of realism. There are two particularly brutal scenes. The defences of camp A107 include a high barbed-wire fence. On the dark night when the NLF at last attack, howling wildly, the defenders switch on the current. For a few moments the battlefield is bathed in light, and we see burning human forms stiffening on the wire. Later, after the base has fallen to the enemy, planes arrive to set fire to the camp. 'It only takes a minute,' says the attacking pilot, before discharging his rocket-load in a matter of fact way. The enemy soldiers are all lying dead, bright red blood staining their black uniforms. It is mass killing beyond all conventions of war, but the message is that it is not at all reprehensible, because it is an act of punishment, almost a visitation of divine justice.

The presentation might seem oversimplified, if the same mechanics of killing had not appeared in other films (in which the victims are also

Stills: The Green Berets – *David Janssen (Beckworth) with orphan; John Wayne in command*

Asian) and if this unthinking contempt for human life were not being expressed daily in assorted battle areas. To a European observer the writhing bodies on the barbed wire might conjure up certain unhappy associations with the German death camps. John Wayne obviously means the audience to follow a different train of thought. In *The Green Berets*, it is the Charlie who burns villages and uses poison. Similar perversion of the truth was evident in the kind of Nazi film intended to shift the guilt for, say, racial hatred or the establishment of concentration camps on to an English or Polish enemy whose evil called for punishment. Wayne's movie is intended to work in the same way. He does not omit to attack US public opinion. A war correspondent, Beckworth, flies in with Kirby to A107. He introduces himself as 'an opponent of the Vietnam war,' and seems ill at ease, squeezed between the uniforms in the helicopter. Since the 'twenties, there has been a kind of tradition in American movies for reporters to seek and tell the truth. They can be relied on to express righteous indignation at any form of corruption or racial oppression, and, after earnest deliberation, to choose the right side.

In *The Green Berets*, the reporter starts out by being sceptical; he remains aloof, as if protecting his integrity. Gradually, however, he begins to warm to the comradeship extended towards him on this isolated base despite his role as the critical civilian. He even befriends a little Vietnamese girl, grand-daughter of the village chief, who has hurt her foot on one of the poisoned sticks planted by the enemy. When she is due to return to the village, he gives her a little medallion to remember him by. He solemnly puts the chain round her neck, and she tells him gravely that she will never take it off, never. Naturally this moving scene indicates that the girl's days are numbered, since it is the ritual method of pointing out who is to be the sacrificial victim. Beckworth is changed after the girl's murder: when the guerrillas attack the camp, he finds himself shooting at them. He says nothing, but his face hardens with a new determination. When the battle is over, we see him holding a gun. He seems to have changed his tools. He suggests to Colonel Kirby that he will probably lose his job if he writes a truthful account of his experiences at A107. 'You can get a job here,' Kirby says, with a grin, and Beckworth stands alone, deep in thought. Wayne is implying that the reports reaching the United States from Vietnam through the mass media are distorted and have misled public opinion.

Children are often used to trigger indignation. Anyone who lays a hand on a small child (or, in certain contexts, a dog) is instantly marked as a bad sort, representing a worthless cause. Two children in *The Green Berets* are exploited

to provide a definition of right and wrong. One is the little girl and the other is Hamchunk, a little orphan boy. We are told that he was brought up by missionaries who were murdered by the Viet Cong. The boy is the mascot of the garrison, a bright-eyed, ubiquitous little figure who has suffered and is looking for affection. He has a little dog as a playmate and his best friend is Peterson, 'the fixer,' a good-natured soldier. Hamchunk soon begins to sleep in Peterson's bed, and the two make a touching pair. When the NLF mount their big attack, the little dog jumps out of a dug-out and is killed in the gunfire. We can be certain that this will not be the only loss.

The Green Berets really consists of two different stories. The first is concerned with the battles around the Vietnamese Dodge City. The second is a simple-minded tale about an expedition carried out by Kirby's group in the Mekong delta. They have set out to kidnap a Communist general, who turns out to have all kinds of vices and to live in colonial luxury; their mission naturally succeeds. When the helicopters return, Hamchunk is waiting at Da Nang airport for his friend. He asks everybody about Peterson, and at last the truth dawns on him. The music rises to a crescendo, the boy's face is bathed in tears. (Peterson has been killed during the raid. Kirby has been surprised by an ominous, sucking noise, and has looked round to see his subordinate crucified on a spiked mantrap.)

Hamchunk runs down to the sea, followed slowly by Kirby. The boy stops to ask, 'Was my Peterson brave?' The Colonel answers, 'He was very brave. Are you going to be brave?' 'I'll try.'

This is the big moment. Everything revolves around these two, the little boy and the big, heavy man. It is sunset; the waves are growing darker. The colonel stoops to place a green beret on the boy's head, while Hamchunk is solemn and still. Then they walk off hand-in-hand, the colonel and the son of the regiment, along the shore to the right, towards the future. Music: 'The Ballad of the Green Berets.'

Still: The Green Berets – *Kirby and Beckworth.*

Hanoi, martes 13 diz.

Santiago Alvarez directed this Cuban film about Lyndon B. Johnson and the Democratic Republic of Vietnam in 1967. First, we are shown a hero in the battle for freedom: José Martí, the great Cuban writer and the country's first real revolutionary, who wrote in 1889 about Vietnam's traditions and her struggle for independence. Martí's words are read in a gentle, sensitive voice and accompanied by shots of heroes and holy men. The next sequence, in colour, emphasises the sensual nature of the Vietnamese people, their passion for freedom and their ability to fight. The commentary describes how the nation freed itself from the Burmese, the Khmers, and the Chinese.

Then a black title, dramatically large, zooms in threateningly: '*Nace un niño en Texas*' (A boy was born in Texas.) The year of his birth was 1908. With this, Alvarez changes to black and white. There is a montage of shock close-ups: the earth opening in a volcanic eruption – a woman in childbirth with the baby's head emerging – a cow giving birth – a buffalo in labour with four men violently tugging the calf free. Santiago Alvarez could be saying that the birth of this child is a great miracle, like the birth of any child, but there is already the suggestion of something monstrous. Alvarez's language is condensed. He uses surprising combinations of images, and moments of sarcasm.

Next, Lyndon Baines Johnson is two years old. (The camera zooms in on his picture.) His life is portrayed in press photographs taken at various ages, in assorted poses. He 'makes himself President' – we see him take the oath in Dallas. He steps out of a plane, raising his arm in a rather Hitlerian salute. He consults with the Asian Fascist, Cao Ky. This rapid accumulation of images carries the political implication that Lyndon Johnson is more or less a Fascist, and that he was behind the assassination of John F. Kennedy.

The section ends with grim scenes of demonstrations: police dragging away young men and women, security personnel with egg-stained clothes, black limousines, evil power hiding in fear of the people. Then the President again scornfully depicted in a montage of thoughtful poses, linked with pictures of clocks ticking away with a loud, hollow sound. The image we get of Lyndon Johnson is certainly not of a warm and spontaneous human being.

This violence is followed by a restful passage.

Stills, this page: Hanoi, martes 13 diz.

The ticking of the clocks leads up to a title: Hanoi, Tuesday the 13th.' The image is still, in slightly varying shades of grey, with water gently gliding to music by Debussy, boats, fishermen and their catch. The same calm seems to reign in the city itself. The camera moves among people eating, chatting and smiling. Then the countryside once more – women planting rice, men ploughing behind their oxen. They carry rifles on their backs, and at this moment the first American plane emitting a flame like a welding torch appears in the upper right-hand corner of the frame. This section of the film seems to slow and drawn-out, but the intrusion of the plane imparts a different feeling to the tranquillity. Alvarez wants to stress the peace-loving character of the Vietnamese people. He takes his time, and our initial reaction might be one of impatience; later, when the attack comes, we see it as a vicious act against people leading such a quiet, simple life. The mild shades of grey begin to seem defiant, representing a way of life which is bound to outlast the attacks. A new title fills the screen: 'We turn our hatred into energy.' Women are repairing a road with their bare hands. The words 'hatred into energy' are repeated once, twice, three times. A camouflaged train moves through the darkness. Faces are briefly illuminated. The force of resistance is marked by drums and percussion instruments.

Back in the North Vietnamese capital, on the morning of 13 December, a cleansing vehicle is at work in the streets. The camera moves among the people: school-children buying ice-cream, young mothers, cyclists, two soldiers walking hand-in-hand, girls giggling at a tramstop. The gravity of the situation is registered in the same forthright way; we witness the cementing of one-man bomb-shelters, concrete cylinders. A few moments are

spent in a department store, among crowds of people. There is a solitary dancing girl – we hear her song and guess at her movements, but the camera concentrates on her hand and we watch it for a few breathless seconds of tense concentration. The image crystallises the civilised refinement of this people. Then comes the explosion, this time closer and more violent. Five planes in formation roar through black smoke. The streets have gun-posts under the trees. Anti-aircraft rockets burst in the sky, spreading like drops of ink on a blotting paper. We see a little boy's anxious, watchful eyes. A missile traces a white zig-zag as it rises; then it slowly falls in a black line after finding its target. Afterwards, we are shown the smouldering houses, the stretchers, the dead and the survivors. Many of the victims are in a state of shock and unable to move, with staring eyes and gaping mouths. The music is shrill.

This view of everyday life in Hanoi is an accusation in itself, and all the more effective as no one raises his voice in accusation. Santiago Alvarez steps up the intensity. He shows us an old woman sitting resignedly in the midst of the devastation. A woman gives a puppy something to drink. Another has to be forcibly dragged away from the grave of her dead child. Unflinchingly, Alvarez cuts to a close-up of Lady Bird Johnson holding a movie camera and roaring with laughter. The effect is devastating, and although we don't feel she is laughing directly at the women of Hanoi, the implication is of a shameless lack of awareness.

Alvarez does not exploit opportunities for propaganda presented by the dead; we glimpse them only briefly. But the camera dwells on the shattered gods. A gutted pagoda with its damaged Buddhas. The association with Cardinal Spellman is stressed: his physical resemblance to Buddha, and the contrast between them. A catholic sanctuary in ruins and Spellman again, the man of God who blessed the weapons.

The climax is still to come. First we catch sight of General Westmoreland and Secretary of Defence McNamara. Then some dark, feverish pictures from Hanoi show captured American pilots moving like sleepwalkers

through rows of onlookers to the hysterical rhythm and bellowing laughter of Jerry Samuel's pop hit, 'They're coming to take me away, ha-ha.' Words, music and image merge into merciless satire on American ignorance, lack of dignity, megalomania. A pilot towers over the tiny, gentle people who have conquered him. Another captured superman sits, crestfallen, on the back of a farmer's cart. From there we switch to the coffins at Saigon airport, the military honours; the image shrinks and ends up inserted into the forehead of a pensive Lyndon Johnson. The end is harmonious, like the beginning: the same bright, gentle voice, the same warm colours.

Hanoi, martes 13 diz. is very much a Cuban film. It is Cuba's comment on US imperialism, and the scorn is Cuba's, not Vietnam's. At the same time, a clear parallel is conveyed between the two situations. Both Cuba and the Democratic Republic of Vietnam are autonomous Socialist states whose existence is threatened by the United States. Alvarez does not refer to the outside help which is important both to Havana and Hanoi. There is nothing about Russian arms shipments, or about China, apart from a brief mention of its imperialist past at the beginning of the film.

Stills. Below: Hanoi, martes 13 diz. *Right:* Omar Guevara and Jack Castro in Che!

Che!

In the days of McCarthyism, Michael Wilson was among the Hollywood scriptwriters blacklisted for their alleged communist sympathies. In 1968, he shared the script credit on Twentieth Century-Fox's *Che!* which starred Omar Sharif as Che Guevara, the world revolutionary. The use of a radical writer and a popular star might look like hypocrisy, but more likely reflects a genuine desire to be fair to Guevara before executing him. What we have here is certainly an execution – or at least an attempted one, because a myth is not going to be destroyed in a film which uses Omar Sharif as its embodiment. The idea of casting the actor who played Doctor Zhivago to be Che Guevara suggests, if not actual malice, a grotesque lack of judgment. It could even be a devious attempt to make Guevara appear absurd.

Similarly, other aspects of the film look like the product of conflict between conscious and unconscious intentions. On some issues, it manifests a curious sensitivity, which probably upset certain pressure groups in the United States. To judge from statements made by Sy Bartlett, the producer and joint scriptwriter, the film was not meant to be political but 'objective'. Maybe Mr Bartlett is actually as

150

naïve as this suggests. If so, his naïvety has in one respect helped to fulfil his (subconscious) political intentions.

Initially, the film does appear to be striving for an open-minded approach to Guevara's character and his historic role. It turns out to be based on interviews with eye-witnesses, even Castroites, who appear to be commenting in their own words on a series of real events. It creates a feeling of solidarity in the audience with the film and its eye-witnesses. This approach might seem courageous or generous or even like a straight search for the truth.

But this pseudo-solidarity is soon being used subtly, possibly subconsciously, for the purposes of persuasion. The film shows Guevara becoming increasingly isolated from his revolutionary comrades. This process has already begun during the guerilla war in Cuba with the hint that Che is conducting a private campaign of terror within his own ranks. After the guerillas have taken Havana, he stages courts martial. Later, the break is clearly defined when he disrupts Cuba's relations with the Soviet Union. It is reasonable to assume that when divisions appear in the film, the feeling of solidarity will also be shattered, causing Che to lose the audience's sympathy.

Fidel Castro (Jack Palance) is consistently drawn as a less significant character than Che. He may be calmer and more circumspect, but Che is the genius with strategic brilliance,

eloquence and vision. Fidel lacks the ambition for global revolution and Che's hatred of America. The Russian nuclear weapons, too, are Che's idea. The reduction of Fidel Castro to a jovial mediocrity is in itself quite a feat of political film-making. But he still seems like a decent fellow, not really guilty of any base deeds and certainly not fitting in with any bogey man image. This tribute at least should be paid to Sy Bartlett's naïve brand of honesty.

The audience's early support for the revolution is taken care of by the treatment of Guevara's activities in Bolivia. Back in Havana, Fidel is concerned that his friend might be losing his grip on reality. We see how unwelcome Che is in the Bolivian freedom movement, how he forces his way into houses and terrorises the occupants.

The Bolivian army which has been trained in accordance with Guevara's principles of guerilla warfare takes him prisoner, but 'the CIA was not involved in any way.' Before his execution, a goat-herd is taken to him by the army and told that Che has come to free him. 'To free me from what?' asks the old man; nobody has asked him what he wants. 'Ever since you came to these mountains with your guns and your fighting, my goats give no milk.' It is through the old goat-herd that the Guevara of the film is really executed. The execution of the myth is followed by the sound of the gunfire which kills the man.

The Aesthetics of Propaganda

Tolstoy wrote: 'Influence is not only a sure sign that something is art, but the degree of influence is also the only measure of the value of art'. Some decades later, a group of Tolstoy's compatriots attempted to adapt this thesis to cinematic theory and practice. They created the classic period of the Russian cinema and a completely new film aesthetic.

One remarkable aspect of their work was that their artistic principles grew from psychological rather than artistic speculation. Eisenstein and Pudovkin turned the director into a dictator able, by means of montage, to direct the audience's experience in the minutest detail – its field of vision, thoughts, associations, emotions and conclusions.

In the 'forties, the French critic André Bazin suggested an alternative in a somewhat belated attack on the totalitarian approach to films of the Russian authorities. Bazin attempted to formulate the aesthetics of a democratic cinema; he wanted a cinema in which reality was not as in the Russian films, robbed of all its complexity for the purpose of creating predetermined emotions and simple effects. Audiences should not have perceptions and reactions forced upon them but should be given freedom of choice and the opportunity to make up their own minds.

In recent years, film-makers all over the world have made movies – even political ones – that have been democratic in Bazin's sense of the word, movies that have questioned rather than asserted, reported rather than suggested, searched rather than directed. But propaganda has followed Eisenstein's road and not Bazin's. It cannot afford to be democratic. Its purpose is to *force* people into a specific commitment.

It would be misleading, however, to see the Russian theories as a *prerequisite* for the current form and aesthetics of film propaganda. The Russians formulated, analysed and developed principles which have always been more or less consciously applied by film propagandists – and would have continued to have been even without the theorists.

Russian theories of montage share the underlying assumption of propaganda films: that by manipulating the cinematic image of reality one can also manipulate the spectators' *concepts* of reality – i.e. the concepts on which they base their attitudes and actions.

In this, documentaries are no different from features. True, they deal with reality, but for the purposes of propaganda this is a distinct advantage: so authentically does documentary seem to mirror the audience's preconceptions that manipulation can be all the more easily concealed. The film-maker builds his own reality even when he seems to be working with objective facts.

British newsreel photographers filming at the front for *The Battle of the Somme* and other World War I documentaries would probably have denied that they were creating politically aimed propaganda (in spite of the fact that their films were considered an important means of strengthening morale on the home front). In one respect they had a considerably greater degree of honesty and objectivity than more recent documentaries on war; the authentic material was not subjected to the subtle slanting that goes with the elegantly confected narrative of a modern compilation film. The films were edited without any adjustments for dramatic or epic effect: one image followed another without any attempt at imposing artificial logic or continuity.

But their material was subjected to a very useful, albeit enforced, principle of selection. The films worked as propaganda because they showed the war solely from the viewpoint of their own side. The photographers got no further than their own front line; they could not register what was said, thought and suffered on the other side. Their picture of the war was possibly true, but it was literally only half the truth.

Selection and half truth are the corner-stones of propagandist documentary, and it is a psychological fact that half truths serve as well as whole truths in supporting cinematic illusions of what is real. The Russian masters of montage discovered that illusion could be solidly constructed out of small, carefully chosen and combined pieces. All that was unsuitable or accidental in reality could be eliminated at the cutting stage, and the effect of the images could be further loaded by rhythmic editing and a didactic approach.

With the coming of sound, documentarists gained the added resources of speakers' voices and musical accompaniment and documentary became even more effective as a political weapon. In Nazi Germany, at least as much importance was attached to newsreels as to feature films, and the Italian cinema during the

Fascist era was rarely propagandist except in its documentaries.

What was true of the front line reportage in World War I remains equally valid for these and other more recent exponents of the propaganda documentary: the veracity of individual images is rarely in doubt as reality is rich enough to provide authentic material for the most disparate interpretations The larger the area of reality the documentarist chooses to describe, the greater are his opportunities for selection and hence for apparently well documented exposition.

In the three first instalments of the American *Why We Fight* series, years of reality pass within the space of a couple of hours and the very density of the presentation precludes any feeling in the audience that some of the truth has been omitted The Nazi documentary *Sieg im Westen* (*Victory in the West*) shows how war can be depicted with authentic images without any suggestion of blood or death. From a comparison of these two efforts, we can see how convincing two diametrically opposed interpretations of the same series of historical events can appear when both are based on what we can actually see to be true with our own eyes. Equally, films about the Spanish Civil War emanating from different political

Still: mercenaries in Gualtiero Jacopetti's Africa Addio.

camps confirm that in any war there is enough material on both sides to enable documentary film-makers to create indignation without having to resort to untruths.

A documentary therefore does not have to be a work of total deception to present reality in the image that suits the director or his taskmasters. Of course, there are also cases of intentional deception, which audiences are unlikely to spot. A mutilated corpse looks much the same whichever side is responsible.

In 1960 the Congressional Committee on un-American Activities presented a documentary about the demonstrations that took place in San Francisco during its hearings that year. The film was called *Operation Abolition* and set out to prove that the demonstrations had been incited by communists and traitors. It was later shown that the shots of communist leaders, for instance, had been lifted from documentaries on a completely different event; one crowd looks pretty much like another.

A few days after the Normandy invasion, German audiences could see documentaries showing the Allies being driven back into the sea by the forces of the Reich. These newsreels actually showed the unsuccessful Allied landings at Dieppe a couple of years earlier.

Falsification can also be achieved by fixing things, reality itself, for the documentary camera to film. The most macabre example is not the notorious one of Gualtiero Jacopetti's

Africa Addio (1963) but a Nazi picture about Theresienstadt, *Der Führer schenkt den Juden eine Stadt* (*The Führer Gives the Jews a Town*, 1944). For a few days, things were doctored so to give the impression that the Jews at Theresienstadt were living in the most idyllic circumstances, that the German state had placed at their disposal a well-developed system of social services, that it had subsidised enjoyable leisure activities, and that every conceivable comfort went with this gift from Hitler to the Jews. For good measure, a Jewish inmate, Kurt Gerron, was chosen to direct the film. Afterwards he was executed.

Feature films do not have documentary's aura of authenticity (and its consequent moral problems). On the other hand, the feature director's resources are in principle unlimited, for he literally creates the film's reality to suit his purposes. Any lack of credibility can be compensated for by added intensity – and feature propaganda guards against any ambivalent reactions by seeking out the most fundamental human responses, the most basic value judgments, the most elementary emotions.

Watching a well constructed propaganda film can therefore be a peculiarly ambivalent experience. The political purpose might well be repulsive, but if one only considers what takes place and what is said and done in the *film*, one must, as a member of the audience, take the intended side. Propaganda films have good and evil so well ordered, with their well-defined characters and clear cut conflicts, that there is little choice but to react with the violent emotions that are called for.

It is of course the emotions, not the intellect, to which propaganda is addressed. Confident that people in an excited state are receptive to influences which would otherwise be subject to scrutiny, the propagandist does all he can to stir up emotions, the more easily to guide them towards his political goal.

When Eisenstein came to formulate his aesthetics in print, the theory of 'attraction' became one of his basic, albeit cryptically expressed, theses. The theory goes back to Eisenstein's pre-film activities as stage director and was born out of the need for sudden, shattering moments in the production, for shocks to provoke violent psychological reactions. These 'attractions' were intended to heighten the degree of the audience's involvement in much the same way as the most hazardous acrobatic acts in the circus. Applied to film the theory meant, in essence, that the attractions were to contribute towards generally building up emotional tension, hence emotional involvement which could then be guided.

Reduced to these terms, the attraction theory turns out to be less than mystifying, in fact

Still: Gustav Ucicky's Morgenrot.

merely one of the basic tenets of all propaganda films. Traditionally the genre has worked on the realisation (whether rational or instinctive) that propaganda has no impact unless it is working on powerful emotions. However, one type of film propaganda deviates to a certain extent from the general pattern. Social realism in the Soviet Union and other eastern European countries was often characterised by a form of puritanism over the use of attractions which rather sympathetically (if precariously from the point of view of effectiveness) eschewed any short cuts to audience involvement. Otherwise, within this art form, which is so well equipped to work on the emotions, hardly any genre has speculated with such a sense of purpose and such lack of prejudice as the propaganda film has in all kinds of emotional attractions.

The favourite emotion here is indignation, as it contains within the same moment of experience both the requisite force and the required bias, leaving no room for moral ambivalence. But even if indignation is one characteristic element of propaganda, it constitutes something of a special case in emotional manipulation. The emotions on which propaganda operates do not need to be intrinsically tendentious. They make up the motive force behind the audience's involvement, the direction can be guided by other elements.

Thus it is perhaps only natural that the great exponents of melodrama are among the most successful propagandist directors (D. W. Griffith, Leni Riefenstahl, Veit Harlan, Michael Curtiz, etc.) Because of the way in which propaganda has developed, the ability to heighten emotional tension has become more important as an asset than political knowledge. Surprise, menace, adventure, love and death – these and other gripping attractions of melodrama expand, in propaganda, into a great sounding board for the message.

Eroticism is a key source of inspiration for melodrama and consequently one of the major catalysts in the emotional laboratory of propaganda. Its applications are legion.

Nazi propaganda, for example, used the emotive value of love stories with great consistency and clarity, to suggest a hierarchy of values connecting love and politics. Love was conceded as a positive factor and propaganda stories were structured to subordinate it to something even more elevated – loyalty to Hitler and death for the fatherland. If two sympathetic young men compete for the affections of the same blonde girl in a Nazi film, it may well be fascinating to discover who gets her, but for example in Gustav Ucicky's *Morgenrot* (*Dawn*, 1933), in *Kampfgeschwader Lützow* (*Bomber Squadron Lützow*, 1941) or in Günther Rittau's *U-Boote westwärts* (*U-Boats Westwards*, 1941) it is the rejected suitor who becomes undisputed hero by winning a prize greater than a woman's love: heroic martyrdom, the intrinsic emotional value of which is here heightened by the love interest.

From a vast multitude of possible examples, one which rewards closer examination is an American picture on the Korean War, Tay Garnett's *One Minute to Zero* (1952). It is virulently anti-communist and superficially appears to be filled with detestation for the war, but beneath this run sophisticated emotional undercurrents – among them the love-story involving Robert Mitchum and Ann Blyth. It is 1950 and Mitchum is colonel of a small UN battalion suddenly faced with the task of establishing a South Korean defence system capable of protecting the existing border against attacks from the north. He meets Blyth, who is working there as a nurse, when the war breaks out. Later, during an enemy bombing raid, their unspoken love is awakened; for the first time they touch. During the fighting Mitchum is wounded and ends up in her care, but he also learns that she is married. Before he returns to the front, they dine together, and over the soup our heroine tells him that her husband was killed in World War II. Over the coffee they kiss, but when it is time to part, she tells him with tears in her eyes that she cannot marry a soldier again and live once more with the fear that her husband might be killed. The lovers are alienated when Blyth watches Mitchum ordering his troops to open fire on a column of fleeing North Koreans. But the more she sees of the war, the stronger her conviction grows that Mitchum acted correctly, and with this her love grows even stronger. She promises to marry him at the moment that he is promoted for his valour.

The subtlety of this story lies in the way that the love interest continually lends added emotional value to war. War that brings the couple together. War, it is revealed, has killed her husband, thereby making it allowable for them to be in love. War gives him the wounds that provide her with the opportunity of caring for him. War convinces her of the inevitability of their love having given urgency to their relationship through an emotional crisis. War gives Mitchum both social status and a wife. Their love is blessed by the war and conversely sanctifies it at every moment of stress, because the audience wants a happy ending to the love-story and the means to provide it is the war.

Love, though, can be dangerous. It can be used as a weapon by the enemy. During the Cold War, for instance, a common plot variation on both sides was to let the hero fall in love with a woman who turned out to be an enemy spy. The revelation is certainly painful, but in the shock lies an emotional charge, an 'attraction' in Eisenstein's sense of the word. The emotional force behind the message becomes even more powerful when political rectitude violently overcomes love, when the partisan woman shoots her lover because he is a German infiltrator or a Czarist officer – respectively in Ivan Pyriev's *Secretary of the District Committee* (1942) and both versions of *The Forty-First*.

But love is usually a great ally of right, and its victory can bring political triumph. It can stand for a symbolic union of two opposed camps in the face of a common enemy, as when liberalism and socialism, personified by Tallulah Bankhead and John Hodiak, are brought together by love in Alfred Hitchcock's *Lifeboat* (1943), or when capital and labour unite against Marxism in the Norwegian Walter Fyrst's Nazi picture, *Unge Viljer* (1943). It conquers frontiers when it wins over Greta Garbo, the Soviet commissar, from Communism in Ernst Lubitsch's *Ninotchka* (1939), or the camp commandant from Nazism in Hasse Ekman's *Excellensen* (1944).

Both the bliss and the pain of love evoke emotional reaction which can be harnessed politically. In war, love becomes afflicted by death and separation; bliss and pain fuse together into one of the most diligently exploited of propaganda's emotional weapons. Love in the face of death can be used to create feelings that go far beyond simple pathos. One standard pattern is to let love awaken and grow at the moment that danger is at its height, when death is nearest and emotional preparedness at its most intense in both the characters and the audience: all the emotional forces are brought together into a single strand ready to be exploited.

Love appears as a positive political force in films from most countries, though predictably with greater emphasis and frequency in films from the United States, which more than any other country has given Love a pre-eminent value in its fictional mythology. Love turns up in Russian films, too, but more as a supplementary theme than as one of central concern. It appears as a tender feeling, vulnerable to loss, a loss which has to be revenged. It is something to be sealed by Stalin, which unites people in their struggle to build a better society, a small alliance within the larger one of the collective.

The puritanical modesty with which it is handled sometimes verges on the comic. But this puritanical streak is not specific to Russian film propaganda, because just as Pure Love is a positive concept, Desire is an almost universal sign of evil.

In the early 'thirties, when Nazism was constructing an ideal image of itself in films like *Hans Westmar* and *Hitlerjunge Quex* (both from 1933), the aversion to sex was particularly striking. Hans Westmar, the flawless young leader, is above all private emotional ties and bodily desires. He is repelled by the moral depravity of Weimar, and spurns the approaches of a rich German-American woman so that he can give the Movement all the concentration and energy which his young body can muster. Heini in *Hitlerjunge Quex*, though a bit younger, is no less contemptuous of the rather promiscuous life led by the group of young Communists and, significantly, the only member of the Hitlerjugend to be tempted by the desires of the flesh is the one who smokes, wears his uniform sloppily and in the end betrays the Nazis to the Communists.

In the American cinema, sexual appetite was long attributed only to the blacks plus, during World War I, German officers whose only desire in life was to rape American innocents. Ever since, the rape motif has been a favourite source of indignation, reinforcing the genre's hostility towards sex. But this puritanism in propaganda is a subtle form of double morality. The anti-semitism in Veit Harlan's *Jud Süss* is among the many examples of committed pornography, and it is ironic but entirely logical

Stills. Top left: sex and anti-semitism – Ferdinand Marian as the lecherous Jud Süss. Left: love and politics – Grigori Chukhrai's The Forty-First *(centre); Tallulah Bankhead and John Hodiak in Alfred Hitchcock's* Lifeboat. *Below: Lewis Milestone's* Halls of Montezuma.

that the actor Ferdinand Marian who played the lecherous Jew received a vast amount of fan-mail, mostly from women. Anger apart, such films also profit from the physiological excitement stirred up by rape fantasies.

Puritanical tendencies were most systematically worked out in the early Nazi movies, which consistently preached a strict pattern of clean living – there is an ancient mystical connection between asceticism and power. Not that the Nazi cinema lacked erotic overtones: in the parades, the shining boots, the fondness for uniform, the power mystique, and the charismatic leader concept, Nazi propaganda possessed a diffuse but very real sexual quality – an ecstatic sublimation of sex drives, a channelling of erotic power towards Party symbols and Führer figures.

Nazi film propaganda differs in degree but not in kind from the latent eroticism of some other examples. Exhibitions of violence and demonstrations of strength in themselves have arousing qualities. The physical ability to excel, the mechanical precision of shooting, the machine-like potency are not simply evidence of overwhelming strength but have a euphoric quality. The aesthetics of power in war films have their own libidinous overtones: there are curious elements of sexual ecstasy in the thrust of torpedoes, the roaring elegance of the parabolas described by rockets, and the apocalyptic beauty of the fires after bombing raids.

Occasionally these particular elements in the aesthetics of war are cultivated into a veritable choreography. The Nazi film *Stukas*, the Russian *Battle of Stalingrad* and the American *Halls of Montezuma* have different chauvinistic points of departure, but they all contain remarkable sequences combining images, cutting, music and the sound and fury of battle into an orgiastic ballet of rhythms, stylised form and symphonic exaltation. In moments like these, when the gory reality is abstracted into pure

form, propaganda gives its most extreme demonstration of just how irrational emotional suggestion can be allowed to become in the cause of patriotism.

The effects of rhythm perhaps offer the simplest illustration of how a heightened emotional level functions in purely physiological terms to reinforce a particular tendency. Russian montage of the Eisenstein and Pudovkin vintage has come to be identified above all by the frenzied tempo of its images. Undoubtedly the optical fury of visual stimuli changing at violent speed had in itself an exciting effect which could then be guided by other and emotionally more distinct factors. Sound brought with it certain limitations in the scope of montage, but accelerated cutting still retained its popularity as a propaganda device. It was employed with particular effectiveness by the Cuban Santiago Alvarez in his anti-American film *NOW* (1965) which bombards the viewer with briefly glimpsed, indignation-producing images of American racism; the montage pulsates to the rhythm and the steady *crescendo* of 'Hava nageela', sung as a protest song by Lena Horne.

The *crescendo* form is a natural one for propaganda films. Aided by the rhythm of images and music emotions are awakened, gathered and heightened towards a climax. Eisenstein has explained how carefully he used the method of progressive repetition on several levels in *Battleship Potemkin*: 'From a tiny cellular organism of the battleship to the organism of the entire battleship; from a tiny cellular organism of the fleet to the organism of the whole fleet – thus flies through the theme the revolutionary feeling of brotherhood.'

Both Russian revolutionary cinema and early Nazi films offer some outstanding examples of the slow build-up of involvement towards a final culmination which appears to gather together and reinforce the whole spectrum of emotions previously aroused but not fully exploited. Without such psychological tactics as these, there are propaganda films that have come unstuck by going flat out and demanding a fully developed emotional involvement from the start, leaving themselves without the chance to build it up. The Chinese documentary *Chairman Mao is the Red Sun in Our Hearts* (1966) is clearly made in the certainty that the audience is already so well geared emotionally in favour of Mao Tse-tung it is ready to respond ecstatically from the very beginning of the film, which presents an endless, enthusiastic crowd of people. It lacks a progressive build-up towards ecstasy and thereby remains monotonous and unengaging for those who do not have the required *a priori* bias.

Stills: solidarity. Below: Battleship Potemkin. *Right:* Aufstand der Fischer (*top*), L'Espoir (*bottom*).

A favourite propagandist motif and one which seems to work with the same emotive force every time it recurs, originates in the Russian cinema's effective use of the crowd. It appears to start in 1925 with Eisenstein's *Battleship Potemkin* and Pudovkin's *Mother*. A small group of people come together and walk towards a goal; they are joined by increasing numbers until the little group has swelled into a vast mass moving forward. The emotions of these people reach out to the spectator and grip him in a way that can only be explained as an instinctive experience of solidarity, not necessarily with the message of the people but with their enthusiasm, and it seems as if the actual growth from group into crowd is the active element, just as the *crescendo* is more suggestive than the *fortissimo*. The motif crops up in a number of Socialist films and eventually reaches its most graphic and meaningful expression in André Malraux's *L'Espoir* (1938). Curiously enough, the growing collective does not necessarily have to consist of people to obtain the desired effect: in *Mrs Miniver* it is the boats coming together in a steadily growing armada, the highly emotional sequence before the miracle of Dunkirk. Nazi film propaganda, which in many respects adopted and revamped formal and psychological ideas from the

Stills. Below: René Clement's La Bataille du rail. *Right: Mark Donskoi's* The Rainbow.

Russian cinema, made use of this motif in a number of films, often expressing it in a visionary, surrealist manner, accompanied by a rising flood of martial music.

Even *Battleship Potemkin* originally had its own music, specially composed by Edmund Meisel. This has long since vanished, but rumour has it that its power in arousing an audience was so great that it was even banned in certain countries where the film itself was shown.

There is, however, no need to rely on hearsay to appreciate the significance of music in emotional manipulation. It has the ability, so valuable in propaganda, to slip past the spectator's consciousness, to comment, sentimentalise and dramatise without being noticed.

The effectiveness of music naturally depends on current convention. Consequently what was once powerfully persuasive may now seem simply ridiculous, because the cinema has adopted new musical principles. Many patriotic films from World War II are virtually drowned by a bombastic score that has to do for intimate details as well as for sweeping panoramas. The German documentary *Blitzkrieg* (1939) is not an isolated instance; its many curiosities include a fanfare suddenly ringing out from the musical background to lend an air of solemn festivity to the moment when the Führer tastes the soldiers' soup. The rousing panoramic sweep is there too, and turns up in virtually all Nazi

documentaries and Ufa newsreels. They brimmed over with martial music, which ground on ceaselessly to create a state of emotional intoxication. This may well have been effective *at that time*. Today this apparently fatal misuse of sound seems to stand only for megalomania, insensitivity and murderousness.

But not all Nazi film music was monotonously ear-splitting; it could occasionally be seductively refined. The propaganda in 'unpolitical' entertainment films was hard to discern but often masterly and frequently achieved its effect through an elaborate use of music. One such film, the highly popular *Wunschkonzert* (1940), largely owes its emotional power to the music, which is part of one of the most sublimely extravagant excesses of heroism in the history of the cinema. Surrounded by crackling fires, a German soldier sits at night in a bombed-out church, playing the organ so that its sound can guide a lost patrol back through minefields and enemy artillery fire. But when his friends have returned safely, thanks to his help, he gets hit by a grenade and slumps down over the keys as the final chord rings out across the sombre, ruined landscape. This heroic death in music is unforgettable, its effect impossible to convey in words.

But then the content and implications of music are notoriously hard to describe in words, though a few points about the aesthetics of music in propaganda movies are worth noting.

No other genre makes such extensive use of ready-made music – no other genre has such a need to use emotional attitudes sufficiently institutionalised to have their own musical symbols. Patriotic marches and national anthems become signature tunes of good or evil forces. In Nazi films, the heroes operate to the accompaniment of the Horst Wessel Lied, 'Deutschland, Deutschland über alles' and 'Wir fahren gegen Engeland' ('We're on our way to England') – tunes to stir up emotions called for by the fatherland and the idea of national revenge. On the other side, the American fleet goes into battle against the Japanese and other threats to the Free World, the sounds of 'Halls of Montezuma', 'Anchors Aweigh' or 'The Battle Hymn of the Republic' burst forth – *They Were Expendable* has all three.

Conversely, the enemy's musical themes can be turned against him. In René Clement's *La Bataille du rail* (1945), for instance, ironic or gloating pastiches of the Horst Wessel Lied keep popping up in the score as the French Resistance sabotages German trains, and in Mark Donskoi's anti-Nazi *The Rainbow* (1944), distorted versions of the German national anthem are heard as German soldiers assault children, women and old people. This is an astute attempt at making the action seem representative – the national anthem generalises the brutality of isolated soldiers to make it seem characteristic of the whole German nation.

When Bertil Malmberg and Hasse Ekman appeal for moral preparedness in *Excellensen* (1944), they do not have to say in so many words where the terror is taking place, for the credits are accompanied by scarcely camouflaged variations on the theme of 'Deutschland über alles'. In the final scene, however, when His Excellency, after having been tortured by the Fascists, dies a sacrificial death, an invisible choir is to be heard singing 'Ave Maria'.

Such heavenly choirs appear in propaganda films with unparalleled frequency. The genre does not attain its full splendour until it has succeeded in mobilising emotions connected with the hereafter. The trilling of heavenly voices invests the message with an extra-terrestrial level of authority which cannot be given either by instrumental music or by a spoken commentary. Even a film with as great a sense of authenticity as Gillo Pontecorvo's *La Battaglia di Algeri* (1966) enshrouds the struggle for freedom in celestial voices to infuse it with transcendental value: the Algerians' sacrifices are holy; their cause is 'good' almost in a religious sense.

In Fred Zinnemann's anti-Nazi movie *The Seventh Cross* (1944), there is a unique attempt at spiritualising a *spoken* commentary. The speaker's voice turns out to belong to someone who dies early in the film but goes on commenting on the action from above. His judgments are somehow raised to a level that is beyond question, and even if this particular gimmick can hardly be recommended for imitation, Zinnemann manages to avoid any comic side effects.

More frequent use is obviously made of earthly commentaries for shaping the audience's conclusions, particularly in documentaries which, unlike features, have conventionally provided narration with their images. Comments can be made, explanations offered and conclusions drawn, insuring that the ambivalences of reality do not allow the audience to stray into political confusion. This may not merely be wise but possibly necessary, as the average spectator rarely draws conclusions or constructs generalisations from the isolated phenomena presented on the screen, at least beyond the degree to which he is already convinced. The decisive importance of the commentary to the message is clearly demonstrated by the ease with which visual material from *Triumph of the Will* has been used for anti-Nazi purposes.

Possibly the most effective and elaborate propaganda commentaries in documentary can be found in the films made around 1960 by Andrew and Annalie Thorndike and their colleagues in East Germany – for instance in *Unternehmen Teutonenschwert* (Operation Teutonic Sword) and *Aktion J*, in which the speaker's voice may be bitingly ironical but remains authoritative – low-keyed but intense, witty and engaging. But more often one has cause to be amazed that commentaries are so

bombastic that they are more liable to dull than to inform. It seems to reflect an effort by the propaganda documentary to find some form of emotional heightening to complement the visual actuality. The same emotional considerations apply to documentaries as to fiction.

In fiction, though, there is another convention available for providing the audience with an easily assimilated summary of the message going outside a naturalistic framework. In an emotional equivalent to the moral of old-fashioned cautionary tales, one of the most forceful propaganda techniques is to include a stirring appeal delivered by the hero or heroine within the framework of the story but intended directly for the audience. When Ann Blyth is ostensibly talking to God in *One Minute to Zero*, she is in fact preaching an anti-communist sermon to the audience. And when Walter Pidgeon, in *Man Hunt*, expresses his passionate condemnation of Hitler and Nazism, he is addressing himself less to the SS man, George Sanders, than to the spectator. However, these sequences often tend to break the stylistic unity of the film: the image suddenly becomes immobile, shot head-on, and the words become unrelievedly solemn. Anti-fascist propaganda from Britain and the United States contains the most numerous and eloquent examples of such addresses to the spectator, whether pleas on behalf of the oppressed or calls for revenge, or even rhetorical masterpieces in the tradition of

Stills. Left: the Führer in action from Triumph of the Will *via* Why We Fight. *Above: George Sanders and Walter Pidgeon in Fritz Lang's* Man Hunt. *Right: Charles Chaplin as The Great Dictator.*

Lincoln, which in the dark days of World War II qualified as universal affirmations of faith in democracy. The best known of these speeches to the audience is in *The Great Dictator*, where Chaplin seems to step out of his role turning to the audience to deliver an impassioned address to the whole democratic world. The comedian gives way to Chaplin the man, who with unconcealed emotion puts all his personal authority behind the message.

Propaganda has always exploited the personal popularity of cinematic idols, thus drawing on credentials from outside the film itself. From Sarah Bernhardt to John Wayne, stars have by their mere presence guaranteed the validity of political messages. They bring with them the charismatic glamour of their earlier roles, and their popularity gives rise to their status as political authorities. This irrational transfer of prestige has lately turned up in reality as well as fiction in the United States, with former stars going into politics.

In propaganda movies, as in other genres, actors take similar parts in one film after another, not simply from force of habit but so that the actor's established image can lend the

role appropriate and already existing associations. Especially in Hollywood, where the star system and the type-casting have been carried to the greatest lengths, constant repetition invests some screen characterisations with an almost ritualistic constancy.

But it is not only in the heroic roles that the movies use actors in this way to generate associations, and type-casting is just as applicable to heavies as to heroes. In wartime, immigrant actors are obviously the most suitable personifications of 'the foreigners', and each is usually of either distinctly positive or distinctly negative character. Thus, from 1940 onwards, the role of Vladimir Sokoloff in American political films was always that of the kindly old man suffering under the terrorist regime; his comedy equivalent was Felix Bressart.

In a couple of extreme cases, political links have been established in macabre contexts: it is hardly a coincidence that Bela Lugosi, the vampire of the Dracula films, was cast as a Russian commissar in *Ninotchka*, or that the refugee actor Conrad Veidt, with his equally horrific screen past, seemed towards the end of his life to personify the Gestapo fantasies of American movies.

As the mechanism of propaganda seems to favour the linking of certain actors to certain roles, it is not surprising that some political figures are customarily portrayed in the cinema by particular actors. Kaiser Wilhelm was caricatured in several American films during World War I, almost always by the same actor, Rupert Julian. In the Soviet cinema, Mikhail Gelovani played the lead in the majority of the pictures glorifying Stalin, while the part of Lenin has had two great specialist interpreters, Boris Shtyukin (who died in 1937) and Maxim Straukh. Between 1920 and 1940, the German Otto Gebühr devoted himself almost exclusively to one part, Frederick the Great, whom he was called upon to portray in about fifteen films; indeed he appeared as the Prussian military genius in every single German film made about him during the years of growingly militant nationalism.

Propaganda does not rely solely on spoken rhetoric: it employs its own visual equivalent. Indeed, with its need for strong emotional appeal, the propaganda film depends on a particular solemnity of visual style, which preserves the genre's rhetorical character even when the rest of the cinema is finding new stylistic forms.

One might ask whether this characteristic always serves propaganda well. Visual rhetoric may easily be accompanied by a sense of formal emptiness, and emotional distancing can replace the required involvement. Eisenstein's failure with *October* was at least partially due to the coldly aesthetic effect of the picture's formal complexities which went right over the heads of the mass audience. His younger compatriot, Mikhail Kalatozov, treated the preliminaries of the Cuban revolution in a similar manner when he made *Soy Cuba!* on location there in 1963. In Kalatozov's hands the revolution turns into grand opera: the gestures are violently exaggerated, the compositions are elaborately expressionist, the camera-movements are full of virtuosity for its own sake, the symbols are overplayed, the visual rhythm chaotic. *Soy Cuba!* is more emotional in form than any other revolutionary film, but its rhetoric is always hollow. It was received with great scepticism in Cuba.

In studies of film aesthetics, propaganda movies tend to be the chief source of examples to illustrate the camera's role in imposing a view of its subjects upon the audience (e.g. low angle to give an impression of power; high angle to give an impression of insignificance, etc.). They would very likely do as well in providing examples of the use of visual symbols and metaphors as well as of various other cinematic figures of style.

Indeed, propaganda films might be said to be rhetorical figures in themselves. Since the aim of the genre to create suitable generalisations out of the isolated incidents shown, events and leading characters always represent more than

Stills. Left: Vladimir Sokoloff (right) in Song of Russia. *Right: Conrad Veidt and Peter Lorre in* All Through The Night. *Below:* We From Kronstadt.

just themselves. They invariably stand for some larger concept – a collective, a movement, an ideology, a nation, an enemy. Thus every propaganda film, as well as every hero and every villain in it, is *per se* a synecdoche.

Theoreticians have often considered the emotional charge carried by objects on the screen because of the sentimental associations they have acquired in the course of a film. Propa-

ganda has borrowed this melodramatic device and refined it to perfection, linking objects with patriotic and heroic qualities and thus equipping them to function as emotional reminders. The method has a special application to sacrificed heroes: when they die their spirit is seen to live on through some particularly evocative object. In the Soviet film *We From Kronstadt*, three caps are quietly washed ashore after the sailors from Kronstadt have been drowned at sea by the White terrorists.

The most important objects in propaganda, however, already possess a firmly established emotional charge and even some magical significance: emblems, standards and flags – patriotic symbols. During World War I, the dignity of the Star-Spangled Banner was exploited with such cynicism by the American cinema that even the most rabid patriots saw it as an insult to the sacredness of the flag. But flags are used as fetishes in all types of film propaganda, even if their visual magic has various forms in different countries. In later American films, national symbols are there as an identification mark with emotional overtones, as a visual fanfare or a final vignette, but rarely as important elements in the drama itself. Nazi films, on the other hand, incorporated their emblems in the action as

Stills. Below: Alexander Nevsky – *the Knights of the Teutonic Order in white. Right:* Ernst Thälmann – Sohn seiner Klasse.

monumental and curiously potent sources of power. In the Soviet cinema, too, the flag becomes a powerful element in the revolutionary fervour – but the people who carry it are more important than their symbol.

Eisenstein attempted to increase the emotional effect of the flag in *Battleship Potemkin* by hand-colouring it red. Ten years later, Nikolai Ekk gave a classic demonstration of the emotional use of colour in *Women's Revolt*: when a woman worker is wounded by a bullet, the blood slowly turns her head-scarf red to provide what is ultimately used as the flag of the uprising.

Later attempts at planning colour schemes to add to the emotional range of the propaganda film include Kurt Maetzig's biographical *Ernst Thälmann* (in two parts, 1954 and 1955). This is carefully constructed to a political colour scheme in which red goes with positive, elevated, Communist contexts, while its complement, green, occurs as far as possible only in 'negative' scenes. Thus Thälmann's heroic walk to his death in the concentration camp is staged all in red, creating a rather odd impression but clearly intended to give his martyrdom a positive emotional value.

The psychological effect of colour is a difficult subject, and Maetzig's symbolism hardly achieves its purpose. The meanings that might be attributed to particular colours are scarcely due to any inherent qualities in the colours

themselves, but rather to the associations obtained through their frequent use in symbolic contexts. This may be a truism, but one can doubt that colour can be separated from this symbolic context, as in *Ernst Thälmann*, without losing its emotional effect. A film like *Chairman Mao Is the Red Sun In Our Hearts* does, however, succeed in conveying a remarkable effect of unity by the constant dominance of red. The décor framing parades and mass rallies is all red: a dense mass of red flags, tens of thousands of people waving the little red books. The colour seems to carry the revolutionary feeling in the film, not because red has an intrinsic revolutionary quality but because it is the colour in which all revolutionary gestures and symbols are dressed.

It would be wrong to suggest that it is usual for colour to play a major role in guiding the emotions. The exception is the opposition of black and white. Among the films that have tried to exploit politically the accepted moral associations of darkness and light, one might note a weird picture called *Address Unknown* (William Cameron Menzies, 1944), in which propaganda operated on a carefully worked-out formal basis and attempted to give Nazism a demonic quality by playing dramatically on the contrast between black and white. In this sort of symbolism, the East German picture *So macht man Kanzler* (1961) goes even further, marking its rejection of Hitler and Adenauer by

showing them in negative as they make speeches on freedom and peace. Here, however, the technique works more on the intellectual level of metaphor than through its emotional effect.

Not even the direct contrast of light and dark, is limited to its traditional meaning. In some of the most elaborate war films, the conventional meanings of light and dark have been inverted. Eisenstein's *Alexander Nevsky* (1938), Hans Steinhoff's *Ohm 'Krüger* (1941) and Veit Harlan's *Der grosse König* (1942) all consciously allow light shades to represent the enemy and dark ones the heroes. Here it is not any quality intrinsic to the particular colours that is significant but the visual emphasis given to the conflict by the contrasting tones.

This accentuation of contrasts is perhaps the most outstanding stylistic device in propaganda. Strong contrasts carry a greater emotional force than subtle shading: they speak with greater clarity, and direct the audience's sympathies with more certainty. It is not surprising to find that Eisenstein's theoretical writing also goes into the significance of contrasts in film aesthetics, for conflict to him was the very essence of art. Just as the play of thesis and antithesis is the fundamental principle of dialectical materialism, so Eisenstein, as a Marxist, saw contrasts as the basic element of film dynamics. He held, for instance, that contrasts and conflicts of movement, depth, direction, volume, rhythm and lighting, were visual aids activating the spectator's *intellect* in the influencing process.

Though it is as difficult here as elsewhere to follow and be persuaded by Eisenstein's arguments, formal contrasts certainly do work as a method of labelling and clarification in propaganda films. The most powerful contrasting effects, however, operate more on an emotional than on a formal level, where they can be given an incisiveness that leaves no room for doubt in the minds of the audience. The genre is full of confrontations between good and evil, beauty and ugliness, purity and filth, order and chaos, poverty and abundance, idyllic past and menacing present – or between past suppression and present prosperity. In each case, the contrast serves to force the spectator into an inevitable and unequivocal commitment.

In this ultimate purpose, propaganda is aided by man's underlying psychological need for moral value judgments in simple black-and-white terms. This need is particularly apparent in attitudes to political issues which are too complex and too momentous for most people's psychological resources, and which can only be coped with on a much simplified, ritual level. It is often in the interest of the authorities to preserve this state of affairs, and the machinery of propaganda uses it to provide the audience with simple, emotionally satisfying ideas worked out in concrete terms.

Politics are thus reduced to a magic game in which unequivocal moral signals are substituted for ideologies and where there is no room for rational argument among the emotional manipulation. Propaganda is particularly fascinating, though, for its orchestration of the emotions. No other film genre uses such an overwhelming range of emotional artillery or plays with such uninhibited abandon on the whole emotional register of the spectator, from the most superficial to the most profound, from the most primitive to the most spiritual.

Of course, the films are in no way consistently successful in achieving their aims, but when they do succeed and when they reach an audience whose emotions are already geared to the objectives of the film, they are able to offer a degree of emotional ecstasy which no other genre can achieve. Magical powers are invoked along with erotic forces at various levels of subtlety. Religious feeling merges with patriotic enthusiasm. The sense of fellowship is heightened as indignation is stirred up. All manner of tensions are aroused to be resolved in an often orgasmic climax which unites fervour from every source to ring out in unison for The Cause.

It is said that Eisenstein, to whom we have referred so extensively in the preceding pages, was toying with the idea of filming 'Das Kapital'. For some reason this plan never materialised – regrettably if only on the grounds of sheer curiosity. A film of 'Das Kapital' would have had a unique position in the emotion-charged history of the political cinema.

From Personality Cult to Apotheosis

Apotheosis, according to the dictionary, means 'deification', but the word is also used for rather less elevated forms of glorification. The apotheosising ceremony of the Romans contained a solemn scene, a kind of magic ritual in which a waxen image of the dead ruler was burnt and an eagle released to fly up, as it were, from the flames.

Apotheosis in our times occurs above all in the mass media and operates on much the same principle as in ancient Rome – a transient image must be sacrificed in order for the apotheosis to take effect. The subject's photographic image must be retouched and enlarged, his biography rewritten, with certain details deleted and others given added emphasis. The 'making' of a political leader or a pop star is equivalent to marketing a product, with the same need to highlight virtues and hide defects. The idol becomes a commodity, and at times a conflict may arise between the product and the person, a schizophrenia which can be destructive (as in the case of Marilyn Monroe). Now it is quite possible that we could tolerate the truth about our idol which is likely to consist of a perfectly normal conglomerate of conflicting qualities. But if our heroes were represented simply as themselves, they would look just like us and could not become objects for adoration.

The public relations firms and propaganda ministries that create these ghost images are frequently subtle in their sales technique. A demonstration of the idol's naturalness, even ordinariness, becomes an important part of the apotheosis; he could be anybody, but at the same time he is something more. The president bends down to pat a child on the head, and the camera catches the gesture. The boxing champion has a soft heart and loves his mother – or so the tabloids tell us. Through these snippets of information or pseudo-information the person briefly comes down to our level. For a personality to be turned into an idol, an element of identification with him must be established in the emotional responses of a large public.

The idol's image and relationship with the

public cannot purely be manufactured by highly paid specialists; in certain situations, they seem to come about unaided. In times of political crisis, people's need for reassurance increases. Given these conditions, a political leader can become a kind of father substitute. A Churchill or a Stalin inspires confidence through his own assurance, his common sense and massive unflappability, or rather through the public projections of these qualities, whether real or attributed.

At various times, the cinema has been used to build up an idol, a leader figure, or to reinforce an accepted image (and equally, though this belongs in a different chapter, to establish and confirm negative images or caricatures). To this personality-cult cinema belong the romanticised biographies, all those highly coloured accounts of the lives of kings, generals, scientists, poets, painters, composers, actors, sportsmen, film stars and – occasionally – politicians.

In a remarkable essay entitled 'The Stalin Myth in the Soviet Cinema' (1950), André Bazin briefly touches on this interesting topic. He finds that certain specific conditions apply to this form of secular hagiography. The apotheosis, he writes, 'can succeed only when it concerns persons already deified in the mind of the public.' They must be figures of indisputable greatness, idols who have either had their greatness confirmed through death or have finished with public life and can be regarded almost as living legends.

These considerations might of course be commercially based; films, after all, are usually a gamble on safe cards. But there are also widely prevalent inhibitions which make apotheoses of living people seem doubtful propositions. There have been exceptions, and Bazin's essay goes on to discuss the most remarkable of them, concerning Stalin.

Bazin's observation seems correct: filmmakers are unwilling to represent living people on a superhuman scale. This surprising modesty is difficult to explain in view of the lack of inhibition with which the personality cult is pursued in the life style associated with the film industry. It might have something to do with Western individualism, with the democratic ideal of equality (contradicted by our needs for gods and idols) or with the competitive instinct – on film, the great one becomes too great. There need be no limits to his greatness once he is dead and no longer in a position to compete.

The taboo might also be due to a vague fear of conflict with Christian ideas of God. The boxer Marcel Cerdan, who took part in two idolising films about himself, was not competing with God, as his superiority was clearly contained within a specific field. On the other hand, through the frighteningly incontrovertible nature of the cinema, a Charles de Gaulle might be turned into something laughable, whether a political Père Ubu or a political Monsieur Hulot. However, he could also be elevated above all debate, above things ephemeral. But this cannot be, for it would be an act against the individual voter, even against God. Perhaps this form of fiction is impracticable when the fictional image can be compared with the authentic one? We have learned to study images critically. Twenty years before Eisenstein, Lucien Nonguet made a short reconstructing the mutiny on the Battleship Potemkin. 'Since that time', writes André Bazin, 'we have learned to distinguish between document and reconstruction and learned to prefer an authentic image, even when it is incomplete and imperfect, to a re-creation, be it ever so perfect.'

An apotheosis can also be achieved by arranging documentary images around a commentary. Again, such compilations tend to be retrospective. A few months after the Dallas shooting, an American film of this kind was made about John F. Kennedy, *Years of Lightning – Day of Drums*. It is an album of moving pictures, rhapsodic without any profound characterisation or any attempt at assessment. The banality in itself is characteristic and in accordance with the rule that a man cannot be raised above other men without obliteration of the subtler shades in his image. The living face becomes rigid and seems to turn to bronze. The history of cinematic apotheosis is a gallery of statues.

In the Western democracies, the cinema is relatively restrained in its representation of public personalities, particularly over their glorification. Not even during World War II were statesmen and generals turned into the unifying symbols that they could have become in the cinema and to a certain extent already were in reality.

The name of the British Prime Minister was used for its symbolic value in a Canadian documentary, *Churchill's Island* (1941), but the film is not about him but about the collective war effort. In Britain, Churchill's voice expressed his country's confidence and spirit of resistance, but on film he appeared only in fleeting newsreel glimpses. At that time an English feature film about the war with Winston Churchill in the leading role would have been unthinkable, and not simply because of Churchill's physical presence. On the other hand, he could appear by proxy. In Carol Reed's *The Young Mr Pitt* (1942), there is a striking parallel between past and present, between Napoleon's irreconcilable enemy and Hitler's.

Similar discretion operates in the American cinema. Behind Henry King's *Wilson* (1944) there were also parallels; Wilson was the president who broke with isolationism, led the nation into war and in the end brought peace to the world. The ambitious indoctrination experiments of the *Why We Fight* series exploit the symbols of democracy to the point

of exhaustion. Among the heroes invoked are three American presidents, Washington, Jefferson and Lincoln. In the first instalment, where the basic principles of the series are most clearly formulated, the New Deal is represented as valuable, something to be proud of, to fight for, but there is no particular emphasis on the living president who was the foremost architect of social reform. We get the opportunity to study the faces of Hirohito, Hitler and Mussolini, but catch only brief glimpses of Churchill and Roosevelt.

A couple of short films were devoted to Roosevelt at an early stage in his presidency, *Roosevelt, the Man of the Hour* and *The Fighting President*, both in 1933. They seem to have been ordinary reportage films with flashbacks, informative sketches without any real glorification. In later newsreels, however, there is one significant omission: hardly any footage exists showing how the partially-paralysed Franklin D. Roosevelt, a polio victim, was lifted into the speaker's chair or helped down from the platform after speaking engagements. Such things were evidently just not photographed.

In democracies, the head of state is not represented as superhuman except in films intended as memorials. (He is, after all, likely to be the hero of one political party rather than of the nation as a whole.) On the other hand, he must not be made to appear *too* human.

Perhaps, though those responsible for such things never seem to have entertained the notion, the public might have even stronger ties with their leader if they were trusted enough to be told about his weaknesses as well as his strengths. Propagandists are possibly right in assuming that the relationship would be disturbed, authority lessened and the dignity of office undermined.

John F. Kennedy, like Joseph Stalin, is a remarkable exception as a leading political figure who became a film hero in his own active lifetime.

Unfortunately Leslie H. Martinson's *PT 109* (1962) is a very feeble film about events which were already twenty years in the past; it is not about President Kennedy, but about Lieutenant Kennedy and his war-time adventures. The actor (Cliff Robertson) does not look very much like the character he portrays. Kennedy appears keen and resourceful, self-confident and modest. He is slightly humiliated by a superior but swallows his anger. Though guilty of a few minor lapses of judgment, he has the courage to take the rap for them. As an

Stills. Above: Alexander Knox as the President in Henry King's Wilson. *Top right:* Prelude to War *('Take a close look at this trio; remember these faces.'). Right: Cliff Robertson as Lieutenant Kennedy in* PT 109.

individual, he is not exceptional but has the distinctive personality of a leader.

The film demonstrates how his character gets toughened. He performs his heroic deeds, but with the same spirit of humorous diffidence that he earlier gave to his routine tasks as an officer. His torpedo boat is sunk and he rescues a member of the crew. Swimming, Kennedy drags the wounded man through four miles of the Pacific and carries him ashore. He has the man on his back like a cross, and is a modern St Christopher, carrying him across the water.

Apart from these vague hagiographical references, Martinson seems to adhere strictly to the facts. Over one detail, though, there is something like the discretion found in newsreels of President Roosevelt's public appearances. There is no mention in *PT 109* of the serious back injury (actually an old injury greatly aggravated) which Kennedy suffered as a result of the adventure which is the film's climax; this never ceased to trouble him throughout his political career. At the end of the film, John F. Kennedy happily takes command of a new torpedo boat. The Star-Spangled Banner is fluttering as the sun glitters on the waves.

It is not known whether this reticence came about in accordance with someone's express wish or quite spontaneously, out of the un-written conventions of the genre. (In any event, it is difficult to imagine that *PT 109* could have been made without the agreement of the

Stills. Wunschkonzert (*above*) – *the lovers at the Berlin Olympics, seen* (*right*) *in* Fest der Schönheit, *the second part of Leni Riefenstahl's* Olympia.

Kennedy family.) Respect for the individual here seems less important than respect for his office as President. If citizens are to have confidence in the President and Supreme Commander of the Armed Forces, they must be convinced that he is in the best of health. (But Theodore Sorensen mentions in his biography that the greatest possible secrecy was maintained on the subject of John F. Kennedy's health, even during his period as a Senator. His visits to hospital were consistently kept away from the public.)

Behind the film's characterisation, lies the same guiding principle. The main consideration has been to give a reminder of heroic deeds and to demonstrate the man's determination, his alertness, his coolness in the heat of battle and his ability to stay firmly in control – in short his statesmanship. At the same time, the film apparently aims to counter the objections ordinary people might have to a man with Kennedy's upper-class background and great wealth. *PT 109* shows John F. Kennedy as just an ordinary chap who is not afraid of buckling down to the job. During a Japanese attack on the American base, he helps to carry ammuni-tion; he is also seen carting his own kit-bag

around. He has a sense of justice – a crew member from his own social stratum is given no special favours: on the contrary, Kennedy gives him a particularly tough assignment. Cheerful and responsible, unpretentious and authoritative, he clearly merits the renewal of his presidential mandate in 1964. Fate, however, directs an altogether different picture.

Triumph of the Will was Adolf Hitler's own film, expressing his will and imprinted with his personality. It was a unique feat, and nothing similar was ever really attempted again, for, strangely enough, the Nazi cinema rarely devoted itself to the cult of the leader, and then only indirectly or in passing.

Hitler himself rarely turns up in Nazi German features. Even in orthodox NSDAP pictures produced during the years just after he came to power, the Führer is only somewhere in the background. Heini's dreams in *Hitlerjunge Quex* are centred on the flag, which is the symbol of the young people's fellowship, and his last words are about this, not about the Führer. In *Hans Westmar*, the image of Hitler appears before the young student's eyes at the moment he decides to join the political activity in the streets, but even he does not die with Hitler's name on his lips: instead he whispers 'Deutschland'. (But at his funeral a wreath arrives bearing the name of Adolf Hitler, and in *SA-Mann Brand* the dying youth says as he

expires, 'I go now to the Führer'.) In the anti-Polish *Heimkehr* (1941), persecuted Germans secretly and solemnly listen to a speech by Hitler, and when they at last get back to their country, 'home to the Reich', he is the first to welcome them. We see the border post, a portrait of the Führer on a roadside hoarding, and then the same portrait in close-up. This unusual ending is still a very subdued expression of a personality cult. *Wunschkonzert*, a music-filled picture about love and sacrifice, also has Adolf Hitler in a minor role. A happy coincidence brings the two lovers together at the opening of the Berlin Olympics; it is as if Hitler is there to officiate not just for the hundreds of thousands in the vast arena but also specially for the two of them. Lenin and Stalin, too, are given a similar solemnising function in a number of Russian films (e.g. *The Fall of Berlin*). In *Wunschkonzert*, however, the lovers do not exist for the sake of the leader, rather the reverse. Anyway, Hitler does not really belong in the context; he has been lifted out of a newsreel and edited into the story.

In the Soviet Union, there were actors who specialised in the portrayal of Stalin, and Lenin is still handled in a similar way. Hitler, on the other hand, has been played by actors only in anti-Nazi films. This apparent policy of the Nazi cinema may have been because reverence for the Reich Chancellor precluded the use of actors or because the Minister of Propaganda was not convinced that it would be effective. Perhaps Hitler would have been made to look ridiculous.

In 'Propaganda and the Nazi War Film', the supplement to Siegfried Kracauer's 'From Caligari to Hitler', the author comments on the character of Hitler in the German cinema. Hitler 'is not portrayed as an individual with a development of his own but as the embodiment of terrific impersonal powers – or better, as their meeting-place; in spite of many a reverential close-up, these films designed to idolise him cannot adapt his features to human existence.'

On this issue, as on so many others, Kracauer is perhaps too dogmatic. Certainly, in *Triumph of the Will*, the Führer has consciously been made into the personification of an idea, a man who comes down to earth to save people (i.e. the Germans) and represents a superhuman force. Disturbingly enough, this superman also emerges in some confusing moments as a human being.

In *Fest der Völker* (1938), the first part of Leni Riefenstahl's film of the 1936 Olympics, Hitler has been humanised even further to become purely a statesman and a spectator at a sports event. He gives the inaugural speech, and is then seen in relaxed conversation with his entourage or tensely following the progress of the Games with the same degree of involvement as an ordinary sports fan; like most fans, he is chauvinistic. He seems worried before shot-putter Woellke makes his final effort in the last round, but when Woellke makes the winning put, he laughs with relief. During the 10,000 metres, his fidgeting indicates a degree of excitement, which makes a good impression as this is not a great event for the Germans, ending in a triple success for Finland.

Leni Riefenstahl has chosen the images to show the dictator as a good soul. This emphasis could be aimed at the export market – the world had to be duped with the idea that Germany wanted peace (while the Condor Legion was bombing Madrid); it was alternately pummelled with bare-faced threats and calmed with assurances. But in the Berlin sunshine, the youth of the world is meeting in healthy contest. Only in the final sequences of the second part, *Fest der Schönheit*, does the tone harden, the darkness draw closer and the emblem overshadow the people.

In wartime documentaries, Hitler the popular leader has become head of the armed forces and the distance from him correspondingly increases. It continues to do so as he shuts himself away at Berchtesgaden and then in the bunker, and becomes only an increasingly noisy voice over the loudspeakers. The power, the hypnotic force of the Nuremberg rallies seems slowly to be ebbing out of him; after a couple of years the demon has been reduced to a psychopath in a long coat, but by then, his demonic spirit has spread to and taken possession of the landscape.

Feldzug in Polen (1939) is the story of the first military victory as German front line photographers saw it under the direction of Fritz Hippler. Here the relationship to the Führer is reverential, the tone almost servile. As Adolf Hitler arrives at the front, the commentator explains, 'As a veteran of the last war, the Führer wants to be with his soldiers.' (The emphasis is not on the visuals but on the words, which are concerned less with the Führer's greatness but with his military experience.) We later witness Hitler, the ascetic vegetarian, ostensibly enjoying a meal from the cook house. Much stress is laid on the fact that he is at the front line – when the soldiers reach a Polish river, the Führer is waiting for them as a 'surprise' – but this attempt at making Hitler play a heroic role (while underlining his simplicity, his presence as a soldier among soldiers) seems rather forced. Furthermore, the presence of ADC's and staff officers undermines the whole image. In that company he appears dressed up, almost over-dressed.

Sieg im Westen (1940) is less Hitler's film than that of the Wehrmacht. Here the Führer is not portrayed as a front-line soldier but merely glimpsed as a rather distant source of inspiration. He makes a speech before the offensive against France and another one after the victory, but the camera turns away from the platform to photograph the soldiers, the geometrical pattern of the units, and the look of isolated individuals beneath their steel helmets. At this point there is an element of mystique, of concentration and isolation, but there is no question, as in *Triumph of the Will*, of an ecstatic communion between the masses and their leader.

When the breakthrough of the French lines occurs, we are told that the Führer's 'ingenious scheme' has been revealed to the world. But this is an isolated act of homage in a picture otherwise concerned with the invincibility of the German soldier and the German war machine.

With the exception of *Triumph of the Will*, the most effective films about the Führer are those that do not actually include him but are apparently about great Germans of the past. The parallel was noticeable in Wolfgang Liebeneiner's films about the Iron Chancellor, *Bismarck* (1940) and *Die Entlassung* (1942), and must have been impossible to overlook in the films in which Otto Gebühr portrayed Frederick the Great.

Before Hitler came to power, a number of popular films about Frederick had already been made in which Prussia (i.e. Germany) was shown to be so threatened by enemies both at home and abroad that its only remaining hope lay in the determination of the king. The subject was a historical ruler, but could equally be the new Reich Chancellor on whom the nation was now pinning its hopes. The story was of degradation and revenge, of the danger of complete freedom of thought and of the duty

Stills. Wolfgang Liebeneiner's Bismark, *with Paul Hartmann as the Iron Chancellor.*

to obey, of the insignificance of the individual and the superior inspiration of the people's leader. Frederick II is the lonely, great man, the leader who sacrifices all and is therefore entitled to demand great sacrifices.

In Veit Harlan's *Der grosse König* the double meaning of this portrait is firmly underlined. Rune Waldekranz writes:

'Through the warrior king, Veit Harlan paid homage to the Führer, man of Fate, supreme ruler, all alone in his responsibilities towards his contemporaries and posterity, sublimely indifferent to individual happiness or misery, raised above all petty considerations and all ungenerous criticism.'

Certain lines in this film sound like quotations from Hitler's speeches, and on a couple of occasions, the king erupts in almost Hitlerian outbursts. He discusses with his supreme commander the problem of a company which has taken to its heels under enemy pressure. The general advances various hypotheses on how the battle might have developed had the regiment stood firm, but the king interrupts him impatiently. If they had not deserted, he splutters, 'they would have built a wall for me out of corpses, a wall of Prussian corpses'.

Other lines seem designed to disarm Hitler's German critics, to deflect any objections whether whispered or merely thought. Thus Prince Heinrich, the king's brother, rebukes Frederick the Great for having turned the whole of Europe against them. (This was a criticism that the German people might well have been levelling against Hitler at the time.) Eventually, however, the king shows himself capable of vanquishing all his enemies. His will cannot be broken, and history is on his side.

From *Der grosse König* (1942) right up to *Kolberg* (which was premièred on 30 January 1945), Nazi propaganda, whether in the cinema or in other media, insists without fail that final victory is assured, however great the difficulties of the moment may be. There is even the breathless suggestion that it is imminent. As in the protestant style of preaching, paradox has become an important device, a method of influencing the audience. The trials and tribulations are only temporary: they are in themselves the proof of the coming victory.

In his autobiography, '*Im Schatten meiner Filme*' ('In the Shadow of My Films'), Veit Harlan confirms that *Der grosse König* was intended as something of an allegory on Adolf Hitler's greatness and solitude. The German press was discreetly informed that the connection between the Prussian king and the Führer was to be emphasised in reviews. If this is correct – and Harlan's memory is somewhat erratic at times – the Ministry of Propaganda subsequently changed its mind. In March 1943, one year after the film was first shown, a directive to the press was still warmly recommending it, but also stating that:

'Comparisons between Frederick the Great and the Führer must be avoided at all costs, as must all analogies with the present, in particular regarding the pessimistic undertone which, in the beginning of the film, often marks the dialogue, and which must not under any circumstances be represented as a parallel to the attitude of the German people during the present war.'

This new line of thought might be explained in various ways, but it is possible that the Führer's propagandists had come to realise that the psychological effect of the comparison might be weakened if the public became aware that it was being pressured in this way.

Among the many people working in literature, the theatre and the cinema today, there is a growing feeling of scepticism about fiction. Disbelief in the omniscient narrator of the traditional novel has grown into disbelief in the story itself. Fiction may not be condemned as being irresponsible or immoral, but there is a feeling that fiction still circles around when it is quite feasible to go straight to the point. This

Still: Veit Harlan's Der grosse König – *Gustav Fröhlich, Otto Gebühr (as Frederick the Great), and Otto Wernicke.*

line of argument would necessarily mean that a documentary account is preferable to a fictional one.

Yuri Hanyutin, a Russian film critic and joint scriptwriter of Romm's *Ordinary Fascism*, sees these current tendencies in art as a fundamental reaction against the falsification of reality by totalitarian movements in the 'thirties and 'forties. 'Fascism has undermined our belief in sermons,' he says; it has created a lingering scepticism towards rousing words and sweeping presentation. A new factual attitude and with it a new interest in documentary techniques is, in his view, gaining ground in the Soviet Union, not least in the cinema.

An outside observer might well feel that such a tendency should also be seen as a reaction against domestic distortions and simplifications, such as the cinematic oleographs that Josef Stalin, according to Khrushchev, regarded as a true picture of Soviet life. (It was revealed during the 20th Party Congress that Stalin had apparently not set foot in a Russian village since January 1928.) One thinks, too, of the super-humanly-scaled portraits of Lenin and Stalin to which for years the citizens of the Soviet Union were treated in the cinema.

Bazin saw an ideological motivation in the portrayal of great living figures in the Socialist countries, in the enlargement and proliferation of the great men's portraits. In the materialistic concept of history, man is a 'fact', and there is

Still: a pastoral view of Lenin in Dziga Vertov's Three Songs of Lenin.

no reason why Stalin's historical significance cannot be expressed in photographic images. Today it seems much more to the point to look for a psychological explanation of the pictures carried on May Day parades or adorning public buildings. These 'Big Brothers' are part of a system of political persuasion, very simple instruments of propaganda. When Socialism becomes less authoritarian, as in Czechoslovakia in spring 1968, they disappear, for they are used to emphasise the presence of authority. They are a kind of super-ego: Socialist icons, surveying, searching, paternally severe or – sometimes – paternally benevolent.

These are the still pictures. When the image starts to move, a transformation takes place, it begins to emanate a kind of humanity. Whether in documentary images or fictional ones, Lenin the authority also becomes Lenin the man. Stalin seems somewhat different in this respect. In film after film, he looks like a walking statue, and functions excellently as a moral exemplar without any confusingly human features.

The Lenin figure we know from feature films appears during and after the Stalin era. Lenin himself does not appear to have wished for any glorification of himself and his work. According to Edouard Tissé, Lenin asked not to be photographed on 1 May 1919 in Red Square, but told him instead to film the soldiers who were on their way to the front. He does not seem to have

been portrayed in any features during his lifetime. The apotheosis came later.

The first Lenin films were two shorts in his memory made by Dziga Vertov in 1925. One of them, *Leninskaya kino-pravda* formed the blueprint for Vertov's 1934 masterpiece, *Three Songs of Lenin* . The middle section of this film, which concerns Lenin's death and his legacy of achievements is highly emotional in a completely controlled way. Vertov does not seek to erect a monument to Lenin and his work. He takes note of the sudden vacuum and sets new developments in Central Asia, women's liberation and their songs about Lenin, alongside the funeral in Moscow. Vertov invokes the people, and seeks out individual faces in the crowd and the experience which they reveal. He invokes nature and man-made reality, the new society. The two separate stands merge into a lament, with Lenin himself as the centre of calm amid the pulsations of gratitude and deep pain.

Among the first features in which he appears are Boris Barnet's *Moscow in October* (1927) and Eisenstein's *October* (1928) (with the famous speech outside the Finland Station). Both films were commissioned for the tenth anniversary of the October Revolution, and in both Lenin is played by Nikandrov, a worker from the

Urals. Mayakovsky is said to have been dissatisfied with his portrayal which was based on nothing more than physical resemblance and a few well rehearsed gestures. What was more, the actor did not really look like Lenin but rather 'like a statue of him'.

A number of Lenin and Stalin films were made in the late 'thirties. In Vera Stroyeva's *Generation of Conquerors* (1936), the young Lenin is played by a fine character actor, Boris Shtyukin. Sergei Yutkevitch's *The Man with a Gun* (1938) introduced Maxim Straukh, another excellent performer, as Lenin. In *The Vyborg Side* (1939), the last part of the Kozintsev and Trauberg Maxim trilogy, Straukh appears again as Lenin, while the part of Stalin is taken by Mikhail Gelovani, who was to play it in more than twenty films.

Mikhail Romm's *Lenin in October* (1937) and *Lenin in 1918* (1939) are marked by the shadows of the political terror then gripping Russian society: tribunals, deportations, executions. The climax of *Lenin in 1918* is an act of sabotage staged by the Social Revolutionaries, and a central element in the film is the debate on the treatment of enemies of the state. This takes the form of a conversation between Lenin and Gorky which begins in the council of the people's commissars and is resumed by Lenin's sick-bed. They discuss the aims and means of the revolution. Maxim Gorky represents a form of humanism. 'Force is necessary, but . . .', he says, dwelling on the 'but'. Lenin's attitude is pragmatic: his concern is what benefits the state, and he asks his friend to set aside his regrets. After the assassination attempt, he can point to the necessity of keeping a check on suspects and dealing severely with elements inimical to the Party. Humanism falls silent, and when the news of victory arrives from Czaritsyn (later to become Stalingrad, then Volgograd), Lenin quickly rallies.

Romm's two films mainly seem dutiful, but their portrayal of Lenin is outstanding. Shtyukin studied the part with sincerity and scholarly thoroughness. In his interpretation, Lenin comes alive not just through his actions; in repose he does not seem feelingless. He is a politician and statesman, but to an even greater extent he is a human being. He may be a monumental figure, but this portrait does not transform him into a monument. In the first of the two films, Lenin has moments of restlessness, living as he does under great stress, and his nervousness finds staccato expression in facial tics, quick gestures, anxious pacing back and forth. In the second of the films, he is just as human but much more relaxed, with an unpredictable gleam in his eye, more like a liberal headmaster than an omnipotent ruler. But maybe Lenin was just like that.

Lenin in 1918 was Shtyukin's last great performance. Maxim Straukh continued his collaboration with Yutkevitch in *Yakov Sverdlov* (1940). *Stories about Lenin* (1958), and *Lenin in Poland* (1964). With a different actor in the role

Stills: Lenin iconography. Opposite page: Maxim Straukh in Sergei Yutkevitch's Stories about Lenin. *This page: top – Nikandrov in Eisenstein's* October; *Straukh with Mikhail Gelovani as Stalin in* The Vyborg Side.

of Lenin, Yutkevitch made *Light Over Russia* (1947), which for some unknown reason was banned.

In *Stories about Lenin* there is a sense of distance and nostalgia. Maxim Straukh is older and less agile; the revolution has become history and then myth. The setting has been tidied up, and the atmosphere is a strange mixture of hagiography and bourgeois intimacy.

In the first story, set in Petrograd in 1917, Vladimir Ilich is sitting at the breakfast table. There is a white table-cloth and spotlessly white walls; the feeling is of deep calm, and four wide shafts of sunlight fall across the room. The white walls recur in the second story, which takes place in the town of Gorky where Lenin is convalescing in the years 1922-23. The idyllic mood has elegiac undertones, expressed in the falling leaves. On his sick-bed, Lenin receives the message that all is not well in Moscow; he decides to go there. In a factory, Trotsky is addressing the workers. He is represented as a demagogue in decline: when he is interrupted by his audience, he cries helplessly: 'If Lenin were here, he would be on my side.' Lenin *is* there; he says no, and as he mounts the platform, a shaft of light falls across the hall in the manner which, in religious art, signifies the presence of saints.

In *Lenin in Poland*, a black-and-white film, Yutkevitch interestingly scaled-down his subject. Lenin is once more played by Straukh, but this time the role is completely without dialogue. Instead, Lenin-Straukh holds an inner monologue, commenting freely on world events (the time is around the outbreak of World War I) and on the everyday occurrences in the film. The tone is light, and Lenin is presented as a humorous man with a gift for empathy; he is a listener, observer and thinker who is pained, even enraged at the follies of mankind, but who is at all times in control

Stills. Below: Straukh in Yutkevitch's Lenin in Poland. *Opposite page: top* – October; *bottom* – Gelovani in · Mikhail Chiaureli's The Unforgettable Year 1919.

of himself and ready to try out new ways of improving the world. This extremely sympathetic portrait is totally devoid of empty gestures. An elderly international revolutionary with whom I discussed this image of Lenin found it insufferably *petit bourgeois*.

Stories about Lenin still proliferate. Since *October*, the overall conception has changed and possibly even very minor alterations of the image carry their own political significance. It is conceivable that the gallery of Russian film portraits of Lenin could be found to reflect the development of the Soviet Union from 1928 to the present day. In a number of films, Lenin and Stalin appear together. Here Lenin seems to fulfil a confirmatory function. Whenever Stalin makes an important suggestion or sets out to wrestle with some problem, Lenin nods approvingly. He thus gives posthumous approval to Stalin's work, discounting the rumours of warnings set down in his will. In these films, Lenin exists for the sake of Stalin. Thereafter Lenin is on his own. But he has somehow slipped away to become no more than an idealised memory. He seems to be the same age whether the events take place in 1905 (as in Dzigan's *Prologue*, 1956) or in 1923 (as in *Stories about Lenin*).

Lately the Lenin figure appears to have been injected with new life, and in the process has possibly been diminished somewhat – that is to say, he has been humanised. In Ilya Olsh-

wanger's *On the Same Planet* (1965), Lenin is played by the famous Innokenty Smoktunovsky, a young man, who portrays him as old, slightly shrunken and rather tired. (In the film, Lenin says how tired he feels.) As in *Lenin in 1918*, there is a discussion about the justification of violence. Lenin and Stalin talk together after the assassination attempt, and Stalin advocates harsh revenge. He suggests that History demands it. Lenin does not say much, but is of a different opinion and in his presence Stalin has no answer. He falls silent, looking darkly at Lenin.

Although it is a subdued, low-key film, there is no doubt about the impression that the leading characters are meant to make. Stalin is portrayed in *On the Same Planet* as definitely the inferior, and isolated in his bigotry. It is as total a reassessment of the great man as was the removal of his body from the mausoleum in Red Square. After Stalin has had his say, he walks alone through the corridors at Smolny. He comes straight towards us and walks into the camera so that the picture darkens menacingly for a moment. This fleeting reference to the darkness of the Stalin era is surely not accidental. It could also contain an allusion to a sequence in *October*, in which Eisenstein has a shot of a white corridor. The screen goes dark for a moment, as in Olshwanger's film, but it is Kerensky who is then seen walking away from the camera with his hands behind his back in

Napoleonic fashion.

Films made about Lenin in the 'sixties show a development towards greater realism. The image has been enriched with a number of small personal traits, and made more profound. Beyond the great pieces of acting, there is now also the message that Lenin was a human being and an example through his humanity. As he is above debate in the Soviet Union, he can now be portrayed, without any loss of authority, as tired or eccentric or absent-minded. He can enjoy good wine or, as in *Lenin in Poland*, visit a village church because a pretty girl has asked him to do so. His importance needs no emphasis; indeed, it is getting more obvious

than ever as he becomes more 'ordinary'.

At the same time, there is a tendency in the latest Soviet films to move from the image of Lenin towards a more general treatment, with Lenin as an invisible presence. He is associated with nature, with the elemental forces. In *Head of State of the Soviets* (1967) there is a description of the Social Revolutionaries' coup – 'They fired at Lenin' – followed by darkening skies, a sudden flash like lightning, and waves rolling fatefully towards the shore. *Flag Flying Over the World* (1969), another documentary stops at 1922 and Lenin's grave illness. It ends in a parkland setting, as in *Stories About Lenin*, with gently falling leaves, a Russian birch forest, poignantly shot through by shafts of sunlight. Lenin may have become human again, but we are not allowed to forget that he is still immortal.

In *The Unforgettable Year 1919*, which was made by Mikhail Chiaureli in 1952, Lenin and Stalin are conferring, and Lenin is explaining the situation. Everything seems to depend on Stalin, who is authorised to go to Petrograd as a trouble-shooter. As he says farewell, Lenin solemnly reads out all the titles to which his emissary can lay claim.

Stalin, his wavy hair immaculately groomed, stands on the steps of an armoured train. People come up to tell him that a bridge has been destroyed. Stalin cheerfully retorts: 'Then

we'll walk.' In Petrograd, the counter-revolutionaries are meeting. A British conspirator, the envoy of Churchill, speaks up: 'Stalin is here. That will make things more difficult.' Stalin himself stands motionless by the river Neva, alone in the summer night. (Billowing music on piano and orchestra accompanies his thoughts.) A commander with leather coat and binoculars, he is the monumental embodiment of power and security. Day breaks, and the British warships approach Kronstadt. Stalin takes off his coat and begins to issue orders to the navy. The British withdraw and Stalin puts his coat back on. Sitting down for a meal with the soldiers, he confides that he is 'as hungry as a wolf' and they all have a good laugh at this pleasantry. At the end Stalin is heartily cheered by carefully arranged groups of people. (The impression is of a grand finale, with choreography being reminiscent of an old-fashioned opera production.) Stalin makes a speech among the gleaming cannons and red flags. The cannons move, aim and fire.

This absurd film has with time gained a certain entertainment value. In his address to the 20th Party Congress in February 1956, Khrushchev rather dwelled on *The Unforgettable Year 1919*, a film which Stalin is said to have loved watching. It is not the sole representative of its curious genre. In Vladimir Petrov's *The Battle of Stalingrad* (1949-50) and in two other Chiaureli films, *The Vow* (1946) and

Stills: Mikhail Chiaureli's The Fall of Berlin. *Opposite page: Gelovani as Stalin, addressing the Soviet Praesidium (below) and at his desk in the Kremlin – in the words of the official caption to this carefully retouched picture, he 'looks at a map, then takes his pipe, smokes it and remarks "Berlin will soon be finished." ' Above: victory.*

The Fall of Berlin (1949), Stalin also appears in the role of superman. He makes vital military decisions after looking once at the map and drawing twice on his pipe. He is omniscient and infallible; as Bazin has pointed out, there is an unbridgeable distance between his cool, well-ordered office and the chaotic reality under his command: Stalingrad, Moscow, Berlin.

Occasionally Generalissimo Stalin steps down to the level of ordinary mortals, like a benevolent god from antiquity who is touched by man's helplessness and in a trice puts everything right. He is a kindly Jehovah who moves slowly to avoid treading on his little creatures.

There is a moving scene in *The Vow*, at dawn, some time during the earliest days of the Soviet Union. Red Square is almost empty when along comes a revolutionary symbol which chuffs and hiccups and then goes dead: it is the first tractor ever manufactured in the Soviet Union. The driver is desolate; he examines the engine and gets advice from various passers-by, but it just won't work. At this point Stalin just happens to come along with some of his colleagues from the Supreme Soviet. With genuine interest, he asks what is going on. Bukharin malevolently suggests that it might be better to import tractors from the United States, but Stalin bends over the engine and listens. 'It is the sparkplugs,' he diagnoses. Then he climbs on the vehicle and drives across the Square a couple of times. Close-up of the great Stalin: 'He thinks, he looks into the future: double exposure of thousands of tractors in a factory, more tractors, tractors ploughing the fields, pulling behind them a long trail of ploughshares . . . ' The words are André Bazin's and these comments are based on his account of *The Vow*. One result of Khrushchev's attack on Stalinism is that most films about Stalin have since been revised or suppressed. Another is that political leaders in the Soviet Union no longer appear on film except in the occasional newsreel, and then with great restraint.

The cult of personality began with the embalming of Lenin and his public lying-in-state in the Red Square mausoleum. This was followed by a period of regrouping, intrigue and power struggles. By 1929, Stalin had eliminated all rivals, and on 21 December of that year, his fiftieth birthday was celebrated as a national holiday. 'His virtues were praised, immoderately and crudely by every party secretary in the country,' wrote Isaac Deutscher in his biography 'The walls of Moscow were covered with his huge portraits.' Afterwards, old comrades were liquidated as real or imagined rivals, followed by almost the entire Party and general staff. As the terror raged with increasing fury, Stalin's image grew larger on the billboards and in films.

But the war with Germany was real – hard and nightmarish perhaps, but still the fight had a positive significance which must have been absent during the purge years. The fight against Fascism demanded national unity, and dogma was pushed aside to make room for more concrete tasks. The cult of personality was no longer pursued with the same rigour – for instance, in Ivan Pyriev's *Secretary of the District Committee* (1942), the partisan hero gives only a brief matter-of-fact nod to Stalin's portrait before going into battle. Stalin has not yet become the hero of the war. The grotesque excesses of glorification come a year or two after its end, when society and art have once more become paralysed, and when Stalin's own personal terror has completely taken over his mind. In the cinema, he becomes less and less real, though retaining his legendary image, with his pipe and grin and slightly remote benevolence, his air of an elderly squire inspecting the farm.

That such a character could be both portrayed and accepted with such deathly seriousness was not due purely to the terror, but also to the extreme economy of the image. In the Pet-

rov and Chiaureli films, Stalin is so simplified – his characteristics are so few and homogeneous, amounting only to superior paternalism – that he becomes obviously exceptional. It would never occur to anyone to compare himself with the man in the field-marshal's white uniform, or to compare him with any other living person. Therefore Stalin could not become ridiculous (though the situations might well appear so). There was no conflict with reality, because reality was not involved, only legend. Bazin's argument is that Josef Stalin is beyond any psychological analysis, like the stars in screen biographies emanating from Hollywood and Western Europe. Like God, he can only be accepted or rejected. However, the portrayal of Stalin could obviously be analysed politically, and its functions examined. Even if we were not aware that a state of terror reigned in Stalin's Russia, a close analysis of the films would reveal it.

The Vow contains a scene which bears eloquent witness to the pseudo-religious nature of the Stalin cult. Lenin has just died, and Stalin goes off to meditate on his own at the spot where the two have often talked together. At this holy place, the park bench where Lenin used to sit, the deceased returns and whispers to Stalin. But this mystical visitation is not

Stills: Gelovani as Stalin, with Straukh as Molotov in The Fall of Berlin *(left);* The Vow.

enough: Stalin looks up to the sky, and (writes Bazin) 'through the branches of the fir-trees falls a ray of sunshine, touching the forehead of the new Moses.' After this spiritual baptism, Stalin-Gelovani can return to his people clearly marked as superior to all others, not just 'through his insight and his genius, but also through the presence within him of the God of History.'

Mao Tse-tung, too, is involved in the cult of personality and has his screen apotheosis. In *The East Is Red* (1965), a film of a Maoist stage musical with a cast of three thousand, he is celebrated as a saviour even in the opening number and identified with the rising red sun. A commentator declares that the people are happy under Mao Tse-tung's rule and goes on to ask: 'But how could we forget our past suffering?'

Darkness falls across the stage. China's degradation is portrayed in a series of mimed tableaux. The first illustrates capitalism; others in cold, dark colours show the Chinese people staggering under the yoke of imperialism. But a rosy dawn eventually breaks: a red sky in the middle of which hangs a medallion with a double portrait of Marx and Lenin. This picture emits a steady stream of darting rays, revolutionary impulses representing force and knowledge. A flag, adorned with a youthful picture of Mao, appears fluttering over the scene.

After this, the action on the stage alternates between darkness and light. There are representations of the Long March and then the wars against Japan and Chiang Kai-shek, 'the decisive struggle between darkness and light.' Light carries the day, and the stage is filled with red flags. Suddenly we find ourselves in the big square in Peking, where the people have come to salute their hero. The various nationalities step forward, while Mao's portrait hovers in the background. For this spectacle, Mao himself is present but invisible. He is somewhere out in front of the Tibetan girls, who are now dominating the stage as they sing songs to his glory. Mao Tse-tung cannot be represented by an actor; he cannot be portrayed by anyone but himself.

Chairman Mao Is The Red Sun In Our Hearts is a colour film about the cultural revolution with Chairman Mao in the flesh. It is a lengthy documentary dated 1 October 1966, when the population of Peking celebrated the 17th anniversary of the birth of the People's Republic.

It begins with the sun, as in *The East Is Red*, a white sun slowly rising in a red sky. Then Mao Tse-tung, his face a red sun, raising his hand to greet the people as they march past. While Lin Piao is delivering the main address in a monotonous voice, we see the dead idols: Marx, Engels, Lenin, Stalin. The speaker ends with cheers for Chairman Mao: he wishes Mao a long life. The people cheer. A white statue of Mao is carried in the procession.

The high point of the film occurs when the young people come forward to pay their respects – schoolchildren of all ages, including girls wiping the tears from their eyes, or leaping up and down with a curiously detached look. Enthusiasm turns to ecstasy, and for a moment, the situation briefly looks like getting out of control.

Chairman Mao has remained very still all this time, waving calmly, rewarding the people with faint smiles. Now he rises to his feet and walks down among them; the excitement mounts even further. 'Our red sun stands before us', says the commentator. 'The greatest teacher of the human race is here.' Chairman Mao walks slowly, like a god, to his big black sedan. There appears to be a secret connection between Mao Tse-tung's majesty and his way of moving – the measured glide, the economy of gesture, the incredible calm of his face, whether smiling or not. It is impossible to visualise Mao (or Stalin, for that matter) ever breaking into a run, or waving with both hands. His is a definitive form which stands above any earthly impulses.

At dusk, there are more shouts for Chairman Mao, and again he walks among the people. The sky is filled with the floral patterns of thousands of fireworks exploding. Mao Tse-tung sits down on a terrace, and people gather round him. He sits on the floor, smoking, as the sky over Peking turns red. The apotheosis is complete, both in heaven and on earth. We have seen God: He is sitting on the floor puffing on a small cigar.

The First Person Plural

In the age of modern advertising it is perhaps surprising to see how the propaganda film, which is not usually distinguished by lack of cynicism, almost entirely refrains from making any appeal to instinctive individual egocentricity. Almost without exception, it is addressed to a wider form of egoism: that of the group, the collective, the class, the nation, or the people. Whereas advertising turns to *me*, propaganda plays on *us*. The 'we' feeling is a goal to strive for and a weapon to be used. It has a curious but, in the context, very useful tendency to establish outer limits to the sense of community, to draw up frontiers against *the others*, and to suggest that beyond these frontiers lie dangers and enemies which threaten *our* community – while at the same time reinforcing our feelings of togetherness within them.

The most exalted form of fellowship is that of the people – the metaphysical union of all that is good – all of 'us'. The people, and above all 'the ordinary people', are harangued, praised and appealed to as if they were some divine authority. Much wartime propaganda consists of patriotic self-glorification, in which all interest is centred on the people's endurance and simple virtue.

The most appealing examples of this form of self-centred propaganda are to be found in a number of British films from World War II, at their finest in Humphrey Jennings's documentaries and, among others, in Launder and Gilliat's feature *Millions Like Us* (1943). It is tendentious art with an exquisite feeling for the charm of self-mocking understatement and every-day heroism. Perhaps the most striking quality of these films is that they pay so little attention to the enemy. Surprisingly often, the enemy is there only as a distant bombing target, a vague threat somewhere in the sky or beyond the Channel: to summon up indignation, it is quite enough to present without comment the results of his deeds. When Jennings, in *The Silent Village* (1943), transferred the Lidice tragedy to a Welsh setting, the German occupiers were represented solely by brief glimpses of uniformed figures and the ear-splitting sounds from loud-speaker cars. It was a film about *us*, the people.

For the same purpose of exploiting and deepening a 'we' solidarity, another form of film propaganda made a virtue out of the very methods the English eschewed. 'The others' get a great deal of attention but are portrayed in distinctive ways – those who do not belong to the fellowship of the people are also put stylistically outside it. The method is used, for instance, in the Russian revolutionary cinema. When the enemies of the people appear, naturalistic characterisation changes abruptly into coarse caricature, which has the curious result of making the enemy seem less dangerous. At times one could as well be at a ritual celebration of victory, with the enemy represented by masked figures who are humiliated for the edification of the people. The analogy is not just emotional, because revolutionary films sprang partly from the curious mass spectacles which were staged in Petrograd in the early 'twenties to celebrate and re-live the October Revolution. These were weird mystery plays in which the masses themselves played the leading role and the actors donned masks.

The British and Russian cinemas tackle the problem in diametrically opposed ways, but both are conditioned by the fundamental need in propaganda for a 'we' perspective.

The aim in propaganda films is almost always to be on the side of the audience, to adopt the same point of view. Generally, and for obvious reasons, propaganda automatically takes up the attitudes of its audience vis-à-vis basic political conflicts, but quite often it also uses various tricks to reinforce the general consensus.

In Britain during the Cold War, Roy Boulting made an anti-communist film called *High Treason* (1951). In it, a solid police inspector begins to suspect a pro-disarmament Member of Parliament of activities amounting to high treason; he checks out the man's coming engagements which include a date to speak at a foreign embassy. 'Guess which one!' says the inspector, looking straight into the camera. The spectator catches on immediately: the Russian. The film never spells this out. But the audience does, implicitly establishing a mutual understanding with the film.

Man Hunt (1941) is not one of Fritz Lang's most significant works, but it has a brilliant introductory sequence which compulsively allies the spectator with the whole motivation of the picture and its main character, an English gentleman and big game hunter. He has come to the forests around Berchtesgaden, not to kill but to experience the satisfaction of having the telescopic sight of his gun aimed straight at Hitler's heart. When that moment comes, we share the experience of looking through the sight and adjusting our aim at this biggest of big game. The instincts aroused within the spectator during these few seconds make him the sworn ally of the hero. The audience has been placed in a situation which forcibly produces exactly the moral perspective that the film itself will eventually arrive at.

Still: Fritz Lang's Man Hunt.

The achievement of a common perspective could be described as a prerequisite for all film propaganda which is not aiming to provoke or antagonise its audience. Every tangible difference in attitude brings with it increased psychological distance between film and audience, and finally resistance which can boomerang.

Film is the one propaganda medium that hardly ever allows itself to threaten its audience. This rule has a single exception in the way the Nazi German government used newsreels of its army offensives at the beginning of World War II. These were actually exploited in psychological warfare against the countries due to be attacked next. Thus on 5 April 1940, highly-placed Danes and Norwegians were invited to the German Embassy in Oslo to watch Hans Bertram's *Feuertaufe* (*Baptism of Fire*), a *documentary* which showed the invincible perfection of the German war machine as it gained a massive victory over the Poles. This screening was a threatening diplomatic prelude to the invasion which was to come a few days later. But this example is not representative; even German war documentaries had their biggest audience at home, where their function was to reinforce an already massive military self-confidence. When the occupation of Norway and Denmark was later described in Tobis's powerful *Wochenschau* (*Newsreel*) *Nr 17 1940*, a very marked 'we' perspective is established even for audiences in the occupied countries; the principal theme, constantly and emphatically repeated, is: 'We come as friends and are received as friends.'

The need for a common psychological perspective uniting film and audience becomes particularly essential where violence plays a big part. The problem is fairly simple when the perpetrators of violence are supposed to be hated by the audience. The genre abounds in indignation-producing scenes, in which the perspective places the audience firmly with the victims – but unavoidably, propaganda sometimes wants to present violent actions as something positive and show them from the viewpoint of the perpetrators. The propagandist is then faced with a rather tricky problem of balance, because there is always a risk that civilised revulsion against violence will induce untimely reservations in the spectator, and undermine his feeling of solidarity.

It may only be an ideological mirage that makes it appear as if Nazi film-makers, more than any others, considered that they could safely ignore this risk of distorting the emotional perspective; without any scruples, they demonstrated German brutality. *Bomber Squadron Lützow* (1941), for instance, contains a horrifying sequence in which hundreds of Poles fleeing along a road are gunned down by Stukas, and another where the pathetic Polish cavalry is massacred by German tanks. These displays of violence do not achieve the desired

effect *today* – maybe they did at the time with an audience whose need for vengeance found satisfaction through these images of terror.

Certain other Nazi films, however, cunningly manipulated justifications for violence. *Heimkehr* (1941), like *Bomber Squadron Lützow*, describes the outbreak of war, but achieves a more subtle effect by adopting the perspective, not of the conquerors but of the oppressed minorities in enemy territory: while the Volksdeutscher are perishing in Polish gaols, German Stukas and German tanks come roaring and crashing across Poland to save them. *Heimkehr* thus ends in liberation, not rape – and therein lies the tremendous difference between the two films. The power of suggestion contained in this sort of emotional relief is enormous, and the same ending, with the same moral sleight-of-hand and the same relief, recurs in Karl Ritter's *G.P.U.* (1942) – except that the heroes are this time languishing in the cellars of Rotterdam when the Germans invade Holland and come to their aid. The perspective creates the moral.

In this context it is surprising to see how frankly some Russian films of the 'thirties can admit to the rule of terror in the previous decade, but it is achieved by way of skilfully surreptitious appeals to the audience as loyal compatriots of those who were hit by the brutality of the regime. In *Lenin in 1918* (1939), Lenin and Gorky are talking, and Gorky is full

Stills. Above: Merited Arts Worker Mikhail Romm's Lenin in 1918 *with Boris Shtyukin as Lenin and Nikolai Cherkassov as Maxim Gorky. Right: bloated capitalist in another Romm film,* Secret Mission – *Gardin as Dillon ('He is one of Wall Street's wire-pullers and has come to Europe to get his share of the booty and to seize German patent rights.').*

of doubts about the Bolsheviks' violent treatment of their adversaries. The discussion is settled in Lenin's favour when a nice, ordinary man of the people – 'our' representative – comes in with simple, straightforward arguments to convince Gorky of the necessity of using tough methods. (In 1939, the real purpose of this scene was probably to defend Stalin's terror rather than Lenin's; the production was personally supervised by Beria.)

There are numerous methods of stimulating and exploiting 'us' feelings and of working up contempt for 'them', but most are rather unsophisticated. Photographically, 'ours' can be separated from 'theirs' in ways which add to the distinction an implicit value judgment. Early Nazi films were particularly fond of lighting Communists and Jews to make them look sinister. They moved about in the shadows and were preferably photographed from a high angle against dreary, limiting backgrounds (such as walls of buildings or pavements), whereas Aryan faces, 'ours', were shown in low-angle shot against open skies and heroic cloud formations. The documentary *Der ewige Jude* (1940) probably offers the most consistent example of a photographically imposed 'us' perspective, but the principle can be found among features from any period and country. In the Russian anti-Nazi film *Swamp Soldiers* (1938), the faces of the Germans were even photographed through distorting lenses.

Propaganda is not the genre to pass up any opportunities for playing on our deeply rooted instincts about faces. Whether the characters belong in our camp or the enemy's is clearly spelled out in their outward appearance which acts as a reflection of their moral value. Various unpleasant-looking American heavies have become firmly identified with enemy agents of different nationalities; the Russian silent cinema also contains numerous examples of how much a propagandist can achieve simply by a careful choice of attractive and unattractive types for the relevant parts. In addition, the Russian cinema developed a full iconography of detestable capitalistic attributes to be linked with the enemy: obesity, umbrellas, gloves, cigarette-holders and bowler hats, have all been so diligently used in this context that they have become instantly recognisable, like signs of evil magic.

These are primitive mechanisms, activated

189

as they are by such simple signs which set in motion conditioned reflexes rather than arguments. The important thing is to use these signs to initiate a distancing process which involves only the enemy. Once the distance has become well established, propaganda can indulge in apparently risky manoeuvres without jeopardising its aims. In the early 'thirties, Upton Sinclair decided, to the horror of the film companies, to run as the Democratic candidate for the Governorship of California. In the short films which were used in the campaign against him, figures with foreign accents and lugubrious looks *recommended* Sinclair's ideas. 'His system seems to work well in Russia, so why can't it work here?' The dissociation of 'us' feelings from the ideas so disingenuously advanced is prompted both by the speaker's unattractive appearance and by another conditioned reflex in the American public, the fear of communism.

In a number of American propaganda films the mere mention of the word 'communist' is apparently thought enough to produce the desired reaction. Such films are likely to appear curiously distorted when they reach audiences other than that to which they are addressed, and without the required ideological perspective. This is particularly striking in *Operation Abolition* (1960), the anti-communist film produced by HUAC – the House Un-American Activities Committee. Apart from the intricate misrepresentations which were subsequently revealed, the most striking thing about *Operation Abolition* is how powerfully its effect boomerangs with audiences that do not share its rabid 'us' attitude to Americanism and Un-Americanism.

The makers have failed to realise the extent to which they are revealing the grossly inquisitorial nature of the Committee's activities, and the genuine indignation of the accused. The attempt of the HUAC film to play on the audience's conditioned reflexes is a typical one in propaganda, a method never so noticeable as when it is failing to work.

One aspect of the 'us' perspective is purely formal but has psychological implications. Propaganda relies heavily on one particular property of the cinema, that the mere fact of the camera being *with* somebody establishes a relationship, an aesthetic commitment. The viewpoint intended for the *Why We Fight* series, is indicated by the title itself, but the third instalment contains a flagrant violation of the perspective principle, and for a few minutes, the effect is fascinatingly ambivalent. *Divide and Conquer* uses sequences from German newsreels and from documentaries like *Sieg im Westen*. Some of the most intense sections show the German air raids on Rotterdam, but are quite literally rendered from a German perspective, shot from the attacking bombers. The subjective camera effect puts the audience right there in the diving planes with

Stills: unattractive people. Opposite page: Die Rothschilds Aktien auf Waterloo. *Above: Herbert Selpin's* Titanic, *with Ernst Fürbringer as Sir Bruce Ismay.*

the Germans; suddenly we *are* the Germans. This dubious but unintentional effect is reinforced by the exciting visual sensations of vertigo and by the immediacy of the images.

Camera position is obviously not the most important factor in producing audience involvement and eventual commitment. True, psychological perspectives are not always identical with visual ones, but wider implications are to be found, for instance, in the British propaganda style, which exploits to the full the psychological advantages of consistent preoccupation with the virtues of the home side, without forays into the enemy camp to disturb the perspective. Although evil is clearly more photogenic than goodness, by all accounts it is extraordinarily risky to attempt propaganda which uses enemies in all the leading roles and thus fails to provide any anchorage for the 'us' feelings.

'In the cinema, the spectator must know, with greater certainty than in the theatre, whom to love and whom to hate.' These words of wisdom, from the pamphlet, 'Betrachtungen zum Filmschaffen', by Reichsfilmintendant Fritz Hippler, would not be very interesting, except for the implied criticism specifically directed at one of the great failures of Nazi film propaganda, the anti-semitic and anti-British costume picture, *Die Rothschilds (Die Rothschilds Aktien von Waterloo – The Rothschilds' Shares in Waterloo)* Hippler goes on to say:

'If, for instance, I am making an anti-semitic film it is obvious that I must not make the Jews attractive . . . But if I put the Jews against the English, that is to say unattractive people against other unattractive people, the effect will be the same as if I were to put a cut-out silhouette in black paper, however artistically executed, on an equally black background, exclaiming: "Look how artistic it is!" The most perfectly shaped profile would be doomed in advance to complete ineffectuality.'

The Rothschilds (1940) is in certain respects skilfully presented, but was a box-office flop. The scriptwriter had committed the fundamental error of staging the story in 'their environment, among Jews and Englishmen'. Consequently none of the central characters could represent an 'us' perspective, and thus identification could not be established between film and audience. In America, similar risks were taken in *The Hitler Gang* (1944) which described 'from within' the emergence of the Nazi regime, but this film was given a solid emotional mooring with the introduction of a commentator who firmly establishes the moral position of the film – and of the audience.

A remarkable instance of the way in which an unintentional 'us' perspective can distort the political intention is offered by Herbert Selpin's *Titanic* (1943), a film which Goebbels hoped would have powerful anti-British propaganda impact – a scornful allegory about a degenerate people *en route* to the final cataclysm.

Evidently the film misfired as it was banned by Goebbels's Ministry of Propaganda. The failure is understandable, because we as spectators have advance knowledge of the imminent fate of the ship. In the face of catastrophe, we cannot but feel for the passengers, and the ensemble which was intended as a symbol for perfidious Albion instead becomes synonymous with 'us'. This was also unfortunate because, in the Germany of 1943, it could have led to associations which would not have suited the Nazis; at the end of the film, the cocky and irresponsible 'Herr Generaldirektor' is alone to blame (although he goes unpunished) for the meaningless deaths of thousands of people.

The boat passengers are a poor choice as the medium for hostile propaganda because one of the most cherished forms for 'us'-glorification is precisely this sort of closed group, isolated from the outside world and on its way towards a common fate. The limited space has dramatic advantages, and the limited cast allows the propagandist to produce identification on an individual level while exploiting the feelings which bind the group together. The sympathy-attracting group may be an infantry patrol in a strange country or a bomber squadron on its way to a target; it may be people in a drifting lifeboat, a ship's crew or that of a submarine; it may be a besieged garrison or, as in Elia Kazan's *Man on a Tightrope*, a circus company. War surrounds such a fellowship with danger, instilling intense feelings of kinship between the audience-group and the group on the screen. This sort of limited 'us' group takes on allegorical dimensions, a nation in microcosm, a symbol of the people and a distillation of their excellence.

In German propaganda, enthusiasm for the war is rarely more fervent than in this type of film. The soldiers seem to merge into a jovial comradeship. With its jokes and tender but manly songs, this image confirms all one's ideas of the Nazis' sentimental and brutal camaraderie. Nowadays it would probably have a strongly negative effect on most audiences, but at the time it evoked hearty 'us' feelings in Germany.

The most striking thing today about *In Which We Serve* – the best known British example of this genre within the genre – is that it lays bare, with such obvious pride, a cross-

Stills. Below: the circus convoy is ordered off the road to make way for the military in Elia Kazan's Man on a Tightrope, *with Fredric March. Opposite page: top –* In Which We Serve, *with Richard Attenborough; bottom –* Western Approaches.

section of the classes. Differences in rank and social demarcations are clearly marked out and never questioned: the 'natural' hierarchy is presented as the basis of stability and efficiency in the crew and in society; across the class barriers flows an unhesitating current of emotional solidarity which reaches all the way to the audience.

In the United States, the propaganda grouping is always composed with a careful eye to the fair representation of ethnic minorities. It was in these incarnations of the American melting pot that the Negro, during World War II, became emancipated as a movie character and was made a fully-fledged American citizen among his Italian, Scandinavian, Indian, Irish, Greek and Polish compatriots – every American should be able to feel himself represented within the fellowship.

Apart from these slight national variations, the films in this sub-genre are in general so confusingly alike that they illustrate in an almost macabre way the extent to which film propaganda is about labels rather than ideas. Alfred Hitchcock's *Lifeboat* (1943) and Pat Jackson's semi-documentary *Western Approaches* (1944), which is also based on the lifeboat motif, are far above the general run of these films. One of the most moving examples, though, is Augusto Genina's Fascist picture, *L'assedio dell'Alcázar* (1939), which describes with deceptive dignity and restraint the siege

of Alcázar during the Spanish Civil War. As scant attention is given to the enemy outside the fortress, Genina can manage without caricatures. Instead, with exquisitely balanced emotions he concentrates entirely on the beleaguered and their heroism. The film reaches an ecstatic climax when the news arrives of Franco's successful advance on Toledo; the besieged defenders burst into rapturous song (which swells on the soundtrack into a magnificent chorus accompanied by a mammoth orchestra).

As a good propagandist, Genina could hardly have failed to exploit this most seductive method of creating a sense of unity between film and audience. Thanks to an instinctive socio-psychological appreciation of its emotive qualities, community singing has become the uniting medium above all others for popular and revivalist movements, mass ideologies and nationalism of every sort. In the cinema, singing in unison almost always retains its power even if the audience does not actually join in. When '*Vorwärts, und nie vergessen*' ('Forward, and never forgotten') is sung in *Kuhle Wampe* (Slatan Dudow, 1932), the enthusiasm seems to spread right through the cinema with an almost physiological inevitability, and when the soldiers of the Third Reich march to the firm beat of their own singing through one Nazi film after another,

one gets an idea of the almost mystical mass attraction of Fascism. Even the low-keyed British cinema of the war years had moments of rapturous community singing, not necessarily of a pronounced patriotic character but giving an impression of enthusiastic unity in difficult times.

Oppressed minority groups tend to demonstrate their defiant hopes in song: in countless films from Eastern Europe, oppressed Communists sing the praises of Socialism in the Internationale and other fighting songs, to the inspiration of the audience as well. In the Nazi *Heimkehr*, an incarcerated German minority sings '*Treue Heimat, sei gegrüsst*' ('True homeland, be greeted') and seems to rise on the wings of song above the miseries of their prison. In the most beautiful sequence of *Casablanca*, freedom-loving exiles sing the Marseillaise until the Nazi officers' noisy rendering of '*Die Wacht am Rhein*' is drowned in the ecstatic harmony of the Allies.

The great power of songs is used in Maoist China's most ambitious propaganda effort which takes the form of a musical. *The East Is Red* (1965) is fairly unique in being a filmed stage production which manages to make cinematic capital out of its theatrical setting. In

Stills. Below: Augusto Genina's L'Assedio del l'Alcázar, *Mireille Balin and Andrea Checchi Right: Michael Curtiz's* Casablanca.

the final scene, the stage is filled with people singing out their enthusiasm in the Internationale; the camera pulls back from the stage to take in members of the theatre audience as they rise from their seats and join in the singing. The border-line separating actors from spectators has dissolved; the enthusiasm takes in a third party, the cinema audience.

This rapturous state of togetherness with the actors is one into which film propaganda aims primarily to seduce its audience. Man is a gregarious animal who needs a sense of belonging. It is only natural that the cinema should try to use mass suggestion as a means of creating political enthusiasm, of welding people together.

Eisenstein, Pudovkin and the other Russians put the people, the masses, firmly at the centre of their films and addressed a proletariat which had already declared its solidarity with the revolution and consequently felt a deep emotional involvement with the mass uprisings which they depicted. In direct opposition to the masses were the instruments of capitalism, the soldiers – they, too, were a mass, but anonymous, a stamping, crushing, pitiless wall. The good masses were never faceless or impersonal. By skilfully controlling the interplay between crowd scenes and close-ups, the Russians succeeded in giving faces and gestures an incredible poignancy which prevented the mass effect losing itself in anonymity. The will and aims of the masses were as one, but the reactions of each of the innumerable individuals were unique and personal.

Eisenstein's *Strike* (1924) was the first major statement of the Soviet cinema. It is a film that gives its undivided loyalty to the people as a mass without giving precedence to any one individual over the rest. After *Strike*, the Russian cinema gradually evolved away from the total dominance of the masses. Increasingly, individual characters were allowed to step out of the mass to be stressed as positive but still representative figures. However, until the definitive breakthrough of Socialist Realism with its dogmatic glorification of the positive hero, the mass remained, in Gestalt-psychological terms, 'figure' rather than 'background'. During the Stalin era, the mass was rendered even more anonymous until it became virtually a backdrop against which the positive hero performed, although it was still used to reinforce fighting spirit, power-station joy, and 'us' enthusiasm.

The most powerful effects involving the masses in the Soviet cinema have not, however, been achieved through joy. The classical revolutionary film consistently works with the mass as underdog, proletarians oppressed by the rich, unarmed people struggling desperately against superior police or military forces. Their emotional effect cannot therefore be attributed entirely to mass psychology. The spectator's

195

sympathies have been determined by the same outrages that justify the mass's intentions and his loyalty is maintained by mechanisms other than simple mass suggestion.

Around the time that the Russians began to adjust themselves to the demands of Socialist Realism, the Germans started to make spectacular propaganda films in which the main ingredient was the sense of fellowship radiated by the mass. German films celebrating the Nazi Party in the early 'thirties created an almost emblematic version of the growing-mass motif, and propaganda directors loved to shape it into an ecstatic vision of ultimate triumph. The vision first appears in an all-German adventure movie called *Der Rebell* (1932) with the director, Luis Trenker, as the hero who is shot and whose soul leaves his corpse to walk upwards among the clouds, followed by a growing mass of cheering people who fill the entire sky behind his flag of freedom. An almost exact copy of the vision occurs in *Hans Westmar* (1933), and in *Hitlerjunge Quex* (1933), its function in conveying fellow feelings is particularly well prepared for in the young hero's earlier misery at being excluded from desirable 'us' contact. When he becomes a Nazi martyr, the last moments of his life are sweetened by a vision of the future which is meant not just for him but for us as well: thousands of Hitler youth stride towards a new world in steadily growing formations which merge together into an enormous mass of young people marching behind fluttering swastika banners to the rhythm of rousing marches. The effect is overwhelming. This manner of turning people into symbols is characteristic of mass scenes in the Nazi cinema. The mass itself becomes an ornament with a well disciplined, symmetrical form. This is very different from the Russian revolutionary film mass with its raw vitality, unified but without uniformity, explosive and unpredictable.

This in no way implies a denial of the psychological force of the Nazi style. The most magnificent example, Leni Riefenstahl's *Triumph of the Will*, has an inhumanly monumental character and a perfection in its symmetry which makes the whole film seem like a moving standard of gigantic proportions. But the heraldic mass formations give rise to a rapturously sincere 'us' feeling, endowing the film with an emotive radiance which is hard to resist. It would therefore be a grave mistake to imagine that the human ornamentation of the German cinema was ever synonymous with mechanical ineffectuality. It can be compared with another genre which, without political intent, also reduces the individual to an element in decorative mass effects, in which people, subservient to perfection, arrange themselves in a disciplined pattern which allows for no embellishment by its individual components. This is the American show picture, and particularly

Stills. Left and right: Luis Trenker as the hero of his film Der Rebell. *Above:* Triumph of the Will.

the Busby Berkeley style which was prevalent at the time when *Triumph of the Will* was being shot in Germany. Watching *Triumph of the Will*, we are not only called upon to observe the crowd's enthusiastic reactions to its leader and symbols, but also forced into a state of participation. We are there among the banners, floating with the flags, standing next to Hitler and jostling with the crowd. We merge into the mass. Other propaganda documentaries have used mass scenes to establish audience involvement, but *Triumph of the Will* is exceptional in the extraordinary sense of being present. Significantly, Leni Riefenstahl (like Humphrey Jennings in some of his best films) has totally excluded any spoken commentary – the film has no middle-man breaking the immediacy by putting himself between the enthusiasm of the mass and the spectator's involvement. Spoken commentaries inherently stand outside, at a distance from their subject, to provide a description instead of a sense of presence. Under favourable conditions the suggestive power of crowds in films may be quite overwhelming. Yet it is surprisingly easy for a commentator to undo the effect – not just minimising it but actually reversing it. *Triumph of the Will* has been used, frequently and successfully, as source material

197

for films with diametrically opposed aims. The most remarkable of these is probably *These are the Men* (1943), which consists largely of sequences from the Riefenstahl film, provocatively accompanied by a hostile English commentary. *These Are the Men* still has the great emotive force which probably still stems in part from the cheering Nazi crowds. Even here the enthusiasm of the mass constitutes a sounding board, but this time for emotions that are directed *against* all that the mass stands for.

In 1966, the English director Peter Watkins made one of the cinema's most remarkable and complex experiments with mass suggestion, attempting in *Privilege* simultaneously to explain it, exploit it, and warn people of its effects. He put pop hysteria in the context of an imagined totalitarian society which exploited it as opium for the masses. But although the structure of *Privilege* is clearly based on detailed study of *Triumph of the Will*, Watkins fails to make his vision frightening because the mass hysteria for its pop idol does not work powerfully enough to reach out and engulf the audience in the cinema. The mass suggestion becomes something to observe rather than to become spellbound and frightened by. The effects of mass suggestion on an audience are not unconditional; here they are annihilated by the critical attitude of the film itself.

One of the factors determining the psychological effect of the mass is obviously the 'us'

perspective of the audience and the film – the mass becomes attractive or detestable or frightening according to the film's intentions and power, and to the sympathies and idiosyncrasies of the audience. Thus, albeit with feigned lightheartedness, spy movies evoke visions of terror about a destructive mass, the hordes from the East. However many Asiatics are shot down, new ones, looking exactly the same, pour forth.

One complication about mass scenes is that the concept of the mass in itself carries a network of associations that are uncommonly sensitive to impulses in a negative direction. A film-maker can easily associate the idea of the mass with that of a mob, but the spectator can do it for himself by activating his own defence mechanisms, even against films aiming to glorify the mass's purpose. Maoist propaganda documentaries like *Chairman Mao Is the Red Sun In Our Hearts*, which seem to rely entirely on the impact of enthusiastic mass events, would thus be unlikely to evoke much sympathy in the West except in those who have already accepted the message.

It is reasonable to assume that such alienating mechanisms would most easily be aroused by the spectacle of an unruly mass in a state of rage or panic, and prepared for violence. Very few Western films parallel or imitate the aggressively

emotional mass which appears in Russian revolutionary films, which were aimed at audiences already loyally siding with the proletariat on the screen. Cinema Nôvo in Brazil sometimes shows striking resemblances to the Russian silent cinema, but its attitude to the mass is descriptive rather than suggestive. In *Os Fuzis* (1963), the mass is neither attractive nor frightening, but pathetic, politically and morally flabby: Ruy Guerra's desperate picture of the inability of the oppressed to grasp their own situation and their own destiny. In the past few years, one political film has very skilfully managed to work in the tradition of the Russian revolutionary cinema, the means and aims of which it uses as its own. This is Gillo Pontecorvo's *La Battaglia di Algeri* (1966), in which the mass hero is the FLN in the bloody struggle for freedom. There is an effective conflict between an oppressed mass and brutal military domination, and this directs our sympathies sufficiently to enable Pontecorvo even to show Algerian atrocities without seriously endangering the audience's 'us' solidarity with the mass.

The ambivalence in the concept of the mass has sometimes left strange imprints on the political cinema, not least in emphatically democratic films. The difference between the good and the evil mass, between the mass as 'people' and the mass as 'mob' is not as distinct and uncomplicated as films like to pretend. Even a sincere anti-Fascist warning like Robert Rossen's *All the King's Men* (1949) turns out to be more concerned with authority and leadership than with the will of the people, because the mass so easily allows itself to be turned into part of the scenery, a chameleon-like phenomenon which changes its moral colour according to the goodness or badness of its leaders. In Chaplin's *The Great Dictator* (1940), the demagogue Hynkel leads the gullible masses through vacuous speeches promulgating his evil ideas, but when Chaplin's alter ego as spokesman for democracy and humanity delivers a terrific final appeal, he draws cheers from the same mass in the same state of ecstatic enthusiasm. The mass on the screen and the mass in the cinema experience a sense of unity which the irony of the situation cannot disturb. Or perhaps the irony is not intentional, just an artistic lapse.

In the mystical qualities of the mass as depicted on the screen, Nazi ideology's almost dogmatic lack of consistency occasionally reveals itself. The mass as incarnation of the popular soul is something positive, yet the campaign against democratic heresies demands that the Führer's genius be contrasted with the irredeemable nature of the mass. One gets the impression that the Nazi authorities realised that the intrinsic contradictions in its indoctrination might produce undesirable psychological effects, and that they preferred to put anti-democratic propaganda in historical films where it made a less provocative impression on the

199

audience while still producing the desired effect on their political attitudes.

On the whole, the ambivalent power of suggestion that the mass wields in the cinema is probably used more often to its detriment than to its advantage. Faced with a conflict on the screen, we almost automatically incline towards the quantitatively inferior party. One archetypal film plot, which has innumerable propaganda variations, is the story of the lonely individual fighting against or fleeing from a superior collective force. Exceptional circumstances are needed to prevent the audience's sympathies from becoming firmly lodged on the side of the lonely man. This process, which psychologists have labelled 'hero identification', is a simpler way of achieving an 'us' feeling than the uncertain suggestive power of the mass. Even in the Soviet cinema, the mass had to make way for the individual hero – it is irrelevant here that the hero who came to represent 'us', the people, was not particularly attractive.

'We – the people,' says the American *ur*-mother, Jane Darwell, in *The Grapes of Wrath*, and she says it proudly about her America, about herself and her own folks, the impoverished and illiterate, 'the ordinary people'. The people is the 'us' group to which all countries address their propaganda, an audience which must be cajoled into agreement. Therefore, in the final analysis, what must be glorified is the people so that the cause of the people, the ideas of the people, the will of the people, can become imprinted on the people themselves. That is why we, the ordinary people, whether sitting in the cinema or featured on the screen, form the infallible gauge of political good and evil to which propaganda invariably refers.

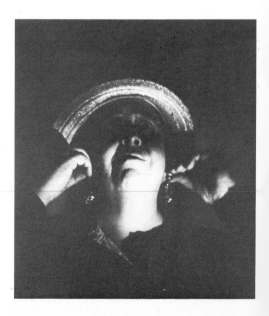

Stills. Above: The Great Dictator. *Right: Jane Darwell in* The Grapes of Wrath.

The Image of the Enemy

When countries are in a state of crisis, or in danger of war, there is an increasing need for things to be simplified. The other side becomes totally malevolent, one's own cause indisputably just, and everyone gathers around the symbols of unity. Social conflicts are rapidly settled or concealed. People often seem to develop a strong need to lose their own individual complexity in a simpler national identity. Political propaganda is at its most effective in such insecure times. Attempts have sometimes been made, as in Nazi Germany, to prolong these situations of stress over long periods so that the public's heightened receptivity could be exploited. Occasionally phoney conflicts have even been staged to preserve a nation's unity and maintain the accepted simplifications. It is perhaps necessary for the political propagandist to 'live from crisis to crisis', as F. C. Bartlett wrote in 'Political Propaganda' (1940). But this brings with it the risk of overplaying the message to an extent that induces either disbelief or hysteria.

It is fundamental to propaganda that the message must be expressed in a way that does not invite discussion. The effect depends upon being received without question, on drowning out all criticism or analysis. Its appeal is purely emotional and excludes all alternatives. As a rule, the propagandist regards intellectuals as unreliable or hostile. Their limited numbers make them of little interest as a target. The best thing is to isolate them and rob them of the opportunity to influence public opinion.

Though the propagandist may not allow any other opinion but his own, he does recognise that there is another side, another cause. A large area of propaganda, possibly the most difficult, has to be devoted to the image of the enemy, both to providing an identikit picture and to guiding reactions to it. The propaganda image of the other side must be of stylised simplicity. Subtlety and realism invite comparisons; if the enemy were represented without distortion, his strength might be recognisable as well as his weakness; the spectator would be exposed to the enemy's point of view, and would discover the human traits behind the unattractive exterior.

In propaganda films, clichés appear unavoidable. Stereotypes generally come ready made, having been evolved over a long period, sometimes as part of myths concerned with other races, nations or groups. They can descend from generation to generation through education or oral tradition; or they may lie dormant in a national subconscious, to be revived by propaganda when the party or state needs an enemy, a scapegoat. They rob others of their humanity by reducing individuals to a lifeless homogeneity. Although such cliché figures may be harmless and occasionally amusing (the stock jokes about foreigners), they can also help prepare the way for genocide. Any effective method of separation – legal, linguistic or physical – between 'us' and 'them', opens the way for 'us' to do anything to 'them'. We no longer need consider them as human beings; we will not see their similarity to ourselves.

Some of the cinema's clichés for people and human relationships are its own, while others appear to be inherited and can be traced back to folk stories. Like fairy-tales, movies rarely make good and evil complicated. Apparently ready-made patterns of development for characters and relationships lead to a feeling of predetermination, so that the ending of most films simply confirms what we guessed in the very first scene. But the cinema is also such an intimate art form that good and evil cannot be represented totally in primary colours. The enemy was the object of an uncomplicated hatred during the early history of the cinema, before it had attained self-awareness. During World War I, hatred of the enemy was beyond the abilities of either side to express in propaganda without resorting to Grand-Guignol. The results did not invite imitation.

The Birth of a Nation (1914) is a film whose greatness we can still recognise: the battle scenes, in particular, come alive, and hardly anyone has done such things better. But at other times, it can now look quite absurd, mainly when Griffith is seized by ambitions to make something more than just a film. He

Still: D. W. Griffith's The Birth of a Nation; *George Siegman, as the evil, lecherous half-caste Silas Lynch, and Mae Marsh.*

decides, for instance, to compete with academicians in the art of historical painting. Certain scenes in *The Birth of a Nation* are conceived as copies of contemporary paintings and photographs. (Robert E. Lee's capitulation is described in a title as a facsimile of the actual scene.) In contrast to the exterior scenes the interiors are musty and lifeless. The most curious aspect of the film, though, is on a per-

sonal, psychological level: the hatred, the story of blacks and whites in black-and-white terms. The whites have clean-cut features and noble souls; they come in touching family groups; the horrors of war have a purifying effect on them; they die with composure. The blacks are undignified; they roll their eyes and jump about like dervishes – detestable creatures who need to be crushed. Worst of all is a half-breed, Silas Lynch. The crime of the rest is that they have set themselves up against the white power structure, but Lynch represents something much more serious to Griffith; he stands for good corrupted by evil, a man of impure blood. Of all the blacks in *The Birth of a Nation*, who include the faithful, sobbing servants, he is the only one credited with any intelligence, but it is destructive, murderous, insane.

To Griffith, the enemy is subhuman yet still lethal; he is close at hand, even if not currently identifiable and it is vital to be on one's guard. In *Orphans of the Storm* (1922), which is about the horrors of the French Revolution, the great director addresses the nation in a long introductory title, issuing an emotional warning

Stills. This page: The Birth of a Nation. *Above: Reconstruction – Southern gentleman in chains, mocked by blacks and Union soldiers; left – revenge. Opposite: top – Lillian Gish in Griffith's* Orphans of the Storm; *bottom – Carl Dreyer's* Leaves from Satan's Book.

about the film's real subject, the Russian Revolution. Griffith speaks of evil and tries to pinpoint it, but it appears as a spectre rather than a reality. His films are reactionary but lacking in ideological substance – the outpourings of a hysterical imagination, a great artist's ghostly fantasies.

Carl Dreyer's *Leaves From Satan's Journal* (1920) is a Nordic Griffith picture about evil and the way it is revealed during different periods of history: at the death of Christ, during the French Revolution, and on the red side during the Finnish Civil War. The dark forces are embodied in the figure of Satan himself; he is briefly glimpsed in various disguises but always seems to be at home with the revolutionary left.

Openly reactionary films would be more common if there were more reactionary film-makers, or perhaps if the film industry gave greater scope to subjective ideas and expression. In the United States, the conspiracy view of politics seems to be quite common – and not only among oil millionaires, but as the driving force behind certain political groupings, yet such attitudes have rarely influenced the American cinema. On the contrary, a number of leftish-liberal films from the 'thirties onwards have warned against political hysteria and hysterical politicians – films like William Wellman's *The President Vanishes* (1934), Archie Mayo's *The Black Legion* (1937), Robert Rossen's *All the King's Men* (1949), and Elia Kazan's *A Face in the Crowd* (1956). With few exceptions, the anti-Soviet films produced in Hollywood during the Cold War do not seem particularly inspired; they are stereotyped, made to order on established patterns, with the communists virtually as gangsters.

The invisible enemy is important in the semi-documentary *Native Land* (1942), directed by Leo Hurwitz and Paul Strand, which tells a story of political violence in the United States, of persecution of the radical trade union movement, of informers, black-listing, assault and murder. The illustrations are partly authentic, partly re-creations of events as they are supposed to have happened. These scenes excite our indignation, and there is nothing to suggest that the crimes were not committed. The strangest aspect of *Native Land* is that the criminal – the enemy – is so hard to catch. This could be taken as realistic: the criminals are rarely caught because the police are politically corrupt; those who are caught are hardly ever the real criminals, merely hired hands. The real enemy does not show his face, and therefore grows into something demonic, an almost omnipotent 'system' which only the people can

Stills. Below: Archie Mayo's The Black Legion. *Right: Broderick Crawford and John Ireland in* All the King's Men.

crush. It is a very powerful image, but possibly capitalism is more effectively exposed if the system is shown to be constructed and held together by people who, superficially at least, resemble everyone else.

Triumph of the Will has the same invisible presence of 'the others'. It is as though we were waiting only for a prearranged sign from the Führer that at last the enemy was right in the arena, for all that incredible energy to be released and annihilate him. The hundreds of thousands of marchers are demonstrating against the past, against Versailles and Weimar, against Germany's humiliation and defeat. But their presence is also a warning and a challenge to the invisible enemy.

The enemy can get close without ever showing his face, and indeed facelessness can be part of his characterisation, as in Humphrey Jennings's documentary allegory of the Lidice massacre, *The Silent Village*. The inhabitants of the occupied Welsh village have human faces and live voices, whereas the enemy expresses himself only through billposted decrees, loudspeaker announcements and machine-gun fire, The voices are mechanical. A loudspeaker car drives repeatedly through the village roaring out threats and later announces the names of those condemned to death. The announcements are preceded by a musical introduction, but it is an ominous kind of music: the funeral march from Wagner's 'Götterdämmerung'.

Where the enemy is concerned, watchfulness seems to be of the essence even in the cinema. Indoctrination is most successful when there is an element of excitement in the presentation; the spectator is left to make his own discoveries, draw his own conclusions, or at least imagine that he does. It is probably not a good idea to label the enemy too clearly – nor too early. He may commit all manner of dirty deeds, but it is for the spectator, not the film, to show indignation. The film is not the vital hater; the audience is.

Sometimes, however, it happens that the mask slips a little and the film-makers reveal themselves. Nazi films rarely give the appearance of having been haphazardly put together, and in the most pernicious of them, *Der ewige Jude*, the very lack of inhibition seems coldbloodedly calculated. At the same time, this film contains brief moments when the horrific lecture (intended to educate its audience towards genocide) appears to falter and uncontrolled emotions come to light. The film describes the Jews as scum, an enemy force, supporting all the evil in the world – war, capitalism, sexuality and modern art. Fritz Hippler speaks in his commentary about the low standard of hygiene among the Jews and goes on to photograph a filthy wall crawling with flies. One can sadly assume that this propagandist landmine was effective, and that German audiences associated vermin directly with Jews. Later, the theme

205

recurs more explicitly. He uses a map to show the global distribution of Jews and then that of the brown rat. Unpleasant pictures of rats are followed by pictures of Jews; the suggested connection is given added emphasis in the commentary. It is hard to believe that this was effective as propaganda. Hippler does not give his audience a chance to make its own discoveries and should thus by rights have forfeited their participation. Even a methodically indoctrinated audience would be likely to reject this kind of forced feeding. It is possible that the director calculated that the impact of the visual juxtapositions and the sheer shamelessness of the sequence would make the audience hesitate to object to the obvious manipulation. It was to be dazzled. But conceivably the propagandist has dropped his mask here without actually realising it, letting his true feelings and those of his political colleagues well out, undirected and uncensored.

A modified version of this startling sequence recurs in *The Grain Is in Danger* (1944), an eight-minute Danish documentary by Hagen Hasselbalch. It is ostensibly about an insect, Sitophilus granariae, which does a great deal of damage to crops, but it is really a viciously intelligent satire on Nazism. The film was passed by the German censor and shown as a short in Danish cinema programmes during the war.

The point of departure is a quotation from Goebbels. On 3 June 1943, the German Propaganda Minister said in a speech in the Berlin Palace of Sport: 'Like the Colorado beetle which destroys, indeed must destroy the potato crops, so the Jew destroys nations. There is only one cure, namely a radical elimination of the danger.'

The Grain Is in Danger describes a visitation of the pest, but this is clearly not an entomological picture. The insects look nasty, and the commentary states that nobody can be safe against their onslaught – they force their way everywhere. (Voices echo ominously: 'Everywhere, everywhere.') In a Danish kitchen, a housewife shows us a slice of bread milling with black creatures, and then the insects are seen fanning out across the map, just like Jews and rats in *Der ewige Jude*. The tone of the commentary is outraged and passionately appealing. Provocative questions are asked: 'How should we organise the counter-offensive? Who will turn the tide? Who will take up the fight?' The final line of this remarkable film is: 'Remember that Denmark's crops are at stake.' (The tone of voice implies that it is talking about Denmark's freedom.) With its mockery of the Germans, *The Grain Is in Danger* was a courageous partisan attack on a superior enemy. It is obviously questionable to equate men with insects. However, this was straight counter-propaganda using enemy material and the insects do not represent German men, women and children but the German war machine, the Nazi threat to Europe and the world. It is not a case of analogy but of metaphor.

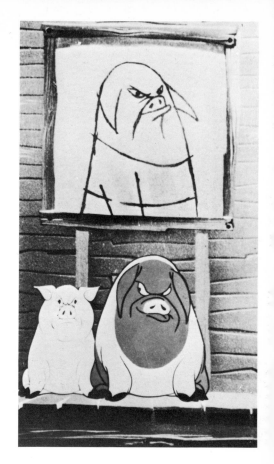

There are less honourable instances of animal symbolism. In the British feature *The Planter's Wife* (1952), communist guerillas in Malaya are identified with snakes. Here the vilification also betrays the feelings of discomfort (and insecurity) evoked by this enemy. Animals can substitute for people in allegorical contexts as in *Animal Farm* (1954), an animated feature by John Halas and Joy Batchelor which is a satire on Stalinism based on George Orwell's famous novel. Animals can also help in the identification of friends and enemies. Features made during World War II include an assortment of fierce-looking dogs to indicate the enemy's unattractiveness before it is revealed by his actions. The malevolent Polish mayor in Gustav Ucicky's *Heimkehr* (1941) looks like Lenin and is followed around by a couple of growling dogs. Members of the Gestapo are generally portrayed as wearing long, stiff, black coats, with black dogs at their sides, and usually rain, thunder and lightning as an accompaniment.

The enemy obviously cannot be represented as good, but he may start off with a semblance of attractiveness which is systematically removed, his disguise proving more and more transparent until the evil which we have suspected in him is finally exposed. In Grigori Alexandrov's *Meeting on the Elbe* (1949), the handsome Russian commandant Kuzmin has a German-American girl-friend. Their relationship is

Stills. Left: the Halas and Batchelor version of Animal Farm. *Above: Erich von Stroheim as the Field Marshal (Rommel) in Billy Wilder's* Five Graves to Cairo.

conducted at a distance – he has her picture in his room and practices saying 'I love', while Moscow Radio plays a request, 'Love of the Home-land.' Eventually it turns out that the girl has only faked affection and is a cold-blooded American agent, a domineering woman who returns to the United States alone in a gigantic airliner. This is not very persuasive stuff, but it creates a clear impression that the capitalist enemy is so lacking in scruples that he exploits even the noblest feelings.

The enemy, while still remaining the enemy, may be treated with a degree of respect, like the Republican officers in *L'Assedio dell'Alcázar*. He may, like Colonel Lemmering in *Det brinner en eld*, half belong on the right side and appear as a regrettable victim of political circumstance. He may be a forceful and complex personality who confuses the strictly ordered categories. The piano-playing White Russian colonel in *Chapayev* at first seems sympathetic and a fine professional soldier. In Billy Wilder's *Five Graves to Cairo* (1943), Erich von Stroheim plays a German field-marshal in the desert war (obviously Rommel, although the name is never mentioned). He is an impressive figure, a great strategist with an

unequalled knowledge of human nature, who is inevitably tricked by simpler people. Nevertheless he has an independent mind and a distinctly humorous glint behind his monocle. Both these relatively agreeable enemy characters are presented as prisoners of a system, but this also indicates a weakness in them; they understand their situation but are unable to escape from it. They are also on the losing side. In the case of Stroheim there is never any real question. He is first and foremost Erich von Stroheim, the man you love to hate, who can therefore never be taken entirely seriously. Usually though, the 'good' enemy is shown to have two faces. Colonel Borozdin in *Chapayev* plays the 'Moonlight Sonata' in his quarters, his eyes half closed. But meanwhile his old servant, who is busy tidying up the room, suddenly notices his own brother's newly signed death warrant on the desk. The piano-playing, which has so far indicated culture and sensitivity, becomes almost perverted. The field marshal in *Five Graves to Cairo* is certainly a humorist, but always at someone else's expense.

Even in the Nazi German cinema, the enemy can occasionally seem sympathetic. This can be taken as a sign, either that he will eventually change sides, or that he will be shown up for the villain he really is. In *Hitlerjunge Quex*, young Heini has a protective older friend in the Communist youth leader, who initially

shows nothing but understanding and thought-fulness. But later he is exposed. The communists in *Hans Westmar*, include an idealist who opposes the party's terrorist activities, speaking up for humane methods. After wrestling with his conscience, he informs the Nazis of the crime that his friends are about to commit. (They attempt to force their way into a hospital to lynch the wounded hero, but are beaten back). In the extraordinary finale, when the Nazi Party marches down the Unter den Linden, a small cluster of Communists watch the enormous turnout. Defiantly they raise their clenched fists – even the sympathetic Bolshevik. However, his fist opens as he slowly lowers his arm, and then, just as slowly, as if spellbound, he raises it again in the Hitler salute.

Communists form the principal enemy in the features made just after Hitler's coming to power. They wear peaked caps and keep their hands in their pockets; their Party officials have pointed beards and soiled, bohemian-looking neckties. Their relationship to Moscow is shown to be completely dependent. In *Hans Westmar*, the secretary of the Communist group announces that its finances are in a bad state, but the chairman comforts her: It doesn't matter – Moscow knows its duty.' Later, it is not Communists at home who are the issue (they are safely in Dachau) but the danger of world communism. A certain amount

Stills. Above: Marina von Dittmar and the Russian secret police in Karl Ritter's G.P.U. Right: Max W. Kimmich's anti-British, pro-Irish pictures, Der Fuchs von Glenarvon (top) and Mein Leben für Irland – water torture in an English boarding school.

of play is given to Soviet atheism, for instance in *Friesennot* (1935), which was about the Volga Germans under the yoke of the godless Bolsheviks. *G.P.U.* (1942), directed by Karl Ritter, is about the Russian secret police and is full of long shadows, sly looks, conspiratorial meetings, underground dungeons, hidden microphones, diabolical machines, sabotage and murder. The familiar terror images naturally had some basis in reality, but on film they assume an air of the commonplace that works against the nightmarishness, and the result is unintentionally comic.

When hatred is the principal aim, documentaries are possibly more suitable than features; the unsuspecting spectator could conceivably experience pictures from reality as a reality. But the Nazis were often too eager to saturate their audiences. The over-indoctrination is exemplified by a short entitled *The Soviet Paradise*, which was sent round the occupied countries in 1942 with a travelling exhibition called 'Europa gegen den Bolschewismus' ('Europe against Bolshevism'). It preaches, in the same overwrought breath anti-semitism and anti-Communism. It demonstrates 'the GPU's torture chambers' and talks of 'the Jewish hangmen.' Corpses are carried out of the prison at Lvov, and the helpers arrange the dead bodies in a row to the accompaniment of Handel's Largo. The commentator describes the faces of the Jews as 'degenerate' and 'murderous-looking,' finally stating that 'this is the true face of bolshevism.'

The Soviet Paradise can scarcely have been enjoyable except for fanatics who were already living in a fantasy world and never had doubts as to who was the murderer and who was the victim. Corpses never provide convincing material evidence on film. Furthermore, unless audiences can feel that they are participating in solving the crime, they are rarely willing to pass sentence. The Nazis would have produced more effective propaganda if they had been better psychologists, if they had been less authoritarian – if they had not been Nazis.

Bolsheviks and Jews appear as the Nazis' major adversaries; they are not just unattractive personally, but also represent dangerous ideas.

The British often appear as enemies in Goebbels's films, but the attitude to them is somewhat inconsistent. In certain pictures it is almost generous. A captured British pilot in Karl Ritter's *Pour le Mérite* (1938) does escape in a slightly underhand manner (through a lavatory window) from his German guards, but after the end of World War I they all meet up and things are sorted out. In a World War II flying film, *Bomber Squadron Lützow*, the British are depicted as formidable enemies – at least, it is particularly honourable to bring down a Spitfire.

More often, however, England is 'perfidious Albion,' a nation of tradesmen surpassed in unreliability only by the Jews. In *Die Roths-*

childs, the emphasis is mainly on the Jews, but the English are robbed of the glory of having won at Waterloo (it was Blücher's victory), and at the end of the picture the director, Erich Waschneck, gives an emphatic warning. The year is 1940 and the Rothschild family have left Europe, but, says the final title, we are carrying on the struggle against their allies, 'the English plutocrats'.

The English are capitalists and imperialists. They enslave brave little nations like the Boers in *Ohm Krüger* and the Irish in two films by Max W. Kimmich *Der Fuchs von Glenarvon* (1940) and *Mein Leben für Irland* (1941). They wage war against civilians and set up concentration camps (*Ohm Krüger*). They inhibit scientific progress in Kimmich's *Germanin* (1943) and impede Germany from establishing colonies in Herbert Selpin's *Carl Peters* (1941). In *Titanic* (1942), a remarkable film by Herbert Selpin, we are first shown a tangled skein of stock-market speculations and capitalist intrigues, followed by the ruthless promotion of the new ship in the hope of winning the Atlantic blue ribbon, and then the cataclysm. The British shipowner, Sir Bruce Ismay, mercilessly harasses the nervous captain, and behaves in a most unmanly way when the ship is sinking. But he is saved and at the inquest blames the catastrophe on the captain who went down with his ship. The only person on board who does not close his eyes to the danger and to responsibility is the first mate, a clear-eyed German. The fact that Ismay does not have to answer for his actions is merely typical of British justice. *Titanic* brands England as a corrupt class society, in which injustice is law and wealth brings absolution from legal and social responsibility. Selpin's film was reissued in West Germany in 1950 but was quickly withdrawn after representations by the British occupation authorities. Apparently a re-edited version was later used in East Germany as anti-capitalist propaganda.

France, too, was a capitalist state and a colonial power, but seems to have been largely ignored in German propaganda. In *Sieg im Westen*, which ends with France's defeat, there are only a few slightly ironic hints about the impenetrability of the Maginot Line (with clips from a film including the Marseillaise, the Arc de Triomphe, and the words 'We are stronger'). Pictures and commentary discreetly suggest that the French were hopelessly organised and inferior soldiers. Prisoners walk past the camera, among them colonial troops, and in a much noted sequence some negroes

Stills. Below: Max W. Kimmich's Germanin *Right: Herbert Selpin films. Top:* Carl Peters *Centre and bottom:* Titanic – Ismay (Ernst Fürbringer), *the Captain (Otto Wernicke), the German first officer (Hans Nielsen) and the unfortunate passengers.*

perform a curious little sketch, miming and dancing. We are aware of the implication that the French made others fight their war and that their well-known frivolity also marked their military effort. But the sequence could also be seen as a bizarre illustration of Hitler's thesis in 'Mein Kampf' that the French, a dying nation, were developing negroid features.

Unlike Stalinist films, Nazi ones contain virtually no caricatures of contemporary rulers and political leaders. Lord Kitchener and Cecil Rhodes are portrayed as malevolent and utterly deceitful in *Ohm Krüger*, and the brutal camp commandant has been taken to represent Winston Churchill. But far from current events are being depicted.

There was never enough time for the propaganda machine to build up a complete system of associations and attitudes to the United States. In his speeches, Hitler raged against Roosevelt and his Jewish-plutocratic advisers. There seems to have been the same murky brew of anti-semitism and anti-capitalism in a propaganda short called *Herr Roosevelt pläudert* (*Mr Roosevelt Chats*, 1942).

Some of the most interesting American films about Germany and the Germans were made by emigrants from Central Europe. Fred Zinnemann, who as a young man had been involved in the making of *Menschen am Sonntag* (1929), directed *The Seventh Cross* (1944), based on a novel by Anna Seghers. It is

a very odd film, and melancholy almost to the point of despair, about evil Germans (a member of the Gestapo is introduced as 'a good German, stone-hearted, mechanical, ruthless'), and about the selfless few who risk their lives by hiding a man who has escaped from a concentration camp. It is about a Germany where almost everyone is guilty, where those who do not take part in the hunt nevertheless turn away from the fugitive. Zinnemann skilfully conveys the claustrophobic feeling inevitable in such a society and the undercurrents of terror beneath the blind obedience.

The Seventh Cross is a serious, low-key film, yet it is also strangely vague. It demonstrates

the existence of an organised resistance, but also seems to stress German collective guilt. The inhabitants of Mainz, where George Heisler (Spencer Tracy) tries to find a place to hide, speak openly of the concentration camp, Westhofen, where seven crosses have been put up for seven escaped inmates. It must have been a burning question in 1944 how the responsibility of the German nation for the Nazi's misdeeds would be assessed after the war, but one cannot be sure how clear Zinnemann's (and Anna Seghers's) attitude would have been to American audiences. Though searching, the film is very restrained and its manhunt story is frequently almost dream-like. There is a timidity even in the characterisation of the few who bravely follow the dictates of their consciences. Heisler can be identified as a fighting socialist (or perhaps communist) from the days before 1933, as can the two men helping him. This is never stated, but is (or appears to be) hinted at with a vagueness which could be understandable: committed proletarians have never been common in MGM pictures. So this beautiful film unfortunately ended up somewhere between realistic story and legend. The scenes inside the concentration camp are enveloped in mist; they have an atmosphere of isolation of night and fog, with shadowy figures and the sounds of dogs barking. This was a way of saying that this was a world without reason, a nightmare within reality, but at the same time, the mists suggested a distance which could not be bridged by emotion or sympathy. They bore witness to the impossibility of contact.

Three years earlier, another emigré, Fritz Lang, had directed a political thriller, *Man Hunt*. It opened in the heart of Hitler's Germany, at Berchtesgaden, and here, too, we were looking at Germany through mists. Lang's *Hangmen Also Die* (1943), a film about the Heydrich assassination, in spite of some sharp dialogue by Brecht, was equally evasive. It teemed with echoes of American gangster films and of what Agee calls 'Middle High German cinematic style', full of shadows and obscurities. The haziness was a result of distance. Nazism was initially something of a horror story in the cinema. Later, when it needed to be made comprehensible for the American public, it was depicted as a kind of underworld and the Nazi Party was made to look like a gangster organisation. Here was a ready-made form, which only needed adapting. A great deal fitted into this pattern, but Hitler himself was too outlandish to be incorporated into any American tradition. *The Hitler Gang* (1944), which showed the rise of the Führer and his apostles to absolute power and their subsequent fall in terms of a very peculiar gangster story, seemed in constant danger of being torn apart by its psychological ambition.

During the war years, even Donald Duck suffered from nightmares about Nazism, which appeared in *Der Fuehrer's Face* (1942). It was easy for the imagination to become preoccupied by Hitler, because of the apparent inconsistency of the image – the terrifying absolute power and the laughable appearance. At a distance, the dictator could only be unreal or comical. In *Man Hunt*, we glimpse him only for a second, centred on the crosswires of the telescopic sight, but Fritz Lang still manages to give him a kind of magical presence in the film. This was 'the genuine fairy-tale version of Hitler,' writes Parker Tyler, 'a tyrant in the untouchable tradition'. By ignoring Hitler's magic, one could see him as a waxwork figure or a grotesque puppet. (Tyler sees Chaplin's *The Great Dictator* as a play of puppets representing dictators.) To view Hitler in this way – something which could be safely done in the United States – was one way of disarming him, of making the superman less of a man. By breaking his spell, one could exact revenge simply by highlighting the ludicrousness of this comedian who rocked the world. There is an

Stills. Donald Duck in Der Fuehrer's Face. *Above: Reginald Gardner and Charles Chaplin in* The Great Dictator. *Left: Arthur Kennedy as Barney Castle with Glenn Ford (right) in Mark Robson's* Trial.

extreme but entertaining variant of this attitude in a pornographic film made in the United States during World War II, which has been described in 'Playboy' magazine. The main character in *Swastika in the Hole* is a man wearing Nazi uniform and a rubber Hitler mask who is being seduced by a dark-haired woman. As he is getting undressed, she notices a swastika on his underwear. 'Hitler' does not manage to satisfy the woman, and when she derides the master of the master race for his failure, he shoots himself. The girl cuts out the swastika on his underpants and pastes it over her vagina.

In general, the attitude of the American and the Soviet cinemas towards each other's country is determined by the political situation. Russians fluctuate between inhumanity and amiability. In Norman Jewison's *The Russians Are Coming, the Russians Are Coming* (1966), they are friendly bears whom the Americans understand without difficulty once the initial strangeness has worn off. In the Russian *On the Same Planet* (1965), the Americans can, at least, be trusted, and the United States is a

country with which Lenin wants to trade. The American military attaché is a Christian and a gentleman but admires Lenin; they are both 'idealists'.

After World War II, UNESCO initiated an ambitious project to examine international differences. One of its results was Siegfried Kracauer's study, 'National Types as Hollywood Presents Them', which in fact deals only with the treatment of British and Russians in American films, and it would perhaps be exaggerating to call it an analysis in depth. However, he stresses the consistent policy of the American film industry in following official political attitudes. At the same time, Kracauer contends that, whatever their disposition, these films depend on conventions that remain unaffected by changes in political climate. Therefore characters and situations are largely interchangeable: Anatole Litvak's *Confessions of a Nazi Spy* (1939), one of the first American films to attack Nazism, is in his opinion virtually the same film as William Wellman's *The Iron Curtain* (1948), one of the pioneer Cold War movies (both scripts were written by the same person).

In American Cold War films the enemy is typified by the intellectual communist. He appears dishonest and effete (*Man on a String*) or immeasurably cynical and ready to sacrifice even his own people (*Big Jim McLain*). Mark Robson's *Trial* (1955) includes a caricature of

215

this kind in Barney Castle, a criminal lawyer and left-wing politician, who is intelligent but completely without scruples. Although he has a certain charm, he is entirely vain and ruthless. Another version of this character appears in Roy Boulting's *High Treason* (1951). Here the intellectual is a Member of Parliament for the People's Progress Party, an aristocratic and almost defiantly elegant character who admits to the police his desire for power and his belief that might is right. Thus a left-wing character is endowed with fascist opinions.

The enemy in 'sixties films was often Asiatic, and, as in the James Bond pictures, of an indeterminate yellow colour – merely

Still: Roy Boulting's High Treason *– Grant Mansfield, M.P. (Anthony Nicholls) visits his constituency.*

oriental. There are plenty of clichés available in this area, and there is no reason to think that they would not be used again, should an opportunity for patriotism arise. The cliché for Asiatics is based on the treatment of the Japanese in World War II films or of the Chinese and Koreans during the Korean War. They are quite anonymous, and therefore cannot arouse empathy. We rarely see their faces. They are gathered somewhere in the jungle, gesticulating and shouting until they start getting hit by the naval bombardment. They emit shrill cries, lay ambushes and hide in burrows like animals, until the flame throwers are brought in to deal with them. Joseph Anderson and Donald Richie (quoting research carried out by the anthropologist Ruth Benedict) report that the Japanese themselves produced some relatively sophisticated propaganda films concentrating on the bravery of their own soldiers in battle rather than on the brutality of the enemy – who were Orientals corrupted by the West, not the people of the West themselves. Frank Capra is said to have expressed admiration for these films.

The Russian cinema also has its own ready-made values and human stereotypes, some of which follow the changes in Soviet society. More interesting than the classic caricatures of capitalists and imperialists in general or of Winston Churchill in particular, are those of Russian opponents – bourgeois elements and kulaks, Mensheviks and Social Revolutionaries, Kerensky and Trotsky. Full appreciation of these demands a sound knowledge of Russian politics from 1905 onwards. Without it, these figures with piercing eyes, oily hair, whining voices and jerky movements are merely grotesque. They are human shapes detached from any reality and reduced to clichéd patterns of treachery.

These caricatures are so crudely drawn as to leave not a trace of ambiguity. Trotsky is divested of his magnetism. His importance in the early years of the revolution, his decisive contribution or (from a Stalinist viewpoint) his monumental treachery, become totally incomprehensible, but evidently the vital aim in these films is to make him an unattractive weakling. Trotsky and less important people of the same kind take the blame for the difficulties of society; their sabotage of the emerging Socialist state, has kept the people that much further from the Communist paradise.

Dovzhenko's *Earth* is an outstandingly beautiful film, but it still contains enemies, who are all the more awful in this warm and vital context – they commit arson and murder; their hair hangs in their eyes; they sweat a lot and make exaggerated displays of anxiety or sorrow. There is something wrong with their character, a discrepancy between expression and feeling, something odd about their eyes. They lack dignity. Dovzhenko shows us the class enemy, the murderer who lumbers strangely across the field of the camera until at the end, he can be seen on the horizon in the bottom right-hand corner of the frame, completely alone and no larger than an insect. We move straight from the enemy of the people to the people, from 'them' to 'us'. It is the hero's funeral, and the whole frame is filled with living people. The enemy is almost invisible, and he cannot work effectively as enemy if he becomes fully visible, if he comes near us, and we can see our own reflection in his eye.

Psychological Defence

There is a widely held belief that propaganda implies nothing less than the art of persuasion, a complex of methods for making people want to do things, for influencing opinions, and for changing attitudes or ideas. Popular suspicion has it that the cinema can exploit unlimited resources in this respect. Fears are occasionally equalled by hopes: President Wilson is said to have expressed the opinion that the cinema would eventually make wars impossible. Literature on the social psychology of the cinema and its influence does not offer much support to any such ideas about the power of the cinema. Man has a remarkable resistance to attitudes which conflict with his own. Film propaganda is constricted by the purely practical considerations which generally prevent it from reaching the unconverted and attempting to undermine the enemy from within. Censorship generally becomes stricter in times of political crisis, even in neutral countries, and consequently hard-hitting national propaganda is directed at audiences who are already emotionally attuned to the message that is being preached.

We are too inclined to regard propaganda solely in terms of the psychology of conversion. Possibly we should, at least in the context of films, talk more often about edification than about conversion and stress psychological defence rather than psychological attack.

One of the most fascinating psychological defence mechanisms is *projection*, our tendency to attribute to other people unsympathetic thoughts, feelings and actions which we would not admit to ourselves. There is a particularly illuminating example of this kind of self-defense in *Ohm Krüger*, in which the anti-British propaganda culminates in a spectacular description of how the British try to undermine the morale of the Boers by imprisoning women and children behind barbed-wire fences to die from typhoid and starvation, watched by sadistic prison guards. The British did in fact establish concentration camps with the purpose of demoralising the Boer, but the point, here, is that the accusation is made in a Nazi film in 1941. *Ohm Krüger* was an ingenious moral sleight of hand designed to salve consciences in the situation at the time.

In the same year, an elaborate example of propagandist projection is to be found in Gustav Ucicky's *Heimkehr* (*Homecoming*), which is also remarkable for its thematic unity. It is about the German minority in Poland in 1939,

and accuses the Poles of treating the Germans with the same viciousness that the Nazis themselves used on the Poles and others.

Heimkehr begins quietly with the closure of a German-speaking school by the Polish authorities. The sense of outrage is gradually intensified in a scene where a group of Germans try to fight the decision but are contemptuously and brutally thrown out by the mayor. The next section mobilises all the resources of audience identification by using a cinema as the setting – the spectator finds himself in exactly the same situation as the principal characters of the film, watching a newsreel about Polish armament (against Germany). When the audience in the film rise in chauvinistic elation to sing the Polish national anthem, the Germans, too, get to their feet, but refuse to join in and are nearly lynched by the excited Polish mob. One of the Germans dies of his injuries after being refused medical attention, and the theme of hatred is constantly escalated through sadistic acts of persecution staged by Polish children, and a shattering sequence in which a young German girl is violated and stoned to death because she wants to protect her virtue and also because she is hiding a swastika chain in her bosom. The Polish terror and Ucicky's incitement of hatred reach their climax when members of the German minority are punished for having listened secretly to one of Hitler's speeches on the radio. They are crowded into

a prison cell where they are all going to be drowned. At that moment liberation comes: the Germans attack Poland.

This is not simple projection, but illustrates another defence mechanism – rationalisation. *Heimkehr* was offering retrospective justification, both emotional and moral for the German attack of 1939. (It is notable that the first death sentence for listening to enemy broadcasts was passed in Germany two months before the film's first showing.)

Heimkehr was not the first such argument to be based on rationalisation. The German propaganda machine had been turning them out ever since Hitler's first public speech on the 'intolerable Polish provocations,' and they were carefully recorded for the screen in a documentary describing the German version of the outbreak of war, *Feldzug in Polen*. Its director was Reichsfilmintendant Fritz Hippler, whose *Der ewige Jude* must also have been partly dependent on processes of rationalisation.

Analyses of the psychology of anti-semitic propaganda usually concentrate on the scapegoat idea, but rationalisation is worth considering as well. The hatred of Jews in Nazi Germany in 1940 is likely to have involved many Germans in a crisis of conscience, whether they were aware of it or not. Those who could not find any rational or emotional reasons for Jew-baiting must have been disturbed and many of them must quite simply have felt a need for emotional arguments to justify the anti-semitism which society demanded. *Der ewige Jude*, *Jud Süss* and *Die Rothschilds* were there to provide rationalisation for the impending mass murder.

Although the most dramatic examples happen to come from the Nazi German cinema of the early 'forties, obviously neither projection nor rationalisation is its sole prerogative. Similar needs exist in every nation fighting for ideological values. Anti-communist films from capitalist countries are fond of using the straightforward projection technique of using millionaires and big industrialists, bankers and negro-haters, to represent the enemy. In films like *Big Jim McLain*, *Blood Alley* and *Man on a*

Stills. Left: British concentration camp for Boer women in Hans Steinhoff's Ohm Krüger. *Below: Alan Napier (seated) as the rich communist in* Big Jim McLain.

String, the communists are enormously rich crooks who call each other comrade, whereas free enterprise is represented by poor, hard-working fellows; in *Ninotchka* the charming spokesman for the capitalist world is poorer than his own valet.

After the mid-'fifties, the West German film industry began to tackle subjects from the Nazi era with a growing sense of commitment. These films were not critical and soul-searching but more like comforting new versions of history, in which all Germans turned out to have been good anti-Nazis, so that the burden of guilt for Nazi crimes was placed entirely on a few influential psychopaths who had been put away for good; professional military honour and the decency of ordinary citizens were shown to have had nothing whatever to do with politics. The rehabilitation of the espionage chief Canaris in *Canaris* (1954), Helmut Käutner's film on air-force general Udet

(*Des Teufels General* – *The Devil's General*, 1954), Paul May's burlesque series about *08/15* (1954-5) and G.W. Pabst's *Es geschah am 20 Juli* (*The Jackboot Mutiny*, 1955) are among the films which offered German audiences moral as well as military rationalisations. These films are nearly always set in a military environment during the final phase of the war, and convey the impression that German soldiers – and officers in particular – were all men of honour who were to blame neither for the crimes nor for the catastrophic outcome of the war. It was Hitler and the other lunatics who lost the war for Germany. A similar version was to be seen at about the same time on cinema screens in other NATO countries like the United States and Britain. It is reassuring to feel that one's friends and allies have an honourable past.

The other side naturally took a different view of history. In the German Democratic Republic, a form of 'documentation film' emerged in the 'fifties accusing West Germany, in an

intelligent, sophisticated manner, of having inherited the legacy of Fascism from Hitler's Reich. The foremost exponents of the genre, Annelie and Andrew Thorndike, produced *Unternehmen Teutonenschwert* (*Operation Teutonic Sword*, 1958), which examined General Speidel's past and ended by asking: 'This is what Hitler's general, Doctor Speidel, did with conventional weapons; what wouldn't the NATO general, Doctor Speidel, achieve with nuclear weapons?' Using similar methods. Walter Heynowski attacked Adenauer's Secretary of State, Dr Hans Globke, in the brilliant *Aktion J* (1961). Joachim Hellwig's *So macht man Kanzler* (*That's how you become Chancellor*,

Stills. West German rehabilitation: top left – Curd Jurgens as Luftwaffe General Udet in Helmut Käutner's Des Teufels General; *left – O. E. Hasse as the Admiral in* Canaris; *above – the plotters are taken away after the failure of their attempt on Hitler's life in G. W. Pabst's* Es geschah am 20 Juli (The Jackboot Mutiny). *Right: the East German documentary on Dr Hans Globke,* Aktion J.

1961) and Kurt and Jeanne Stern's *Unbändiges Spain* (*Unconquerable Spain*, 1962) brought out other parallels between the chancellorships of Adenauer and Hitler. In all the films there was an uneasy and contemptuous emphasis on West Germany's connections with high finance, which continued the pattern of the Greater Reich, and also on the lack of prejudice of the Bonn regime about fraternising with former Nazis.

This same accusation was a standard feature in film propaganda from both the great powers in the Cold War. Western propaganda attempted to link ex-Nazis with officialdom in the Iron Curtain countries and with Communist espionage. In films from Eastern Europe, ex-members of the SS needed to make no adjustment to carry on as before – for the American authorities. These accusations became monotonous and silly, but the almost ritualistic black-and-white of standardised propaganda functions on the level of liturgy – not to convert but to encourage the faithful.

If we cease to look upon propaganda solely as an attempt at conversion and realise that, even here, cinematic fiction tries to give the audience what it wants, it is no longer surprising that the effort so often results in the improbable pattern of nobly attractive heroes representing 'us' and villains wearing all the insignia of diabolism standing for 'them'. Propaganda satisfies our moral or political desires, and credibility is not a characteristic of wishful thinking.

If, however, the believers themselves find the message convincing, this is understandable, for they can rejoice at the sight of the hero up there on the screen defending values which they share. This makes him even more attractive, and the attitudes are reinforced through being held by such a splendid figure. Drawn into this circle of sympathies, we as the audience might even imagine that the film has given us something to think about, when it has done nothing but pamper our own attitudes and ideas. The cinema can aid our self-delusion by disguising preconceived notions as objectivity. Credit titles often mention an authentic event on which a film is based; documentary sequences are worked into the action; enemies are made to express their own diabolical aims. There is one particularly important character in the cast list of propaganda movies whose well-informed testimony is generally called upon to confirm our suspicions. He is the one who defects from the other side after having seen through it all and is often a figure of commanding dignity and high moral standards, epitomised by the tragic and noble German officer in *The Life and Death of Colonel Blimp*, who was played, for good measure, by a German exile (Anton Walbrook) so that his opinions on Nazi Germany seemed particularly authoritative.

The image of reality in propaganda films is largely determined on the level of wish-fulfil-

Still: good German – Anton Walbrook in Life and Death of Colonel Blimp.

ment by the audience's own preconceived ideas. The emphasis placed on the suffering of 'our' side might therefore seem a little odd, but is the product of a culture in which goodness is often associated with suffering. The sacrificial mystique becomes a necessity in times of war. Suffering also stands as the antithesis of violence, the most revealing sign by which evil may be recognised. However, there is a small problem here as violence is also a sign of strength. Suffering arouses indignation, which is the keystone of all propaganda. But it is always the weaker side that attracts such feelings which therefore conflict with the need to appear strongest. However, women, children and old people provide convenient victims, whose defencelessness can never be rationalised, in the spectator's mind, into military or political weakness.

At the same time, indignation serves to legitimise violence from 'our' side. We can thus expand the scope of political rationalisation almost endlessly. It would scarcely be an exaggeration to say that indignation in propaganda has always served the purpose of rationalisation, helping, with ritual assiduity, to strengthen the emotional, ideological, hygienic, humanitarian and ethical motives for considering an enemy as such.

Nevertheless, ingenious methods have been devoted to reduce even further the risk of guilt feelings in the audience arising from violence. As 'our' guys are so brave and incorruptible, the enemy has to develop increasingly barbarous methods of torture without ever managing to extract any information beyond name, rank and number. But when, for instance in Zoltan Korda's *Sahara* (1943), our boys are about to use force on their prisoners, the cowardly fellows spill everything straight away. There is then no need for further brutality, and no slur on our heroes' morality. (It is often remarkable how ingeniously the basic patterns of propaganda dovetail together.) There is, in the same film, another elaborate variation on the rationalisation of violence, perhaps the most common. When the enemy leader quite simply has to be killed, for plot and audience-manipulation reasons, by someone on our side, the murder is committed by a Sudanese in a fit of blind rage: violence on the good side is almost exclusively perpetrated by individuals who are definitely allies but somehow not the same as us. We do not have to regard them as our representatives.

It is often important to satisfy 'forbidden' impulses in the audience by transferring them, as it were, to peripheral characters in the film. William Wyler's *Mrs Miniver* (1942) was made as a tribute to the brave British but had the added purpose of inspiring the Americans to fight. Therefore, enthusiasm for the war and hatred of the Germans had to be given some sort of expression, but such primitive emotions could not be attributed to the adult Minivers. Their little boy, on the other hand, has the instinctive goodness and purity of innocence but also its frankness, and can be allowed quite openly to act out both feelings.

It is interesting that propagandists use indignation in what might seem a paradoxical way. The immediate object of indignation is to stimulate the spectator's aggression, but on the assumption that the main purpose of propaganda is to win new sympathisers or to inspire aggression towards the enemy, propaganda films should, in theory, stop as soon as they have stirred up the requisite indignation. It is surprisingly rare, however, for the audience to be allowed to retain a sense of outrage when the film is over. The aggressive feelings are satisfied by the development of the plot, into which justice and revenge are worked. The power of unreleased indignation is balanced by pleasurably violent discharges of aggression.

In times of war, film propaganda first turns to the home front, where there is no active warfare but a definite need for aggression. This is satisfied by providing on the screen legitimate and concrete objects for hatred. Any latent guilt feelings are defused by the hatred-justifying indignation. Finally, the audience's equanimity and balance are restored by the graphic execution of acts of violence which it wants to see committed against the object of hatred.

Still: Gregory Peck fixes drinks in Nunnally Johnson's Night People.

This pattern in the psychological mechanisms of propaganda is clearest in films about collaborators, renegades and turncoats, whose fates are so horrible that they would inspire compassion in an audience not totally committed in advance. Only audiences already filled with hate can enjoy the Kafka-esque situation in *Hangmen Also Die* (1943) where the informer is nearly driven mad as the Resistance manipulates the evidence to make it point to him as Heydrich's murderer. The same is true of *Night People* (1954), in which the double agent Anita Björk is dispatched in an anaesthetised state by Gregory Peck to the East German authorities who are likely to exact brutal retribution. In Karl Ritter's Nazi *Verräter* (*Traitor*, 1936), the traitor Paul Dahlke is fated to fall into a marsh and get slowly suffocated. In this and many other films, fate acts as a super-ego for the faint-hearted: always on the side of justice, it punishes the unrighteous. The hanging of the Jew at the end of Veit Harlan's *Jud Süss* should, in traditional propaganda terms, be a psychological blunder, since the situation would seem to arouse compassion rather than antipathy for Süss. But an audience which had already chosen the Jews as scapegoats for its national frustration, could regard the execution as a symbolic act, and enjoy it as

revenge. The film's ending was described by a contemporary German critic as 'a joyous crescendo'.

Hatred for the enemy does not always have to find violent expression to appeal to the audience. It is not to convince anyone of anything that *Action in the North Atlantic* contains a scene in which Alan Hale, interviewed as spokesman for the American crew of a submarine rammed by the Germans, asks to send a special greeting to Adolf Hitler, and with a snarling grimace at the microphone makes a derisive noise. He does it for the audience – a primitive gesture of aggression, which gratifies on a purely ritual rather than realistic plane those who are already involved emotionally.

It is relevant here to mention the primitive but pleasant emotion of *schadenfreude* in propaganda. This may be found in Alberto Cavalcanti's highly disrespectful 'documentary' about Mussolini, *Yellow Caesar* (1941), in which the narrator delightedly tells how Il Duce once got some shrapnel in his behind and was unable to sit down for several weeks. This is less than persuasive politically but its witty treatment reinforces the image of Mussolini as a clown and, above all, it is enjoyable as humiliation, even if the victim is no more than an image on a screen.

There are more serious instances of *schadenfreude* which have the same functions. In *The Battle of Russia*, one of the films in the *Why We Fight* series, the German soldiers' terrible suffering after Stalingrad is described in terms that do not conceal the satisfaction at this revenge. The images are shattering but the narrator guides our emotions towards unholy joy. In 1944, near the end of the Quisling regime in Norway, Roar Øye and Börje Mellvig made an unusual short which strikingly expresses harsh contempt and the anticipation of revenge. The title, *Fem i tolv* (*Five Minutes to Twelve*), seems ominous in itself and the narrator speaks for the audience, addressing Quisling directly in half irreverent, half serious comments on images taken from his days of power. The background music, Saint-Saëns' 'Danse Macabre', hints tantalisingly at what is going to happen when the time comes for revenge, at 12 o'clock.

Propaganda functions in the same ritualistic manner when it uses fiction to allow the spectator to experience a surrogate reality in which the enemy suffers constant defeats. An outlet is offered to audiences whose aggressions cannot otherwise be released because the object of their hatred is so distant. Audience indignation is aroused not to create anxiety, but to provide an even greater satisfaction when fortunes change in the film and 'our' side triumphs. Satisfaction does not lie simply in the release gained from revenge and retribution after injustices have been suffered, but also in the anticipation of final, decisive triumph.

Film propaganda always finds good omens for this victory, mostly dug up from the past. The primitive reaction of escape from a crisis by going backwards in time to a safer period is the propaganda cinema's own special form of regression. Thus, when Britain is at war, Admiral Nelson and the Battle of Trafalgar are brought up for consideration: the first film financed by British Government money was *Life of Nelson* (1917), and Alexander Korda's prestige production *Lady Hamilton*, with Laurence Olivier as Nelson, appeared in 1941. In the American cinema, heroic material from World War I, like Howard Hawks's *Sergeant York* (1941), was brought out for World War II. Later, the Korean War and America's strained relationship with Communist China gave rise to films about the previous Pacific war with Japan. In Italy, Mussolini's African imperialism of the mid-thirties was the obvious reference in Carmine Gallone's bombastic epic about Imperial Rome, *Scipio Africanus* (1937). In the Soviet Union, victory over Napoleon provided a popular source of comforting subject matter after Hitler started his war against bolshevism.

Thus chauvinist memories emerge whenever the national consciousness needs the encouragement of victorious fantasies – if possible, closely paralleling the current situation. Eisenstein's

Stills. Left: the execution of Jud Süss. *Right: heroic material from the past. Top: Gary Cooper as the hero of Howard Hawks's* Sergeant York. *Bottom: Carmine Gallone's* Scipio Africanus.

Alexander Nevsky (1938) was banned for the duration of the pact between Russia and Germany, but when it was eventually released in Russia, its anti-German details made it a first rate propaganda weapon. The story of Alexander Nevsky's legendary victory over the German knights who were rampaging through thirteenth-century Russia clearly implied that the Germans could not be relied upon to uphold peace treaties, and showed the cunning high-priest of the Teutonic order with an emblem like a swastika on his collar and hat.

This film had a counterpart in Veit Harlan's film on Frederick the Great, *Der grosse König*, which was banned until the start of the war with Russia in 1941. It was then altered on the instructions of the Minister for Propaganda (disregarding historical facts) to remove any chance of sympathy with the Russian rulers. (These corrections produced the sudden, very noticeable, collapse of the film's dramatic balance.)

One consistent characteristic of historical films produced by the Nazis is the attempt to suggest parallels between then and now. Military parades from the past are shown as lightly disguised Nazi demonstrations, and well-known statements by Hitler are voiced by Bismarck, Frederick the Great and others to complete the association of the heroic past with the present.

A number of Russian films from various periods seem not to comply with the propaganda principle of intimating victory. *Strike*, Pudovkin's *Mother*, *New Babylon*, and Efim Dzigan's two films *We from Kronstadt* (1936) and *Prologue* (1956), are not the only revolutionary stories from the Soviet Union to end in heroically tragic defeat. But they are the product of a country where the victory of the proletariat had long been burnt into public consciousness as a fact, so that awareness of this worked as an extension of the plot beyond the framework of the picture.

The response of the film industry to genuine military setbacks which threaten the fighting morale of the people, is of particular interest. The Nazi German cinema towards the end of the war was certainly able to produce emotive propaganda for endurance, like *Kolberg* (1945), but on the whole it abandoned political and military subjects, opting instead for total escapism – faithfully fulfilling the most important task of film propaganda: giving the public what will make it feel good.

A different picture emerges in Anglo-American films from the early war years. Billy Wilder's *Five Graves to Cairo* (1943), is set at a time when the African campaign is not going well, and we are told at the end that the heroine cried out, before being murdered by the Germans, 'The British will be back!' And

Franchot Tone, the hero, whispers beside her grave in the desert: 'Next time you hear the ground tremble, it won't be the Germans coming but us – Englishmen, Americans, Frenchmen. And we'll be after them.' This theme of revenge and the promise of return recurs in a number of films from the period. It appears at the end, as a flourish of self-confidence, which will linger in the spectator's mind after the end-title. It may take the form of an epilogue showing how the heroes, after their humiliating experiences, set out with

Stills. Opposite page: top – the Germans in Eisenstein's Alexander Nevsky; *bottom – Efim Dzigan's* Prologue. *Above: Billy Wilder's* Five Graves to Cairo. *Below: Napoleonic troops in Veit Harlan's* Kolberg. *Right: Leslie Howard and Mary Morris in the last scene of* Pimpernel Smith.

determination to face the enemy again, this time better equipped for victory. Both Fritz Lang's *Man Hunt* (1941) and Michael Powell's *One of Our Aircraft Is Missing* (1942) end with the principal characters boarding aeroplanes to return with avenging zeal to the countries where they have previously been hunted.

Carol Reed's *The Way Ahead* concludes with the words 'The Beginning' to imply return and victory, just as General MacArthur's words 'We Shall Return' form the end-title of John Ford's *They Were Expendable* (1945), a war story which had up to that point conveyed a growing sense of defeatism. Most memorable of all is Leslie Howard whispering through the fog at the end of *Pimpernel Smith* (1941): 'I'll be back. We shall all be back.'

During both World Wars, one of the principal topics of German propaganda was military

superiority and the inferiority of the enemy. *Feldzug in Polen* (1939) and *Sieg im Westen* (1940) are both documentary celebrations of the unparalleled mechanical efficiency of the army which advanced apparently unopposed. Such assurances of strength carry certain risks, however attractive they may be to audiences at home. In 'Mein Kampf', Hitler had angrily put a large measure of blame for the German defeat in World War I on their propaganda precisely because it thoughtlessly encouraged the Germans to overestimate their own strength and underestimate that of the enemy.

Such demonstrations of strength occur in all propaganda and are symptoms of military wishful thinking; the danger to morale is proportional to the extent to which the demonstrations are believed. Credibility paradoxically becomes a drawback. In this light, unrealistic exhibitions of patriotic resourcefulness become explicable: the tall stories about quick-thinking young lads outsmarting the enemy and overwhelming military victories won by small, ill-equipped armies. The first successful feature made in Soviet Russia was Ivan Perestiani's *Red Imps* (1923), the story of three small boys (one of them a negro) who set out, inspired by adventure stories, to fight in the Russian Civil War eventually capture and destroy the 'white' leader, Machno. The film was such a success at the box-office that it was shown, with soundtrack added, during World War II, when these stories had become wishful escapism. The level of seriousness is higher but the mechanics are the same, for instance, in the American *Sahara*, in which the cunning, resourcefulness and bravery of two men enable them to capture an entire German battalion.

This form of reassuring propaganda does not belong to any specific age or nation but it does flourish mainly in the form of satire, farce or caricature. All anti-fascist satire – from *Pimpernel Smith* to the equally elegant *To Be or Not To Be* – wildly underestimates the resources of Nazism. Stupidity, weakness, arrogance and a gullibility that stems from lack of imagination seem to be the Nazis' most prominent characteristics. But the disparaging

approach is precisely the point, turning the whole thing into a pleasantly wishful fantasy which allays anxieties. It is not important to believe what one sees. Anxiety and our resources for reducing it are not so much intellectual as emotional problems, even in times of war. Laughter can be used as collective therapy against national despair.

International politics were given a farcical treatment with great success in Chaplin's *Shoulder Arms* (1918). Private Charlie captures the Kaiser himself as well as Hindenburg and the Crown Prince, thus winning the war for the United States. Chaplin's film is atypical in that the wishful dream is formally revealed as such: when the comedian wakes up, his life as a soldier is as hopelessly trivial as ever. In all the later farces in which the comedian is called upon to perform militarily decisive acts of valour – for instance, Danny Kaye's first film, *Up in Arms* (1943) – it is never stressed that these wild demonstrations of strength are obviously just an entertaining fantasy.

If propaganda is considered solely as a means of conversion, such films must appear very confusing. The intentions are so transparent and the falsification so obvious that rationally the films should lack any persuasive capacity. This sort of satire implies an admission that what is being shown does not accord with the truth; it is inherently an exaggeration and makes no attempt to conceal its unreality.

The combination of farce and propaganda is a surprising and perhaps dubious phenomenon. It is in the nature of patriotic propaganda to reinforce the established values which are being threatened. It aims to create a desire for stability. The essentially destructive and subversive nature of farce would seem to oppose this. The military successes of Chaplin and Kaye produce a rather ambivalent situation as they consistently conflict with the normal principles of strategy. The comedian almost always appears latently dangerous, a disruptive element, even to his own side. Even more doubtful is the sympathetic madness of the comedian portraying the enemy. René Clair's *Le Dernier Milliardaire* (1934) is intended as a satirical portrait of Hitler, showing how the dictator goes mad after a blow on the head and starts spreading terror in a totally absurd state of insanity. What is so disastrous is that because it is a farce, he is the one who attracts the sympathy of the audience, as he single-handedly renders bourgeois administration powerless. It is interesting to wonder whether Chaplin was really aware of just how much Adenoid Hynkel, the Hitler character in *The Great Dictator*, resembled the mustachioed Charlie figure who was so well loved by the public.

The classic Russian films about the revolution often contained strange and startling variations of style between the extremes of earnestness about the heroic proletariat and burlesque of the capitalist scoundrels. The fluctuations are equally abrupt in several of the post-war epics glorifying Stalin. His

Stills. Bottom left: Sig Ruman as a Gestapo leader on the make for Polish actress Carole Lombard in Ernst Lubitsch's To Be or Not To Be. *Top left: Danny Kaye in a perilous military situation in* Up In Arms. *This page: caricatures of Churchill, Hitler, Göring and Goebbels in Mikhail Chiaureli's* The Fall of Berlin.

apotheosis is built up with a respectful solemnity that is strengthened by contrast with the ridiculous clowns of the West. Mikhail Chiaureli was the master in this school of stylistic contrast, which went furthest in *The Fall of Berlin* and *The Unforgettable Year 1919*. The latter deals with the months following the end of World War I. Wilson, Clemenceau and Lloyd George are so caricatured as to look like utter madmen. Towards the end of the film, when they are conducting their pitiful War of Intervention against bolshevism and planning to partition Russia between them, the Big Three are seen crawling about on the floor over a big map of Europe, bickering about where to look for the Ukraine. But the most grossly caricatured figure of all is Churchill (anachronistically looking as he did in the 'forties). His bulldog appearance is exaggerated and its comic potential is fully exploited in his final appearance in the film: a long, silent close-up in profile until he suddenly turns towards the camera and barks. Cut to dignified popular celebrations of victory going on around the heroic victor, comrade Stalin.

Caricature can be used to deprive adversaries of the dignity of power. Film propaganda emerging from the allied countries during World War II sometimes used edited documentary material to ridicule the enemy. 'I was working on counter-propaganda and everything seemed so gloomy, there was nothing to laugh

Still: Il Duce caught in a moment of relaxation in Alberto Cavalcanti's Yellow Caesar.

about anywhere,' John Grierson has stated apologetically to explain the celebrated newsreel image, reproduced in several documentary compilations, which shows Hitler doing a little dance of delight at the news of France's capitulation in 1940. Grierson doctored the original, authentic image by extending a few frames of the movement to achieve the effect of a ridiculous jig. A documentary caricature on a larger scale is Alberto Cavalcanti's film about Mussolini, *Yellow Caesar*, and there is a magnificent piece of faked humiliation in another British work, Charles Ridley's *Germany Calling* (1940) in which Nazi parades from *Triumph of the Will* have been skilfully re-edited to the music of 'The Lambeth Walk' to give the impression of comical dance formations directed by a preposterous Hitler. Such reduction of a frightening enemy to the level of visibility is perhaps most accurately described as a method of achieving magical power over him. Another, and most remarkable, expression of a magical defence on the screen, a ritual act to demolish the enemy and edify the initiated is *The Grain Is In Danger*. Even today, this film can be rented from Statens Filmcentral in Copenhagen where it is listed under 'Diseases and Vermin Affecting Plants'. This short, though made for the Danish Agricultural Pests Committee during the German occupation, is one of the weirdest political films ever made. It is easy to see that the content of *The Grain Is In Danger* is not as innocent as it might appear, and few Danes failed to realise which obnoxious insects Hagen Hasselbalch was really talking about. But what did the uninitiated, the occupiers themselves, see? Possibly they did not understand the reason for all the laughter in the cinemas. At any rate, the Germans made no effort to ban the film. After all, nobody becomes an anti-Nazi through seeing a film about ways of fighting harmful insects. *The Grain Is In Danger* was a cryptic message to the initiated, a secret expression of communion for those already united by a sense of shared experience.

Propaganda films are generally aimed at audiences which already share their values. To this audience they offer fictions which satisfy pre-existing needs. The needs are rather specific during the periods when most propaganda films appear, but the film industry does not stop being a dream-factory in times of war. The only thing that changes is the content of the dream. Certain reservations must be made here. Functions are not the same as intentions or effects, and the three concepts have a fairly complex interrelationship. Thus, it is in no way certain that propaganda film-makers are ever fully aware of the functions of film as entertainment. It is quite possible that their intention is often solely to convince, persuade and admonish, as they have constructed visions that respond to collective needs and reactions. There is no contradiction here: propagandists and film-makers are themselves subject to the general psychological laws which find expression in the movies. On the other hand, the pattern is complicated by the fact that film-makers often identify with the authorities rather than the audience when shaping their myths. Vast portions of Socialist Realism in the Soviet Union never met with any response from the audience: it was produced entirely by and for Party bureaucrats and served to edify them, not the people. It is more remarkable that the American cinema, which enjoyed a greater measure of freedom, produced so much anti-communist propaganda around 1950, persisting in spite of consistent lack of box-office success. Solidarity with American foreign policy was more important at the time than financial returns or any instinctive sense of what the audience wanted.

Finally, the effects are not as isolated from the functions as might have appeared above. This play on psychological needs and their satisfaction, on moral wishful thinking and latent aggression, on *schadenfreude* and the primitive magic of security, must still have certain effects on attitudes, loyalties and patriotic enthusiasm. Each satisfaction of this kind also serves to reinforce the values and symbols that represent 'us' in the ritual pattern of propaganda.

Myth, Magic and Politics

Since much film propaganda looks like a politically coloured distillation of 'collective unconscious', it should provide a rich source of the kind of archetypal patterns that have been discovered in dreams and traditional art forms. Study of the characteristics of European folk stories seems to suggest that they are based on a much simplified conflict between good and evil in which every quality is reduced to its simplest expression: courage is set against cowardice, corruption against innocence, malice against good will, self-sacrifice against licentiousness. Good triumphs in the end, sometimes through some form of supernatural intervention. The hero often succeeds in an alien environment by his courage, cunning, humour or luck. Evil is nearly always punished; usually it is destroyed, but sometimes it is only driven off. Frequently it brings about its own downfall. The stories reflect very little of the complexity of human relationships and the demands of realism are reduced to a minimum. Instead, the stories are clear-cut and work through pure cliché to depict a consistent, fictional world in pleasant contrast with the threatening uncertainties and complexities of the real world. It might seem rather surprising that all this should apply equally to film propaganda, since here the aim is supposedly not to entertain but to influence.

Several of the reasons which could be suggested for this contain elements of the truth. When things come in a predictable order, they certainly attain a degree of reliability that reality lacks, particularly in times of unrest or war – when most propaganda films are made. It can also be assumed that the need in propaganda to involve the deepest levels of consciousness, provides a strong motive to try and reach them in ways which have already been established by myths and archetypes. C. G. Jung, the prime interpreter of our collective unconscious, gives the following summary:

'The moment when the mythological situation appears is always characterised by a particular emotional intensity; it is as if forces were liberated that we did not know existed. All that relates to the archetype is "moving", i.e. functions by waking up a stronger voice than our own. Whoever speaks in primordial images moves and overwhelms and releases all the helping forces which, again and again, have made it possible for humanity to save itself from all danger and to survive the longest night'.

What more can the propagandist want?

The myth of the knight saving the virgin from the clutches of the beast is one of propaganda's favourite motifs. The appearance of the characters is adjusted to contemporary political demands, but the pattern is still firmly ritualistic. The dragon is obviously symbolic of the enemy, the knight represents 'us', and the virgin's prospects are hopeless unless the hero wins – which, for good magical reasons, he always does.

Leslie Howard's *Pimpernel Smith*, one of the most successful British films of World War II, illustrates how well propaganda may be served by mythological elements from various sources. Smith is a latter-day version of the quick-thinking folk hero who confounds everyone else's expectations by outsmarting evil. The villain is as gross, stupid and evil as any fairy-tale giant. The beautiful, fragile heroine is held captive by the giant – in this case, blackmailed into running the villain's errands. Characters who have been spellbound or led astray are very common, in both folk lore and film propaganda: they are forced to serve an evil master but are forgiven when the spell has been broken (in propaganda fiction, such a character is likely to wake up and sacrifice his life to win salvation).

The archetypal content of *Pimpernel Smith* is enlivened with some more up-to-date British 'mythology'. Snatching precious human lives from the clutches of Nazism, was a motif that occurred in a number of British films, and derived from a story pattern which had captured the British imagination. The whole of *Pimpernel Smith* – including the title – came from a successful film made six years earlier with Leslie Howard, *The Scarlet Pimpernel*. This was based on Baroness Orczy's popular novel sequence, which in turn echoed the theme of Charles Dickens's *A Tale of Two Cities*. The theme can be traced even further back, to the knight and the dragon.

Pimpernel Smith may also be examined from a religious standpoint. This satire of Nazism does not have any explicit religious references, but it is not surprising that Western propaganda fiction should reflect Christian mythology, or in this context, that the Leslie Howard character should show striking parallels with Christ. The most active myths in any cultural environment are those connected with its religious beliefs. Simply on the strength of this, they seem fated to crop up all the time in stories which aim to exploit deep-seated emotions and to impart the highest possible associations to political objectives and heroes. These associations do not have to be intentional or evident; the use of religious mythology here is not primarily meant as a declaration of faith but as a basis for the plot structure.

But the connection between propaganda and religion is probably not quite this casual. Political involvement can assume forms which compare with revivalist fervour. The experi-

Stills: Leslie Howard as Pimpernel Smith and as The Scarlet Pimpernel, with Raymond Massey.

ences accompanying salvation and missionary zeal look very much the same whether conversion is political or religious. Bible quotations and political slogans appear to satisfy related emotional needs. Extremists movements seem to impel the same joyous devotion to a charismatic leader and a comparable need for strict orthodoxy whether they are political or religious – and to fulfil the same psychological functions. Religion has long been regarded as an expression of conservative forces, a means of reinforcing the established system through reference to a divine order. The demands of the god symbolise those of society. This view of religion implies several points of contact with propaganda. In any case, propaganda is generally intended to back the form of society in which it is operating.

Pimpernel Smith is a saviour in the literal sense, who has arrived in an evil world where his origins seem very mysterious and the authorities go all out to destroy him. No one else has his ability to pass from this evil world to the ideal one. He is a teacher, surrounded by a small group of disciples who at first do not understand his greatness and his mission – even if they are unconsciously speaking of him when they talk about 'the greatest man in the universe'. They are not convinced of his identity until, at a later stage, they see his 'pierced' hands. These wounds have been explained, with perfect consistency, in a scene, in which Smith, disguised as a scarecrow erected in a concentration camp, is on a cross, hanging with arms outstretched and head falling forward as if in a Passion painting. His hand is gorily pierced by a guard. The film ends with Smith announcing that he will soon be back.

It is not unreasonable to regard these mythical parallels as purely coincidental, and

they are far from being the only explanation for the film's emotional impact.

But Smith is not the only character in political features to be elevated by religious associations. It is surprising how elaborately the Soviet cinema makes use of Christian iconography, even when it is fighting religion. Lenin and several other Russian film heroes are bathed in overhead light in the manner of saints. This had turned into a cliché at an early stage in the Soviet cinema and was elaborated upon in personality cult films about Stalin. In *The Vow*, Stalin retains his celestial glow even after the end of his conversation with the spirit of Lenin, when he has given his vow for the future; in *The Battle of Stalingrad* he is presented, by allegorically unequivocal means, as God himself.

The American cinema has tacit biblical allusions even in a crude propaganda film like William Wellman's *Blood Alley*, where John Wayne is at once Noah with the Ark and Moses leading the children of Israel (pro-Chiang Chinese) out of Egypt (Mao's China). The David and Goliath pattern constantly recurs with the weak proving to be unconquerable because they are Chosen.

The most frequent religious references, though, occur in Nazi films, which include the most moving martyr legends, complete with the promise of paradise. The Nazi films that appeared in praise of the *Party* for a short time after Hitler's assumption of power systematically built up a quasi-religious myth of sacrifice as part of the National Socialist hagiology. The young heroes die fighting evil (i.e. communism), but not until they have glimpsed salvation and the millennium. 'Now I go to my Führer,' gasps young Erich to his friend Brand as he expires in *SA-Mann Brand*, and 'Deutschland . . . ' is Hans Westmar's last word before the soul leaves his body to march with The Flag towards Eternity. The heroic legend which is

the most finely drawn psychologically, *Hitlerjunge Quex*, is also the most closely linked with Christian ideas of salvation, which is attained by Quex at the end of a process which starts with him being led astray and continues with conversion, rebirth, dedication and martyrdom. And when Adolf Hitler, at the beginning of *Triumph of the Will*, steps out of his plane, he is the god descending from the heavens to his people.

Film propaganda looks for ways of transcending the profane limitations of the message and firmly linking it with values, forces and laws more powerful than those of human existence. Solemn allegories and mythical associations offer one method, echoing 'heavenly choirs' another. It is completely in keeping that many propaganda films are so obviously intended to arouse the audience to a state of religious ecstasy, so that conviction is no longer shackled to earthly arguments. However, the similarity in form between film propaganda and Christian literature and legend is just as remarkable. There are countless tales of martyrdom, although the hope here is of political, rather than religious salvation. Conversion, too, is a popular topic in the propaganda films like Pudovkin's *Mother*, Lubitsch's *Ninotchka*, Hasse Ekman's *Excellensen*, or Allan Dwan's *Sands of Iwo Jima*. The pattern and the frequency are particularly noticeable in Soviet propaganda. There is a recurrent theme involving a politically ignorant soldier in the service of the Czar, who happens to encounter Lenin (or Lenin's wife or mother or someone connected with him) who makes the soldier aware of what is right, so that, when the time comes for him to decide, he is ready to give his life for bolshevism.

These conversion stories – like the Christian ones – are notably lacking in persuasive force except to believers. The changes of mind seem to stem from a superimposed pattern rather

than a psychological development. Like magic formulas, they realise developments which are *desirable*, but not necessarily persuasive. Their edifying function is reinforced by dramatic suspense, and the emotional reward is the relief when the expected conversion occurs.

Michael Curtiz' *Casablanca* (1943) is a masterly exercise in edifying propaganda. We love the hero (Humphrey Bogart), for his brutal commonsense and bitter cynicism; his one disturbing quality is his political ambivalence. This develops into the chief source of tension. Eventually, of course, he commits himself, naturally in the right way. His choice

Stills. This page: relations with the communists – Lauren Bacall and Chinese soldier in William Wellman's Blood Alley; *Melvyn Douglas and Russian Greta Garbo in Ernst Lubitsch's* Ninotchka. *Right: Marcel Dalio and Humphrey Bogart in Michael Curtiz's* Casablanca.

is the emotional climax which every member of the audience expects and desires but which such a relief still gives pleasure when it arrives. To see such a sympathetic character being lost in this war for men's souls would have been unendurable.

Propaganda may thus exploit a religious slant without explicitly calling in religion itself. But there are obviously a great many propaganda films where religion, as such, has become a means of influencing the audience. When heroes uphold piety in the face of godlessness, they place propaganda on the side of religion, and the persuasion becomes doubly effective, using both sympathy-fostering and magical means.

In highly industrialised Hollywood-style film production, it is fairly clear that the values reflected by the films will be those supposedly held by the largest possible part of the audience. Radical or advanced opinions and standards that are struggling to make an impression only reach the cinema screens at a very late stage; conservative attitudes are favoured, even if indirectly. Religious values are a force at the box-office even in countries where religion is on the decline.

This tendency is not exclusive to capitalist film industries. The Soviet cinema, which has at times pursued a systematic campaign against the Church completely changed its tone when the nation as a whole was threatened by an external enemy, for propaganda had to mobilise every popular resource for its patriotic aims (in films like *Secretary of the District Committee*, 1942, and *The Rainbow*, 1944). Anti-religious indoctrination could wait until after the war; religion became an instrument, piety a sympathetic quality to be exploited.

An added explanation of the increased role played by religion in war-time propaganda is provided by the fact that people are especially likely to seek comfort from religion in times of crisis. Religion is a convenient refuge and there are signs that propaganda can function in the same way. There is a primitive form of political magic in the conviction that the side dedicated to God enjoys His protection and thus a guarantee of victory.

American propaganda made enthusiastic use of godliness as a magic formula. At the height of McCarthyist activity even the Virgin Mary emerged as an anti-Soviet propagandist in *The Miracle of Our Lady of Fatima* (1952). The ritual use of pious language is most clearly illustrated when it goes with the hearty killer instincts in adventure films about war. The last spoken or written words of soldiers are often ceremoniously quoted after their deaths and generally contain a few simple, pithy phrases about liberty and God. Such a letter was read out in Lewis Milestone's *Halls of Montezuma* (1950) just before the final offensive

against the Japanese, asserting that God needs us Americans and we must not fail Him. One of the dead man's comrades starts reciting the Lord's Prayer, and after the 'Amen', Richard Widmark yells 'Give 'em hell!' and the attack begins with God as their ally.

Conversely, the godless can never win, and in American films an atheist is frequently also politically suspect and likely to be a collaborator. An anti-communist episode in *The FBI Story* (1959), even suggests that going out for a walk on Sunday morning, without going to church, is an un-American activity. Ritual confrontations between godliness and impiety assume their most grotesque proportions in anti-communist propaganda.

The science fiction opus, *Red Planet Mars*, produced during the Cold War years, portrayed the Martians as good Christians, who are prompted by the Sermon on the Mount to stage an anti-Communist revolution in the Soviet Union. (In this sort of propaganda there are always extra-terrestrial powers on our side.) In *One Minute to Zero*, the nurse (Ann Blyth) is sitting tearfully in a decoratively bombed-out church like a lonely figure in a painting by Caspar David Friedrich. She is praying for Robert Mitchum and victory in a strikingly primitive religious service during which there is a mystical invocation of assistance from America's God.

It is not altogether surprising, then, that two of the most rabid pieces of anti-communist propaganda – *My Son John* (1952) and *Satan Never Sleeps* (1960) – were made by Leo McCarey, a virtuoso of the religious tear jerker, who made *Going My Way* and *The Bells of St Mary's*. The nobility and suffering of the Catholic clergy is embodied in *Satan Never Sleeps*, this time not by Bing Crosby but by Clifton Webb and William Holden, who are missionaries in China when the Communists take over. There is a systematic demonstration of how the Chinese break every one of the Ten Commandments, while the two priests suffer bravely and turn the other cheek (even if Father O'Banion – Holden – like the American Marine he was, eventually gets the chance to show who is really the strongest). The local Communist chief is Ho San, a roughneck who at some point attended the mission school. In due course he reverts to Christianity after realising that he has been led astray by 'the men from Moscow'. Ho San's conversion coincides with some curious initiation rites: he shoots his Chinese chauffeur, saying, 'That was my last act as a non-Christian', and then proceeds to kill a few other Communists with a smile and the words, 'That was my first act as a freshly converted Christian.'

Before Ho San suddenly becomes a new and better man by reverting to Christianity, he has revealed his godlessness by dishonouring and humiliating his Christian parents in the lowest

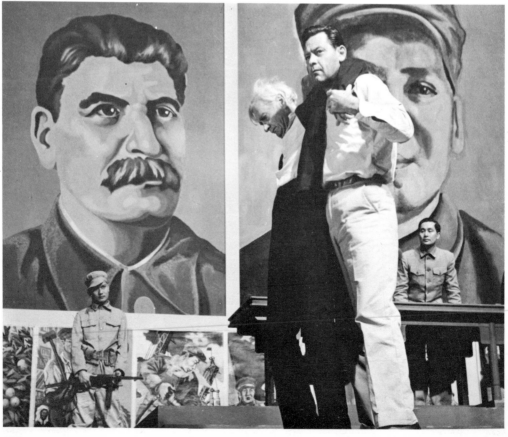

possible manner. The relationship between parent and child is very important in propaganda, where the mystical and emotional implications appear to be derived from religious precepts. The Commandment says, 'Honour thy father and thy mother' and continues with a political promise on the part of God 'that thy days may be long upon the land that the Lord thy God giveth thee.' The heroes of propaganda generally honour their parents in an exemplary fashion, and their parents' pride is a guarantee that our heroes will forever rule the land that God has given them. On the other hand, the parents of hell-bent sons and daughters must deny their children, thereby magically condemning them – and, indirectly, their entire brotherhood – to death as the hard-working elderly parents of a communist do in *Big Jim McLain*.

But propaganda may also exploit the emotive power of such conflicts between the generations in the opposite way. In *Address Unknown* (1944), a father joins the Nazis, and the son obviously does the right thing from a propaganda viewpoint when he drives his father to his death, since the parent has rendered the Fourth Com-

Stills. Left: priests Clifton Webb and William Holden in Leo McCarey's Satan Never Sleeps. *Below: son stabs traitorous father in Lewis Milestone's* The Purple Heart. *Top: Frank Reicher and Paul Lukas in* Address Unknown.

mandment inapplicable. One might compare this particular patricide with the one in another American film of the same year, *The Purple Heart*. A group of captured American airmen have been brought before a Japanese war tribunal; they face torture and execution. A Chinese traitor makes false accusations against them, but his son, who has followed him into the courtroom, jumps up and kills him. As the murderer is being taken away, the American commander, Dana Andrews, turns to his men and says 'Come on, fellows, stand up for a man.' The Americans all rise and stand to attention as a mark of respect.

Traumatic patricides in ancient mythology

have given rise to many frequently challenged psychological interpretations. Freud, after his explanation of the Oedipus situation, would probably have seen a profound mythological significance in the young man being described as 'a man' at this juncture, but it does not take psycho-analysis to uncover the political function of this moment in *The Purple Heart*. By the standards of propaganda, the father is evil, and so the son has a moral justification for the murder. But the breaking of the Fourth Commandment retains an immense emotional charge even when it is justified, and the conflict between parents and children can be exploited to strengthen the impact of the political message. You must honour your father and your mother – within certain limits. Even little Heini in *Hitlerjunge Quex* breaks the Fourth Commandment. He tries for as long as he can to please his father, but when forced to choose between father and Führer, he abides by his conviction – because it is also written that 'whoever loves his father and his mother more than me, he is not worthy of me.'

Heini's political choice is the more moving because he is still a child. Bright-eyed children are regularly used in propaganda for their disarming effect. As in folk-tales, their sympathetic and blameless aspect makes them ideal as carriers of the message. Cruelty to children has always figured among the accusations

levelled at an enemy: in World War I, the Germans were accused of breaking the fingers off Belgian children to take home as souvenirs. (These charges were answered by German documentaries in which soldiers distributed food to young Belgians, with the message in the titles: 'Is this how barbarians behave?')

Russian agitprop films appear to have gone furthest in developing enemy outrages against children into a favourite theme. *Strike* contains a long-shot in which a Cossack, standing on a viaduct, lifts up a small child, and holds it for a horrifying second over the edge before committing the final senseless act of evil by dropping it on the road below. We get a closer view in the Odessa Steps sequence of *Battleship Potemkin*, when a little boy who has been shot down is held up before the audience, while a pram bounces down the steps through a hail of bullets. And no verbal description can convey the impression of cold fury in Mark Donskoi's *The Rainbow*, where children are continually subjected to viciousness, which reaches its climax when the Germans torture a pregnant woman, force her to give birth in a stable and then shoot both her and the baby.

But children do not play an exclusively tragic role. Heroes on the run in foreign lands are often found by children who are prompted by a natural sense of good and evil to become their accomplices and helpers. In propaganda, children have taken over the part played by

Stills. Left: The Rainbow. *Above:* Battleship Potemkin. *Right:* The Battle of Russia.

kindly animals in folk stories.

Love of children is always attributed to great dictators in their own propaganda – and not only for the sake of cuteness. It is not just the dictator loving children; the love has to be reciprocal. This love of children is pointedly indicated in propaganda documentaries, and is of equal importance in the relatively few features that are made about statesmen. In Mikhail Romm's *Lenin in* 1918, the great man discovers a starving little orphan girl in a corridor at his headquarters. He takes care of her, reading to her, playing and drawing with her in spite of the war that is raging outside between Red and White (or good and evil). In the fictional reality of propaganda Lenin has every reason to do this, because the child embodies the very concept of goodness, and those who have the children on their side will emerge victorious. When *The Battle of Russia* (1943) was made to reinforce American solidarity with the embattled Russians, much emphasis was laid on the fact that even children were joining in the fight on the Soviet side – not because of the children's strength in a military sense, but because of their goodness.

There are mystical functions behind the ubiquitous presence of children in propaganda. Legend has it that the failure of the Crusades to the Holy Land at the end of the twelfth century was supposed to be the result of all-too-great a burden of sin on the adult crusaders. Consequently the children decided to form a crusade of their own, as they were without sin and should, with God's help, be able to win a victory for Christianity. Children still stand as personifications of Right and the Ultimate Victory.

This is why children are born in so many propaganda films; birth represents for us the promise of a new future when all pain and suffering will be over. The striker in *Salt of the Earth* is tortured by the company heavies, while his wife, Esperanza, gives birth to his child. In *Blockade*, Henry Fonda saves a baby from the

ruins of Spain, and in the Fascist version of the same Civil War, *L'Assedio dell'Alcázar*, a child is born in a stable, and the mother's name is Maria.

Religious and political propaganda differ on one very important point in their psychological tactics. Political propaganda in the cinema has hardly ever appealed to the audience's feelings of guilt. Admittedly, there are tendencies in that direction among the Nazi films (such as *Hans Westmar* and *Pour le mérite*) aimed at denigrating the depraved and spineless Weimar era for its treason against German nationalism, and in the *Why We Fight* series with its penitence over American isolationism in the thirties. But on the whole, propaganda has concentrated on comforting excuses and the careful avoidance of anything which might give rise to doubts about the ideological or moral probity of its country of origin. It is vital to the ritual of politics that one's own side should be represented as unequivocally good, and this is not just to attract the sympathies of the audience.

Considering how negative the very word 'propaganda' has become, it is remarkable to see how fundamental a role moral values play in all propaganda films. The battle never appears primarily to be waged between ideas, ideologies or nations, but between good and evil.

In some of the less ornate types of film – as in myths and traditional folk stories – there appears a type of villain who seems to act according to a predetermined behavioural pattern of evil rather than from any psychological motives. The type is naturally common in a genre like the propaganda movie based on a morality-play view of life. There is a ritualistically evil character who represents the very spirit of evil and does evil entirely for its own sake. Evil is his sole characteristic, intention and desire, and he incarnates the concept of evil, the enemy – 'them'. The reason is to be found in psychologically deep-rooted, mythical ideas associated with evil, the most important being that evil carries with it its own fated destruction.

Thus the enemy, simply by virtue of being an enemy, is condemned to defeat at the hands of 'us', the good. 'Captain of murderers', Leslie Howard says to the leader of the evil forces in *Pimpernel Smith*, 'you will never rule the world – because you are *doomed*!'

This is why propaganda films are so fond of investing a power struggle with metaphysical overtones, like an introductory stage to Armaggeddon. And this is also the reason why the assurances of victory have so inalienable a feeling of predestination, and why omens from the past are rehearsed on the screen before the impending showdown.

When a country goes to war, propaganda

Stills: Madeleine Carroll in Blockade. *Right:* Why We Fight – The Battle of Britain. *Bottom right: rejoicing at the end of* Kolberg.

films revive the memories of past victories and glories, and embellish them with tolling bells, banners and other symbols worthy of the transcendental significance of the struggle. The standard propaganda of the boastful historical film is there, not just as a pleasant memory or admonishment, but also as a power rite, to conjure up past victories. There is reassurance in the belief that fate will realise the wishes expressed in the rite. This magical quality emerges more strongly than ever in *Kolberg* (1945), the last film to be produced at Goebbels's initiative. Shooting was started at the point when Germany's elation began to turn to premonitions of defeat. The film described how the besieged town of Kolberg bravely held out in the fight against Napoleon, to be saved at last by a military miracle in which fate, against all odds, gave victory to the right side. Fate or God – the propaganda magic is the same.

As described by Terry Ramsaye, John Stuart Blackton's *Tearing Down the Spanish Flag* (1898), probably the world's first propaganda film, showed quite literally the hand of fate intervening in the Spanish-American war over Cuba, tearing the Spanish flag down from the government building in Havana. The film was a great success and produced a great swell of American patriotism. It is remarkable that this vision of the Spanish defeat was already produced and shown in April 1898, when war had only just been declared. This pattern has been repeated at later stages in the history of film propaganda. In the last two years of the 'thirties for instance, a number of films appeared in the Soviet Union anticipating the coming war against Nazi Germany. Audiences were shown how easily Russian border guards annihilated German attackers in films like Efim Dzigan's *When the War Comes* (1938) and Abram Room's *Squadron Number Five* (1939). This is quite simply a magic formula for shaping the future to suit patriotic interests. Just as

ritual dancing imitates the hunt in order to bring success in hunting, film propaganda constantly enacts the happy outcome of political conflicts. Propaganda films have predominantly been like magic ceremonies in which ritual figures invoke the reality which the public wishes to see brought about. Here propaganda is not just attempting to influence the spectator but is a magical means of influencing reality itself.

PART FOUR-CONCLUSION

Politics and Film— A Tricky Subject

Man Hunt, Hangmen Also Die and Ministry of Fear, three of the most trenchantly anti-Nazi features of World War II, were made by the German emigré Fritz Lang, who has become something of a symbol of the cinema's resistance to Fascism and Nazism. His first important works were made in Germany during the Weimar Republic, where he ranked among the most talented and visionary of film-makers. This first phase of his career ended at about the time that Hitler came to power with Das Testament des Dr Mabuse, which was banned and confiscated by Goebbels's Ministry of Propaganda and which has since been interpreted, among others by Lang himself, as an anti-Nazi allegory. After Das Testament des Dr Mabuse, the non-Aryan Lang escaped from Germany and eventually attained importance in Hollywood. There he directed the three films mentioned above, works of unequivocal propaganda which confirmed him to be irreconcilably anti-Fascist.

From a political standpoint, however, Fritz Lang's career is considerably more complex than is suggested by the outlines generally given in histories of the cinema, paradoxically illustrating some of the difficulties inherent in the relationship of film and politics.

1922: The first Mabuse film, Dr Mabuse der Spieler, a contemporary crime thriller about a terrorist organisation which exploits the German inflationary crisis to give its leader dictatorial powers. Critics have described the film as a prophecy of what was to happen in Germany a decade later. But according to the producer, Erich Pommer, Mabuse was conceived as a personification of the Spartacist movement. It is hardly likely that the film was understood as having a political commitment, even less so that it exerted any very precise influence. It is also doubtful whether an analysis of the film would

provide conclusive proof for any political interpretation. However, the intention behind the allegory is clear: the terrorists were to be identified with the recently crushed political left, not with the extreme right.

1924: Die Nibelungen, a monumental two-part film version of the Siegfried legend. There is no reason to look for any conscious political intention here, nor to assume that contemporary audiences saw any political significance in it. Nevertheless, in Die Nibelungen Lang created a visual style for cinematic mythology which could very well be taken as a foretaste, even as a model, for a Nazi fantasy world. The power of the film is based on the contrast between supermen and inferior beings, between the Germanic and the racially impure, between the elevated and the crawling, the masters and the oppressed. In its compositions, too, Die Nibelungen can be regarded as a direct precursor of the official architectural style of the Third Reich: the reduction of humanity to ornamental masses, weighed down by vastness, monotonous rhythm and symmetry.

1926: Metropolis, a vision of the future. The workers are slaves under a capitalist dictatorship. Its eminence grise is a wizened, malevolent scientist whose distinguishing sign is a five-pointed star. The slaves attempt to stage a revolution, which results only in chaos. The conflict is resolved when both dictator and workers realise that 'the brain and the hand cannot work together unless they are united by the heart'. The wizened scientist is destroyed; capital and labour unite in an ideal state with no conflicts and, in particular, no class struggle. Whether intentionally or not, Lang created a mythological vision of society which tallies perfectly with Fascist ideology. Hitler's enthusiasm for Metropolis is well documented.

1928: Spione, a thriller which is pointedly anti-Communist. The leader of the gang, played by Rudolf Klein-Rogge, the creator of the Mabuse role in two Lang films and the scientist in Metropolis, is made up to look like Lenin; his gang is obviously working for the Soviet Union. Here intentions and the political interpretation appear self-evident.

1929: the curious Frau im Mond, a science-fiction story which is vaguely political in content. The scientific adviser was Professor Hermann Oberth, later to lead the Peenemünde tests of the V-1 and V-2 rockets.

1931: 'M', a psychological thriller based on the case of Peter Kürten, the Düsseldorf murderer. Its working title was Mörder unter Uns – Murderer Among Us, and shooting was initially sabotaged by the Nazis who suspected that the title referred obliquely to them. In later years, the film has often been interpreted as relating to Nazism.

1933: *Das Testament des Dr Mabuse* showed the crazed genius building up an evil organisation to dominate the world. Posterity has seen the film as an anti-Nazi document, thanks partly to Lang's own retrospective comments, partly because the film was immediately banned in Nazi Germany, but also because the interpretation seems to fit perfectly once it has been pointed out. It is still startling that this alleged anti-Nazi allegory was so cryptic that it escaped even Lang's wife, Thea von Harbou, who collaborated on the script of this and all the German films mentioned here as well as being a member of the Nazi Party.

Immediately after Hitler came to power and *Das Testament des Dr Mabuse* was banned, the regime took the extraordinary step of offering Fritz Lang, as an 'honorary Aryan', the post of head of the German film industry. The main reason was probably enthusiasm for *Die Nibelungen*, which was singled out by Goebbels as a model for the Nazi cinema. Instead of becoming the Führer of the propaganda cinema, Lang escaped from Germany, eventually to Hollywood, where he built up a new career.

Still: Rudolf Klein-Rogge looking like Lenin as the gang leader in Fritz Lang's Spione.

Fritz Lang's films between the wars pose a number of problems concerning the relationship of politics and film. What criterion of political commitment can be valid if not even the scriptwriter is aware of it? One has to ask whether it is intentions or effects that make a film a political act, and how far this depends on external factors like the audience's way of looking at it, even critics' analyses or the judgment of posterity. How, then, does one discover what implications are genuinely to be found in film?

Even a seemingly precise term like 'propaganda' becomes vague in the face of such elementary questions. *Triumph of the Will* has been represented throughout this book as a landmark in film propaganda. There is little doubt that Leni Riefenstahl's picture has functioned as propaganda, in the same measure as the Nuremberg rallies themselves did. Nor can it be doubted that the intention of the people who conceived the idea for the film was propagandist (even if Frau Riefenstahl is speaking in good faith when she assures us that she had no political intentions). All the same, the question remains whether these intentions can really be gathered from the film itself as unequivocally as is usually taken for granted. Would a cinematic genius like Leni Riefenstahl have made an essentially different film if the intention had been to expose Nazism? No anti-Nazi film ever presented as clear an image of the Nazi spirit and no film-maker would ever have succeeded in portraying the nature of Nazism without allowing the spectator, as Riefenstahl does, to sense the magnetism of mass feeling and the inspirational quality of power.

The difficulty in dealing with film and politics is that what takes place must be assessed not only at the production level but also at the consumer level. The question of effects and functions of propaganda for the audience is as complex as that of intentions and awareness in the producers.

Cecil B. DeMille felt that Hollywood cinema (of the 'unpolitical' variety) offered an excellent method of disseminating information about American thought and the American way of life. President Sukarno is said to have stated that Hollywood films form the most efficient political cinema, as they keep the masses away from politics. Others, again, have suggested that Hollywood paves the way for revolution in the developing countries by revealing most clearly the great gulf that exists globally between prosperity and poverty. It is hard to dismiss any one of these ideas.

How, then, can one define the political effect of a film? Should it be seen purely in terms of election results and of changing attitudes, or should it cover the less obvious matters of satisfying political needs and confirming attitudes? The problem is further complicated by the difficulties of separating the effects of a film from among the range of influences in one direction or another which are brought to bear on people. There are also effects to be considered which appear to have no motivation in the intended content of the film. In sum, the question is whether the consequences of a cinematic experience are ever possible to define and assess.

Fritz Lang's *Die Nibelungen* came to fulfil a political function by providing visual images for the concept of the master race; it provided a form for future political content. This is not entirely a statement of fact but contains an element of hypothesis, for there is a risk in supposing that a political effect can always be predicted from conscious intentions and obvious distinguishing marks. Confirmation for this

243

can be found in a number of other surprising phenomena in film history.

The Grain Is In Danger is a cryptogram which cannot be understood unless one has the key. In occupied Denmark, the key was the current political situation, which made the code decipherable for every Danish spectator. In Vichy France, Jean Delannoy's historical film *Pontcarral* (1942) was received with incomprehensible acclaim simply because it happened to contain the line that 'nowadays only decent people are being put in prison'. Louis Malle's adventure film *Viva Maria* (1965), which was seen at least in Sweden as a piece of cynical and dubious enterprise, appears to have acted as powerful inspiration to the revolutionary spirit in Peru in 1966.

It is the situation that creates the function – a film's consequences do not seem to be exclusively dependent on its political gestures. A depressed social situation may create the need for some form of political stimulus which occasionally appears in the most surprising and apparently quite irrelevant film contexts.

Film propaganda very rarely seems to have actively educational objectives, but there are exceptions. The *Why We Fight* series gives historical instruction (and was made with the specific purpose of stimulating Americans to an active war effort). *Kuhle Wampe* (1932) contains a very illuminating didactic discussion on contemporary economics and politics. The Chinese *Tunnel War* (1965) centres on the successful resistance against the Japanese during World War II but it is also a concrete guide to guerilla tactics. *Destination Tokyo* (1944) is a Cary Grant picture crammed with all the simplest propaganda tricks, but at the same time it is technically so clear and realistic that it has been used as a submarine instruction film by the US Navy. In general, though, surprisingly little practical teaching can be expected from feature film propaganda, which has usually been content to indeterminate political edification.

One could argue about the reasons for this, but research on the influence of films provides indirect justification for the concentration on edification at the expense of instruction. The results of this research offer very little evidence to support the theory that feature films are able to effect changes of behaviour, inspire actions or even alter opinions. Maybe this is partly due to the ambivalent situation of the audience in front of the cinema screen. With a feature film, everybody can remind himself that he is watching a series of constructed, artificial and unreal events. Feature films never have quite the genuineness of real experience. However absorbing they may be, they nevertheless take place in a 'fictional space' which is definitely separate from reality. This explanation gains credibility if feature films are seen in the context of rapid news dissemination through the mass media. There is no longer much doubt that television reportage has a considerably greater effect on group reactions than the dramatic fictions of the feature cinema ever had, particularly in bringing about political repercussions.

Even if feature films do not have the authority to determine political opinions and actions to any significant degree, they can operate covertly with political consequences which might be diametrically opposed to the apparent intention. Even in entertainment films from the capitalist countries, rich men have tended to be suspicious characters – they occupy an almost institutional position as scapegoats. When the rich man does not reform into a decent fellow (as in *Metropolis*, for instance), he often gets punished or destroyed in much the way that villains do. Superficially, such a convention might be seen as a latent threat to the established economic machinery, as it keeps alive the stereotype of the capitalist as exploiter. But to the extent that films containing this figure can be said to have any political effect at all, it is probably the exact opposite: by restoring the justice and balance lacking in society, the film offers a form of comforting compensation. The cinematic villain functions ritualistically as a representative victim for the audience's social rancour. Far from being a threat, such films are a political safety valve.

Similar arguments could be applied to other supposedly standard political ingredients of the movies. Since World War II, the American cinema has treated the race problem from various liberal standpoints. These films have often been prestige opuses which have helped patch up Hollywood's tattered reputation as a dream-factory: it has been shown to be capable of producing 'mature' films and has laid claim to a social conscience. Problem films about racial discrimination have surprisingly often been box-office successes, although the motivation behind them has usually been quite sincere.

But people do not choose to go to the movies simply to have their consciences disturbed. However thoughtful and sincere these problem films may be in their indignation, they are all constructed to guide the audience as simply as possible into taking the side of the blacks against the whites. They shape the spectator's experience in such a way that everyone can feel that the social accusation must be directed against people other than himself. The really guilty ones exist only in the film, and no guilt feelings are induced in the cinema audience. Certainly these films offer a form of catharsis for the white audiences, but as purifying rites they are characterised less by social soul-searching but rather by social self-satisfaction. They function as substitutes for reform.

Hidden propaganda takes many forms. Every society which is built on a reasonably firm and homogeneous set of values, strives to reinforce and maintain them through times of change. Social outlooks and standards are passed on in upbringing and education, but attitudes can

Still: Louis Malle's Viva Maria.

also be conveyed and implanted in ways which are more unsystematic and less intentional – for instance, through the various forms of entertainment. Here, myths and values are not presented as such but camouflaged and, going unnoticed, are taken as self-evident and indisputable. This prodding in the direction of conformity is not a measurable didactic factor. Nevertheless it is an active process of reinforcement: we watch the realisation of our values in escapist drama with a sense of unreflecting emotional satisfaction.

On the other hand, influences which openly conflict with established values are easily distinguished and rejected. Our defence mechanisms against experiences which run counter to our accepted ideas and attitudes are extraordinarily efficient; we safeguard our values as fiercely as if they were part of ourselves – which, strictly speaking, they are.

Empirical research has enabled social psychologists to confirm that the cinema rarely causes any changes in attitude. It is tempting to conclude that films never contribute greatly to any readjustment of standards. But such a conclusion deserves to be regarded with scepticism – we know from historical experience that attitudes are subject to change, and it is unlikely that the cinema is completely without effect. It is quite a different matter to try distinguishing film from the mass of other factors which contribute to the changes.

It should be kept in mind that social psychologists base their conclusions on investigation of the effect of individual films, whereas the cumulative effect of a number of similar influences can be measured only to a very limited extent. The revelation that a film directed against certain values can often help to reinforce these same values in an audience does not necessarily warrant the conclusion that the same

defence mechanisms will always be effective against further influence. Political censorship of films in totalitarian countries operates on the opposite assumption in order to produce a basic conformity so that no information or fiction could ever give rise to unsuitable values. When the individual has been so forcefully besieged, he loses the resilience necessary to keep rejecting the indoctrination.

Consideration of the research methods used gives further reasons to doubt this claim that the cinema is only rarely able to effect changes in attitude. Experiments have been based on narrow concepts of attitude which are quite possibly too crude as measuring devices to be used on the dynamic, interdependent system of human values. Attitude as defined for the purposes of research is a construction based on the available techniques of measurement. It could well be that the most significant influencing processes of the cinema take place on more subtle levels. This is suggested by *Die Nibelungen*, and there are other examples. For instance, Leni Riefenstahl's film of the Berlin Olympic Games in 1936 can be defined as propaganda only to the extent that, like so much film entertainment, it reflects and idealises a way of life, a vision of Man, an atmosphere. It might seem strange to suggest that a documentary about an international sporting event could mirror a specific way of life. But comparison with another brilliant piece of reportage on an Olympic Games gives some indication of the special character of the Berlin film. Kon Ichikawa's *Tokyo Olympiad* records the effort in all its agonising, ugly detail with sweating, dishevelled victors and frustrated losers. In *Olympia*, Riefenstahl concentrates on the perfect beauty and elegant strength; the human body appears to float weightlessly in a ballet of power in a mystical setting of fire, cloud and massive pageantry. Man himself is portrayed, quite literally, as a statue endowed with the

245

Stills. Left: Stukas. *Above:* Olympia. *Opposite:* The Sound of Music.

ability to move. The Berlin film did not manipulate opinion but quite possibly opened a particular path for the imagination and introduced a view of humanity which helped prepare the ground for Nazism. Our perception of reality is shaped by our ideas about reality, by which it is filtered and evaluated. How many people actually got their ideas about revolution from *The Scarlet Pimpernel*?

Although the studies of attitude suggest that deeply rooted values are difficult to change, propaganda can, nevertheless, manipulate ideas and thereby, indirectly, attitudes. Without openly threatening any basic values, it can find substitutes for undesirable ideas.

But Nazi anti-semitism, supported by films like *Der ewige Jude* and *Jud Süss*, could hardly have banished so effectively all sense of humanity and justice, unless certain deeply rooted values had been erased from the German nation. To some extent, at least, the concept of Man is based on a set of values, which include definite principles of justice. On the other hand, it also comprises means of distinguishing categories like 'sub-human' or 'animal', towards which our attitudes are different. Basically, the technique in *Der ewige Jude* was to exclude Jews from the human race by such means as investing them with animal characteristics. This made it possible to launch anti-semitic propaganda without threatening any deep-rooted ideas of human dignity – it could even be claimed that man's dignity was being upheld. There are, then, quite simple ways of getting round the problem of immovable basic values.

The deceptive and confusing way in which film propaganda can influence ideas is most clearly illustrated by the ambivalence of its attitude to War. Very few films make the mistake of describing the war verbally as something positive – the officer cadet in Karl Ritter's *Verräter* (1936) says about his profession: 'It's not a game but certainly a joke.' But it is in the nature of propaganda to represent death as a gain, possibly reconciling those in danger to the prospect of sudden death and making it seem worth something to those they will leave behind. There are many ways of unobtrusively building up a view of the war as attractive. In propaganda, the enemy often dies quite differently from 'us'. The Germans in *Action in the North Atlantic*, for example, shout and scream in panic, whereas the Americans face death with dignity. This is partly an extension of the 'us' perspective, but it is also a way of making it seem that the war is worse for the enemy. Nazi propaganda preferred to envelop the war in symphonic sentiment (as in *Wunschkonzert*) or boy-scout-like heartiness (as in *Stukas*), while pretending to abhor it. It is really only in historical films that the Nazi cinema allowed war to appear as an affliction, and even there it seems almost an enviable way of life, a profession for kings. Not only in Nazi films but in all patriotic propaganda, war is the experience that turns boys into men. War in the movies is also an unfailing weapon in the service of justice, an exciting adventure and a field of honour, the setting for heroic deeds.

The effects of these variations on the theme of war would hardly show on an attitude scale. A survey using conventional measuring techniques might even indicate that war films tend to reinforce a negative attitude to war. A possible explanation for these misleading results is that such films are generally full of disclaimers that 'war is hell', which satisfy the values sanctioned by society. Such phrases stimulate a conditioned reflex, but that is hardly the most essential effect of the film. This is perhaps the most important problem with traditional attitude research. As a rule, the results are likely to gauge the intensity of superficial reactions while ignoring the fact that significant learning processes might be going on below the surface. Even very striking results must therefore be regarded as less telling than they appear. From the results of attitude research, *Pimpernel Smith* should powerfully reinforce a negative attitude to Nazism (or more precisely to Germans), but it seems to do so chiefly in terms of signals. It is true that the effect may be significant in itself, but there is nothing to indicate that anyone who has seen the film would be less receptive than before to ideas which could lead to Fascism.

Another example will show the ambivalence more clearly. Imagine an entertainment film set in a middle-European country in the 'thirties and entirely hostile to Nazism. Suppose, too, that all the sympathy is directed towards a wealthy, property-owning family persecuted by the Nazis, thus appealing to the audience's *Blut und Boden* instincts and their need for authority; that it glorifies a patriarchal view of man and woman not unlike that of Nazism; and furthermore that it presents chauvinistic nationalism as the noblest of emotions and has as its hero an Austrian Fascist. Would the double morality be obvious to the audience? Could such a film have an effective influence on attitudes? Would its values, disguised as anti-Nazism, find any response? At any rate, *The Sound of Music* is one of the biggest box-office successes in the history of the cinema.

Wartime propaganda has had every reason to make use of the power attitudes have to elicit responses and create patterns of conditioned reflexes rather to manipulate slower and more complicated mental processes. It is useful to replace the 'enemy' concept with a stereotype so unpleasant that reactions of hatred become as automatic and unavoidable as the salivation of Pavlov's dogs.

But to the extent that propagandist drama has succeeded in conditioning the audience to react in a Pavlovian way to the enemy as well as its own side, it has also disconnected the response from any basis of reasoning or ideology. Unfortunately, this has happened with reactions to Nazism and Fascism, which were originally ideologies that had to be fought but were gradually reduced to symbols of evil with almost exclusively metaphysical significance. Anti-Nazism lost its real meaning and became no more than a signal; beneath it, diametrically opposed ideas have managed to get insinuated into both propaganda films and apparently innocuous entertainments.

This is not at all surprising in the realm of propaganda. Research has shown that a number of American voters claim to be opposed to socialism when they are unwittingly propounding its ideas; their vague concept of socialism has been obscured by traditional American images of leftist terror. The way people vote is determined by deceptive images, not by ideas.

Politicians themselves accept the importance of illusion and the mass media support it. As political issues become increasingly complex the tendency towards simplification grows and political leadership assumes more smoothly stereotyped forms of attractiveness. Election campaigns turn into spectacular exercises in public relations without any political substance. Image counts for more than ideology – the spectacle is more important than the content. Politics become a carefully arranged performance, both on the television screen and in the minds of the audience.

Television has confirmed its position as *the* medium for transmitting political information. Politicians have the opportunity to express their ideologies in conditions of intimacy combined with mass impact. The era of primitive political concepts should by rights be making way for a more thinking, factual approach. But the medium shapes the message – some contend it *is* the message – and television has created a stronger demand than ever for politics to be exciting and attractive.

There is another trend which might appear to exercise a corrective influence: news is gaining in importance for television audiences. There is even occasionally the impression that the news is assuming a number of the dramatic functions which used to be fulfilled by the cinema, the novel, theatre and radio. But here, too, certain frightening possibilities have to be reckoned with. In the same way that the audience's expectations and demands for certain experiences have come to determine film production, so they are also guiding the communication of news. Demand creates the news, the pseudo-events and even the interpretation of these events. It seems likely that the mechanism of self-confirming ideas will be kept going by the mass media, even if film propaganda as examined in this book will soon be an anachronism. The ritual treatment of politics is being taken over by television.

Bibliography

WORLD WAR I

Maurice Bardèche and Robert Brasillach: History of the Film (London 1938)
Karl Demeter: 'Die Filmpropaganda der Entente im Weltkriege' – Archiv für Politik und Geschichte, 3(8): 214–231 (1925)
Filmbladet, years 1915–1917
Lewis Jacobs: The Rise of the American Film (New York 1949)
René Jeanne and Charles Ford: Histoire du Cinéma (Paris 1947)
Winifred Johnston: Memo on the Movies; War Propaganda 1914–1939 (Norman, Oklahoma 1935)
Harold D. Lasswell: Propaganda Technique in the World War (London–New York 1927)
Rachael Low: The History of the British Film 1914–1918 (London 1950)
Terry Ramsaye: A Million and One Nights (New York 1964)
Curt Riess: Das gabs nur einmal (Hamburg 1957)
David Robinson: 'The Old Lie' – Sight and Sound, vol. 31, no. 4 (1962)
Georges Sadoul: Le Cinéma devient un art II (Paris 1952)
Marie Seton: 'War' – Sight and Sound, vol. 6, p. 182 ff (1937–1938)
Jack Spears: 'World War I on the Screen' – Films in Review, vol. 17, nos. 5–7 (1966)
H. H. Wollenberg: Fifty Years of German Film (London 1947)

RUSSIA AFTER THE REVOLUTION

Paul Babitsky and John Rimberg: The Soviet Film Industry (New York 1955)
Johan Bergengren: 'Tio års töväder' – Chaplin, no. 37 (1963)
Le Cinéma Soviétique par ceux qui l'ont fait (Paris 1966)
Thorold Dickinson and Catherine de la Roche: Soviet Cinema (London 1948)
Sergei Eisenstein: Film Form and the Film Sense (New York 1959)
H. Herlinghaus, H. Baumert and R. Georgi (ed.): Sergei Eisenstein, Künstler der Revolution (Berlin 1960)
Ulrich Gregor and Friedrich Hitzer (ed.): Der sowjetische Film 1930 bis 1939. Herausgegeben von Verband der deutschen Filmclubs e. V. anlässlich der Retrospektive (Bad Ems 1966)
Ulrich Gregor and Enno Patalas: Geschichte des Films (Gütersloh 1962)
George A. Huaco: The Sociology of Film Art (New York–London 1965)
Bengt Idestam-Almquist: Eisenstein. Ett konstnärsöde i Sovjet (Stockholm 1951)
Bengt Idestam-Almquist: Rysk film (Stockholm 1962)
Bengt Idestam-Almquist: Polsk film och den nya ryska vägen (Stockholm 1964)
Boris Lawrenjew: Der Russische Revolutionsfilm (Zürich 1960)
Jay Leyda: Kino. A History of the Russian and Soviet Film (London 1960)
Herbert Linder: 'Die Kamera im Waffenverzeichnis' – Filmkritik, no. 7 (1966)
A. W. Lunacharsky: Der Russische Revolutionsfilm (Zürich 1929)
Vsevolod Pudovkin: 'Stanislavsky's System in the Cinema' – Sight and Sound, vol. 22, no. 3 (1953)
Philippe Sabant: 'La Crise de scénarios en U.R.S.S.' – Cahiers du Cinéma, nos. 15–16 (1952)
Marie Seton: Sergei M. Eisenstein, a Biography (London 1952)
Robert Vas: 'Sunflowers and Commissars' – Sight and Sound, vol. 31, no. 3 (1962)
Dziga Vertov: Aus den Tagebüchern (Vienna 1967)

GERMANY: THE RED FRONT

H. Baumert, H. Lohmann and H. Schneider (ed.): 'Beiträge zur deutschen Filmgeschichte' – Filmwissenschaftliche Mitteilungen 1: 1965
R. Borde, F. Buache and F. Courtade: Le Cinéma Réaliste Allemand (Neuchâtel 1965)
Alan Bullock: Hitler, A Study in Tyranny (revised edition, London 1962)
H. Herlinghaus, H. Baumert and R. Georgi (ed.): Sergei Eisenstein. Künstler der Revolution (Berlin 1960)
Hermann Herlinghaus: Slatan Dudow (Berlin 1965)
Ruth Herlinghaus (ed.): 'Slatan Dudow zum 60. Geburtstag' – Filmwissenschaftliche Mitteilungen 4 (1962)
George A. Huaco: The Sociology of Film Art (New York 1965)
Arthur Koestler: 'Piscators Fischer von Sankt Barbara' – Das neue Tagebuch, 9: 2 (1935)
Siegfried Kracauer: From Caligari to Hitler (New York 1960)
Jay Leyda: Kino (London 1960)
Ernest Lindgren: 'Revolt of the Fishermen' – Sight and Sound (Summer 1955)
Marcel Martin: Le Langage Cinématographique (Paris 1962)
Erwin Piscator: Das politische Theater (Berlin 1929)
John Hans Winge: 'Brecht and the Cinema' – Sight and Sound (Winter 1956–1957)

PRODUCED BY JOSEPH GOEBBELS

F. C. Bartlett: Political Propaganda (Cambridge 1940)
Curt Belling: Der Film in Staat und Partei (Berlin 1936)
Helmut Blobner and Herbert Holba: 'Jackboot Cinema. Political Propaganda in the Third Reich' – Films and Filming (December 1962)
Hildegard Brenner: Die Kunstpolitik des Nationalsozialismus (Hamburg 1963)
Alan Bullock: Hitler, A Study in Tyranny (revised edition, London 1962)
Hamilton T. Burden: The Nuremberg Party Rallies: 1923–39 (New York 1967)
Sergei Eisenstein: 'On Fascism, the German Cinema and Real Life' – International Theatre (October 1934)
Veit Harlan: Im Schatten meiner Filme (Gütersloh 1966)
Fritz Hippler: Betrachtungen zum Filmschaffen (Berlin 1942)
David Stewart Hull: 'Forbidden Fruit: The Harvest of the German Cinema, 1939–1945' – Film Quarterly (Summer 1961)
Stig Jonasson: Nazismen i dokument (Stockholm 1965)
Hans-Peter Kochenrath (ed.): Der Film im Dritten Reich (Cologne 1963)
Siegfried Kracauer: From Caligari to Hitler (New York 1960)
Erwin Leiser: 'Filmen i Tredje riket' – Ord och Bild, no. 1 (1966)
Roger Manvell and Heinrich Fraenkel: Doctor Goebbels (London 1960)
C. Neumann, C. Belling and H.-W. Betz: Film-'Kunst', Film-Kohn, Film-Korruption (Berlin 1937)
Arthur Maria Rabenalt: Film im Zwielicht (Munich 1958)
A. U. Sander: Jugend und Film (Berlin 1944)
Derrick Sington and Arthur Weidenfeld: Goebbels experiment (Stockholm 1943)
Rune Waldekranz: Modern film (Stockholm 1951)
Gösta Werner: Kameran går (Uppsala 1944)
Joseph Wulf: Theater und Film im Dritten Reich (Gütersloh 1964)
Z. A. B. Zeman: Nazi Propaganda (London 1964)

THE SPANISH CIVIL WAR

James Agee: On Film, vol. I (New York 1958)
Madeleine Chapsal and Frédéric Rossif: Mourir à Madrid (Paris 1963)
Wolfgang Klaue and Manfred Lichtenstein (ed.): Filme contra Faschismus (Berlin 1965)
Jay Leyda: Films Beget Films (London 1964)
Artur Lundkvist: Buñuel (Stockholm 1967)
Gerd Osten: Det förlorade paradiset (Stockholm 1947)
William L. Shirer: Berlin Diary, The Journal of a Foreign Correspondent, 1934–1941 (New York 1941)

Jonas Sima: 'En film, ett vapen' – Chaplin, no. 73 (1967)
Vilgot Sjöman: Jag var nyfiken (Stockholm 1967)
Hugh Thomas: The Spanish Civil War (London 1961)

HOLLYWOOD AND THE WORLD

'Annual Communications Bibliography' – supplement to vol. I, Hollywood Quarterly (1946)
André Bazin: 'A propos de Pourquoi nous combattons' – 'Qu'est-ce que le cinéma? I (Paris 1958)
Alvah Bessie: Inquisition in Eden (New York 1965)
John Cogley: Report on Blacklisting: I: Movies (New York 1956)
Film Comment, vol. 4, no. 1 (1966)
Walter Goodman: The Committee (New York 1968)
Richard Griffith: 'The Use of Films by the U.S. Armed Services' – in Paul Rotha et al.: Documentary Film (London 1952)
C. I. Hovland et al.: Experiments on Mass Communication (Princeton 1949)
Image et Son, no. 188 (1965)
Lewis Jacobs: The Rise of the American Film (New York 1939)
Gertrude Jobes: Motion Picture Empire (Hamden, Connecticut 1967)
Gordon Kahn: Hollywood on Trial (New York 1948)
Siegfried Kracauer: National Types as Hollywood Presents Them (UNESCO 1951)
John Howard Lawson: Film in the Battle of Ideas (New York 1953)
Göran Palm: Indoktrineringen i Sverige (Stockholm 1968)
Karel Reisz: 'Hollywood's Antired Boomerang' – Sight and Sound, vol. 22, no. 3 (1953)
Georges Sadoul: Le Cinéma pendant la guerre 1939–1945 (Paris 1954)
Adrian Scott: 'Histoire de la Liste noire' – Cahiers du Cinéma, nos. 54–55 (1955–1956)
W. M. Seabury: Motion Picture Problems. The Cinema and the League of Nations (New York 1929)
Roger Tailleur: Elia Kazan (Paris 1966)
Rune Waldekranz: Modern film (Stockholm 1951)
Walter Wanger: 'The Motion Picture Industry and the War Effort' – John Gassner and Dudley Nichols (ed.): Best Film Plays of 1943–1944 (New York 1945)

BRITAIN: DEMOCRACY AT WAR

Michael Balcon, Ernest Lindgren, Roger Manvell and Forsyth Hardy: Twenty Years of British Film, 1925–1945 (London 1947)
Wolfgang Klaue and Manfred Lichtenstein (ed.): Filme contra Faschismus (Berlin 1965)
Arthur Knight: The Liveliest Art (New York 1957)
Roger Manvell (ed.): The Cinema 1950 (London 1950)
Roger Manvell (ed.): Film (London 1944, 1950)
Ib Monty and Morten Piil (ed.): Se – det er Film II (Odense 1965)
C. A. Oakley: Where We Came In (London 1964)
Eric Rhode: Tower of Babel (London 1966)
Paul Rotha: Documentary Film, Third Edition (London 1966)
Rune Waldekranz: Modern film (Stockholm 1951)

CESARE ZAVATTINI

André Bazin: Qu'est-ce que le cinéma? IV. Une esthétique de la réalité: le néo-réalisme (Paris 1962)
George A. Huaco: The Sociology of Film Art (New York 1965)
Robert Hughes (ed.): Film: Book 1 (New York 1959)
Ib Monty and Morten Piil (ed.): Se – det er Film II (Odense 1965)
Rune Waldekranz: Italiensk film (Stockholm 1953)

CINEMA NÔVO: BRAZIL BEFORE THE REVOLUTION

Jan Aghed: 'Samtale med Glauber Rocha' – Kosmorama, no. 93 (1969)
Georg Alexander: 'Versuch über das Cinema Nôvo' – FILM (1967). Chronik und Bilanz des internationalen Films vorgelegt von der Zeitschrift film (Hanover 1967)
Cahiers du Cinéma: no. 176 (1966)
Th. Christensen: 'Filmen i det revolutionaere Samfund'

– A. Bodelsen (ed.): Filmen nu (Copenhagen 1966)
Artur Lundkvist: 'Cuba Si' – Chaplin, no. 56 (1965)
Artur Lundkvist: Buñuel (Stockholm 1967)
'Noveau Cinéma Latinoamericain' – Cine Cubano, vol. 7, nos. 42, 43, 44 (1967)
P. B. Schumann (ed.): Retrospektive Dokumentation zu den filmhistorischen Vorführingen der XVI. Internationalen Filmfestspiele Berlin 1966 (Berlin 1966)

NEW BABYLON

Le Film Muet Soviétique (Brussels 1965)
Bengt Idestam-Almquist: Rysk film (Stockholm 1962)
V. I. Lenin: State and Revolution (second revised edition, Moscow 1965)
Jay Leyda: Kino (London 1960)
P. O. Lissagaray: Histoire de la Commune (1876)
Ebbe Neergaard: Hvorfor er filmen sådan? (Copenhagen 1931)

HITLERJUNGE QUEX

G. Bateson: 'An Analysis of the Nazi Film Hitlerjunge Quex' – Margaret Mead and R. Métraux (ed.): The Study of Culture at a Distance (Chicago 1953)

TRIUMPH OF THE WILL

Alan Bullock: Hitler, A Study in Tyranny (revised edition, London 1962)
Hamilton T. Burden: The Nuremberg Party Rallies: 1923–39 (New York 1967)
Michel Delahaye: 'Leni et le loup' – Cahiers du Cinéma, no. 170 (1965)
David Gunston: 'Leni Riefenstahl' – Film Quarterly (Fall 1960)
Siegfried Kracauer: From Caligari to Hitler (New York 1960)
Leni Riefenstahl: Hinter den Kulissen des Reichsparteitag-Films (München 1935)
Joseph Wulf: Theater und Film im Dritten Reich (Gütersloh 1964)

THE SPANISH EARTH

Robert Grelier: Joris Ivens (Paris 1965)
Wolfgang Klaue and Manfred Lichtenstein (ed.): Filme contra Faschismus (Berlin 1965)
Hans Wegner: Joris Ivens (Berlin 1965)
A. Zalzman: Joris Ivens (Paris 1963)

DER EWIGE JUDE

Hildegard Brenner: Die Kunstpolitik des Nationalsozialismus (Hamburg 1963)
Cinéma d'aujourd'hui (Geneva–Paris 1945)
Veit Harlan: Im Schatten meiner Filme (Gütersloh 1966)
Fritz Hippler: Betrachtungen zum Filmschaffen (Berlin 1942)
Hans-Peter Kochenrath (ed.): Der Film im Dritten Reich. Stencil (Cologne 1963)
Siegfried Kracauer: From Caligari to Hitler (New York 1960)
Erhard Kranz: Filmkunst in der Agonie (Berlin 1964)
Derrick Sington and Arthur Weidenfeld: Goebbels experiment (Stockholm 1943)
Joseph Wulf: Theater und Film im Dritten Reich (Gütersloh 1964)

OHM KRÜGER

Ohm Krüger. Ein Emil Jannings-Film der Tobis. Programme booklet (Berlin 1941)

VI ER VIDKUN QUISLINGS HIRDMENN

Sigurd Evensmoe: Det store tivoli. Film og kino i Norge gjennom 70 år (Oslo 1967)

DET BRINNER EN ELD

Den tyska propagandan i Sverige under krigsåren 1939–1945 (SOU 1946: 86, Stockholm 1946)

THE HITLER GANG

James Agee: On Film. Reviews and Comments (New York 1958)

THE BATTLE OF STALINGRAD

André Bazin: 'Le mythe de Staline dans le cinéma soviétique' – Qu'est-ce que le cinéma? I (Paris 1958)

SÅNT HÄNDER INTE HÄR

Jörn Donner: Djävulens ansikte (Lund 1962) translated as The Personal Vision of Ingmar Bergman (Bloomington, Indiana)

TORN CURTAIN

Alfred Hitchcock: 'Den vita rektangeln' – Interview in Chaplin no. 67 (1966)
François Truffaut: Hitchcock on Hitchcock (New York 1968)

THE GREEN BERETS

'Propaganda Films about the War in Vietnam' – Film Comment, vol. 4, no. 1 (1966)

THE AESTHETICS OF PROPAGANDA

Henri Agel: Esthétique du cinéma (Paris 1962)
Jan Andersson and Mats Furberg: Språk och påverkan (Lund 1966)
André Bazin: Qu'est-ce que le cinéma? I: Ontologie et langage (Paris 1958)
Sergei M. Eisenstein: Film Form and the Film Sense (New York 1960)
Gunnar Fredriksson: Det politiska språket (Malmö 1963)
Ph. Haudiquet: 'Le Film de Montage' – Image et son, no. 188 (1965)
Joachim Hellwig and W. Weiss: So macht man Kanzler (Berlin 1961)
Erwin Leiser: Om dokumentärfilm (Stockholm 1967)
Jay Leyda: Films beget Films (London 1964)
Marcel Martin: Le Langage Cinématographique (Paris 1962)
Vladimir Nilsen: The Cinema as a Graphic Art (New York 1959)
V. Pudovkin: Film Technique (New York 1949)
Karel Reisz: The Technique of Film Editing (London 1960)
Parker Tyler: 'The Eyewitness Era in Film Fiction' in The Three Faces of the Film (New York 1960)
Fifty Years of Italian Cinema (Rome 1954)

FROM PERSONALITY CULT TO APOTHEOSIS

André Bazin: Qu'est-ce que le cinéma? I: Ontologie et langage (Paris 1958)
Isaac Deutscher: Stalin, A Political Biography (revised edition, London 1966)
Yuri Hanyutin: 'Modern rysk film' – Filmrutan, no. 1 (1968)
Veit Harlan: Im Schatten meiner Filme (Gütersloh 1966)
Siegfried Kracauer: From Caligari to Hitler (New York 1960)
Erwin Leiser: Om dokumentärfilm (Stockholm 1967)
Jay Leyda: Films Beget Films (London 1964)
Roger Manvell (ed.): Experiment in the Film (London 1949)
Theodore C. Sorensen: Kennedy (New York 1965)
Rune Waldekranz: Modern film (Stockholm 1951)
Joseph Wulf: Theater und Film im Dritten Reich (Gütersloh 1964)

THE FIRST PERSON PLURAL

J. A. C. Brown: Techniques of Persuasion from Propaganda to Brainwashing (London 1963)
M. Choukas: Propaganda Comes of Age (Washington 1965)
Jaques Ellul: Propaganda (New York 1964)
Fritz Hippler: Betrachtungen zum Filmschaffen (Berlin 1942)

L. Linhart: 'Darstellung von Masse und Volk im "Panzerkreuzer Potemkin"' – Sergei Eisenstein, Künstler der Revolution (Berlin 1960)
Raymond Williams and Michael Orrom: Preface to Film (London 1954)
Joseph Wulf: Theater und Film im Dritten Reich (Gütersloh 1964)

THE IMAGE OF THE ENEMY

Joseph Anderson and Donald Richie: The Japanese Film (New York 1960)
F. C. Bartlett: Political Propaganda (Cambridge 1940)
Siegfried Kracauer: National Types as Hollywood Presents Them (UNESCO 1951)
Siegfried Kracauer: From Caligari to Hitler (New York 1960)
Jay Leyda: Films Beget Films (London 1964)
Parker Tyler: Magic and Myth of the Movies (New York 1947)
Rune Waldekranz: Modern film (Stockholm 1951)

PSYCHOLOGICAL DEFENCE

J. A. C. Brown: Techniques of Persuasion from Propaganda to Brainwashing (London 1963)
M. Choukas: Propaganda Comes of Age (Washington 1965)
Jacques Ellul: Propaganda (New York 1964)
Lars Forssell: Chaplin (Stockholm 1953)
Adolf Hitler: Mein Kampf (unexpurgated English translation, London 1939)
Pauline Kael: 'Morality Plays Right and Left' in I lost it at the Movies (New York 1966)
E. Kranz: Filmkunst in der Agonie (Berlin 1964)
M. Mardore: 'Age d'or, âge du fer. Notes sur la politique et le cinéma' – Cahiers du Cinéma, no. 175 (1966)
Helmut Regel: 'Autoritäre Muster' – Filmkritik, no. 11 (1966)
G. Wagner: Parade of Pleasure. A Study of Popular Iconography in the U.S.A. (London 1954)

MYTH, MAGIC AND POLITICS

André Bazin: Qu'est-ce que le cinéma? I (Paris 1958)
M.-L. von Franz: 'The Problem of Evil in Fairy Tales' – in *J. Hillman* (ed.): Evil (Evanston 1967)
Otto Fridén: Makt och magi (Stockholm 1942)
C. G. Jung: Modern Man in Search of a Soul (London 1933)
Siegfried Kracauer: From Caligari to Hitler (New York 1960)
Thomas F. O'Dea: Sociology of Religion (New York 1966)
Terry Ramsaye: A Million and One Nights (New York 1964)

POLITICS AND FILM – A TRICKY SUBJECT

H. J. Eysenck: Uses and Abuses of Psychology (London 1953)
Leif Furhammar: Filmpåverkan (Stockholm 1964)
George A. Huaco: The Sociology of Film Art (New York–London 1965)
Siegfried Kracauer: From Caligari to Hitler (New York 1960)
M. Meucci: Political Cinematology. How Motion Pictures and Television Will Shape the Political Destiny of America (Newark, N.J. 1943)
Robert Merton and Paul F. Lazarsfeld: 'Studies in Radio and Film Propaganda' in *Merton*: Social Theory and Social Structure (Glencoe, Illinois 1951)
Kjell Nowak et al.: Masskommunikation och åsiktsförändringar (Stockholm 1966)
Eric Rhode: 'Fritz Lang' in Tower of Babel (London 1966)

ADDITIONAL REFERENCES

David Stewart Hull: 'Film in the Third Reich' (Berkeley 1969)
Gerald Reitlinger: 'The Final Solution' (London 1961, third edition 1968)

Index

Page numbers in *italic* indicate references within illustrations captions.

Under the name of each director are listed the films by him referred to in the text: page references may be found under the main index entry for each film.

252

255